Holocaust Restitution

Holocaust Restitution

*Perspectives on the Litigation
and Its Legacy*

EDITED BY

*Michael J. Bazyler and
Roger P. Alford*

New York University Press

NEW YORK AND LONDON

NEW YORK UNIVERSITY PRESS
New York and London
www.nyupress.org

Library of Congress Cataloging-in-Publication Data
Holocaust restitution : perspectives on the litigation and its legacy /
edited by Michael J. Bazyler and Roger P. Alford.
p.   cm.
Includes bibliographical references and index.
ISBN-13: 978-0-8147-9943-7 (cloth : acid-free paper)
ISBN-10: 0-8147-9943-4 (cloth : acid-free paper)
1. Holocaust survivors—Legal status, laws, etc.—United States.
2. Holocaust, Jewish (1939–1945)—Reparations. 3. World War, 1939–
1945—Claims.   I. Bazyler, Michael J. II. Alford, Roger P.
KF6075.H65 2005
940.53'18144—dc22   2005017564

New York University Press books are printed on acid-free paper,
and their binding materials are chosen for strength and durability.

Manufactured in the United States of America
10 9 8 7 6 5 4 3 2

To Mari

— MICHAEL BAZYLER

To Leslie, Mason, and Andrew

— ROGER ALFORD

Contents

     Website: www.holocaustlitigation.com

Acknowledgments

The genesis of this book originated on March 9, 2001, when both of us were participating in the Stefan A. Riesenfeld Symposium at Boalt Hall School of Law in Berkeley, California. The topic of the symposium was "Fifty Years in the Making: World War II Reparation and Restitution Claims." After the conference, we remarked about how wonderful it would be if someone put together a book that gathered all the different voices in the Holocaust restitution movement and did a postmortem review of the litigation.

With Michael's relationships with Holocaust plaintiffs in the United States and Roger's experience with the Claims Resolution Tribunal adjudicating Holocaust Swiss bank claims in Zurich, our sense was that we both had dozens of wonderful contacts, very few of which overlapped. We both remarked, "Someday we should do that." Years passed and the Holocaust restitution movement slowly edged toward conclusion. As soon as Michael finished his book *Holocaust Justice,* we sat down in earnest in 2003 and began the project that is now before you.

From the beginning, we recognized that a book of this magnitude would be a collective effort from persons of great significance. It would require the protagonists in the Holocaust restitution drama to trust that we would give each of them the freedom to give their own unadulterated perspective on this controversial subject.

We are extraordinarily grateful for the time, energy, and trust that the contributors provided us. This book is ultimately a result of their commitment to memorializing the historic moments of the past ten years. The success of their work inspired us to write this book in the first place, and our admiration for them has increased with their latest contributions.

We are deeply indebted to Bonny V. Fetterman, our independent editor, and Jennifer Hammer, our editor at NYU Press, for their critical editorial assistance. We would also like to acknowledge our research assistants, Wendy Yang at Whittier Law School and Jennifer Black at Pepperdine Law

School, for their truly excellent work in helping us prepare this manuscript.

Our home institutions, Whittier and Pepperdine Law Schools, were very supportive and encouraging in this work. As always, our colleagues are simply a delight to work with, and they provided continuous support for our work.

As coeditors, when we began this work we had great respect for one another. That respect continues but is now combined with great affection. We're not sure whether it's traditional for coeditors to recognize one another in an acknowledgment. But if it is (and even if it is not), we do.

As for our families, Michael's wife, Mari, and Roger's family, Leslie, Mason, and Andrew, provided much love, support, and richness to our lives and to this project. We feel truly blessed that when we think of family, their smiling faces fill our hearts and minds.

Finally, we are grateful to God that we have had the privilege of working on a project such as this. Although it has been arduous, it has rarely felt like work. We understand the meaning of Theodore Roosevelt's great words that one of the "best prize[s] that life has to offer is the chance to work hard at work worth doing."

Holocaust Restitution Timeline

1942   *Buxbaum v. Assicurazioni Generali,* the first Holocaust-era lawsuit, was filed in the United States
against a major Italian insurance company for
policies purchased by a Holocaust victim. Relief
granted.

1949   *Bernstein v. N. V. Nederlandsche-Amerikaansche
Stoomvaart-Maatschappij* was filed by a Holocaust
survivor seeking compensation for the forcible
transfer of his business to a Nazi trustee. Relief
granted.

1985   *Handel v. Artukovic,* the first Holocaust-era class
action, was filed in the United States by Holocaust
survivors from Yugoslavia against a former pro-
Nazi Croatian official in violation of the Geneva
and the Hague Conventions, war crimes, crimes
against humanity, and violations of the Yugoslavian
Criminal Code. Suit dismissed.

April 23, 1996   U.S. Senate Banking Committee, headed by Senator
Alfonse D'Amato, held hearings on the Swiss banks
dealing with World War II dormant accounts.

May 2, 1996   The Swiss Bankers Association created the
Independent Committee of Eminent Persons
(ICEP), chaired by Paul Volcker, to audit records of
the Swiss banks on wartime dormant accounts.

October 1996   The modern era of Holocaust asset litigation began
with the filing of the first of three class action
lawsuits against the Swiss banks in federal district
court in Brooklyn, New York.

January 1997   The third class action suit was filed against the
Swiss banks by the World Council of Orthodox
Jewish Communities.

January 8, 1997	Christoph Meili discovered the Union Bank of Switzerland attempting to shred pre–World War II financial documents.
March 25, 1997	French Prime Minister Alain Juppe created the Prime Minister's Office Study Mission into the Looting of Jewish Assets in France ("Mattéoli Commission") to study various forms of theft of Jewish property during World War II and the postwar efforts to remedy such theft.
April 1997	The three class action suits against the Swiss banks were consolidated in federal district court in Brooklyn, New York, before Chief Judge Edward R. Korman, and collectively titled *In re Holocaust Victim Assets Litigation.*
May 7, 1997	The United States government issued a report, coordinated by Undersecretary of State Stuart Eizenstat, criticizing Switzerland for its World War II dealings with the Nazis.
July 1997	Swiss banks issued a list of 1,756 dormant Swiss bank accounts.
October 1997	Swiss banks issued a supplemental list of 3,500 additional names.
October 10, 1997	Alan Hevesi, New York City comptroller, barred the Union Bank of Switzerland (UBS) from leading a $1.3 billion letter of credit deal.
March 8, 1998	The first German slave labor lawsuit, a class action against Ford Motor Company for the forced labor performed at Ford-Werke A.G., between 1941 and 1945, was filed in New Jersey.
June 19, 1998	Swiss banks publicly announced in a press conference that they were ready to settle the claims for $600 million and insisted that it was their final offer.
July 12, 1998	New York State Controller H. Carl McCall and New York City Controller Alan Hevesi released a statement outlining sanctions they would place upon the Swiss banks in an effort to force the continuation of negotiations in the Swiss bank litigation.

August 7, 1998	The first Nazi-looted-art lawsuit, filed in 1996, *Goodman v. Searle,* over a disputed Degas, *Landscape with Smokestacks,* was settled on the eve of trial, when the parties agreed to share ownership of that Degas and to place it for public viewing in the Art Institute of Chicago.
August 13, 1998	Swiss banks agreed to a $1.25 billion settlement with Jewish groups regarding long-lost assets of Holocaust victims and their heirs.
August 25, 1998	Signed by six European insurance companies, a Memorandum of Understanding (MOU) created an International Commission of Holocaust Era Insurance Claims (ICHEIC) and charged it with establishing a just process to collect and facilitate the signatory companies' processing of insurance claims from the Holocaust era.
December 3, 1998	Forty-four governments endorsed the Washington Conference Principles on Nazi-Confiscated Art ("Washington Principles") to develop a consensus on nonbinding principles to assist in resolving issues relating to Nazi-confiscated art.
December 23, 1998	First French class action bank Holocaust-era lawsuit, *Bodner v. Banque Paribas,* filed by Holocaust survivors for the banks' theft of their assets in the aftermath of the German occupation of France in 1940.
December 23, 1998	A class action suit against Chase Manhattan Bank and J.P. Morgan & Co was filed in Brooklyn federal court alleging confiscation of Jewish bank account holders' assets during the German occupation of France.
March 11, 1999	Suits against German banks were consolidated in the Southern District of New York as *In re Austrian and German Bank Holocaust Litigation* before Judge Shirley Wohl Kram.
September 12, 1999	*U.S. v. Portrait of Wally,* a lawsuit over disputed Schiele paintings, was filed in New York.
September 14, 1999	The House of Representatives Banking Committee, chaired by Congressman Jim Leach, held hearings

	on French financial institutions' past misappropriations of Holocaust victims' assets in wartime France.
September 19, 1999	Two New Jersey district judges dismissed five German slave-labor class action lawsuits, holding the suits were nonjusticiable and also time barred.
October 14, 1999	The Presidential Advisory Commission on Holocaust Assets in the United States (PCHA) issued a preliminary report on the so-called Hungarian Gold Train. The report told the story of a 42-wagon freight train loaded with goods stolen by the Germans and their Hungarian allies from the Jews of Hungary, captured by the U.S. Army at the end of World War II.
December 1999	Under the guidance of U.S. presidential envoy Stuart Eizenstat and German representative Otto Graf Lambsdorff, a comprehensive settlement was reached over all claims against Germany and its industry relating to World War II conduct.
December 6, 1999	The Volcker Committee report on dormant accounts was published, finding 53,886 accounts in Swiss banks that could have been linked to persons persecuted by the Nazis.
September 5, 2000	*Abrams v. Societe Nationale des Chemins de Fer Francais* was filed against the French national railroad for its role in transporting Jews in cattle cars from both occupied and unoccupied France to death camps in Germany and Eastern Europe.
July 17, 2000	The United States and the Federal Republic of Germany signed a formal agreement concerning the German settlement and allowing creation under German law of the "Remembrance, Responsibility, and Future" Foundation ("German Foundation").
November 27, 2000	The Austrian Fund for Reconciliation, Peace, and Cooperation was established to compensate former slave and forced laborers of the Nazi regime.
January 18, 2001	An agreement was signed between the Government of the United States and the Government of France concerning Payments for Certain Losses Suffered

	during World War II ("Washington Agreement"), in which French banks agreed to pay $172.5 million to sixty-four thousand known account holders and other undocumented claimants. The payments to the victims would be made through the French government's Drai Commission.
May 2001	Hungarian Gold Train litigation began with the filing of a class action suit against the United States in the Southern District of Florida by Hungarian Holocaust survivors, *Rosner v. U.S.*
March 22, 2002	The Swiss government's Bergier Commission published its "Final Report" detailing Swiss activities during and after World War II.
August 2002	Federal Judge Patricia Seitz rejected the U.S. government's motion to dismiss the Hungarian Gold Train litigation.
June 23, 2003	The U.S. Supreme Court issued *American Insurance Association v. Garamendi*, finding unconstitutional the California law aiming to force European insurance companies doing business in the state to disclose their prewar and wartime insurance records.
June 7, 2004	The U.S. Supreme Court in *Republic of Austria v. Altmann* held that the Foreign Sovereign Immunities Act (FSIA) could be applied to all actions of a foreign government, regardless of when the acts underlying the claim took place, even before the enactment of the FSIA in 1976. The litigation involved artworks of Gustav Klimt, which are claimed to be Nazi-looted art by Holocaust survivor and plaintiff Maria Altmann. The case was remanded by the U.S. Supreme Court to federal trial court and set for a November 2005 trial date.
December 20, 2004	The U.S. government settled the Hungarian Gold Train litigation.
January 2005	Under an agreement reached between the Swiss banks and the plaintiffs' representatives, the Swiss made public an additional twenty-one hundred names of Holocaust-era bank accounts.

April 2005   The Swiss Claims Resolution Tribunal issued, and Judge Edward R. Korman approved, the largest Swiss dormant account award, $21.8 million, to the Bloch-Bauer family, formerly of Austria.

April 2005   The Ninth Circuit Court of Appeals, in a 2-1 panel decision, overturned the dismissal by the federal trial judge of the lawsuit against the Vatican Bank and related entities by Holocaust survivors for slave labor and looted-assets profits which were earned by the Nazi puppet regime in Croatia and which allegedly passed through the Vatican Bank and related entities.

Introduction

Michael J. Bazyler and Roger P. Alford

Holocaust restitution is not about money. It is about victims. It is about individuals who have waited sixty years for something. Of course it is not about "perfect justice," a phrase that may never pass one's lips in the same breath as "Holocaust." But it is about waiting for some recognition, some voucher to validate the misdeeds that have been perpetrated.

Excerpts from the letters of one claimant appearing before the Claims Resolution Tribunal for Dormant Accounts in Switzerland give voice to this yearning for recognition:

We had not been able to locate [my grandfather's] personal account. My grandmother tried on several occasions, without success. She gave up in quiet desperation. Sometimes not so quiet. There were a lot of tears. She felt betrayed and deceived, frustrated and powerless. You see, she knew money had been put into Swiss accounts, but she had no power to open the doors.

I look at the amount of money now in the account, and I see how little money it is. So little for so much grief! Inconsolable grief. But I also have to remember that in the refugee camps we had nothing, not even a pair of shoes. We ate black bread and lard for months and were lucky to have it. So this money, which I now think of as a little amount, at that time in history, fifty years ago, was indeed a good sum. . . .

My grandmother never dreamed, nor did I, that this moment in history would come. Who could have known. I thought about not pursuing this claim. I said it's not worth it. But I changed my mind. I have to do this for my grandmother, even though she is dead. For her suffering, for her pain, for her incredible losses. I owe her memory. To pursue and possibly attain the impossible. To be validated! This small amount of money represents more than this to me. It represents a cleansing, a true release and forgiveness of the past. This money needs to be circulated, and therefore cleansed. So I now bless and release this to you to be in right action as your conscience guides you. For me it is an opportunity to wash the pain from the past away, to have a truly new and honorable beginning.

Holocaust restitution is not only about the victims. It also is about those who victimized. As German president Johannes Rau put it in the December 1999 ceremony on the signing of the German slave labor settlement,

> [A]ll contributors to the Foundation Initiative, both government and business, accept the shared responsibility and moral duty arising from the injustices of the past. . . . I know that for many it is not really money that matters. What they want is for their suffering to be recognized as suffering, and for the injustices done to them to be named injustices. I pay tribute to all who were subjected to slave and forced labor under German rule and, in the name of the German people, beg forgiveness.

Such an apology is, in the words of one survivor, a "moral victory that will live forever." It is a recognition that promises a cleansing for the children and grandchildren of those who victimized. It offers, if you will, a release from their past too. Holocaust restitution, then, is about satisfying the victims' and victimizers' historic need for a moral accounting regarding the horrific events that transpired during and after the Second World War.

A brief synopsis of the Holocaust restitution movement is in order. The first chapter in that story concerns the fifty-year interregnum. Since 1952, Germany has paid over $50 billion to Holocaust survivors, pursuant to federal indemnification laws. Many Germans believed that this action closed the book on Holocaust restitution. But that indemnity was limited; it did not include many survivors, particularly in Eastern Europe, and excluded many crimes, such as slave labor. The Swiss delay was due primarily to obfuscation by the Swiss banks, who in self-audits required by Swiss law in the 1960s, reported only 1 percent of the actual number of Holocaust accounts. As for insurance, Jewish insurance policies were confiscated by the Nazis and dishonored after the war because companies either denied their existence or deemed them to have lapsed from unpaid premiums. Looted art was a much more complicated affair. With hundreds of thousands of pieces of art confiscated by the Nazis during the war, the Allies' approach was one of repatriation to the country of origin, with each government responsible for the ultimate return of the art to the rightful owners. Not surprisingly, many governments did not rigorously pursue this objective, leaving thousands of pieces of looted art subject to claims for restitution by their previous owners. As Judge Thomas Buergenthal puts it, "it seemed . . . in those years that the Holocaust would soon become one more of those historical events that mankind wanted to forget."

But many refused to forget. And as they held to the memory, a perfect storm gathered on the distant horizon. Even as the last Holocaust victims were soon to pass from this realm, the Cold War ended, the human rights movement was born, government doors flew open, and Holocaust images captured on film and in museums transfixed the public imagination. Holocaust restitution came into its own.

The most recent initiative for Holocaust restitution began in 1996 with Edgar Bronfman and Israel Singer of the World Jewish Congress persuading Senator Alfonse D'Amato to hold Senate Banking Committee hearings on Holocaust-era dormant Swiss bank accounts. Those hearings were followed by the filing in 1996–1997 of three class action lawsuits against the Swiss banks in a Brooklyn federal district court, which began the modern era of Holocaust restitution litigation and opened the door for the subsequent suits and settlements. In August 1998, the banks settled the class actions for $1.25 billion. The distribution of these funds is being supervised by Judge Edward Korman, who for the last six years has been called upon to make various "Solomonic" decisions on how best to allocate the Swiss bank settlement funds. As we write, a new list of twenty-one hundred additional names of dormant Swiss bank accounts has just been made public in the hope that further claimants will come forth to make claims upon the $800 million set aside for them.

At the same time when the Swiss bank settlement was being negotiated, a new front began with the Holocaust slave labor and related litigation against German industry. The German companies vigorously defended these lawsuits while simultaneously moving to establish a national foundation to compensate Germany's former slave laborers and other victims. These negotiations, conducted under the leadership of Count Otto Lambsdorff for Germany and Stuart Eizenstat for the United States, incorporated a "big tent" approach with dozens of interested parties, including numerous foreign countries, class action lawyers, and representative Jewish groups, present at the negotiating table. They concluded with a December 1999 settlement in which German public and private funds would be used to establish a DM 10 billion (approximately $5.2 billion) foundation to pay slave labor claimants and other victims. In keeping with the settlement's objective of "legal peace," virtually all related outstanding claims in U.S. courts against German public and private entities have been dismissed.

Claims against insurance companies began much like the claims against the Swiss banks, with class action lawsuits filed in 1997 against over a dozen European insurance companies. State regulators stepped in with legislation that strengthened the plaintiffs' hand. Insurance companies responded through the establishment of an ad hoc commission, the International Commission of Holocaust Era Insurance Claims (ICHEIC), chaired by former secretary of state Lawrence Eagleburger. The United States endorsed ICHEIC pursuant to the insurance component of the German settlement, which called for ICHEIC resolution of German insurance claims. Such endorsement was of monumental importance, for in 2003 the Supreme Court issued a decision in *American Insurance Association v. Garamendi* finding that state laws designed to facilitate litigation against European insurance companies were preempted by the executive preference for voluntary resolution of claims under the auspices of ICHEIC. This left ICHEIC as virtually the only vehicle for resolution of such claims, with subsequent lower court cases broadly construing the import of that opinion and dismissing outstanding claims against European insurance companies.

Holocaust looted-art claims are different. With looted art, most claimants do not want reparation but rather actual restitution of the looted art object. Ill suited for consolidated class action litigation, Holocaust art litigation has ensued piecemeal, with marked successes in some cases and notable failures in others. But several significant developments have occurred as a result of the Holocaust restitution movement. In December 1998 the United States brokered an agreement with over forty countries for the establishment of the so-called Washington Principles to require public museums to research the provenance of their art and develop claims processes for disputed works. Another significant development was the Supreme Court's 2004 decision in *Altmann v. Austria* that denied immunity to Austria for claims seeking restoration of art.

The purpose of this book is twofold. First, it is intended to present an up-to-date analysis of the Holocaust restitution movement. The essays in the book all were written after the major Holocaust claims had been resolved, permitting the contributors the luxury of a more accurate look backwards as they analyze the various aspects of this entire movement and compare its disparate parts. The timing of this book affords the opportunity to thoughtfully reflect on the legacy of this litigation, in terms of both unfinished Holocaust business as well as future claims to address other historical wrongs.

Second, this book presents the drama of Holocaust restitution from the perspective of almost all the major players, including plaintiff counsel, defense counsel, judges, diplomats, administrators, corporate defendants, and Jewish representatives. It also includes outside viewpoints from respected commentators, including historians, academics, and Holocaust survivors. These voices are authentic and disparate, displaying a range of emotions and a panoply of perspectives. Of course, not all of these perspectives are ones that we share.

For readers who want to study the legal history of the restitution cases in greater depth, we created a dedicated website, www.holocaustlitigation .com. It includes a Holocaust restitution timeline, a list of significant cases, and an appendix of primary source documents.

This volume is divided into six sections. Part 1 is the overview, which takes a panoramic look at the Holocaust restitution movement. The next four sections address the specific subjects of Holocaust litigation involving banks, slave labor, insurance, and art. The final section addresses the legacy of Holocaust litigation, with chapters that focus on unfinished Holocaust business and also feature competing prognoses for the future of other human rights litigation.

Part 1: Overview

Part 1 begins with an essay by Judge Thomas Buergenthal, who brings a unique perspective to the subject of Holocaust restitution as a Holocaust survivor, human rights scholar, former vice-chairman of the Claims Resolution Tribunal for Dormant Accounts in Switzerland, and now American judge on the International Court of Justice (the "World Court"). His chapter introduces the topic of restitution with a background survey of how reactions to the Holocaust became the impetus for the modern human rights movement.

William Slany, as the State Department historian, was the chief author of the so-called Eizenstat Reports, which proved so instrumental in launching the Holocaust restitution movement. Here he offers a succinct summary of how the Clinton administration came to be intimately involved in addressing the issue of Holocaust restitution. He views the noble efforts of the United States in the modern Holocaust restitution movement as making partial amends for the State Department's deplorable failures in aiding Holocaust victims before and after the war.

For Holocaust historian Michael Berenbaum, one of the most important results of the Holocaust restitution movement was that it forced dozens of countries to reexamine their role in the Second World War. He cites the Swiss, Austrian, and Romanian investigations as prime examples of countries that are thoughtfully reconsidering their wartime roles and recrafting their historical narratives.

Attorneys Robert Swift and Burt Neuborne offer plaintiff perspectives on Holocaust restitution, with Swift focusing on the events that led to the settlements and Neuborne focusing on postsettlement activities. Swift's chapter explains some of the antecedents for Holocaust litigation and the successes and problems encountered in settling Holocaust claims. Neuborne, as one of the leading plaintiffs' representatives in the Swiss and German settlements, provides a vital overview on the settlements as well as the postsettlement activities.

Following the chapters by two leading plaintiff lawyers, we turn to the essay by Roger Witten, who served as lead counsel for corporate defendants in both the Swiss and German settlements. Witten compares and contrasts the two settlements, pointing out that the "Swiss issues were resolved through a unique agreement among private parties that affected significant government interests" while the "German issues were resolved through a unique government-to-government agreement that affected significant private interests."

Si Frumkin's provocative chapter entitled "Why Won't These SOBs Give Me My Money?" expresses an authentic voice of survivor outrage—at the German corporation, Philipp Holzmann A.G., that employed him as a slave laborer; at European insurance companies that sold Holocaust-era insurance; and at Jewish organizations that he claims speak in his name without his consent. When the Holocaust restitution negotiators speak of "imperfect justice," Frumkin's frank and incisive chapter underscores just how inadequate these attempts at justice seem to those who were victims of such opprobrious conduct and its aftermath.

Part 2: The Bank Litigation

The genesis of the modern Holocaust restitution movement began with litigation against Swiss banks. Part 2 focuses on this litigation, which was based on allegations that private banks unlawfully retained monies that Holocaust victims had voluntarily deposited prior to and during the events of World War II. The lead plaintiff perspective on Holocaust bank litigation (and the later German settlement) is presented by Melvyn Weiss, a prominent American class action lawyer and one of the principal architects of the $1.25 billion Swiss bank settlement. Weiss views the litigation as a just battle that produced a worthy legal legacy. He also responds to critics, from those who argue that any compensation is unseemly to those who deem the results inadequate to those who contend that the entire restitution movement threatens to malign the memory of the Holocaust.

Chief Judge Edward Korman was the Brooklyn federal district court judge who presided over the Swiss bank litigation and approved its settlement. He currently oversees the distribution of the settlement fund. His chapter stands as a stinging indictment of "decades of improper behavior by [the] Swiss banks."

Eric Freedman and Richard Weisberg provide a plaintiff's perspective on the French bank litigation. Their chapter discusses the events that led to the Franco-American Washington Accords, which ended the litigation, and then outlines the current status of the processing of the settlement claims under the French government's Drai Commission. In their view, the French bank litigation "signifies a momentous victory for those trying to right some of the enormous financial wrongs committed against the Jews in wartime France." Shimon Samuels, head of the Paris office of the Simon Wiesenthal Centre, provides a perspective from an official of a major Jewish organization involved in Holocaust restitution, and one that is decidedly critical of the process. Here he presents a scathing critique of the French banks, asserting that the "French Bank settlement ends without apology and a very qualified measure of justice."

The section concludes with a chapter by law professor and human rights activist Lee Boyd, who is counsel for plaintiffs in the final episode of the Holocaust bank cases, this time pertaining to the Vatican bank. She makes a strong case that Holocaust cases should not be dismissed because they implicate political rather than legal questions within the competency of the judicial branch.

Part 3: The Slave Labor Litigation

Part 3 turns to the most emotive aspect of the Holocaust restitution move-ment: claims for reparation arising from Nazi Germany's use of slave and forced labor and related crimes. Gideon Taylor speaks from his experience as executive vice president of the Conference on Jewish Material Claims against Germany, the group created in the aftermath of the West German reparations settlement in the 1950s, which has been at the forefront in the struggle to assist Holocaust survivors and is presently involved in the ad-ministration and distribution of many of the recent settlement funds. His chapter seeks to offer a representative voice for survivors who seek a reck-oning, while outlining the moral dimensions of the pecuniary settlement.

Otto Graf Lambsdorff was the principal German negotiator responsible for resolving the wartime claims against German industry. Lambsdorff asserts that the impetus behind the German negotiations was not fear of failure in American courts but rather the general threat the litigation posed to German-American economic and political relations. Lambsdorff defends the use of German public funds as the primary resource for com-pensating the victims, forthrightly admitting that the "bulk of moral re-sponsibility" lay on the shoulders of the government of the Third Reich, not German corporations.

The next chapter in this section offers the German corporate perspec-tive. Lothar Ulsamer outlines the reasons why forced labor claims became a subject of public attention in the 1990s and details the constructive na-ture of negotiations, which he describes as far more conciliatory than con-frontational. He offers his own postmortem on the settlement, expressing regret over the absence of "legal peace" but hope that Foundation funds will be instrumental in improving the protection of human rights.

The final essay in the trilogy of German perspectives is offered by Ro-land Bank, general counsel for the German Foundation. Bank presents a detailed discussion of the eligibility requirements, standard of proof, and review of forced and slave labor claims. He also explains the difficult bal-ance between accuracy and efficiency, with the Foundation opting for the prompt processing of claims as the concern of paramount importance in light of the advanced age of most survivors.

Holocaust historian Peter Hayes offers a dissenting view on the forced labor settlement. Following detailed investigation of the historical rec-ord, Hayes contends that the rhetoric of "disgorgement" of unjust profit is misplaced. His historical analysis suggests that, much to his own surprise, while the German corporations undoubtedly engaged in grave criminal misdeeds, the profits procured by the corporations as a result of such malfeasance was marginal and fleeting at best.

Roman Kent's chapter offers a haunting perspective on the German slave labor negotiations by a Holocaust survivor. Intimately involved as a participant in the negotiations, Kent argues that "the basis for these negotiations on the part of the Germans, as well as the great majority of class action lawyers, was not founded on moral and humanitarian purposes. It was strictly business." His essay offers a disheartening portrait of some of the major players in the litigation and negotiations. For Kent, the German Foundation represents a small, imperfect form of justice, the most critical component being the apology issued by Germany concomitant with the settlement.

Deborah Sturman conceived of the idea of suing German companies in U.S. courts for their use of slave and forced labor in wartime Europe and was actively involved in the litigation as cocounsel with Melvyn Weiss. Her chapter attributes few benevolent motives to the Germans, concluding that German corporations fought the litigation with all their collective might and recognizing the impact the litigation had upon the various generations of present-day Germans.

Hannah Lessing and Fiorentina Azizi, the leading Austrian officials working with survivors and their monetary claims, present the Austrian component of the saga. Speaking on behalf of the two Austrian funds created to assist victims of National Socialism in Austria, they offer a historical perspective on Austria's self-understanding of its complicity for the war, which they characterize not as "collective guilt" but as "collective responsibility" to remember. The chapter outlines the steps that led to Austrian compensation for Holocaust victims and concludes with an assessment of the impact such compensation has had on Austria's view of its wartime role.

Part 4: The Insurance Litigation

With the essays on the insurance litigation, the Holocaust restitution movement turns the page to a far more equivocal chapter. Lawrence Kill and Linda Gerstel's piece outlines the history of the Holocaust-era insurance litigation, beginning in 1997, and reviews the regulatory oversight that led to the establishment of ICHEIC and, ultimately, to U.S. executive branch intervention. The signal moment in the insurance restitution process was the Supreme Court's resounding endorsement of executive branch authority in *Garamendi*. With federal endorsement of ICHEIC, they note, it became the exclusive albeit imperfect mechanism for resolving insurance claims.

Kai Hennig's chapter offers an update to the insurance litigation, with detailed discussion of the claims process established under ICHEIC pursuant to the Foundation Law. He outlines the difficulties associated with implementation, including concerns regarding eligibility, appeal, disbursement, and expeditious processing.

Sidney Zabludoff, former CIA analyst and current expert on Holocaust-era claims, concludes this section with a sharp critique of ICHEIC. Although it was initially successful, Zabludoff argues that beginning in early 2000 ICHEIC lost its way, with growing signs of inept management, poor communication, and the insurance companies' lackadaisical performance of their commitments. He concludes that ICHEIC was a good idea gone awry, with ICHEIC personnel lacking "the skills, patience, and interest to deal with day-to-day governance and management."

Part 5: The Looted Art Litigation

Part 5 briefly addresses the one aspect of Holocaust restitution that has been the least susceptible to mass resolution: looted art. The nature of the wrongdoing and the claims for return of Nazi looted art render mass claims settlement inappropriate. As Monica Dugot notes of her work in the New York Holocaust Claims Process Office (HCPO), because "each art claim involves a specific and identifiable object, art claims have been resolved on a case-by-case basis." She views the absence of a wholesale approach as an opportunity to establish creative, fair, and swift solutions to provenance disputes. Her conclusion is that litigation is not necessarily the preferred approach for resolving Holocaust art claims.

The balance of this section is provided by the lead plaintiff counsel in two of the most celebrated looted art cases. The chapter by Howard Spiegler summarizes the history of litigation over Egon Schiele's *Portrait of Wally* and poses the perplexing question of the propriety of committing U.S. government resources to the resolution of private art disputes. Spiegler argues that government intervention in such private disputes, like his

Portrait of Wally litigation, is consistent with government interests and instrumental in achieving a satisfactory result.

E. Randol Schoenberg's chapter describes the tortured path that his client, Maria Altmann, has taken to secure restitution of some of the most valuable paintings in Austria, including Gustav Klimt's painting of her aunt, Adele Bloch-Bauer. The most notable aspect of the *Altmann* case is the U.S. Supreme Court's monumental decision allowing the lawsuit against Austria to go forward in American courts by denying Austrian sovereign immunity. That decision opens the door for further claims against sovereigns arising from historical misdeeds.

Part 6: The Litigation's Legacy

The final section of this book surveys the legacy of the Holocaust litigation. Part 6 begins with a chapter by Stuart Eizenstat, arguably the most prominent figure in the Holocaust restitution movement. As President Clinton's special Holocaust envoy, Eizenstat rendered a great service to the world with his steady hand in navigating the Holocaust restitution claims. His essay focuses on the still unfinished business of Holocaust restitution, and he offers valuable prescriptions for the work yet to be done.

Public interest lawyers David Lash and Mitchell Kamin address Holocaust restitution as it relates to indigent survivors. The authors offer a heartfelt appeal that residue funds be distributed consistent with the needs of the most impecunious survivors. With the settlement fund facing "an unfortunate confrontation between right and right" the chapter argues that "those who have suffered the most brutal blows of history and society . . . have the greatest claim to whatever funds justice has acquired in their name."

Arie Zuckerman's chapter reviews Israel's ambivalent attitude towards monetary restitution coming from the perpetrators. He traces this ambivalence from the 1950s—when there was a public outcry against Israel's Prime Minister David Ben-Gurion for accepting reparations from the West German government—to the present day, as Swiss, German, French, and Austrian funds become available for individual survivors. Zuckerman, the lead Israeli negotiator in the Holocaust restitution negotiations and himself the grandson of Holocaust survivors, observes that in recent years Israel has "clearly moved towards a policy of increased involvement." The presence of the Israelis inevitably raises the question, "Who speaks for Jewish victims at the close of the final chapter of the Holocaust?"—a question that puts the Israeli government at times in an uncomfortable relationship with other Jewish representative groups.

Two final essays scan the future horizon. Owen Pell reflects on his experience as defense counsel in the French bank litigation. Pell sees a future in which corporate defendants in subsequent litigation will be more prepared, more attuned, and more publicly adept in the face of claims for compensation for historical wrongs. He cautions defendants—whether being accused of profiting from African-American slavery or sued for doing business in apartheid South Africa—to become more knowledgeable about their company's history, more strategic in their litigation response, and more cautious in their public response to claims of injustice.

Plaintiff attorneys Morris Ratner and Caryn Becker raise one of the most important questions of the Holocaust litigation legacy: whether the successes achieved in Holocaust litigation may signal hope for other victim groups. The authors outline the reasons why Holocaust restitution proved so successful and conversely examine why "there has not been a repetition to date of the success of the Nazi-era cases in the context of litigation efforts intended to address other historical wrongs."

The Holocaust restitution movement now comes to a close. The settlements have been brokered. The funds have been allocated and are being distributed. To be sure, there is unfinished business. But relative to what has been accomplished, such concerns are secondary. For what has been accomplished is the impossible. Holocaust claims have been pursued and validated. Apologies have been made. Restitution money has been circulated and cleansed. And for the children of many victims and victimizers, a balm has healed some of the pain from the past.

We close with one of the most difficult questions in Holocaust restitution: Why so late? Ambassador Eizenstat posed this question at a B'nai B'rith International ceremony honoring him with its Humanitarian Award. Eizenstat enumerated the usual reasons given: the end of the Cold War; a desire to attend to the unfinished business of World War II; the advanced age of the survivors; and a smaller world that makes multinational companies subject to foreign judicial scrutiny. To this list, he added his own observation:

The fifty years following the Holocaust have seen the gradual development of an international consensus for justice and human rights that did not exist before World War II. . . . It was first applied in the Nuremberg trials, was carried to the Helsinki Declaration in the 1970s, and can be seen in the war crimes trials that have recently been conducted by an international court in The Hague. . . . This higher moral standard explains the increasing appreciation in the non-Jewish community of the moral dimensions of the Holocaust, and the hold that terrible crime still has on the conscience of the world.

As international law professors, we try to make our students aware of this higher moral standard. For litigators seeking to apply this standard through human rights suits against public and private perpetrators of international crimes, we emphasize the direct line from Nuremberg to the current litigation. It is the "Nuremberg principles" of nonimpunity, increasingly accepted and applied by American judges in the last quarter-century, that made these suits possible. The Holocaust restitution suits were not created out of whole cloth. Without the human rights precedents laboriously fashioned over the last twenty-five years, these lawsuits—brought for acts committed on another continent over a half-century ago—would have been summarily dismissed.

But there is an another, more personal answer to the question "why so late?"—and it comes from Abraham Foxman, a child survivor of the Holocaust, and now long-time head of the Anti-Defamation League:

> [T]here's another reason that we didn't deal with this issue for 50 years—because the trauma of the human tragedy was so tremendous, so enormous, so gargantuan, that nobody wanted to talk about material loss for fear that it will lessen the human tragedy. Because when you begin talking about property, then what about life? . . . Not that we didn't know that there were bank accounts, that there was insurance, that there was property. . . . But nobody ever raised it. Nobody ever said, look what we lost. I don't remember conversations of material loss. Now I realize how significant the loss was, but nobody talked about it. Because what they talked about was that they lost 16 members of their family.

We offer this volume to all those who yearn for and work towards a world in which the question "why so late?" should never have to be asked again.

Part I

Overview

Chapter 1

International Law and the Holocaust

Thomas Buergenthal

This chapter reproduces one part of the lecture on "International Law and the Holocaust," delivered by the author at the United States Holocaust Memorial Museum in 2003. The omitted part of the lecture dealt principally with international criminal law and the impact of the Holocaust on this branch of contemporary international law.

Introduction

I am profoundly honored to be this year's Joseph and Rebecca Meyerhoff Lecturer here at the United States Holocaust Memorial Museum. The museum evokes very special feelings of awe and gratitude in me. When I came to the United States in 1951 as a boy of seventeen, no one in my high school in Paterson, New Jersey, ever asked what it was like in the camps; they were either afraid to ask or did not care to know. And when in my sophomore or junior year in Bethany College, West Virginia—the only college, incidentally, that was willing to give me a scholarship despite my only three years of formal education—I published an article describing my experiences on the death march out of Auschwitz, most of my fellow students thought that I had written a piece of fiction.

It seemed to me in those years that the Holocaust would soon become one more of those historical events that mankind wanted to forget because of the pain, vicarious shame, and guilt they evoke. It was not until much later that things began to change, and the trend to reverse our self-induced amnesia set in.

For me this museum symbolizes a permanent commitment to ensure that the crimes of Nazi Germany will not be forgotten, not only in order to honor the memory of its victims but also to serve as a permanent reminder to all mankind of the risk to humanity itself from those forces of evil who kill, enslave, and torture to advance their false ideologies of racial, religious, or ethnic superiority and hatred or simply to maintain themselves in power.

I believe very strongly that this museum is not for the tears of those of us who lived through the Holocaust; it is for the young people who daily line up outside the museum doors waiting with their teachers to get in; it is for the people from all over America and the world who come and who, I fervently hope, will never again be the same for the experience of seeing and learning what the Holocaust was all about. We will have to count on them and the future generations who will follow in their footsteps in this building to ensure that "Never Again" becomes humanity's pledge that no people, no human beings, will ever again be treated as we were. And this brings me to my lecture this evening.

It is sad but true that throughout history the impetus for many significant advances in the field of international law in general and international human rights in particular can be attributed to wars or other catastrophes in which millions and millions of human beings lost their lives. But all prior advances in this regard are dwarfed by the impact of the Holocaust and the Second World War on the creation of the international law of human rights. To understand and appreciate these developments, it is useful, initially, to take a snapshot of what international law looked like before World War II as far as human rights are concerned.

The Individual and Pre–World War Two International Law

In the second edition of the most authoritative English-language treatise, Oppenheim's *International Law,* published in 1912, the author had the following to say on the subject of human rights:

> [W]hat is the position of individuals in International Law. . . ? Now it is maintained that, although individuals cannot be subjects of International Law, they nevertheless acquire rights and duties from International Law. But it is impossible to find a basis for the existence of such rights and duties. International rights and duties they cannot be, for international rights and duties can only exist between States.

But what then is the real position of individuals in International Law, if they are not subjects thereof? The answer can only be that they are objects thereof. . . . When for instance, the Law of Nations recognizes the personal supremacy of every State over its subjects at home and abroad, these individuals appear just as much objects of the Law of Nations as the territory of the States does in consequence of the recognized territorial supremacy of the States.[1]

In other words, individuals as such had no rights under international law. They could not claim rights under international law since they were not subjects of international law. As objects of international law, their status did not differ from the state's territory or its other sovereign possessions.

In another part of his treatise, Oppenheim points out that whatever protection individuals enjoyed under international law derived from their nationality. That is, the state of the individual's nationality had the right under international law to protect its nationals on the theory that any injury sustained by the individual was deemed to be an injury to the national's state. One cruel consequence of this rule of law was that a stateless person, that is, a person who had lost or otherwise lacked a nationality, enjoyed no protection under international law. Here is what Oppenheim had to say on this subject in 1912:

As far as the Law of Nations is concerned, apart from morality, there is no restriction whatever to cause a State to abstain from maltreating to any extent such stateless individuals. On the other hand, if individuals who possess nationality are wronged abroad, it is their home State only and exclusively which has a right to ask for redress, and these individuals themselves have no such rights.[2]

This, for all practical purposes, was the international law of the pre–World War I era, and it remained the law until World War II. The status of the individual under international law did not change in the period following the publication of Oppenheim's treatise in 1912 and the years preceding World War II. Thus, the fourth edition of Oppenheim's book, published in 1928, and the fifth edition, published in 1937, reproduce almost verbatim the language I quoted from the 1912 edition. What is interesting about the fifth edition is that it was edited by Hersch Lauterpacht, an eminent British international legal scholar and one of the strongest early international human rights advocates.[3]

In a footnote to his 1937 edition of Oppenheim's treatise, Lauterpacht reproduces some parts of the Declaration on the Rights of Man, adopted in 1929 by the Institute of International Law, a private association of leading international legal scholars. The Declaration proclaimed certain fundamental human rights principles. While expressing the view "that the development of International Law in accordance with its true function is, in the last resort, bound up with the triumph of the spirit of these principles [proclaimed in the Declaration]," Lauterpacht hastened to emphasize that these principles "are not expressive of the law and practice of many states; neither is their non-observance treated by other states as a breach of International Law."[4] Lauterpacht's edition of Oppenheim's great treatise was published in 1937, one year before Kristallnacht. But even this brilliant international lawyer and human rights proponent had to admit that the international law in force at that tragic moment in history provided no protection for German Jewish victims of Nazi persecution and brutality.

One important consequence of the international legal doctrines in force before World War II was that the manner in which a state treated its own nationals or stateless persons in its territory was a matter exclusively within its own domestic jurisdiction. As a result, no other state had the right to complain about their treatment or to protest against it. To do so would have constituted intervention in the domestic affairs of the other state, which was deemed to be a violation of international law. Thus, when the United States wished to express its concern over the pogroms and mass killings of Jews in Romania and Russia in the late nineteenth and early twentieth centuries, it took care to avoid being charged with interference in the domestic affairs of these countries. To get around the domestic jurisdiction barrier, the United States argued that the maltreatment of Jews in Romania, for example, led many poor and sick Romanian Jews to come to the United States, thereby imposing social and economic burdens on the United States.[5] Note that it was these interests and not humanitarian concerns which provided the United States with something of a valid international law basis for protesting against the pogroms.

The domestic jurisdiction principle also limited the humanitarian role the United States sought to play in confronting the Armenian genocide, particularly during its early stages.[6] And it kept some countries from interceding with Germany in any meaningful way when Hitler embarked on his persecution of German Jews. Of course, the domestic jurisdiction doctrine also provided the many countries that wished to remain silent in the face of these Nazi measures with an excuse for not speaking out. More importantly, and outrageous as it may sound to contemporary ears, Hitler would not have violated the international law in force at the time had he limited himself to the extermination solely of German and stateless Jews. It is important to keep this sad truth in mind in order to fully appreciate not only how far international law has come since the days of the Holocaust but also how much this development is the direct result of the Holocaust.

The Impact of World War Two

Efforts to change the status of individuals under international law gained increasing support as the scale of Nazi atrocities became known. As early as 1941, President Franklin D. Roosevelt, in his "Four Freedoms" speech, called for a "world founded upon four essential human freedoms," namely, "freedom of speech and expression," "freedom of every person to worship God in his own way," "freedom from want," and "freedom from fear." Roosevelt's vision of "the moral order," as he characterized it, became the clarion call of the nations that fought the Axis in the Second World War and founded the United Nations. The war also quite naturally led to the realization that traditional international law concepts about the rights of individual human beings had to be drastically revised in order to empower the international community to deal with large-scale violations of human rights, irrespective of the nationality of the victims, and that it also had to provide for the punishment of those responsible for these violations.

When we compare the position of individuals under international law as it existed before the Second World War with their status under contemporary international law, it is evident that a dramatic legal and conceptual transformation has taken place.[7] This transformation has "internationalized human rights and humanized international law."[8] As a consequence of the internationalization of human rights, the way a country today treats human beings generally, whether they are its citizens or not, is a legitimate subject of international concern and diplomatic discussion. Due to the humanization of international law, individuals as such now have internationally guaranteed human rights, and to that extent are subjects of international law. Moreover, as we shall see, more and more international tribunals and institutions have been and continue to be created to permit individuals to assert their international human rights directly against states that have violated them. Of course—and this needs to be emphasized—we still have a long way to go as far as the effective international enforcement of these rights is concerned, but a great deal of progress is being made nevertheless.

A. The United Nations and Human Rights Law

The modern international law of human rights begins with the Charter of the United Nations, despite the fact that it contains only some vague statements relating to human rights.[9] Given the experience of the Second World War, the Holocaust, and the other horrendous crimes which had been committed by the Nazis, there was hope in San Francisco, where the Charter was drafted, that it would proclaim an enforceable bill of rights. That was not to be, despite the support for such a document by many smaller countries participating in the San Francisco meeting and the extensive lobbying by nongovernment organizations (NGOs), particularly by Jewish organizations and individual Jewish leaders.[10] The strongest opposition to the inclusion in the Charter of any meaningful human rights provisions came, not surprisingly, from Stalin's Soviet Union. But Britain, France, and the United States were also not too eager at the time to support strong UN human rights provisions.

The reluctance of the United States was no doubt due to de jure racial discrimination, then still in force in the South, and to states' rights concerns. These policies and concerns would have posed serious obstacles to U.S. ratification of the UN Charter had it contained binding human rights obligations barring racial discrimination. At the time, the U.S. Senate was still controlled by a coalition of segregationist southern Democrats and conservative midwestern Republicans.[11] They violently opposed any treaty provisions that would have permitted U.S. courts to override existing discriminatory laws and practices in force in many states of the Union. This Senate coalition would have blocked the ratification of the UN Charter if it had contained such provisions since, as a treaty of the United States, the charter would have superseded any state laws in conflict with it as well as earlier federal laws.[12] The Truman administration, well aware of President Woodrow Wilson's inability to get the U.S. Senate to approve the ratification of the Covenant of the League of Nations, was not willing to risk making the same mistake with regard to the UN Charter. The United States preferred therefore to have the UN Charter contain only very vague human rights language.

But that vague language—"the United Nations shall promote . . . universal respect for, and observance of, human rights and fundamental freedom for all without distinction as to race, sex, language or religion"—buttressed by a pledge of the UN member states to cooperate with the UN in these promotional activities, set the stage, together with the Universal Declaration of Human Rights, for the contemporary human rights revolution.[13]

The Universal Declaration of Human Rights, drafted by a distinguished UN committee consisting, among others, of Eleanor Roosevelt, René Cassin of France, and Charles Malik of Lebanon, was proclaimed by the UN General Assembly in 1948. Although adopted as a nonbinding UN resolution, the Universal Declaration has over the years joined the Magna Carta, the French Declaration of the Rights and Duties of Man, and the American Declaration of Independence as a milestone in mankind's struggle for freedom and human dignity, becoming the foremost international instrument on the subject.[14]

Following the adoption of the Universal Declaration, the UN embarked on a drafting effort designed to convert the lofty language of the Declaration into binding treaty obligations. The result has been a large body of international human rights agreements, now widely ratified, including such important instruments as the Genocide Convention, the International Covenants on Human Rights, the International Convention on the Elimination of All Forms of Racial Discrimination, the Convention on the Elimination of All Forms of Discrimination against Women, the Convention on the Rights of the Child, and the Convention against Torture and Other Cruel, Inhuman, or Degrading Treatment or Punishment.[15] Some of these treaties provide for committees, consisting of independent experts, to supervise the implementation of the rights these instruments guarantee. Many states now also recognize the right of individuals to file complaints with these committees if their rights are violated. Additional human rights treaties have been adopted by the UN and its specialized agencies, among them the United Nations Educational Scientific and Cultural Organization (UNESCO) and the International Labor Organization, some with their own mechanisms of supervision.[16]

Before addressing the question whether the vast body of UN human rights law now on the books is being complied with by the states that are legally bound to give effect to it, let me say a word about the human rights law and institutions created within the framework of regional intergovernmental organizations, such as the Council of Europe, the Organization of American States, and the Organization of African Unity.

B. Regional Human Rights Systems

In the early 1950s, the Council of Europe, a regional intergovernmental organization then comprising only Western European democratic states, adopted the European Convention of Human Rights. The preamble of the Convention expresses the resolve of "the governments of European countries which are like-minded and have a common heritage of political traditions, ideals, freedom and the rule of law, to take the first steps for the collective enforcement of certain of the rights stated in the Universal Declaration [of Human Rights]."

The adoption of the European Convention by the Council of Europe was prompted in large measure by the Holocaust and the lessons Europe's post–World War II democratic leaders had learned when watching Hitler's rise to power. Explaining the need for a European treaty guaranteeing human rights, one of its leading proponents, a former French minister of justice, put it as follows:

> Democracies do not become Nazi countries in one day. Evil progresses cunningly, with a minority operating . . . to remove the levers of control. One by one, freedoms are suppressed, in one sphere after the other. Public opinion and the entire national conscience are asphyxiated. And then, when everything is in order, the "Führer" is installed and the evolution continues even to the oven of the crematorium.
>
> It is necessary to intervene before it is too late. A conscience must exist somewhere which will sound the alarm in the minds of a nation menaced by this progressive corruption, to warn them of a peril and to show them that they are progressing down a long road which leads far, sometimes even to Buchenwald or to Dachau.[17]

Since the end of the Cold War, the membership in the European Convention of Human Rights has grown to more than forty European countries, among them Russia, Germany, France, and the United Kingdom. It now also includes some former Soviet Republics and most of the Soviet Union's erstwhile Eastern European allies. The catalog of rights guaranteed by the Convention has been enlarged over the years by means of additional protocols. The Convention also established the European Court of Human Rights, the first ever such international institution where individuals may institute proceedings against any state party to the Convention allegedly violating their rights. In the past, the court has found many states in violation of one or more provisions of the Convention and required them to pay compensation or to repeal or amend national laws in conflict with the Convention. The Convention now enjoys the status of domestic law in almost all of its states parties. In some states, moreover, it has acquired constitutional law status. The United Kingdom, where for decades the Convention could not be applied directly by British courts, eventually adopted legislation removing that obstacle. Over the years, the European Court of Human Rights has for all practical purposes become the constitutional court of Europe for questions of human rights and fundamental freedoms. What is more, its judgments are complied with as a matter of course.

The European Convention system is rightly considered to be the most effective international system for the protection of human rights in existence today. It has served as a model for other regional human rights treaties, notably the American Convention on Human Rights, adopted within the framework of the Organization of American States. In force since 1978, the Inter-American Commission and Court of Human Rights have increasingly played an important role in promoting and enforcing human rights in the Americas, without as yet being able to match the successes of the European system. With the exception of Canada, the United States, and a number of smaller Commonwealth Caribbean countries, all Western hemisphere nations have now become parties to the Convention and accepted the jurisdiction of the Inter-American Court of Human Rights. A similar regional human rights treaty, the African Charter of Human and Peoples' Rights, has been in force for a number of years, but it has still not had a significant impact on the protection of human rights in Africa. That is not surprising, given the African continent's political and economic problems.

C. Failures and Achievements

It would be dishonest not to admit that despite the vast body of international human rights law in existence today—I know of no other branch of international law which has produced more law—many states merely give lip service to that law without complying with it. Put another way, international human rights law continues to be blatantly violated in many parts of the world despite often valiant efforts by democratic governments, by governmental and nongovernmental organizations, and by individual human beings around the world to prevent such violations.

Let us not lose sight of the other side of the coin, however. To start with, it is clear that international human rights standards and international efforts to enforce them have over time helped to improve human rights conditions in various countries around the world. The existence of these standards has also served to legitimate efforts by democratic governments to press for compliance and to tie trade preferences, development aid, and military assistance to the improvement of human rights conditions in many countries. None of this would have been possible before World War II given the absence of the normative framework applicable to human rights now in effect.

It is important also to remember that the various UN human rights institutions, such as the treaty bodies established to supervise compliance with the UN human rights treaties and conventions, have gradually been able to engage governments in ever more intrusive human rights dialogues, publicly exposing significant shortcomings.[18] These dialogues have not necessarily always or even frequently proved successful in remedying specific human rights violations, but they have made people around the world ever more aware of the existence of international human rights guarantees and of the obligations assumed by their governments to honor them. These expectations of compliance tend to put pressure on governments to comply, making it increasingly more difficult for them simply to shrug off their international human rights obligations. Instead, governments find that they are being compelled to explain their noncompliance or to deny that they are guilty of alleged human rights violations. By thus implicitly acknowledging their human rights obligations, governments are frequently forced to rethink their human rights policies and to improve their human rights practices.

The international climate that has produced the expectations of compliance has been reinforced by the work of regional human rights institutions and UN specialized agencies. An important role in this regard has also been played by the periodic UN-sponsored World Conferences on Human Rights, among them in particular the Vienna World Conference or the Fourth World Conference on Women. Important, too, have been the Follow-Up Conferences of the Organization for Security and Cooperation in Europe. Today, moreover, it is rare for major intergovernmental meetings or conferences not to deal with some aspect of human rights.

Many governments have now established human rights departments in their foreign ministries because of the growing foreign policy implications and importance of the subject. All these developments strengthen the public's perception of the centrality of human rights and expectations of governmental compliance, putting ever greater pressure on governments to act accordingly.

Equally relevant is the dramatic expansion in recent decades of the number of national and international human rights NGOs. Their existence and ever more important status is the direct result of the normative and institutional developments I have described. They provide NGOs with the legitimacy they need to function effectively. Specifically, these developments facilitate NGO efforts to investigate and publicize human rights violations, to lobby for appropriate legal and institutional changes to prevent future violations, and to file complaints on behalf of victims of human rights violations. NGOs have played, and continue to play, a vital role in deepening mankind's expectations with regard to human rights and the obligations of governments to respect them.

Skeptics frequently forget that the human rights revolution played an important role in hastening the end of apartheid in South Africa; it no doubt also contributed to speeding the demise of the Soviet Union. The fall of many oppressive regimes in different parts of the world can be attributed to it. This is not to say, of course, that other factors may not have played an equally or more important role in bringing about some of these changes in one or the other country. It should also not be forgotten that the human rights revolution was not able to prevent the Rwanda genocide or the horrendous crimes that were committed in the former Yugoslavia. But it would be a mistake not to recognize that, in today's world, human rights issues are closely intertwined with political and economic considerations, and this to such an extent that governments are frequently no longer able to separate one from the other. That, in turn, has an impact on their international human rights policies and, in general, on improving human rights conditions and preventing human rights violations. If only some such system had existed before the Holocaust!

Conclusion

The contemporary international law on human rights that I have described in this lecture has taken many decades to evolve. The development of this law owes much to the impact of the Holocaust and its influence in shaping mankind's consciousness of and reaction to the crimes against humanity and the genocides that the world has experienced since the Holocaust.

Although I have in this essay focused on international human rights, it should be noted that since the Second World War, international law in general has become ever more responsive to international humanitarian needs and to social, cultural, and educational concerns. The largely sterile international law of the pre–World War Two era, with its almost exclusive emphasis on political diplomacy, state prerogatives, and national sovereignty, has taken on a more humane face. Although many other factors account for this gradual transformation, the Holocaust and the Second World War certainly contributed to it by getting governments to realize that international law must address mankind's concerns if it is to play a meaningful role in promoting and preserving a peaceful world.

The preamble to the constitution of UNESCO, adopted shortly after the end of the war, expresses in almost lyrical terms the thinking that influenced the post–World War Two transformation of international law. "Since wars begin in the minds of men," it declares, "it is in the minds of men that the defences of peace must be constructed." The preamble further emphasizes that "the great and terrible war which has now ended was a war made possible by the denial of the democratic principles of the dignity, equality and mutual respect of men, and by the propagation, in their place, through ignorance and prejudice, of the doctrine of the inequality of men and races."

Similar ideas are reflected in the preamble to the Charter of the United Nations, which expresses the determination of its founders "to reaffirm faith in fundamental human rights, in the dignity and worth of the human person, in the equal rights of men and women and of nations large and small . . . and to promote social progress and better standards of life in larger freedom."

Contemporary international law now regulates many spheres of human endeavor previously deemed to fall within the domestic jurisdiction of states. This has forced international law to expand the scope of its legislative reach and to establish new international institutions to cope with contemporary societal problems. The dramatic transformation in international law owes much to the lessons of the Holocaust. What a pity that it took the Holocaust to provide the impetus for these changes.

NOTES

1. L. Oppenheim, *International Law: A Treatise*, 2d ed., H. Lauterpacht, ed. (1912), I: §§ 289–90.

2. *Ibid.*, § 291.

3. *See* H. Lauterpacht, *International Law and Human Rights* (1950), the most important early post–World War II text on the subject.

4. L. Oppenheim, *International Law: A Treatise*, 3d ed., H. Lauterpacht, ed. (1937), I: § 292, n.4.

5. Letter from U.S. Secretary of State Hay (Aug. 11, 1902), [1902] U.S. Foreign Relations 42.

6. *See* Letter from U.S. Secretary of States Root to O. Straus (Jan. 25, 1906), 2 U.S. Foreign Relations 1417–19, *reprinted in* L. Sohn and T. Buergenthal, *International Protection of Human Rights* (1973), 183.

7. *See generally* T. Meron, *International Law in the Age of Human Rights*, Hague Academy of International Law, Collected Courses (2003), 301: 9 *et seq.*

8. For what may well have been the earliest use of this phrase, *see* T. Buergenthal, *Human Rights: A Challenge for Universities*, 31 UNESCO Courier 25 (1978), 28.

9. *See generally* T. Buergenthal, *The Normative and Institutional Evolution of International Human Rights*, 19 Human Rights Quarterly 703 (1997).

10. W. Korey, *NGOs and the Universal Declaration of Human Rights* (1998), 33.

11. *See, e.g.*, Robert Caro, *Lyndon Johnson: Master of the Senate* (2002), 96–97.

12. *Restatement (Third) of the Foreign Relations Law of the United States* (1987), § 115.

13. *See* L. Sohn, *The New International Law: Protection of the Rights of Individuals Rather Than States*, 32 American U. L. Rev. 1 (1982).

14. *See generally* B. Van der Heijden & B. Tahzib-Lie, eds., *Reflections on the Universal Declaration of Human Rights* (1998).

15. For these texts, *see Human Rights: A Compilation of International Instruments* (United Nations, 2002), I: first and second part. *See also ibid.*, II, for the regional human rights instruments.

16. For the work of these and related UN bodies, *see* P. Alston, ed., *The United Nations and Human Rights: A Critical Appraisal* (1992). *See also* T. Meron, *Human Rights Law-Making in the United Nations: A Critique of Instruments and Process* (1986).

17. *See* A. H. Robertson, *Human Rights in Europe*, 2d ed. (1977), 4 (quoting Former French Minister of Justice, Pierre-Henri Teitgen, speaking to the Consultative Assembly of the Council of Europe in August 1949).

18. For the work of one such body, *see* T. Buergenthal, *The U.N. Human Rights Committee*, 5 Max Planck Yearbook of United Nations Law 341 (2001).

Chapter 2

The State Department, Nazi Gold, and the Search for Holocaust Assets

William Z. Slany

Introduction

During the last years of the twentieth century, an unprecedented international campaign to achieve long-delayed justice and compensation for the victims of the Holocaust and their heirs gathered strength until it became a powerful moral and political incentive to act. Stuart Eizenstat and the State Department gave essential leadership and vision to the United States' management of the international negotiations for Holocaust-era restitution. In a unique occurrence for policymakers and historians, the historical staffs of the State Department and ten other federal agencies joined together to provide historical research that gave U.S. government negotiators important and essential insights and impetus. This brief and rather spontaneous episode of historical research led by State Department historians gave context and form to the confused early steps of the U.S. government's struggle to seize leadership of the Holocaust restitution movement. It also reflected the maturing of some liberal humanitarian tendencies in the government, and especially in the State Department.[1]

Like other remarkable episodes in history, the movement for Holocaust-era restitution in the 1990s advanced as a result more of unexpected concatenations of events than of the far-sightedness of individuals. The movement started with efforts for the restitution or compensation of Holocaust victims languishing in post-Communist Eastern Europe. The rampant economic and financial expansion in the Western industrial nations at the time made redressing the plight of the victims, who were isolated and neglected for so long, more urgent and more possible. Initiated and inspired by the World Jewish Congress (WJC), the movement gained its first U.S. government support in the person of Stuart Eizenstat, first as ambassador to the European Union in 1995 and then as Under Secretary of Commerce in the spring of 1996. All branches of the U.S. government were soon drawn into the restitution campaign when the prosperous Swiss banking industry proved insensitive and resistant to claims to the dormant accounts of Holocaust victims. The Senate Banking Committee hearings in April 1996 were a sensational introduction of the Swiss banking issue to the public and the press, where the Clinton administration made clear that it regarded restitution to victims as an important moral issue for the United States. Class action suits were filed in federal court on behalf of survivors, and this pending litigation—reinforced by the threat of punitive action by banking officials in various states—sparked investigations and negotiations. Potential resolutions and settlements in the hundreds of millions of dollars became real possibilities. Each step in the campaign for restitution, in the various government and private venues, was accompanied by sporadic revelations of tantalizing and troubling bits of Holocaust-era history. It was into this confusing but emotionally charged situation, where huge indemnities were being discussed, that U.S. government historians made their brief but essential contribution to government policymaking.

The State Department and the Origins of the First U.S. Report on Nazi Gold (the Eizenstat Report)

The State Department's involvement in the pursuit of dormant Swiss bank accounts of Holocaust victims and the related issue of Nazi-looted assets began with Senator D'Amato's Senate Banking Committee's request in the summer of 1996 to executive branch agencies to produce relevant historical records on Nazi assets. The committee staff had begun in the spring of 1996 its own preliminary exploration of government wartime and postwar files at the National Archives and Records Administration. During the summer, researchers working on behalf of Jewish organizations and class action lawyers joined the hunt. They soon identified records that made clear the important role of Swiss banks as gold clearinghouses for Nazi Germany both before and during the war. Senator D'Amato and his staff, as well as the WJC, focused public attention on the Nazi gold issue with their periodic release of documents with sensational and even shocking historical evidence concerning the role of Swiss banks. This early research engendered interest in Holocaust assets questions at the National Archives, but it lacked focus and required the professional expertise and access that only federal historians could provide. The success of the U.S. intervention in Holocaust restitution efforts turned on historical research in the records of wartime government agencies, an area where the State Department's Historian's Office and its staff of professional historians had special expertise. The office had a tradition of preparing narrative studies for policymakers, and could follow the example of the British report on Nazi gold. In September 1996, the State Department authorized the Historian's Office to respond to the Senate request for documents and produce a comprehensive study of the diplomacy surrounding the Nazi gold issue. The study was intended for State Department policymakers, based on a close review of U.S. government records, and aimed at demonstrating what U.S. officials knew and did about the theft of assets by the Nazi regime.

Even before the State Department study had gotten underway, it became the nucleus of a broader interagency study. In September 1996, in response to the inquiries from WJC president Edgar Bronfman, President Clinton directed Under Secretary of Commerce Stuart Eizenstat[2] to expand his responsibilities for Holocaust assets issues to include the coordination of a government-wide, executive branch review of the gold remaining with the Tripartite Gold Commission and the larger question of the past policies and actions regarding gold looted by the Germans. Eizenstat decided to make the State Department's proposed historical study the basis of this broader interagency review. Interagency working groups were formed to coordinate U.S. policy on the diplomatic and legal aspects of the issues, particularly the disposition of undistributed gold recovered from the Nazis.

Why the State Department?

President Clinton's decision to give Eizenstat the lead in coordinating the broad U.S. government review set in motion six years of U.S. involvement in Holocaust investigations, negotiations, and litigation. Eizenstat inspired and directed the government effort that gave the United States the leadership of these international efforts. His position in the State Department provided means and context for his successful shaping of a final international accounting. Holocaust restitution issues, almost always freighted with intensely painful memories, strained some ongoing diplomatic relationships. But the State Department proved an effective instrument for Eizenstat's efforts.

Human Rights and the State Department

Nearly twenty years of human rights battles in American diplomacy sensitized the State Department to the issues of justice for the Holocaust victims. The national despair over the Vietnam War and the turbulent campaign for domestic civil rights in the 1960s and 1970s impacted American diplomacy, as the advancement of human rights around the world became a dominant component of U.S. foreign policy. A separate Bureau of Human Rights within the State Department was established in 1978, and the observance of human rights became an increasingly important component of U.S. foreign aid programs. A new generation of American diplomats grew accustomed to addressing human rights around the world, and the State Department became an articulate and practiced international advocate of such rights.

The State Department Revisits the Holocaust

The State Department's new emphasis on human rights underscored the need for the United States to confront the indifference, even anti-Semitism, that marred the U.S. government's conduct during the Holocaust. Historical scholarship published in the 1970s and 1980s clarified the indifference of State Department leaders to the plight of the Jews, resulting in prewar and wartime immigration and visa policies that prevented the escape of hundreds of thousands of Jews from occupied Europe. The rising public demand for a post–Cold War reexamination of these forgotten episodes found a receptive ear in the State Department during the Clinton presidency. In 1995 Secretary of State Warren Christopher publicly acknowledged the State Department's moral and legal failure to act in saving the hundreds of refugees aboard the ill-fated ship *St. Louis* as it languished off Florida in May 1939. In 1996, he honored activist Varian Fry's actions in rescuing Nazi victims from southern France in 1940 in the face of State Department indifference and even hostility. These early steps to make amends for the State Department's silence during the Holocaust led directly to the steady support for Eizenstat's diplomatic intervention regarding Holocaust assets restitution. The Nazi gold study launched in 1996 was another manifestation of that commitment.

The Interagency Effort and the Reports of May 1997 and June 1998

The interagency historical review, launched by Eizenstat and led by State Department historians, resulted in the May 1997 publication of the so-called Eizenstat Report, formally known as *U.S. and Allied Efforts to Recover and Restore Gold and Other Assets Stolen or Hidden by Germany during World War II*, and its June 1998 supplement, *U.S. and Allied Wartime and Postwar Relations and Negotiations with Argentina, Portugal, Spain, Sweden, and Turkey on Looted Gold and German External Assets and U.S. Concerns about the Fate of the Wartime Ustasha Treasury.* These reports relied on federal historical records and provided historical context for Eizenstat's diplomatic initiatives. The reports also accelerated examinations by other governments of their own past actions regarding Holocaust assets. In particular, the reports' uncompromising look at past policies dramatized the scale of injustices inflicted on Holocaust victims and promoted an atmosphere of urgency for the ongoing restitution and compensation negotiations.

The Eizenstat Report

The first report of May 1997 was researched, written, and published in seven months by an unprecedented alliance of U.S. government historians, researchers, policymakers, and diplomats. Of greatest importance was the personal involvement of Under Secretary Eizenstat, who brought to the project vision, leadership, enthusiasm, and drive. Eizenstat marshaled within the government a powerful priority, without which the reports most certainly would have been endlessly delayed and deflected. Heads of the relevant government agencies eagerly cooperated with Eizenstat, on the few occasions when he intervened, to ensure that sufficient resources were assigned and appropriate documents were declassified. Eizenstat was deeply concerned about all aspects of the research and writing of the reports, demanding clarity and debating points of historical evidence and analysis, as well as mediating the occasional interagency conflict. While always acutely sensitive to the policy implications of the developing research, he never sought to dictate lines of analysis or conclusions.

Even with Eizenstat's leadership, the reports could not have been written by mobilized federal historians and researchers without the enthusiastic support and full resources of the National Archives, which became the headquarters for the international research in Holocaust-era assets. Even that unprecedented cooperation would have come to naught if the State Department's Historian's Office had not harnessed the resources in support of the policymakers engaged in the emerging international dispute over Holocaust-era assets.

Once Eizenstat established the interagency working group in October 1996, research and writing went forward on the basis of an agreed distribution of responsibilities. The State Department historians, researchers, and editors prepared the largest part of the report and assembled the contributions of the other agencies into a comprehensive text. Interagency participation included

- State Department historians who explored the development of wartime allied policy regarding the German looting of monetary gold in Europe and the postwar Allied policies for the restitution of the gold from the neutral nations;
- Treasury Department officials who, with no historical staff, arranged for the speedy declassification and transfer to the National Archives of more than a million pages of wartime records;
- the historical staffs of the U.S. Holocaust Memorial Museum and the Justice Department's Office of Special Investigations (OSI), who prepared narrative texts based on original historical research outside of U.S. records regarding the army's evolving policy on the disposition of looted assets recovered by the occupation forces in Germany;
- CIA history staff, who prepared the chapter on the "Safehaven" project, which sought to discover and prevent efforts to hide German assets abroad for a possible revival of the Nazis after Germany's defeat;
- U.S. Army Center for Military History officials, who provided information on the army's recovery and disposition of looted monetary gold and other valuables in the U.S. Zone of Occupation;

- National Security Agency officials, who identified and declassified several hundred 1945 and 1946 "intercepted" messages between the Swiss Legation in Washington and the Swiss Foreign Ministry; and
- the Federal Reserve Bank of New York, the repository of the U.S. share of looted gold held by the Tripartite Gold Commission, which provided information on the wartime operations of the Bank for International Settlements (BIS) regarding the sale of gold by Germany.

Agreement on a Final Text

From the beginning, the State Department secured a consensus that in answering the questions of what the government knew about Nazi gold issues and what it did as a result of such knowledge, research would be restricted to U.S. government records. It was also agreed that the complete opening of the records for public review at the National Archives was equally important. This consensus was generally easily maintained. Only the Justice Department's OSI took issue with the project's focus on the origin and nature of diplomatic policy decisions. OSI was strenuous, at times rancorous, in its criticism of the State Department's drafts of the report for allegedly exculpating American officials from responsibility for failure to achieve substantial postwar restitution, especially from Switzerland, and for inadequately acknowledging the presence of victim gold mixed in with the looted monetary gold recovered after the war. Only Eizenstat's mediation avoided an embarrassing fracture of the consensus.

The Conclusions of the Report

The participating historians eventually reached agreement on the basic content and major conclusions of the report: (1) Nazi Germany looted more than $700 million in gold from both occupied nations and private individuals; (2) gold from the personal possessions of victims of the Holocaust had been included in Germany's wartime gold reserve; (3) the restitution of looted gold and other property to their rightful owners after the war had been far from complete; and (4) the policies and actions of the United States and its wartime allies in the search for stolen gold and other properties had been flawed in its implementation and premature in its end.

The Reaction to the Report

Under Secretary Eizenstat's foreword to the report provided an "executive summary" and placed the interagency historical research effort into a political and moral context. The foreword, which owed much to the drafting skill of Deputy Assistant Secretary of State for Public Affairs Bennett Freeman, drew together the major conclusions of the report in a clear and accessible form.

The State Department diplomats, dismayed by the condemnatory conclusions in the early drafts of the foreword regarding the conduct of the neutral states, argued that the conclusions in the foreword were not supported by the report and could harm current relations with the governments whose support the United States was seeking. After weighing the possible danger to ongoing diplomacy posed by the report, Eizenstat and his advisers concluded that policy and political imperatives on behalf of the Holocaust victims required going forward with publication. Critics in Switzerland tried without success to fend off the report's impact by focusing on the foreword, claiming it was arbitrary, political, and not reflective of the full text. In fact, however, there was no difference in substance or spirit between the two.

The May 1997 report gained substantial media attention and the resulting public awareness of Holocaust assets issues put the State Department and the U.S. government in the forefront of the international Holocaust restitution movement. The report was not without its negative consequences, however. As some diplomats had feared, a few of the wartime neutral nations, particularly Switzerland, were both angered and chastened by the publicity and resisted American initiatives to acknowledge wartime behavior and compensate survivors. The class action lawsuits by American lawyers against Swiss banks no doubt benefited from the publicity, but American diplomats were often distressed by the strains the report placed on bilateral relations and the rather ugly backdrop such historical information provided for ongoing negotiations on other matters.

Openness and the Interagency Project

Unfettered public access to all Holocaust-era records, not just those dealing with Nazi gold, was a principal objective of the interagency project. The State Department's Historian's Office had by 1996 a prominent role in this drive for openness of the historical foreign affairs record. Congress adopted legislation in October 1991 that made the State Department officially responsible for preparing and publishing the comprehensive record of American policy in the official *Foreign Relations of the United States* documentary series. The Clinton administration strongly supported the principle of openness, and Executive Order 12958 of April 1995 expanded and accelerated the declassification of all such government records. The president's order gave impetus to the entire federal government for the organized opening of historical records.

At the urging of the Historian's Office, and with the strong support of Under Secretary Eizenstat, agencies moved quickly to ensure that the National Archives accessioned not only records used in the Nazi gold studies but also the whole realm of Holocaust-era records. Eizenstat sought to encourage other governments to follow the U.S. example. The National Archives was tireless and unsparing of its resources and became the world center of Holocaust-era assets research. By 1998 the National Archives' printed guide to the records relevant to Nazi gold studies exceeded six hundred pages, and it grew still larger in later years. It was also a guide to the history of the Holocaust-era policies of many other governments. The volume of records at the National Archives in Washington bearing on the policies and actions of other governments during the war—allies, belligerents, and neutrals—was far greater and far more accessible than almost anywhere else in the world.

The Need for a Second U.S. Report

The interagency report released by Under Secretary Eizenstat in May 1997 was published as a "preliminary report" because it was clearly the product of hasty research that left many issues inadequately examined. Eizenstat and his close advisers urgently needed the initial report to clarify unanswered questions about looted gold and to provide some leverage for diplomatic intervention into the increasingly heated negotiations among the Swiss banks, American lawyers, and Jewish organizations. They could not wait beyond the spring of 1997 for this initial report, which became the first Eizenstat Report.

By the end of the summer of 1997, Eizenstat decided that the State Department's Historian's Office should head another interagency team to prepare a second report. The goal of this "supplementary study" was to provide a more comprehensive historical account of Allied negotiations with the neutral nations regarding wartime and postwar use of Nazi looted assets. The second report sought to more intensely assess the financial and economic roles of the neutral nations during the war and to encourage these nations to be more positive toward U.S. initiatives for compensation to Holocaust survivors. There were also those at the State Department, myself included, who wanted to try to probe further into U.S. government policies regarding other aspects of wartime and postwar decision making regarding the Holocaust.

The June 1998 Interagency Report

The supplementary Eizenstat report published in June 1998 was the product of a reconstituted interagency team, again led by the State Department. The State Department's Historian's Office did nearly all of the drafting of the text, with small but important contributions from historians and experts from the Office of Special Investigations, the Central Intelligence Agency, the Center for Military History, and the Federal Reserve Bank of New York. Once again, Eizenstat closely monitored the research and writing of the report and devoted long meetings to carefully critiquing the evidence and analysis presented in various drafts.

The report of June 1998 focused on U.S. and Allied policymaking regarding the trading relations between Germany and major neutral nations, Switzerland excepted, and explored in greater detail the nature of the inadequate postwar restitution negotiations with these neutrals. The inquiry into the movement of monetary gold was expanded to include German commerce with Argentina and the gold reserve accumulated by the puppet state of Croatia, which mysteriously disappeared at war's end. The report accumulated more evidence of what the United States and its Allies knew of the gold acquired by the neutral nations (other than Switzerland) from Germany in exchange for vital commodities that enabled Germany to prolong the war. Some of the historical commissions had issued reports by this time, and the findings in their reports were incorporated into the text where appropriate.

The second report concluded that the United States and its wartime allies failed to press the neutral nations for the return of looted monetary gold in the postwar years, did little to recover the gold and other valuables of the victims, and fell far short of even modest goals of applying recovered assets to the relief and succor of Jewish refugees in Europe in the postwar years. A significant portion of the report dwelt on the record of wartime Allied efforts to curb and end the trade between the neutrals and Germany, trade substantially paid for by looted monetary gold. A foreword by Under Secretary Eizenstat emphasized the conclusion that the neutrality practiced by the neutral nations, including Switzerland, facilitated Germany's industrial effort and prolonged the war. The foreword also made more explicit the relationship between the historical research for the U.S. report and the investigations of other historical commissions and the way these efforts all related to the ultimate goal of compensating the victims of the Holocaust.

The End of the Interagency Historical Project

The June 1998 report signaled the end of State Department and interagency historical research into Holocaust-era assets. The international negotiations among governments, lawyers, and organizations had moved beyond looted gold and Swiss bank accounts into looted art, unpaid insurance policies, and the wartime suffering of slave laborers. Under Secretary Eizenstat, supported by a new special staff in the State Department's Bureau of European Affairs, continued to take the lead in these intense and complex negotiations for the next several years.

A new phase in the Holocaust assets effort was launched at the Washington Holocaust Assets Conference, convened at the State Department in December 1998. Representatives from forty-four nations and thirteen nongovernmental organizations debated how to achieve the restitution of stolen art, compensation by insurance companies, and restitution of other cultural valuables and Jewish communal properties in Eastern Europe. A Presidential Advisory Commission on Holocaust Era Assets in the United States, authorized by Congress in June 1998, ensured that U.S. policymaking on the issues was responsive to a broad range of interests. The Advisory Commission's historical research staff was entirely independent of the historians of the various federal agencies, including the State Department's Historian's Office, whose involvement in the restitution and compensation campaigns had ended. U.S. diplomats engaged in the ongoing

international negotiations did not want or need other government historical research that risked inflaming public opinion at home and abroad.

Conclusions

The Eizenstat reports were the serendipitous product of the brief concate-
nation of political forces in the last years of the twentieth century. The end
of the Cold War and the lifting of the Iron Curtain, the dwindling numbers of Holocaust survivors, and the financial boom in the major industrial countries all combined to make possible the international struggle to
provide compensation and justice to Holocaust victims and their heirs.
Jewish groups interested in unresolved issues concerning Holocaust victims, reinforced by a new generation of aggressive attorneys, stirred all
three branches of the U.S. government into action. The courts responded
to class action suits on behalf of victims, Congress aired many of the issues and authorized historical studies, and the Clinton administration
turned to Stuart Eizenstat to manage the executive response. Eizenstat
brought to bear both passion and skill in leading the international effort
to bring closure and compensation for the nearly forgotten tragedies of
the Holocaust era. The State Department, which had become sensitized
to the nation's more humanitarian activist tendencies, was the locus of
Eizenstat's efforts. A coalition of federal historians and researchers, led by
State Department historians, gave Eizenstat two timely research reports
that illuminated failed government policies for the rescue of the assets of
Holocaust victims at the end of the war, and that provided much of the
early rationale for Eizenstat's bold diplomatic intervention for restitution.
The role of the historians in the overall Holocaust-era assets effort was
brief and small, but it did demonstrate that historical facts were potent for
successful policymaking. And just as important, the interagency Nazi gold
reports of 1997 and 1998 were a clear acknowledgment and a partial redress of the State Department's deplorable failures in recognizing and aiding Holocaust victims both during and after World War II.

NOTES

1. Space constraints preclude taking up here the important parallel historical
studies on various Holocaust assets issues that were undertaken by or under the

auspices of various European governments, especially those of Britain and Switzerland.

2. Stuart Eizenstat held many important government posts over a more than thirty-year span. During the years covered by this essay he was U.S. representative to the European Union from 1993 to 1996, under secretary of commerce from May 1996 to June 1997, under secretary of state for Economic, Business, and Agricultural Affairs, from June 1997 to July 1999, and deputy secretary of the treasury, from July 1999 to January 2001.

Chapter 3

Confronting History
Restitution and the Historians

Michael Berenbaum

The major drama regarding Holocaust restitution issues was played out by political leaders and Jewish communal officials, diplomats and lawyers, bankers and insurance company executives, businesspersons and survivors. Historians played a significant but clearly supporting role, reviewing archival findings and leading international commissions to establish or recreate the national narratives that had been so decimated by the new historical information. When called upon, their skills—combing archival records, reconstructing events, determining who was present where and when and what they did—proved useful in strengthening or counteracting the evidence that was being gathered. They also uncovered new evidence, as well as evidence that was not quite new but was received in a rather different way due to the changed political climate.

What then have we learned for history from the restitution cases of the last decade? The great Holocaust scholar Raul Hilberg, whose work *The Destruction of the European Jews*[1] is now regarded as the most influential historical work on the Holocaust, is a political scientist by training. He identified six stages of the destruction process: definition, expropriation, concentration, deportation, mobile killing, and death camps. Definition was the first stage of destruction. In the Nuremberg Laws of 1935, Jews were defined on the basis of the religion of their grandparents. Jews were defined by blood lines, according to race, not religion, and thus there could be no escape by conversion. This legal definition, once enacted in 1935, became the norm whenever Germany conquered new territory.

In the classical understanding of the second stage, expropriation, the process began in 1933 with the Nazi ascent to power and continued through 1945. The first manifestations of expropriation were designed to make it impossible for Jews to live in Germany—and later in the countries that the Germans occupied—and thus to coerce their emigration while giving the local non-Jewish population the bounty of the departing Jews. In the later stage of expropriation, the confiscation of Jewish property was designed to give collateral economic benefits to the destruction process.

Two basic conclusions must be drawn from what we have learned in the past few years: first, that the expropriation did not end in 1945 with the end of the Nazi regime but continued with the failure to make restitution to survivors; and second, that expropriation was limited neither to Germans and their collaborators nor even to the local populations who lived under German occupation. It also affected neutral countries during the Holocaust and long thereafter, as well as entire industries, including banking, insurance, and the art world. These participants would have been the permanent beneficiaries of their ill-gotten gains had not the political-judicial processes intervened.

While antisemitism was undeniably a major factor in initiating and sustaining the process of expropriation, it was by no means the only factor, and it may not even have been present among those who participated in the processes of expropriation. More routine motivations included greed, the exploitation of weakness, and bureaucratic considerations, although antisemitism may have spurred expropriation along and salved the consciences of those involved. In looking at the motivations, we can never deny the presence of antisemitism as the engine of initiation that presented various parties with the opportunity to benefit from the confiscation and expropriation of Jewish wealth, but we should also look for a more complex dynamics of explanation. Yet the fact remains—as the restitution movement brought to light—that expropriation continued long after the defeat of Germany and, indeed, continues even in our day.

Almost fifteen years ago, Judith Miller published her study of historical memory of the Holocaust, One by One, by One,[2] which described the way in which the Holocaust was being remembered in many different countries. Since then much has happened. Many of the countries involved have been forced to reevaluate their role in the Holocaust and forced—by dint of circumstances and by important historical work—to rewrite their own history and to recraft their own historical narratives or historical myths. (A word of caution is in order: I use the term "myth" in the way that it is used in the history of religion, i.e., not as something opposed to truth but as the story we tell that underlies our deepest beliefs.)

In fact, as Stuart Eizenstat, who led the American restitution efforts, reported in his work *Imperfect Justice,* "twenty-one countries, from Argentina and Brazil to Latvia and Lithuania, have established some twenty-eight historical commissions to examine their role in World War II and their relationships with looted Nazi assets, the most comprehensive being the Swiss Bergier Commission and the French Mattéoli Commission."[3]

What has this reexamination wrought?

Let us consider three examples. Switzerland had portrayed itself as heroically resisting the Germans. Because of geography—the Alps—and the strength of its army, goes the Swiss myth, the Germans did not dare to invade. As a result, Switzerland could remain neutral, untainted by the corrupting and deadly impact of occupation. Years ago that self-depiction was challenged by a film, *The Boat Is Full,* which described Switzerland's unwillingness to accept refugees and its readiness to send Jews back into Germany. The banking scandal of the 1990s forced a much more systematic reevaluation of Switzerland's role and most especially of the way in which Swiss neutrality served the interests of the German state. The Bergier historical commission contributed significantly to this reevaluation and the process of revision. ("Revision" is an honorable task in history and not to be confused with revisionism, i.e., Holocaust denial, which deliberately misappropriated the term.) Today any discussion of Switzerland must include the role that it played in financing the Third Reich, most significantly by knowingly purchasing Nazi-stolen gold, as well as the mishandling by Swiss banks of the assets of Jewish depositors before, during, and after the war. Swiss neutrality is seen as a result of German needs, and the significant measure of its cooperation with Germany is no longer ignored.

As late as 1990, Austria had a vested stake in portraying itself as the first of Germany's victims rather than as a perpetrator of the Holocaust. (Stuart Eizenstat cites—as he puts it—"an ironic witticism straight from a Viennese coffeehouse" to the effect that "the Austrians had convinced themselves and the world that Hitler was a German and Beethoven was an Austrian.")[4] The controversy surrounding the election of Kurt Waldheim as president of Austria and the antisemitism that was stirred up in the process suggested that amnesia with regard to the Nazi years, most specifically 1938–45, was both permitted and indeed encouraged within Austrian society. While serious historians did not accept the Austrian narrative, it had widespread acceptance within the country and abroad, and indeed it insulated Austria from outside criticism. The Holocaust restitution movement of the 1990s led to greater acceptance of Austrian responsibility and a greater willingness to acknowledge culpability. There was a direct national statement regarding responsibility and a public apology that would never have been forthcoming in a different political climate. This apology sets the stage for very different types of research by Austrian historians and for Austrians' willingness to hear the findings of historians from abroad.

In 1985, President Ronald Reagan was invited to visit Bitburg by German chancellor Helmut Kohl as an effort to put behind the antagonisms of the war years and to cement the preferred narrative that the Nazis were few and not representative of the German nation. The American Jewish community, in an effort led by Elie Wiesel, tried to dissuade the president from laying a wreath on the graves of German soldiers at Bitburg. In retrospect, it seems that the fears that Germany would rewrite its history and exonerate itself for the Nazi years may have been exaggerated. There is a paradox relating to Holocaust memory: the innocent feel guilty. No one is more innocent that the young generation of Germans, who were born well after the war and are the grandchildren of the perpetrators. And yet, they are asking questions of the German past that their parents were reluctant to ask. What Anna Rosmus first confronted in her book and later in the film, *The Nasty Girl*—namely, the rewriting of the history of her town and her refusal to accept that falsification of history—has become commonplace among young Germans. Three of four Germans who saw *Schindler's List* were under the age of thirty. An exhibition on the Wehrmacht's role as the handmaiden of genocide—the Wehrmacht cooperated with the *Einsatzgruppen* (mobile killing squads) in initiating and carrying out the murder of European Jews in the East—was widely viewed in Germany. New questions were asked, questions that could not be faced a generation ago. Similarly, the debates surrounding Daniel Jonah Goldhagen's *Hitler's Willing Executioners,*[5] a work that engendered heated debate in the United States, provoked widespread discussions on college campuses throughout Germany on how responsible ordinary Germans were, and how supportive they were, of the mass murder of Jews.

The settlements negotiated by German businesses and the German government had an important effect on this process that goes well beyond the cash settlement. In the aftermath of World War II, it was assumed that proximity to the crime was directly related to responsibility. Business leaders often got off with the lightest sentences and served the least prison time. The long, tense negotiations over slave labor have imposed the distinction between slave labor and forced labor and detailed the scope of German corporate involvement. In the past few years, some German businesses have written serious histories of their corporate involvement with the Nazis; others, such as publishing giant Bertelsmann, were forced by dint of the historical records to write the history of their own companies and their record during the Nazi years. Volkswagen issued an unusually detailed and meticulous report. Some German firms that merged with American corporations or that do extensive business in the United States through local subsidiaries and therefore are very sensitive to their image in America produced histories of their involvement with the Third Reich as a public relations effort to rid themselves of accusations of guilt—to control the bad news by getting it out quickly and completely rather than having it exposed by others in an uncontrollable manner. These included Daimler-Chrysler, Degussa, and Deutsche Bank. In the United States, General Motors and Ford reexamined the roles of their subsidiaries during the war years. IBM was forced on the defensive by Edwin Black's sensationalistic account of its history,[6] but it has yet to produce a serious history of its role and the role of its technology in the "Final Solution."

Recent events in Romania also prove instructive. In the immediate aftermath of the collapse of communism, there was an attempt at the rehabilitation of Marshall Ion Atonescu, the Romanian dictator during World War II, and the fascist Iron Guard. One might well have expected that the Romanians would rewrite their history and exonerate themselves, not only of collaboration and alliance with the Germans but also at the killing of their own Jewish community.

Under pressure and with a strong desire to join the West, Romania, however, established a commission chaired by Elie Wiesel and with Radu Ioanid, a distinguished scholar of Romanian Holocaust history, as vice chairman and the driving force of the commission, to investigate its wartime record. The result has been a unanimous, well-documented report that pulls no punches regarding Romania's historical role and the responsibility of its wartime leadership.

Yet, as of this writing, one must also record some problematic consequences of restitution efforts. One hesitates to ask the question, for it seems to blame the Jews for their own victimization and yet we must ask: Have the Holocaust restitution efforts contributed to the resurgence of antisemitism in Europe? We should note that many factors have contributed to the new wave of European antisemitism, such as the joining together of forces on the Right and on the Left, forces of nationalism and antiglobalism, the presence of large and unassimilated Muslim populations, and the hyperintensity of anti-Israel rhetoric with overt antisemitic overtones, which has been taken by some as license to attack local Jews. The extreme—and needless to say unwarranted—equation of Israel with Nazism, of the IDF with the SS, and of Prime Minister Ariel Sharon with Adolf Hitler can be viewed in part as a pathological reaction to the perceived humiliation that many Europeans feel regarding the collapse of their national myths of the past. In his brilliant new work on antisemitism, *Those Who Forget the Past*,[7] Ron Rosenbaum observes, "The more European nations can focus one-sidedly on the Israeli response to terror and not the terror itself, the more they can portray the Jews as the real villains, as Nazis, the more salve to their collective conscience for their complicity in collective mass murder in the past."[8]

In Austria, the Kurt Waldheim affair led to new outbreaks of antisemitism. The same can be said of the Swiss reaction to the banking scandal. The antisemitic rhetoric with which the Israelis are attacked manifests that something more is at stake than specific policies of the Israeli government. The virulence of these accusations suggests that something subliminal is forcing itself to the surface.

Finally, there is a risk that the final word of the Holocaust will not be justice, nor education, nor remembrance, but money. As pointedly asked by Abraham Foxman, head of the Anti-Defamation League and himself a child survivor, will the demand for compensation make money the "last sound bite" of the Holocaust?[9] The monetary nature of the settlements reinforces in some quarters the deepest antisemitic stereotypes in the European mind. For those who would regard the restitution movement as a "shakedown"[10]—as opposed to an opportunity to acknowledge history and make amends—perhaps there is no response that can reach them. Nevertheless, for the current generation of Europeans, a thoughtful and engaged reckoning with history has been therapeutic and long overdue. It can allow them to develop their own future based on a more honest confrontation with the past.

NOTES

1. Raul Hilberg, *The Destruction of the European Jews,* 3d ed. (2003).
2. Judith Miller, *One by One, by One* (1990).
3. Stuart Eizenstat, *Imperfect Justice: Looted Assets, Slave Labor, and the Unfinished Business of World War II* (2003), 347.

4. Ibid. at 279.

5. Daniel Jonah Goldhagen, *Hitler's Willing Executioners: Ordinary Germans and the Holocaust* (1997).

6. Edwin Black, *IBM and the Holocaust: The Strategic Alliance between Nazi Germany and America's Most Powerful Corporation* (2002).

7. Ron Rosenbaum, ed., *Those Who Forget the Past: The Question of Anti-semitism* (2004).

8. Ibid. at 173.

9. Abraham H. Foxman, "The Dangers of Holocaust Restitution," *Wall Street Journal,* Dec. 4, 1998.

10. Norman Finkelstein, *The Holocaust Industry: Reflections on the Exploitation of Jewish Suffering* (2000). *See also* my review of Finkelstein in "Is the Memory of the Holocaust Being Exploited?" *Midstream* (April 2004).

Chapter 4

Holocaust Litigation and Human Rights Jurisprudence

Robert A. Swift

The Holocaust litigation was both about achieving a sense of justice and obtaining a fair financial recovery. No attorney, class member, or defendant came away satisfied that either objective was fully satisfied. However, from the standpoint of providing material assistance to two million human rights victims or their heirs, the Holocaust settlements have achieved great success.

In this chapter, I will explain some of the antecedents for the Holocaust litigation and the successes and problems encountered in settling Holocaust claims. The Holocaust cases represent a stage in the development of human rights jurisprudence, especially as those cases focus on property rights. I was the only lawyer pursuing these cases with either a background in human rights litigation or litigation experience with Swiss banks. A constant concern of mine was positioning the Holocaust claims so that they would be consistent with, and could benefit from, developing human rights jurisprudence. Stated another way, I wanted to transform the cause of Holocaust survivors into a viable case. Ultimately that was accomplished by creating credible claims and negotiating meaningful settlements.

What is human rights jurisprudence? It is the body of substantive and procedural law that provides remedies for the vindication of violations of the fundamental rights of human beings. A subset of international law, human rights are sometimes called "*jus cogens*" because their primacy and universality transcend national boundaries. Certainly human rights include prohibitions against summary execution, genocide, slavery, or piracy. These rights stand in juxtaposition to violations of domestic law adopted by individual nations (e.g. murder, theft, assault) and the counterpart body of law we call "civil rights." A notable, but not consistent, difference is that human rights violations are often perpetrated "under color of law," that is, by governmental officials.

International treaties, principally the Geneva Conventions, in the late nineteenth and twentieth centuries delineated prohibited actions during war. War crimes tribunals following World Wars I and II laid down guidelines for assessing the conduct of military and governmental officials in waging war. Most notable among these were the Nuremberg Principles, which recognized and prosecuted crimes against humanity. According to the modern concept of command responsibility embodied in international and American law,

> [A] higher official need not have personally performed or ordered the abuses in order to be held liable. Under international law, responsibility for torture, summary execution, or disappearances extends beyond the person or persons who actually committed those acts—anyone with higher authority who authorized, tolerated or knowingly ignored those acts is liable for them.[1]

The Holocaust litigation extended this concept to corporations that knowingly tolerated, or by their actions aided and abetted, the abuses.

The development of civil remedies in human rights jurisprudence in American law began in 1980 with *Filartiga v. Pena-Irala*, 630 F.2d 876 (2d Cir. 1980), a case establishing federal court jurisdiction under the Alien Tort Act (ATA), 28 U.S.C. 1350, for tort violations of international law. The ATA was adopted by the First Congress in 1789[2] but was rarely invoked during its 200-year history and was never used to prosecute human rights claims. The human rights cases of the 1980s were largely individual actions; the defendants fled the United States; judgments were by default; and victims never collected compensation. *Filartiga* is a case in point. The plaintiffs received a default judgment of $10 million but never collected. The number of uncollected human rights judgments is staggering, in part because collection procedures in countries where the abuses occurred are inadequate or fraught with politics.

The human rights litigation against Ferdinand E. Marcos marked a watershed for human rights litigation in the United States. During his 21-year rule in the Philippines, Marcos not only committed gross human rights violations but also built a billion-dollar personal fortune. Following a popular uprising in 1986, Marcos fled to Hawaii, where he lived until his death in 1989.

Marcos was sued in Hawaii in 1986 in a class action suit under the ATA on behalf of a class of almost ten thousand Filipino victims (and their heirs) of torture, summary execution, and disappearance. It was the first use of a class action in human rights jurisprudence. What also differentiated the litigation from prior human rights lawsuits was that Marcos was a kingpin, not a rank and file abuser, as were defendants in other cases. The lawsuit was certified as a class action and tried in three trial stages: liability, compensatory damages, and exemplary (punitive) damages. Despite a strong defense by Marcos and his family, as well as opposition from the Philippine government, the class prevailed at each stage, and the court of appeals affirmed a judgment consisting of $766 million compensatory and $1.2 billion exemplary damages.[3]

The *Marcos* case demonstrated that a large, contentious, and well-defended human rights case could be managed and adjudicated efficiently in American courts as a class action. It also showed that a class action leveled the playing field for human rights victims. Capable lawyers would be motivated to devote the time and resources that they regularly invested in class action antitrust and securities cases where fees and collection of judgments are more assured. Proof could be adduced more ably in a class action than in a non–class action. Instead of prosecutors having to prove linkage between defendant and victim, evidence of a pattern and practice of abuses would suffice. Compensatory damages could be proven on the basis of benchmark awards. Moreover, the availability of injunctive relief could enhance collection of an ultimate judgment.[4]

The Holocaust cases were modeled on the architecture of the *Marcos* litigation. The Holocaust cases claimed class action status but also sought to extend the coverage of human rights to financial abuses by private businesses. The first cases were filed against three Swiss banks. The cases asserted that these banks had violated the rights of persecuted individuals by confiscating their bank accounts during World War II. Following the war, the Swiss banks had made it difficult, if not impossible, for heirs of murdered Holocaust victims to identify and recover deposited assets.

Yet in prewar Europe, only a small minority of eventual Holocaust victims had either the assets or the ability to travel to Switzerland to establish accounts. Therefore, the totality of Holocaust-related Swiss bank accounts numbered in the tens of thousands, not hundreds of thousands. The litigation's more provocative, and larger, claim was a "looted assets" claim.

The Swiss banks, the complaints alleged, laundered property stolen from Holocaust victims that the Germans then used to buy war materiel. Although the merits of the class's claims were never developed in discovery, the factual basis was substantiated in both the reports of the International Committee of Eminent Persons and the Bergier Commission. The far more daunting task was to quantify damages.

The $1.25 billion Swiss banks settlement may owe more to political, diplomatic, and media pressure than to the likelihood of a court verdict. But the case could not have settled without the assertion of viable legal claims that could eventually be tried in a courtroom. The Swiss banks looked upon the United States as fertile ground to expand their overseas business, and the Holocaust cases—well publicized in the media—were embarrassing them. The Senate Banking Committee held hearings on Holocaust claims against Swiss banks at which Holocaust survivors testified. When urged to commence negotiations in 1997 by Stuart Eizenstat, then under secretary of state, the banks agreed. A month and a half later, the cases settled for $1.25 billion.

The settlement with the Swiss banks was the opening shot for future litigation of Holocaust claims against German, Austrian, and other corporations that benefited from the Axis's wartime use of slave labor and the plunder of Holocaust victims' assets. An important development arising out of the Swiss banks settlement was a new cooperation between U.S. government and plaintiffs' counsel. The executive branch of government had rarely supported human rights claims. But here Eizenstat had the support of President Clinton and used it as a catalyst for settlement. As a lawyer, Eizenstat understood litigation. As a diplomat, he understood that there were limits to how hard he could press American allies. In the Swiss banks settlement Eizenstat proved his mettle. Despite the Swiss government's vehement opposition to any settlement that exceeded $600 million, the banks became convinced that it was in their best interest to settle for more than double that amount.

Eizenstat's skills and influence shaped the whole-country settlements with German and Austrian companies and brought more money to the table than the plaintiffs' attorneys would have been able to do alone. Yet the role of the plaintiffs' lawyers was crucial to the settlement process. Credible, triable, and quantifiable claims had to be presented. Swiss, Austrian, and German companies demanded closure from litigation so that there would be an end to Holocaust claims. This demanded a legal solution. The German government's announcement in the spring of 1999—

that it was prepared to compensate wartime forced laborers from Eastern Europe as part of an overall settlement between victims and German industry—opened the door to the largest Holocaust settlement—over $5 billion. Once the German agreement was in place, Eizenstat quickly mediated a comparable agreement with the Austrian government and industry.

But the Swiss bank settlement also opened up fissures and demonstrated weaknesses. The Swiss banks insisted on closure for themselves and all Swiss entities—an unprecedented nationwide release for any type of Holocaust-era claim. While releases are often broader than the actual claims compensated, due process requires that there be some congruence between the claims released and the claims compensated. Congruence is acutely sensitive when the plaintiff class is worldwide. Problems abound in identifying types of claims, finding class members, and allocating compensation to all. Because all Holocaust claims against Swiss entities were over fifty years old and the distribution process was flexible enough to fashion relief to compensate various types of claims, a nationwide release was an appropriate solution.

The Swiss bank litigation highlighted another fissure: the conflict between Holocaust victims and the nongovernmental organizations (NGOs) that purport to advance the victims' interests. The conflict between NGOs and human rights victims is not new. In the *Marcos* litigation, a Philippine NGO demanded that any distribution of the judgment proceeds pass through it and further demanded that class members agree to pay it 15 percent of whatever they received. While the Swiss banks litigation was ongoing, the World Jewish Congress (WJC), a well-known American NGO, attempted to settle all claims with the Swiss banks by creating an unworkable alternative to litigation. When the WJC's ploy failed to derail the litigation, the WJC successfully intervened in the litigation (over the objection of plaintiffs' counsel) by asserting a right to recovery of "heirless" claims. Heirless claims do not exist as a matter of law since, by definition, there are no heirs with standing to pursue the claims. An NGO receives no legal right from dead Holocaust victims to represent their interests. The WJC's interest was to achieve a recovery for itself so that it could fund the goals of the organization. In other words, instead of the full funding going to victims with real claims, a significant portion of the funds would go to the WJC.

Still another weakness in the Swiss banks settlement was the difficulty in distributing $1.25 billion to victims and heirs worldwide. Counsel who negotiated and drafted the Swiss Banks Settlement Agreement fully intended that the $1.25 billion be distributed to all subclasses in proportion to the claims settled, and informed the court of the relative amounts negotiated for each subclass. During settlement negotiations, $50–100 million was allocated for deposited assets and $1 billion for looted assets. Ultimately, the intent of the settlement agreement was not carried out. The court, adopting the Volcker Committee's high range for deposited assets losses, allowed up to $800 million for deposited assets claims and nothing for looted assets. The high range was premised on a string of assumptions divorced from reality, notably that where information is missing for an account, the account is deemed confiscated. Following Class Notice, over four hundred thousand persons completed detailed questionnaires as to their looted assets. Yet the court concluded that monies could not be distributed to the looted assets subclass. The court ruled that it lacked standards to fairly adjudicate either the validity or the amount of the claims, and the court of appeals agreed, in an unreported decision. This decision disappointed the justifiable expectations of hundreds of thousands of victims and heirs, once again frustrating them in their decade-long struggle to achieve some accounting for the wrongs perpetrated. Three years of handling deposited-assets claims has demonstrated that the $800 million estimate was wrong. Only $131 million has been distributed despite the use of relaxed evidentiary standards and victim-favorable assumptions. The fig leaf used to justify the original allocation of $800 million is a continued coverup by Swiss banks that fails to take into full consideration the loss of records in the intervening sixty years.

The overallocation of funds to deposited-asset claims has created another problem in the Swiss banks settlement. With the court unable to distribute the full $800 million to deposited-asset claimants and having ruled that looted-asset claims would not be paid, the money must be distributed on a *cy pres* basis. *Cy Pres* is a legal doctrine in class action law that requires that any monies that cannot be distributed on a claims-made basis must be distributed for the benefit of the class members. Since other subclasses received compensation on a claims-made basis, that leaves only the looted-assets subclass for *cy pres* distribution.

The court presiding over the Swiss banks settlement is now engaged in the largest *cy pres* distribution of monies in judicial history, where it will distribute a total of about $800 million to NGOs. If the *cy pres* fund were a private foundation, it would be the sixtieth largest by asset size in the United States.[5]

Approximately seventy-five NGOs have submitted proposals seeking to distribute the *cy pres* funds. An alliance of Jewish NGOs has stated publicly that it will seek the money to distribute to Jewish old-age homes.[6] The question will not be whether the NGOs are trustworthy or their causes laudable; the question will be whether distribution to them benefits the intended recipients of the settlement. Illustrative of the conflicts that arise with such large sums of money, the court approved *cy pres* distributions of $205 million to several NGOs serving poor Jewish Holocaust survivors, principally in the former Soviet Union, prior to any meaningful analysis of whether the distribution benefits the subclass of looted-assets victims.[7]

Whether that money is truly assisting Holocaust survivors—as opposed to the aged Jewish population in that territory—is unknown to either class counsel or the public because neither the court nor the court-appointed Special Master disclosed that information.

It was never intended by the framers of the Constitution that Article III judges (federal judges) would have discretionary spending of vast sums of money. A court, even with the assistance of a Special Master, lacks both the expertise of sophisticated foundations and the controls that foundations apply both before and after making grants. In this case, the court declined to implement accounting controls over recipients of its discretionary largesse. A watchdog independent of the Special Master should have been appointed and should have published a report of findings. In these circumstances, the appearance of impropriety from a lack of transparency is rife and invites attack.

Learning from the weaknesses of the Swiss banks settlement, negotiators in subsequent settlements improved both the mode of settlement and the distribution of compensation. Early in the German negotiations, the German side insisted that a settlement be arrived at by executive agreement between governments—not as part of a class action—with the parties signing separate agreements pledging to carry out its terms. Surprisingly, the German side abandoned legally enforceable class action releases in favor of a pledge by the American executive branch that it would seek the dismissal of any existing or future Holocaust-related case against German entities that were not voluntarily dismissed by claimants. This meant that the pending class actions would have to be dismissed with no judicial scrutiny of the fairness of the settlements. Yet a primary judicial control assuring the integrity and transparency of class actions is a rigorous scrutiny of settlement. There was no legal precedent for this kind of class action settlement. Nonetheless, courts approved this new procedure, largely relying on the executive branch's participation in the settlement negotiations.[8] Subsequently the Supreme Court gave sanctity to this form of closure by ruling that an executive agreement between the United States and a foreign sovereign preempts litigation of Holocaust claims in the United States.[9]

This form of closure—when accompanied by fair compensation for the victims—can be a model for future human rights settlements. It avoids the strictures of formal releases and allows more flexibility in allocating compensation to victim groups.

Unlike the Swiss settlement, the German and Austrian settlements created mechanisms for a wider variety of property claims. These settlements created foundations charged with overseeing the distribution of settlement proceeds. The foundation boards were drawn from government, industry, and NGOs. Accounting and auditing procedures were adopted. The $230 million property settlement with the Republic of Austria, signed on January 17, 2001, did what the court in the Swiss banks settlement was unwilling to do.[10] That property settlement created a fair and workable methodology for the distribution of looted assets to individual Holocaust survivors and heirs. Amounts were specified for each property classification. The settlement established two equal funds, one for pro rata claims and one for per capita claims. Persons with large, substantiated claims could seek payment from the pro rata fund, while persons with smaller or less substantiated claims could seek a fixed-amount payment from the per capita fund. Claimants who needed money because of old age, infirmity, or other circumstances could obtain payment promptly from the per capita fund. While not perfect, this distribution solution delivers money to the intended recipients instead of to NGOs with mixed missions and limited accountability. The solution also achieves justice for the small number of persons who long to have a ruling on the amount of their losses.

Another good example of a successful distribution was the class action settlement for $40 million reached with two Austrian banks several months after the Swiss banks settlement. The settlement was approved and endorsed by both the district court and court of appeals as fair and adequate.[11]

The Austrian banks settlement preceded any negotiations with Germany and included three provisions not found in other Holocaust settlements.[12] First, it was a relationship settlement and required that a claimant have evidence linking the banks to the looted assets or confiscated accounts. Second, the banks would make their archival records available for use in litigation against German banks. This was the first breach in the wall of secrecy surrounding World War II banking practices and the only instance in which European banks permitted plaintiffs' counsel to enter the banks and inspect their records. Third, a historical commission was established and funded to write a history of the banks' role during the Holocaust. The final report, in book form, is scheduled to be released shortly.

Though criticized by other lawyers, the Austrian banks settlement compares favorably with other Holocaust settlements. The average payout to fifteen hundred claimants, either survivors or heirs, in the Austrian banks settlement is $20,000. In the 1950s, Austrian restitution legislation had already distributed 40 percent of the value of accounts taken during World War II. By contrast, the Swiss banks settlement paid out $131 million to 1,590 deposited account claimants as of September 30, 2004. The Austrian banks settlement was limited to the two banks; the Swiss banks settlement covered over 125 banks. Subsequently, a nationwide Austrian property settlement of $230 million included the country's remaining banks and a claims program for banking claims not covered by the Austrian banks settlement. Under the settlement with Germany, only $75 million was allocated for countrywide banking claims. The average payout in the Austrian banks settlement was three times the amount awarded to slave labor victims in the German settlement.

As outlined above, therefore, the Holocaust cases as a whole had mixed success. To focus on the deficiencies and conflicts is to lose sight of the overall benefit to the victims. The Holocaust litigation generated over $7.5 billion in compensation for human rights abuses committed before and during World War II. The result was unprecedented in the human rights field. The litigation also demonstrated the potential for what can be done to compensate human rights victims when the executive branch and plaintiffs' attorneys cooperate to achieve a result.

NOTES

1. Rep. No. 102-249, 102nd Cong., 1st Sess. (11/26/91) at 9.

2. The ATA provides that "[t]he district courts shall have original jurisdiction of any civil action by an alien for a tort only, committed in violation of the law of nations or a treaty of the United States."

3. *Hilao v. Estate of Marcos*, 103 F.3d 767 (9th Cir. 1996).

4. *See Hilao v. Estate of Marcos,* 25 F.3d 1467 (9th Cir. 1994) (affirming injunction freezing Marcos assets); *Hilao v. Estate of Marcos,* 103 F.3d 762 (9th Cir. 1996)

(affirming contempt violation against representatives of Marcos estate for transferring assets in violation of the injunction).

5. *See* www.fdncenter.org for rankings of U.S. foundations by assets and annual giving.

6. Amy D. Marcus, "Painful Choices: As Survivors Age, Debate Breaks Out on Holocaust Funds," *Wall Street Journal*, 15 Jan. 2003, p. 1.

7. *In re Holocaust Victims Assets Litig.*, No. CV 96-4849, 2000 WL 33281701 (E.D.N.Y. Dec. 8, 2000).

8. *See In re Nazi Era Cases against German Defs. Litig.*, 198 F.R.D. 429 (D.N.J. 2000).

9. *See Am. Ins. Ass'n v. Garamendi*, 1235 S. Ct. 2374 (2003).

10. The property settlement was in addition to countrywide settlements with Austria for slave and forced labor ($400 million) and household property ($150 million).

11. *See D'Amato v. Deutsche Bank*, 236 F.3d 78 (2d Cir. 2001); *In re Austrian and German Bank Holocaust Litig.*, 80 F. Supp. 2d 164 (S.D.N.Y. 2000).

12. *In re Austrian and German Bank Holocaust Litig.*, 80 F. Supp. 2d at 170–71.

Chapter 5

A Tale of Two Cities

Administering the Holocaust Settlements in Brooklyn and Berlin

Burt Neuborne

Introduction

Holocaust-era litigation in American courts against Swiss banks and German industry has played a major role in assembling approximately $6.5 billion for distribution to hundreds of thousands of Holocaust victims who fell between the cracks of prior reparations programs.

The Swiss bank cases were settled for $1.25 billion on January 26, 1999.[1] The German industry cases were settled on July 17, 2000, through the creation of a DM 10 billion ($5.25 billion) German Foundation, "Remembrance, Responsibility, and the Future," which acts as a conduit for payment to designated categories of Holocaust victims.[2] In addition, slightly more than $1 billion has been assembled in connection with settlements involving Austrian and French Holocaust-era claims. An additional $500 million has been assembled to pay Holocaust-era insurance claims through the efforts of the International Commission on Holocaust-Era Insurance Claims (ICHEIC), a collaboration between the European insurance industry and state insurance regulators. ICHEIC was established without the participation of lawyers or courts. All told, approximately $8 billion has been assembled for payment to Holocaust victims or their heirs. And if litigation in connection with recovery of looted art is included, at least another $1 billion must be added to the total.

I serve as court-designated lead settlement counsel in the Swiss bank settlement, which is being administered in Brooklyn federal court as a classic Rule Twenty-Three class action, and as one of two U.S. appointees to the 27-person Board of Trustees of the German Foundation, which is being administered in Berlin under the supervision of the trustees and the German Ministries of Finance and Foreign Affairs.[3]

Not surprisingly, the bulk of the commentary on this remarkable spate of litigation has focused on the merits of the claims, the personalities of the lawyers, and the tactics of the diplomats, Jewish community leaders, and litigators who made the Holocaust-era settlements possible. Little attention has been paid to the postsettlement activities of the two funds in distributing settlement monies to actual victims. This essay serves as an interim report as of January 1, 2005, on the progress of both funds. While I draw on the official data released by both funds, the assessment is, of course, a personal one.

The Long Road to Distribution

The Swiss Bank Settlement

The road from settlement to distribution in both the Swiss bank and German Foundation proceedings was enormously complex and time consuming.

In the Swiss banks case, before distribution could begin, it was necessary to comply with the strict legal formalities imposed by Rule Twenty-Three of the Federal Rules of Civil Procedure governing class actions. Since a class action invites one or more "named plaintiffs" to act as the legal representative of thousands of similarly situated strangers whose rights will stand or fall on the success or failure of the unelected representative, federal law is peppered with time-consuming rules designed to protect absent class members.

One of the most important protections is a requirement that the class members be kept informed. Notice to the class is particularly important when the named representatives decide to settle the lawsuit, since the terms of a class action settlement will bind all absent class members. Federal law requires that any proposed settlement be fully described to the class so that individual class members can object to its terms, or even elect to "opt out" of the class in order to pursue the claims on their own. No federal class action settlement can become effective until such notice is given and until a federal judge holds a public hearing on the settlement's fairness, at which hearing any class member can contest the settlement's terms.

In the Swiss bank case, the notice requirements were particularly demanding. Once the terms of the settlement had been hammered out in late January 1999, it was necessary to identify and notify all known Holocaust survivors and their heirs of the terms of the $1.25 billion settlement and of their right to object to the terms of the settlement or to "opt out" of the class in order to pursue their own claims individually. The ensuing massive worldwide notice program was one of the most extensive ever undertaken. Notice of the settlement's terms was mailed to all known surviving Holocaust victims. Notice was also given to every known organization serving Holocaust victims, and the settlement's terms were widely advertised and reported in the media. When the dust had settled, 584,000 questionnaires were returned, and fewer than three hundred persons had decided to opt out.

The notice phase was successfully completed by September 1999. Chief Judge Korman then scheduled hearings on the Swiss bank settlement's fairness for November 29, 1999, in Brooklyn, and December 14, 1999, in Jerusalem. He invited all class members to comment on the settlement's fairness in writing or in person. Judge Korman's invitation elicited hundreds of written comments and numerous requests to comment in person.

At day-long hearings in both Brooklyn and Jerusalem,[4] the settlement's terms were critiqued by class members. While the response to the settlement was generally positive, concerns were raised that the $1.25 billion settlement was too small and that settlement funds might be diverted from actual survivors to institutional beneficiaries. Judge Korman took pains to explain that the settlement, while morally inadequate, was the best that could be achieved. He promised that settlement funds would go to actual victims, not to institutions.

At the close of the hearings, Judge Korman notified me that he was troubled by three issues that had been raised by class members. First, he was concerned that the terms of the settlement might inadvertently interfere with the recovery of looted art; second, he was troubled that no formal, written provisions had been made to assure access to information that was in the hands of the banks and was needed to administer a fair bank account claims process; and, third, he was concerned that Swiss insurance companies were being released from liability without the establishment of an insurance claims program. Until those problems were solved, Judge Korman told me that he could not approve the settlement as fair.

At his direction, beginning in January 2000, I launched into an intense six-month renegotiation of aspects of the settlement that resulted in added protections for recovery of looted art; specific guarantees concerning publication of, and access to, information concerning Swiss bank accounts; and a modest insurance claims program involving two Swiss companies. I also negotiated an accelerated payment schedule designed to speed up the banks' transfer of funds to the settlement in order to generate the additional interest needed to fund the bank account claims program.

The amended version of the settlement agreement was reported to Judge Korman in June 2000. The judge approved the settlement's fairness in an extensive opinion issued on July 26, 2000, and in a final order issued on August 9, 2000. Thus the process, from the settlement's signing in January 1999 to its approval as fair by Judge Korman in August 2000, took eighteen grueling months.

Once the basic fairness of the Swiss settlement was approved in August 1999, Judge Korman directed Judah Gribetz, a New York attorney who was well versed in Jewish community affairs and who had been unanimously endorsed by the parties, to serve as a Special Master with a mandate to develop a detailed proposed plan of allocation and distribution of the settlement proceeds. Gribetz was instructed to complete his work as quickly as possible and to make his recommendations public.

The Special Master's proposed plan of allocation and distribution was unveiled on September 11, 2000. The plan recognized claims for unpaid Holocaust-era bank accounts as the core of the Swiss bank case. Accordingly, Gribetz recommended allocating $800 million to bank account claims, subject to reallocation to other beneficiaries if it ultimately proved impossible to trace all the accounts. The Special Master chose the $800 million figure in response to information revealed by an audit of Swiss banks conducted under the auspices of Paul Volcker. The Volcker audit was made public on December 8, 1999, and identified fifty-four thousand potential unclaimed Holocaust-era accounts. Subsequent "scrubbing" by the banks moved the figure down to thirty-six thousand. The Special Master estimated that once interest was added, the unpaid accounts identified by the Volcker audit might exceed the value of the entire settlement.

Special Master Gribetz then turned to the victims' slave labor claims, which were linked to the Swiss banks' repeated decisions to provide knowing financial support to Swiss and German clients for the establishment and maintenance of Nazi slave labor camps in violation of international law. Noting that slave laborers were scheduled to receive $7,500 per person from the German Foundation, the Special Master fixed individual payments from the Swiss settlement at a modest $1,000 per survivor (subsequently raised to $1,450 through accumulation of tax-free interest). Gribetz estimated that the total payments to slave laborers from the Swiss bank fund would exceed $200 million. In fact, the Swiss slave labor payments to surviving slave laborers will exceed $250 million.[5]

The Special Master then dealt with looted assets claims linked to the banks' having knowingly acted as "fences" for the disposal of Nazi loot obtained in violation of international law. Given the enormous size of the looted assets class—the Nazis stole from virtually every conquered person —and the impossible task of proving which item of Nazi loot was knowingly disposed of through a Swiss bank, Gribetz recommended that no attempt be made to set up an individualized looted assets claims process. Instead, he urged that looted assets funds be distributed to a subset of the looted assets class most in need. He recommended the allocation of $100 million (subsequently increased to $205 million through addition of tax-free interest) to the looted assets class, to be distributed worldwide to social services agencies serving the poorest survivors. Finally, the Special Master recommended modest individual payments of between $500 and $3,500 to identifiable refugees who had been excluded from, or were mistreated by, Switzerland during World War II because they were Jewish, or belonged to another victim group.

After another round of invitations to class members to comment on the Special Master's allocation and distribution plan, Judge Korman approved the plan on November 22, 2000, after a full day of hearings on November 20, 2000.

The last legal hurdle to distribution was finally cleared two and one-half years after the settlement was signed when the Second Circuit formally approved the plan of allocation and distribution on July 26, 2001.

The German Industry Settlement

The path to distributing the German Foundation's assets was equally tortuous. After eighteen months of intense negotiation and vigorous litigation, the parties, meeting in Bonn, Germany, on December 17, 1999, agreed on a DM 10 billion (approximately $5 billion) German Foundation settlement in return for dismissal of all Holocaust litigation pending against German industry in American courts. Neither side was happy with the figure.

Lawyers for the victims viewed the sum as far too low but were badly shaken by the recent rejection of their legal theories by two federal judges in Newark, New Jersey (see discussion infra). Representatives of German industry had initially offered DM 1 billion, and had gradually increased their offer in response to progress in the American litigation. Lawyers for the victims believed that a settlement of DM 15 billion was possible. But, buoyed by the New Jersey decisions, German industry refused to budge from its final offer of DM 8 billion.

After a flurry of letters between President Bill Clinton and Chancellor Gerhard Schroeder, German industry, aware that the German government was willing to foot half the bill and had granted generous tax credits for the industry's contribution (thereby raising the German state's contribution to two-thirds of the settlement amount), reluctantly agreed to raise their offer to DM 10 billion. Lawyers for the victims, after seeking an increase to DM 11 billion, equally reluctantly accepted the DM 10 billion offer.

Once the parties had agreed upon a DM 10 billion foundation, allocating the DM 10 billion between and among the categories of victims became the subject of intense bargaining over the next six months. Since a fund of DM 10 billion was not nearly large enough to satisfy all legitimate claims, it became necessary to choose between and among slave labor, insurance, and looted property claims, and to apportion scarce slave labor funds on a national basis.

In the Swiss bank case, the complex allocation formula was developed and proposed by Special Master Gribetz (who consulted widely with class members before recommending a plan) and was subjected to scrutiny in a court hearing before being approved by two levels of federal judges. The German allocation process, on the other hand, involved bare-knuckle, back-room negotiations between and among various contesting groups of Holocaust survivors. It was not pretty. Jews were pitted against non-Jews. Property owners were pitted against surviving slave laborers. Each Eastern European country was pitted against every other in an effort to maximize its relative share of the slave labor funds.

In the end, with the active involvement of the United States, an allocation plan emerged that apportioned approximately 80 percent of the Foundation's funds to slave and forced laborers, with payments graduated from $7,500 per person to surviving concentration camp inmates to $3,000 per person to forced laborers confined in less brutal conditions to nominal payments of several hundred dollars to forced agricultural laborers. DM 500 million was allocated to German insurance claims, with administration of the claims program to be shared with ICHEIC. Approximately DM 1 billion was allocated to property claims, and DM 700 million was set aside for the establishment of a forward-looking Future Fund, designed to foster toleration in Europe.

Agreement on an allocation formula was finally made possible by a reminder from Ambassador Stuart Eizenstat—who served as President Clinton's special envoy on Holocaust issues and who played an indispensable role in achieving the settlements—that the DM 10 billion would earn at least DM 400 million in interest in the years before it was disbursed to victims. DM 100 million of the anticipated interest was formally factored into the final allocation formula, resulting in a DM 10.1 billion fund, with the rest of the anticipated DM 400 million in interest being held in reserve to assure full payment to all beneficiaries.

Unfortunately, a dispute over payment of interest by German industry has arisen that has threatened a decrease in payments to slave laborers. German industry had promised to pay "at least" DM 100 million in interest in connection with the deferred payment of its DM 5 billion obligation. Although the deferral period lasted almost a year longer than the parties anticipated, German industry has refused to pay more than the DM 100 million figure, pocketing as a windfall the DM 100 million interest earned on the unpaid funds during the unexpectedly long deferral period. Unless the interest is restored, concentration camp inmates will receive $6,900, not $7,500.

Once the allocation formula had been hammered out, the parties met in Berlin on July 17, 2000, to sign a statement of principles, setting forth the promise to create the DM 10 billion German Foundation in return for the dismissal of all Holocaust-era litigation against German industry in American courts. At the same time, Germany and the United States signed an executive agreement protecting German industry against future Holocaust-era litigation in the United States. Finally, the German Bundestag (German parliament) enacted a law establishing the German Foundation "Remembrance, Responsibility, and the Future," which codified the allocation formula as German law.

Pursuant to the statement of principles, the German government agreed to place its DM 5 billion contribution into the Foundation by the close of 2000, but insisted that no distribution to victims take place until "legal peace" was attained by the dismissal of the pending litigation against German industry. German industry was even more cautious, refusing to place any funds into the Foundation until all the cases pending against German companies had been dismissed. Instead, German industry agreed to collect its contribution, to hold it in escrow for the Foundation, and to pay "at least" DM 100 million in interest in connection with the deferred payment of principal to the Foundation, which would take place as soon as the American cases were dismissed. Thus, dismissal of pending litigation in the United States became the last hurdle to distributing the German funds.

Since the American cases were almost all class actions, federal law forbade dismissal as part of a settlement unless and until a federal judge accepted the settlement as fair. Even before the signing of the statement of principles on July 17, 2000, the parties had approached the Federal Panel on Multi-District Litigation, a kind of superjudicial traffic cop with power to move complex cases around within the federal system, and had asked the panel to consolidate all pending Holocaust-era lawsuits against German defendants in one court in order to facilitate the dismissals needed to empower the German Foundation to distribute funds to victims.

All parties recommended transfer of the cases to Judge William Bassler, a widely respected federal judge in the district of New Jersey, who had the confidence of all parties. Instead, responding to an apparent overture from federal Judge Shirley Wohl Kram of Manhattan, before whom the German and Austrian banking cases were pending, the panel consolidated only the slave labor cases before Judge Bassler, leaving the German banking and German insurance cases before Judge Kram and Chief Judge Michael Mukasey, respectively, in Manhattan. The panel's decision to leave the German banking cases before Judge Kram significantly complicated the process of clearing hurdles to distribution of funds by the German Foundation, and may ultimately cost the victims DM 100 million.

As the parties had expected, Judge Bassler acted swiftly and thoughtfully in connection with the fifty slave labor cases that had been transferred to him. He accurately characterized his role as passing on the basic fairness of using a German Foundation to settle the German cases. After holding a hearing to assure that the German Foundation was an acceptable method of satisfying the victims' claims, on November 14, 2000, Bassler granted leave to dismiss virtually all slave labor cases, writing a thoughtful opinion that painstakingly describes the German Foundation.[6]

Chief Judge Mukasey quickly followed suit on December 7, 2000, with an order granting leave to dismiss the German insurance cases.

On January 21, 2001, however, Judge Kram stunned the parties by refusing to permit the dismissal of the German banking cases, thus freezing the German Foundation. She demanded that the German Foundation's allocation formula be modified to shift a portion of German Foundation funds to certain Austrian banking victims whose claims had apparently been extinguished by the Austrian State Treaty of 1955. When the German government and the victims refused to alter the carefully negotiated allocation formula, Judge Kram refused to grant permission to dismiss the German banking cases, making it impossible to begin payments to victims from the German Foundation and artificially extending the deferral period during which German industry refused to make any payments to the Foundation.

Judge Kram's intransigence made it necessary for us to seek from the Second Circuit a writ of mandamus, an extraordinary remedy reserved for judges who are acting in clear violation of their legal duties, directing Judge Kram to permit the dismissal of the German banking cases in order to permit the German Foundation to come into being.

On May 17, 2001, eighteen months after the parties had agreed on the DM 10 billion German Foundation, the Second Circuit issued a writ of mandamus directing Judge Kram to permit dismissal of the German banking cases.[7] She promptly complied. The German Bundestag quickly responded on May 30, 2001, by declaring that "legal peace" had been obtained. German industry thereupon transferred DM 3.4 billion to the Foundation on June 20, 2001.

Inching towards Jerusalem: Distributions Finally Begin

The lag between agreement on a Swiss bank settlement fund and the clearing of the last legal hurdle to distribution was two and one-half years—from January 29, 1999, to August 17, 2001. The corresponding lag in the German cases was one and one-half years—from December 17, 1999, to May 30, 2001.

The complexity of the two processes is reflected by the fact that I defended sixteen appeals to the Second Circuit challenging multiple aspects of the Swiss bank settlement; litigated three extensive ancillary adversary proceedings in the district court seeking to enforce the Swiss bank settlement against the banks; appeared in at least seven formal district court Rule Twenty-Three hearings needed to administer the settlement; participated in innumerable informal administrative conferences with Judge Korman; and engaged in three extensive negotiations with the banks, each of which led to important alterations in the original settlement.

In the German Foundation proceedings, I participated in fourteen two-day Board of Trustees meetings in Berlin, as well as three district court proceedings and an appeal to the Third Circuit designed to enforce the provisions of underlying settlement. In addition, I appeared in three district courts seeking approval of the German Foundation and obtained a writ of mandamus from the Second Circuit to permit the establishment of the German Foundation. That's a total of fifty-one formal legal proceedings *after* the settlements were reached.

Once the legal obstacles to distribution were finally cleared, payments to victims have proceeded relatively quickly in both the Swiss and German settings.

The Swiss Bank Distribution

As of May 15, 2005, the Swiss bank settlement fund has distributed $735 million to, or for the support of, individual Holocaust victims.

Slave Labor Distribution

Approximately $260 million has been distributed from the Swiss bank settlement to surviving slave laborers. Under Judge Korman's supervision, the Jewish Conference for the Material Claims against Germany, created after World War II to administer German reparations to Jews who survived the Holocaust and popularly known as the Claims Conference, administers the slave labor claims program for Jewish victims. The International Organization for Migration (IOM), an NGO headquartered in Geneva, administers the slave labor claims of non-Jews, who are overwhelmingly Sinti-Roma, more commonly known as gypsies.

Excellent German records and extraordinary work by Claims Conference and IOM researchers made it possible to identify approximately 150,000 surviving Jewish, and almost 20,000 of Sinti-Roma, slave laborers. Each surviving slave laborer receives a payment of $1,450 from the Swiss bank settlement. When added to the $7,500 payable to slave laborers from the German Foundation, payments to Jewish and Sinti-Roma slave laborers approximate $9,000 per person.

Dormant Accounts Distribution

In addition, approximately $260 million has been distributed to owners of approximately three thousand Holocaust-era Swiss bank accounts. Information concerning twenty-one thousand potential Holocaust-era accounts was published on the Internet by the Swiss settlement fund on February 5, 2001. Approximately three thousand additional names were published in early January 2005. As of January 1, 2005, just over thirty-three thousand bank account claims have been filed with the Claims Resolution Tribunal (CRT), the body, headquartered in Zurich, that was established by Judge Korman to administer the bank account claims process. In addition, sixty thousand initial questionnaires mentioned bank accounts and are being treated as formal claims. Each claim has been matched against a database of thirty-six thousand accounts identified as "probably or possibly" owned by Holocaust victims or their heirs by an audit of the Swiss banks conducted under the auspices of Paul Volcker.

Unfortunately, long before the litigation began, the Swiss banks had destroyed almost all of the records needed to validate the bank account claims in an efficient manner. Of the 6.8 million Swiss bank accounts open during the Holocaust era, all records of 2.7 million accounts have been completely obliterated, making it impossible to validate claims for the lost accounts. Moreover, only fragmentary records exist for the remaining 4.1 million, making the matching task extremely difficult. The task has been made even more onerous by the banks' insistence on adherence to Swiss bank secrecy, which often makes it difficult, if not impossible, for the CRT to gain access to needed information in the banks' files.[8] After protected negotiations, an agreement has been reached with the banks to match particularly promising claims against databases that include the entire 4.1 million accounts for which any records remain.

In short, the task of matching Swiss bank account claims has been herculean. Thus far, more than three thousand accounts have been identified and returned to their true owners, with an average value of more than $130,000 per account. Each award contains an interest component.

The largest award to date has been a $21 million award to the Bloch-Bauer owners of prewar Austria's largest sugar refinery. Other multimillion-dollar awards have been made as well.

The tedious task of matching bank account claims against surviving fragmentary records is continuing in both Zurich and New York in an effort to return the full $800 million allocated to bank accounts. If it ultimately proves impossible to trace all the accounts, any undistributed funds will be reallocated to assist poor survivors.

One of the CRT's most dramatic achievements has been the issuance of written opinions explaining the facts and legal basis for each of the three thousand bank account awards issued through May 15, 2005. The opinions (with names occasionally redacted) are posted at www.swissbank claims.com.

The CRT opinions chronicle the efforts of Jews and other victims of Nazi persecution to use Swiss banks to shield their property from Nazi looters, and the failure of the Swiss financial community to keep its promise to safeguard the assets.

The $21 million Bloch-Bauer award reflects the widespread failure of Swiss banks to protect Jewish depositors from Nazi efforts to seize their assets. One week before the *Anschluss* that annexed Austria into the Third Reich, the Bloch-Bauer family journeyed to Zurich and placed their enormously valuable shares in OZAG, Austria's largest sugar refinery, in a custody account with a Swiss bank, with instructions that the shares were not to be sold without the unanimous consent of the family members. One week later, after the Nazis had assumed control of Austria, the Nazis arrested Otto Bloch-Bauer and commenced bogus tax proceedings against the company, but they were unable to get their hands on the shares in OZAG, which were safely tied up in a Swiss bank. After forfeiting virtually all their property, the family members fled to Zurich, where they were approached by a designated Nazi purchaser, who offered a fraction of the company's value. When the offer was refused, the bogus tax proceedings were intensified in an effort to drive down the value of the company. When the family still refused to sell at an unfair price, the Nazis approached the Swiss bank, which calmly betrayed the family by turning the shares over to the Nazis for a fraction of their value. As soon as the company was safely in Nazi hands, all tax proceedings were dropped. The pittance of a purchase price was confiscated by the Nazis as a so-called flight tax.

The CRT ruled that the Swiss bank was liable for its breach of trust and would be obliged to make good any losses caused by the transfer of the shares. Accordingly, the settlement fund awarded the family the true value of the shares on the date the bank turned them over to the Nazis, less any amounts received for the shares or in any prior restitution proceeding. Disturbingly, no record of the Bloch-Bauer account can be found in the bank's records. If the family had not preserved their copies of the documents, the bank's breach of trust would never have been discovered, and the family's claims would have been rejected. Since the Swiss banks admit to having destroyed all traces of 2.7 million accounts, one wonders how many awards similar to Bloch-Bauer will never be made because the banks have covered their tracks.

Looted Assets Distribution

Judge Korman has ruled that funds allocated to the looted assets class could not be the subject of an individual claims program because the size of the class and the problems of proof precluded individualized awards. Instead, he directed that the $205 million allocated thus far to the looted assets class be administered on a *cy pres*[9] basis on behalf of the poorest survivors. The funds are paid to social services agencies over the life span of the needy recipients.

As of May 15, 2005, 90 percent of the looted assets funds has been allocated to poor Jewish survivors, with the remaining 10 percent allocated to poor Sinti-Roma. Within the Jewish community, 75 percent of the funds has been allocated for the relief of destitute survivors in the former Soviet Union, 12.5 percent to destitute survivors in Israel, 4.7 percent to needy survivors in the United States, and the remaining 7.8 percent to the very poor elsewhere in the world.[10]

When distribution is finally over, I estimate that Jewish victims will receive approximately 90 percent of the Swiss settlement funds, with the bulk of the remaining 10 percent being paid to Sinti-Roma victims. Payments from the Swiss fund will also be made to Jehovah's Witness, disabled, and gay victims, the other groups persecuted by the Nazis.

The German Foundation Distribution

The German Foundation is on target to spend itself out of existence by the end of 2005, after having distributed more than $4 billion to partner organizations in each affected country for delivery to identified Holocaust victims and having created a DM 700 million Future Fund to support tolerance in the new Europe. Approximately DM 4 billion ($2.5 billion) has already been distributed to partner organizations. Periodic audits verify that the funds are actually being received by victims.

Disputes have arisen. German banks working for the Foundation mishandled a huge distribution to the Polish partner organization by failing to hedge against currency fluctuations, ultimately costing the Polish victims almost 10 percent of the award. The Foundation made much of the loss good out of general Foundation funds belonging to the victims. Despite my efforts, no attempt was made by the Foundation to place the ultimate loss where it belonged—on the banks. Disagreements also arose over whether certain places of confinement were sufficiently brutal to be treated as "slave labor" facilities. The disagreements were resolved by negotiations and thoughtful historical research. Italian prisoners of war who were required to perform forced labor by the Nazis sought forced labor status. The Board of Trustees quite properly excluded prisoners of war from eligibility, since the numbers would have swamped the available funds. Finally, a bitter disagreement erupted over the power of the Board of Trustees to disagree with the German Ministry of Finance about the existence of unpaid interest obligations by German industry.

In an effort to avoid litigation over unpaid interest, I offered to resolve the dispute over interest by putting it to an up-and-down vote by the 27-person Board of Trustees, consisting of fourteen German and thirteen non-German members. I placed the item on the board's agenda at the February 2002 meeting. During the debate, the German Ministry of Finance intervened and purported to block the vote, ruling that it possessed unilateral power to resolve the issue. Rather than provoke an open split between the Board of Trustees and the German government, I placed the interest issue before the American courts, where it is currently pending.[11]

Despite disagreements, the German Foundation has worked extremely well in distributing a huge amount of money to more than one million victims in a relatively short time. When all the funds have been distributed, non-Jewish victims, especially Slavs residing in Eastern Europe, will receive approximately 75 percent of the German Foundation funds, with approximately 25 percent payable to Jewish victims, primarily surviving concentration camp slave laborers.

The Myth That the Holocaust Settlements Are a Triumph of American Law

Given the general success of the enterprise, the tendency is to view the Holocaust-era cases as a triumph of the rule of law, and there has been much self-congratulatory rhetoric about the role of the class action and the American courts as guardians of justice for the downtrodden.

Not surprisingly, other victim groups have sought to use the Holocaust-era cases as a template in an effort to obtain reparations for past historical injustices, ranging from black slavery to the sexual enslavement of Korean women by the Japanese during World War II to South African apartheid.

As a matter of theory, the Holocaust-era litigation model should travel. The Swiss and German cases were based on classic principles of restitution and unjust enrichment. In each case, a private entity was unjustly enriched by the transfer of identifiable property from a victim of a crime against humanity. The remedy sought by plaintiffs in the Holocaust cases consisted of a simple reversal of the unjust wealth transfer. Assuming that it is possible to replicate such a model on behalf of other victims of slavery and oppression, no reason exists to deny other, similarly situated victim groups similar relief.

But it will never happen. The Holocaust cases are not legal launching pads for other efforts to right historical wrongs precisely because there is no legal platform from which to launch. The sad fact is that American courts have too often turned their backs on Holocaust victims. The truth is that, with the important exception of Judge Korman and his colleagues in the Brooklyn federal courthouse, the Holocaust settlements were attained despite American judges, not because of them.

In *Garamendi*,[12] California, acting pursuant to traditional regulatory authority exercised by states over foreign insurance companies, had directed that all European insurance companies doing business in California disclose the existence of unpaid Holocaust-era insurance policies. The companies counterattacked with a lawsuit in federal court challenging the constitutionality of California's disclosure requirement.

The Supreme Court, in a 5-4 decision, ruled that California lacked power to compel the disclosures. In one fell swoop, the Supreme Court majority in *Garamendi*—to the astonishment of those of us who had worked on the German negotiations—transformed the results of the German negotiations from a complex settlement of a series of private lawsuits into a federal legal ceiling that made it unconstitutional for any state to seek to provide greater protection to Holocaust victims.

Even when the Supreme Court thinks it's helping Holocaust victims, it gets it wrong. In *Republic of Austria v. Altmann,* the Court construed the Foreign Sovereign Immunities Act to permit a suit against the government of Austria to recover looted art currently hanging in the Austrian State

Museum. But the narrow theory adopted by the Court doomed virtually all other efforts to seek relief for Holocaust victims against foreign governments. Indeed, the principal practical effect of *Altmann* was the reluctant dismissal by the Second Circuit of a suit by Holocaust survivors against the French National Railroad system for having been a little too enthusiastic in deporting French Jews to the death camps.[13]

Bad as *Garamendi* is, the decision pales when measured against the genuinely appalling refusal of two federal judges in the district of New Jersey to recognize the powerful legal claims of slave laborers against their German corporate enslavers.[14]

At the end of the war, American policy initially insisted that German industry compensate surviving slave and forced laborers. The Treaty of Paris of 1946 contemplated turning the assets of German companies over to the victims in order to provide them with compensation. As the Soviet threat grew in Europe, however, Germany was increasingly seen as a crucial bulwark against communist expansion. In 1953, the United States reversed course and signed the London Debt Agreement, which subordinated the claims of Holocaust victims to the need to rebuild German industry. Under the London Debt Agreement, all Holocaust-era claims against German industry were suspended until the signing of a peace treaty with Germany, by which time the German economy would have recovered from the war. In fact, the Cold War made it impossible to agree on a peace treaty with a divided Germany. Thus, the "temporary" suspension of Holocaust victims' claims against German industry imposed by the London Debt Agreement remained in effect for over forty years.

In 1996, the German Federal Constitutional Court, to its credit, ruled that the 2 + 4 Treaty of 1991, defining Germany's borders and paving the way for German reunification, had functioned as a de facto peace treaty, finally lifting the suspension of Holocaust victims' rights to seek compensation for World War II enslavement.[15]

In the wake of the German decision, multiple federal class actions seeking relief against the giants of German industry were filed in federal court in Newark, New Jersey. Surviving slave laborers chose to sue in the United States because German law does not recognize a class action, making it impossible to obtain mass relief on behalf of all victims.

On September 13, 1999, in what were clearly coordinated decisions, Greenaway and Debevoise dismissed plaintiffs' claims for relief on the same day. Both judges acknowledged the powerful legal nature of the claims and recognized their factual accuracy. Moreover, both judges acknowledged that the federal court had power to grant the victims compensatory relief. Instead of enforcing the victims' legal claims, however, both judges simply abandoned the victims.

Judge Greenaway held that claims under German law to compensation for forced labor were subject to an absurdly short two-year statute of limitations. He claimed to be obliged to accept the two-year limitations period because postwar German courts in the 1950s, staffed by Nazi judges, had imposed a similar two-year limitations period on German slave labor victims. The judge rejected overwhelming evidence that no modern German court would impose such an unfairly short deadline.

Moreover, both judges held that claims for compensation under customary international law had been implicitly erased by the failure of the 2 + 4 Treaty to have made explicit provision for the claims. Both judges rejected the argument that the decision of the German Federal Constitutional Court showed that the 2 + 4 Treaty was intended to help victims by lifting the suspension imposed by the London Debt Agreement of 1953, not to hurt them by implicitly destroying their claims through silence.

Although the victims immediately appealed and sought expedited review in the Third Circuit Court of Appeals (the federal appeals court for New Jersey), the two decisions, coming at a crucial point in the settlement negotiations, dealt the victims a terrible blow. I believe that if the Newark federal court had upheld the claims, the size of the German Foundation settlement would have doubled to DM 20 billion. Even if the two judges had simply remained silent and had allowed the negotiations to continue in the shadow of the litigation, as Judge Korman had done in the Swiss bank cases, the settlement would have reached DM 15 billion.

Unfortunately, the coordinated one-two punch by the Newark federal judges dismissed the slave labor claims at a crucial point in the negotiations, placing plaintiffs' lawyers in a severely weakened position. We pressed the appeal to the Third Circuit in order to keep some pressure on the defendants, but when the offer of DM 10 billion was placed on the table in December 1999, three months after the dismissals, there was no choice but to accept it, even though every lawyer believed that the sum was shockingly low and would have been much higher but for the actions of the two Newark federal judges. Subsequent academic criticism of the decisions has been savage, and every appeals court that has considered the matter has rejected the New Jersey decisions as wrong.[16] But the damage was done.

In retrospect, very few American judges went out of their way to help Holocaust victims. Some judges, including the Supreme Court majority in *Garamendi* and the two federal judges in Newark, were actively harmful; some, like Judge Kram in her stubborn effort to force a change in the German Foundation's allocation formula, were well-intentioned victims of bad judgment; some were just plain timid.

In fairness, there were a few federal judges willing to flex their Article III muscles in favor of Holocaust victims. Judge Korman's orchestration of the final phase of the Swiss bank negotiations, which unfolded in his chambers over a twelve-day period, was masterful. Negotiations culminated in an informal dinner at Gage & Tollner's Restaurant in downtown Brooklyn, where Korman, after hearing a presentation of plaintiffs' proposed case made by Michael Hausfeld, suggested the settlement figure that he deemed fair. The parties accepted the figure the next day. Korman's stewardship of the settlement fund has also been intensely dedicated and principled.[17]

Judge Korman's colleagues in the Brooklyn federal court—Judges Jack Weinstein,[18] Frederick Block,[19] and Sterling Johnson[20]—have lent a helping hand whenever possible. Judge Bassler, in Newark federal court, was instrumental in bringing the German Foundation into being, but even Judge Bassler ultimately proved unwilling to enforce the German settlement's terms when German industry apparently reneged on its interest commitments.

In the end, my interim report on the Swiss and German Holocaust settlements is unequivocally positive—$6.5 billion distributed to victims is nothing to sneeze at. But it should be better.

NOTES

1. The most complete judicial description of the Swiss bank settlement is *In re Holocaust Victim Assets Litig.*, 105 F. Supp. 2d 139 (E.D.N.Y. 2000) (upholding fairness of settlement).

2. The best judicial description of the circumstances leading to the creation of the German Foundation is *In re Nazi Era Cases Against German Defs. Litig.*, 198 FRD 429 (D.N.J. 2000)(upholding fairness of German Foundation).

3. This essay is based on my personal experience with the Swiss bank and German industry settlements. Since I lack personal knowledge concerning the administration of ICHEIC and Austrian and French settlements, those proceedings are beyond the scope of this essay.

4. Judge Korman presided over the Brooklyn hearing in person, and over the Jerusalem hearing through an all-night telephone hookup to his chambers.

5. Unlike the bank account claims, slave labor payments from both the Swiss settlement fund and the German Foundation are made only to survivors. It would have been impossible to identify and pay heirs of the six million Jews and millions of non-Jews who were murdered by Nazis during the war after being forced to work as slaves.

6. *In re Nazi Era Cases Against German Defs. Litig.*, 198 FRD 429 (D.N.J. 2000).

7. *Duveen v. United States District Court* (*In re Austrian & German Bank Holocaust Litig.*), 250 F.3d 156 (2d Cir. 2001).

8. Judge Korman's remarkable opinion excoriating the Swiss banks for having destroyed the data is reported at *In re Holocaust Victim Assets Litig.*, 302 F. Supp. 2d 59 (E.D.N.Y. 2004) (describing destruction of Swiss bank records and questionable postwar conduct by banks in denying information to claimants).

9. "*Cy pres*" is a Norman-French phrase used to describe a "second-best" procedure that gets as close as possible to an unattainable ideal. Since it is impossible to follow the ideal course of an individual looted assets claims process, Judge Korman found that the second best approach would be to distribute the funds to the poorest members of the class.

10. The national percentages may change if it becomes impossible to return the full $800 million allocated for bank accounts. Any such unreturned residual funds will be distributed to assist poor survivors throughout the world.

11. *Gross v. German Foundation Indus. Initiative*, 320 F. Supp. 2d 235 (D.N.J. 2004) (dismissing plenary action seeking to enforce interest provision—appeal pending).

12. *Am. Ins. Ass'n v. Garamendi*, 539 U.S. 396 (2003) (invalidating California law requiring publication of unpaid Holocaust-era insurance policies as condition of doing business in California).

13. *See Abrams v. Societe Nationale des Chemins de fer Francais*, 389 F.3d 61 (2d Cir. 2004).

14. *Iwanowa v. Ford Motor Co.*, 67 F. Supp. 2d 424 (D.N.J. 1999); *Burger-Fischer v. Degussa AG*, 65 F. Supp. 2d 248 (D.N.J. 1999).

15. Krakauer v. Federal Republic of Germany, Federal Constitutional Court, BvL33/93 (March 13, 1996).

16. Two circuits have repudiated the district court's reasoning. *Ungaro-Benesch v. Dresdener Bank*, 379 F.3d 1227, 1236 (11th Cir. 2004); *Deutsch v. Tuner Corp.*, 324 F.3d 692, 713 n.11 (9th Cir. 2003).

17. Even Judge Korman has been reluctant to use his full Article III power. He never issued an opinion on the merits of the Swiss bank case, preferring to broker a settlement. Subsequently, he has characterized (erroneously, I believe) plaintiffs' international law claims as "worthless" and has declined to direct the Swiss to make information available to the bank account claims process, choosing to rely

on a series of negotiated information concordats. In fairness, I should note that his settlement strategy was masterful, the international law claims are far more difficult than the traditional bank account claims, and a negotiated resolution over information disputes may well have been a more efficient way to deal with the issue.

18. Judge Weinstein was helpful in persuading German insurance companies to make their final payment to the Foundation. He also tried to force the Foundation to take action against the German banks that had mishandled the Polish distribution.

19. Judge Block ruled that the Swiss banks were obliged to pay compound, not simple, interest on settlement funds held in escrow awaiting judicial approval of the settlement. He was also helpful in resolving disputes over the definition of the Slave Labor II class and in establishing secure facilities for the transmission of banking information from Switzerland to CRT offices in New York.

20. Judge Johnson courageously upheld the victims' claims against French banks in *Paribas,* one of the few cases upholding the legal rights of Holocaust victims.

Chapter 6

How Swiss Banks and German Companies Came to Terms with the Wrenching Legacies of the Holocaust and World War II
A Defense Perspective

Roger M. Witten

In 1996, long after World War II ended in Europe, the demands of Holocaust victims and others for compensation from Swiss and German companies began to receive sustained attention in the United States and abroad. Litigation and complex international negotiations ensued. This chapter offers a general perspective on how these difficult and emotional issues came to be resolved, as this resolution was viewed by a defense counsel who was intimately involved with the Swiss bank settlement and German Nazi-era negotiations and related litigation.

Introduction

Switzerland, of course, was not a belligerent during World War II; it was a neutral. Nevertheless, probing questions about Switzerland's role during that war arose after the Cold War ended. Had Swiss commercial banks unfairly retained deposits in accounts opened by Holocaust victims? And had the Swiss, while technically neutral, provided too much practical assistance to the Nazi regime in Germany? These questions implicated the policies and conduct of the Swiss government and the Swiss National Bank (the country's central bank), as well as those of the Swiss commercial banks. But it was the commercial banks, particularly those with operations in the United States—Credit Suisse Group, Union Bank of Switzerland, and Swiss Bank Corporation (the latter two merged in 1998 to become UBS AG)—who bore the brunt of these inquiries.

For Germany, the issues that arose in the late 1990s were altogether different. Nazi Germany had admittedly waged an aggressive war on its neighbors and had heinously sought to exterminate Jews and other groups. No questions lingered about German responsibility for these horrors; the open question was whether Germany's unprecedented postwar reparations, restitution, and compensation programs, amounting to over DM 200 billion in today's value (or approximately $100 billion), had adequately compensated certain categories of victims, particularly slave and forced laborers. Again, although the questions clearly implicated the policies and conduct of the Nazi dictatorship, German companies with substantial operations in the United States became the focus of attention.

Switzerland and Germany responded quite differently. This chapter discusses how and why.

The Swiss Response

In 1996, Jewish groups, particularly the World Jewish Congress, supported by Senator Alfonse D'Amato and others, brought considerable public attention to the so-called dormant accounts issue. Essentially, the allegation was that after the war, Swiss banks failed to return assets in accounts that Jews who perished or otherwise suffered in the Holocaust had previously opened. It was also alleged that Swiss banks, principally the governmental central bank, extensively exchanged hard currency for gold the Nazis may have looted from national treasuries of conquered countries or from Holocaust victims. These allegations were thrust on a country whose people prized their stalwart independence and who were particularly proud that they alone had managed to preserve a democracy on the continent of Europe during World War II.

Although the ghosts of World War II were distinctly unwelcome in Switzerland, the Swiss absorbed the need for an historical reckoning and reacted pragmatically. First, the Swiss Bankers Association (SBA) entered into an agreement with Jewish groups in May 1996 (before any lawsuits had been filed against Swiss banks) to form the Independent Committee of Eminent Persons (ICEP) to conduct, at the banks' expense, a comprehensive, independent forensic audit of virtually all Swiss banks in search of accounts that could have belonged to Holocaust victims. Paul Volcker, former chairman of the U.S. Federal Reserve, chaired this group. In connection with the ICEP process, the SBA and Jewish groups also created the Claims Resolution Tribunal, which resolved claims to some two hundred dormant accounts published by the banks in 1997, resulting in payments by the banks of approximately $11 million. Second, in a parallel action in early 1997, the Swiss government passed legislation creating the Bergier Commission, a group of esteemed Swiss and non-Swiss historians who were charged with performing a review of Switzerland's role during the Nazi era. The establishment of these two investigative commissions reflected an extraordinary Swiss commitment to national self-examination, and both commissions have since produced "no holds barred" reports. Third, in early 1997 the large commercial banks, the Swiss National Bank, and other Swiss companies established a $200 million Humanitarian Fund for Holocaust victims, which was distributed on the basis of need, without regard to anyone's entitlement to an account at a Swiss bank. Finally, the Swiss banks, while maintaining their position in court that the purported class action lawsuits, filed against them in Brooklyn in October 1996, should be dismissed on legal grounds, entered into negotiations with plaintiffs' lawyers and representatives of Jewish groups, under the aegis of a U.S. government mediation effort chaired by Stuart E. Eizenstat.

The good start the Swiss made toward resolution and reconciliation then foundered, and a period of acrimony and stalemate ensued. Why did that happen? Fundamentally, and perhaps to oversimplify, there were two main reasons.

First, the Swiss banks had reached the correct strategic conclusion that it would be fruitless for them to settle the disputes on a piecemeal basis with some or all of the plaintiffs' class action lawyers without securing approval for such a settlement from the relevant Jewish organizations who, if unhappy with such a court settlement, could continue to bring political and economic pressure to bear on the banks. Likewise, it was pointless to reach some accommodation with the organizations but leave the litigation unresolved. The problem, from the Swiss perspective, was that "the other side" was not monolithic; to the contrary, it was badly fractured along multiple fault lines, with various factions in seeming competition with one another to make the most aggressive public attacks on the banks or the most extreme financial demands. In a very real sense, there was and could be no one with whom the Swiss could reliably settle until "the other side" overcame the rifts that bitterly divided it and until all parties on "the other side" began to act in a more pragmatic, realistic fashion.

Second, the Swiss populace, once convinced of the need to engage in national self-examination and restitution, came to feel strongly that Switzerland should devise and implement its own steps for addressing the questions that had arisen. Swiss citizens did not want the United States to dictate to their country, and they felt abused by what they saw as an unappreciative, unfair, and unremittingly anti-Swiss attitude emanating from America. Senator D'Amato's colorful Swiss-bashing was one such provocation. In addition, a 1997 U.S. government report asserting, with little factual basis, that Swiss actions prolonged World War II particularly aggravated public opinion. Likewise, a campaign by Jewish groups and plaintiffs' lawyers to block the merger between Union Bank of Switzerland and Swiss Bank Corporation, which needed the approval of New York State banking authorities, provoked widespread feelings in Switzerland that the country and its banks should not bow to outside pressure. As Swiss public opinion moved toward a decidedly more nationalistic and less cooperative stance, the Swiss government retrenched from playing a leadership role in attempting to resolve the controversy and instead adopted the view that Switzerland's problems in the United States, relating to World War II, were something the Swiss banks, who did business there, had principal responsibility for resolving.

Although the banks wished to resolve the lawsuits and to avert increasingly menacing threats of state and local economic sanctions, the banks could not easily allow themselves to be seen by their government or their important Swiss domestic constituency as "betraying their country" by submitting to American pressure. While the banks' interlocutors in the United States (plaintiffs' lawyers, Jewish groups, and state and local officials) focused on what pressures they might bring to bear on the banks in the United States, they generally gave scant attention to, and lacked a sufficient understanding of, the Swiss domestic pressures that constrained the banks' conduct.

As a consequence of these and certain other factors, the settlement negotiations the U.S. government had been mediating foundered during the early summer of 1998. In the end, however, the two largest Swiss banks who had significant operations in the United States (Credit Suisse Group and the merged UBS AG) succeeded in ending the imbroglio without the involvement of the Swiss government or the U.S. government. In August 1998, the banks reached an agreement in principle on a unique class action settlement resolving the lawsuits: in return for payments totaling $1.25 billion over several years, the banks secured an "all-Switzerland settlement" that released claims asserted by all class members not only against the banks who had been sued but also against the Swiss government (for such things as its refugee policy), the Swiss National Bank (for such things as gold trading with Nazi Germany), and against all Swiss companies (e.g., other banks, insurers, industrial concerns, etc.). Significantly, every major Jewish organization in the world endorsed the settlement as bringing closure to these issues. The U.S. government and later the Swiss government also endorsed the settlement, as did state and local officials who terminated their sanctions campaign. Later, the Brooklyn federal court approved all aspects of the settlement as fair, just, and reasonable.[1] Nothing quite like this "all Switzerland" settlement had ever happened before.

In December 1999, after the settlement agreement had been signed, the ICEP completed its forensic audit, at a cost borne by the Swiss banks of several hundred million dollars, and issued its report. The report concluded that the ICEP "has provided as full and complete [an] accounting of the status of the accounts in Switzerland of victims of Nazi persecution as is now reasonably feasible" and that "a line can [now] be drawn under this contentious and difficult matter."[2] The ICEP ultimately identified approximately twenty-one thousand dormant and closed accounts that had a "probable" connection to a Holocaust victim and an additional fifteen thousand that had a "possible" connection. The report did not reach any conclusion as to the value of the assets "probably" or "possibly" involved. Significantly, the independent ICEP concluded that "there was no evidence of systematic discrimination [against Holocaust victims], obstruction of access, misappropriation, or violation of document retention requirements of Swiss law."[3] Further, the report found "no evidence of systematic destruction of account records for the purpose of concealing past behavior."[4] Indeed, the ICEP audit found that a "surprising amount of old records were in fact preserved."[5] Following the recommendation of the ICEP, the Swiss Federal Banking Commission authorized publication of the names associated with the roughly twenty-one thousand "probable" accounts. That publication went forward, with court approval, as part of the implementation of the class action settlement agreement.

One critical question, however, was not resolved either by the settlement agreement or the ICEP report: how to allocate the settlement money. It was clear that class members who demonstrated entitlement to a particular account would receive from the settlement fund the assets in, or estimated to have been in, that account, grossed up to account for the passage of time. But because of the "all Switzerland" nature of the settlement, it was also clear from the beginning that the $1.25 billion fund far exceeded the likely sums that could rightfully be awarded to specific account holders. The vexing issue of what to do with the excess was deemed too difficult for the fractured plaintiff/Jewish constituencies to resolve as part of the settlement, and the Swiss banks did not believe they properly had a voice in this matter, so it was left for judicial consideration. A court-appointed Special Master took a full year to make recommendations, which the court ultimately endorsed. Regrettably, distribution of the Swiss settlement money has encountered significant delay. As of April 2005, seven years after the settlement, only approximately $242 million had been distributed via about three thousand awards, which were all certified by the Claims Resolution Tribunal and approved by the court. An additional approximately $485 million has been distributed to slave labor and refugee claimants and, on a *cy pres* basis, to especially needy Holocaust survivors in former Soviet Union countries. The Swiss banks play no role whatsoever in the distribution process or in considering the validity of any class member's claims.

The German Response

Germany resolved its World War II and Holocaust-related issues in a fundamentally different manner. Although Germany had provided extensive restitution and compensation, beginning under the Allied occupation and continuing throughout the history of the Federal Republic, no specific program directly compensated slave and forced workers for their work per se. In 1998, leading German companies recognized the lingering slave and forced labor issue and proposed the establishment of a private German foundation that would make payments to those who had suffered. At roughly the same time, Gerhard Schroeder was elected chancellor to head a coalition government formed by the Social Democrats and the Greens. Both parties had, while previously in the opposition, long pressed the German government to establish a fund for slave laborers. On February 16, 1999, the chancellor and leading German companies, calling themselves the German Economy Foundation Initiative (GEFI), announced an extraordinary government-business coalition formed to pursue these aims and, at the same time, to obtain legal peace for German companies who were being sued over these issues in purported class actions in the United States.

Eschewing the Swiss model, which had involved a class action settlement overseen by a U.S. court—indeed, eschewing the word "settlement" —GEFI and the German government sought to resolve the remaining Nazi-era issues on a government-to-government basis with the United States and other interested nations. There followed an extraordinary international negotiation, which the German and U.S. governments (represented respectively by Otto Graf Lambsdorff and Stuart E. Eizenstat) convened and vigorously cochaired and in which the governments of Israel, Belarus, the Czech Republic, Poland, Russia, and the Ukraine participated alongside representatives of GEFI, Jewish groups, and lawyers who had brought purported class action suits in the United States. The negotiations, whose situs alternated between Bonn and then Berlin and Washington, struggled with the following four main issues: (1) how to structure and govern a fund for making payments to victims of Nazi persecution; (2) how much money would be in the fund and who would supply that money; (3) how to allocate the funds among the categories of potentially eligible claimants; and (4) how to achieve reliable legal peace for German companies, who were both being sued and being threatened with economic sanctions at the state and local level in the United States.

Each of these daunting issues was substantively complex and emotionally charged, and the resolution of each was to a certain extent intertwined with and dependent on the resolution of the others. Some of the dynamics that had formed the context of the Swiss negotiations reappeared. The German side, for strategic reasons, correctly concluded that it would pursue only a global resolution that brought an end not only to legal skirmishing in court but also to sanctions imposed by state and local governments and to potentially image-damaging public attacks. But, again, "the other side"—composed of American class action lawyers, American and international Jewish organizations, and, quite significantly, non-Jewish victims represented by Eastern and Central European governments— was badly splintered. As a result, the substantive and emotional fabric of the talks was highly fluid and volatile, and it was difficult for the German side to secure a reliable negotiating partner whose views could command a consensus. Significantly, during these protracted negotiations, a measure of realism was injected when two federal district court judges in New Jersey dismissed World War II class action slave labor cases against German companies and American companies that had German affiliates during the Nazi era, finding in both cases that they raised nonjusticiable political questions, and in one that the doctrine of international comity and applicable statutes of limitations also barred suit.[6]

On July 17, 2000, after a year of difficult talks, including interventions by President Clinton and Chancellor Schroeder, the parties endorsed instruments that became known as "the Berlin Agreements." The Berlin Agreements consisted of an Executive Agreement between Germany and the United States and a cognate Joint Statement signed by these two governments and the other participants in the negotiations. Pursuant to the Berlin Agreements, Germany agreed to enact legislation establishing a German Foundation named "Remembrance, Responsibility, and the Future" as a sovereign instrumentality of the German government and to endow it with DM 10 billion (approximately $5 billion) in principal, half contributed by the German government and half through voluntary contributions from German companies raised by GEFI. The parties agreed further that the Foundation would operate as the exclusive remedy and forum for all asserted claims against German companies arising out of World War II and the Nazi era, including claims relating to slave labor, forced labor, property losses (including "Aryanization"), and other personal injuries. Unlike in the Swiss case, the parties to the German talks resolved the vexing allocation issues in advance rather than leave them to the Foundation to resolve. This was possible only because of the political will that the participating governments brought to the talks. Notably, the participants agreed to allocate the considerable sum of DM 700 million (approximately $350 million) to a Future Fund at the Foundation that would combat racial hatred and bigotry.

The parties also adopted an unprecedented mechanism for achieving "all-embracing and enduring legal peace" for German companies with respect to asserted claims against them arising out of the Nazi era and World War II. First, as noted, the agreements established the German Foundation as the exclusive forum and remedy for such asserted claims, which German legislation confirmed. Second, the class action lawyers who participated in the talks agreed to dismiss their suits and to refrain from bringing new ones. Third, in a unique step that had initially been proposed by GEFI's representatives, the U.S. government promised the German government in the executive agreement, which bound succeeding administrations, that it would press for dismissal of all current and any future cases against German companies by filing a Statement of Interest in such cases urging the court to dismiss on any valid legal ground. The United States agreed to this because President Clinton and Secretary of State Albright formally determined that legal peace for German companies was not only in the interests of the companies and Germany but also in the fundamental foreign policy interests of the United States, because it would remove a serious irritant between friendly allies.[7]

Under the Berlin Agreements, the Foundation was not obligated to distribute its funds until legal peace had been secured through dismissal of all pending cases against German companies. Following the execution of the Berlin Agreements, U.S. courts ultimately dismissed almost seventy lawsuits against German companies. The German Bundestag then declared that legal peace had been sufficiently achieved and the Foundation thereupon began distribution of funds in 2001. In contrast to the slow progress made by the U.S. court administering the Swiss settlement, the German Foundation has made admirable progress: as of September 2004, it had paid over 3.603 billion Euros (approximately $4 billion) for distribution to over 1.585 million people.

Comparing and Reflecting on the Swiss and German Agreements

The Swiss issues were resolved through a unique agreement among private parties that affected significant government interests. In contrast, the German issues were resolved through a unique government-to-government agreement that affected significant private interests.

Several important considerations led Germany to follow a different strategy from the Swiss. First, Germany viewed the slave labor issue as a national problem; by contrast, Switzerland came to view its World War II problems in the United States as centered on the conduct of Swiss commercial banks. As a result of these different national policy perceptions, the German government, unlike the Swiss government, steadfastly pursued a "hands on" approach. Second, the German Foundation was created through legislation enacted by the German Bundestag as a German public body with significant German public funding. In these circumstances, it was unthinkable that the German Foundation would be supervised by a U.S. court, and therefore, a class action settlement mechanism was unacceptable for German companies. By contrast, the Swiss settlement fund lacked sovereign attributes, even though it conferred benefits on sovereign entities like the Swiss National Bank, so U.S. court supervision of a class action settlement fund was not anathema. Third, the issues affecting Germany, a belligerent in the war, were viewed by many—certainly the German side—as reparations issues that, as a matter of public international law, could not give rise to adjudicable private claims but only to sovereign interests resolvable solely through diplomacy by governments. This too excluded the possibility of a court settlement, because such a settlement would imply that private claims could be asserted in a court.

The Swiss class action settlement had one major advantage: it provided broad binding releases running from all class members to "all Switzerland," thereby legally precluding new lawsuits by class members. In contrast, the Berlin Agreements did not provide German companies with binding classwide releases; putative class members remain technically free to sue. This exposure was limited in two practical ways, however. First, any person receiving a payment from the German Foundation automatically gives a blanket release in favor of all German companies (and others) on all issues arising from World War II and the Nazi era; the universe of releasors thus created includes most potential plaintiffs, because the Foundation offers them a speedy way to receive dignified payments for the harms they had suffered. Second, if someone does sue a German company in the United States, the German company can depend on the highly persuasive effect of a U.S. government Statement of Interest that urges the court to dismiss such suits with prejudice. In fact, this procedure has brought dismissal of all cases that have reached a decision on defendants' dispositive motions. The objective of legal peace has in this manner been substantially achieved, although, regrettably, several cases have since been filed against German companies. These cases have all been dismissed as of September 2004, although several plaintiffs have filed appeals.

The role of the courts in the Swiss and German cases is noteworthy. No legal rulings on the merits of the asserted claims were ever issued in the Swiss cases. The banks had moved to dismiss the suits on legal grounds (including nonjusticiability, international comity, failure to state a claim, and lack of subject matter jurisdiction), but the judge never ruled on these motions. Clearly, the judge hoped the cases would settle, thereby sparing him the rigors of decision; and he eventually played a role in helping the parties forge a settlement. By contrast, courts both recently and in the past have uniformly dismissed World War II suits against German companies. The majority of courts have held that plaintiffs present no justiciable claims in light of the extensive postwar government-to-government resolution of these issues. The basic thrust of these decisions has been that such disputes do not belong in U.S. courts. Thus, no case against a Swiss bank or German company has yet to produce a judgment for a claimant. The legal hurdles confronting plaintiffs make success in court highly unlikely.

Further emphasizing that point, in June 2003 the U.S. Supreme Court upheld the president's power to enter into the German-U.S. Executive Agreement and struck down a California law seeking to regulate German insurance companies in a manner inconsistent with that agreement.[8] The Supreme Court held, among other things, that the California law compromised "'the very capacity of the President to speak for the Nation with one voice in dealing with other governments' to resolve claims against European companies arising out of World War II."[9]

Why then would Swiss banks or German companies pay large sums in connection with these agreements? Here, the reasons are similar for the Swiss and the Germans. First, a court victory standing alone, in the highly charged context of claims asserted by Holocaust victims, may well have had only limited long-term strategic value. It could have exposed the company to allegations that it was "stonewalling" vulnerable people and, for that reason, generated intense political and economic pressures, which in an increasingly globalized economy can be more menacing than a lawsuit. Second, leading Swiss and German companies had an overarching desire to "do right," to acknowledge moral (but not legal) responsibility for historical wrongs, to make material amends, and to ground closure on a sound moral and financial footing. In the end, these altruistic considerations, while thoroughly blended with pragmatic considerations, supplied the driving dynamic that made constructive resolution of both the Swiss and German disputes possible.

The key to the successful resolution of these difficult, emotional problems of historical dimension was the creation and preservation of goodwill among those charged with the responsibility for finding a way forward. Without abiding goodwill on all sides, no lawsuit, no sanction, and no other strategy could have produced results in both the Swiss and German cases that were fair, that promise to endure, and that simultaneously serve both the public interest and each party's private interests. In such difficult and complex endeavors, goodwill is a precious resource, to be husbanded and cultivated and not to be squandered in the emotions of the moment or for perceived short-term advantage. This lesson should not be lost as postagreement implementation issues arise in both the Swiss and German arenas.

NOTES

1. *In re* Holocaust Victim Assets Litig., 105 F. Supp. 2d 139 (E.D.N.Y. July 26, 2000).

2. *See* Independent Committee of Eminent Persons, *Report on Dormant Accounts of Victims of Nazi Persecution in Swiss Banks* (Dec. 1999), 18 (ICEP Report).

3. *Id.* at 81.

4. *Id.* at 6, 13, 17, 109–10.

5. *Id.* at 15, 17, 108, 111.

6. Burger-Fisher v. Degussa AG, 65 F. Supp. 2d 248 (D.N.J. 1999); Iwanowa v. Ford, 67 F. Supp. 2d 424 (D.N.J. 1999).

7. Letter from Samuel R. Berger, Assistant to the President for National Security Affairs, and Beth Nolan, Counsel to the President, to Michael Steiner, National Security Assistant, Office of the Federal Chancellor, F.R.G. (June 16, 2000); Statement by Secretary of State Madeleine K. Albright (Oct. 20, 2000).

8. *See* Am. Ins. Ass'n v. Garamendi, 123 S. Ct. 2374 (2003).

9. *Id.* at 2391–92 (quoting Crosby v. Nat'l Foreign Trade Council, 530 U.S. 363, 381 (2000)); *id.* at 2391 (noting the executive agreement serves "to resolve the several competing matters of national concern [including] . . . the national interest in maintaining amicable relationships with current European allies; survivors' interests in a 'fair and prompt' but nonadversarial resolution of their claims . . . ; and the companies' interest in securing 'legal peace.'").

Chapter 7

Why Won't Those SOBs Give Me My Money?
A Survivor's Perspective

Si Frumkin

Actually, this is a rhetorical question. I know why they won't. Isn't it obvious? It is because they would rather keep it. They figure that if I got along all this time without them paying what they owe me, well, then I can wait a while longer and then, well, eventually I will be gone and that will be the end of the story. If they bother to talk or think about what I and the other survivors are bitching about, they probably say, "they shouldn't bitch; they are lucky to be alive."

You know, they are right. I am lucky to be alive. I have survived, I have lived a good life, I have seen much beauty, I have known much ugliness, and I am coming to the end of it all. Maybe I should just relax and let it go. Maybe, but not yet.

I am angry. I am angry with the SOBs in Germany. With our own SOBs in Washington. With the SOBs running the Jewish organizations that presume to speak and negotiate for me and others like me. With the criminals who run European insurance companies that stole hundreds of millions of dollars from those who died prematurely in the gas chambers, and who used the money to hire stooges to make sure that the money is not given back.

I am a law-abiding American citizen. I pay my taxes and my traffic tickets. I vote. I have served on a jury. I fly my flag on national holidays. I know how to recite the Pledge of Allegiance.

In return, I expect my government to fulfill its obligations to me, at least when it comes to the foundation on which everything else is built: the U.S. Constitution, or, more precisely, my constitutional rights. One of them is my right to a trial by a jury of my peers. This has now been denied me because, apparently, my government prefers to uphold and defend the rights of giant German corporations rather than mine. The SOBs that anger me are many. The one I know best is the one whose slave I was, the one that worked my father to death, the one my government is protecting from me. It is called Philipp Holzmann A.G. It is a biggie—the second largest in Germany and one of the largest in Europe. During World War II, Holzmann owned me and my father for slightly more than a year. I wasn't an American then, of course; I was just a 13-year-old Jewish kid from Lithuania given to Holzmann as a slave by the Nazi government. I didn't even have a name. I was Jew #82191. My dad was #82192—he stood in line behind me when the numbers were given out. There were about nine or ten thousand of us from Lithuania who were loaded into freight cars and shipped to Landsberg, a town in Bavaria, where the Holzmann corporation was constructing a giant underground factory to build jet fighters for Hitler's air force.

Hitler needed the jets. The dozen or so prototype ME-262s flew about one hundred miles per hour faster than anything the Allies had. In their first month of operation they downed almost one hundred U.S. and British bombers over Germany. Holzmann's job was to get the factory built in a hurry, and they did their best. Work went on twenty-four hours a day, in twelve-hour shifts, seven days a week. There were no days off, no holidays. We lived on starvation diets—after all, unlike Jewish workers, food cost money; when people died, more would be brought in for free. There was no shortage of slaves in Hitler's Europe.

The factory was never finished. I was liberated at the age of fourteen, twenty days after my dad died. After wandering around Europe and South America for a few years, I ended up in California. By 1954, I had an American wife, a job, a college education, a tract home, and a newborn son. Holzmann went on to much success and fortune. We didn't keep track of one another; they never wrote to apologize and I never contacted them for a slave and master reunion.

In the late 1990s, people started talking about German companies paying compensation to those who worked for them for free during the war. Just for fun, I figured out what Holzmann owed me.

We worked 84-hour weeks when the minimum wage for unskilled labor in Germany was about twenty-five cents an hour for a ten-hour day. Not even allowing for overtime and all the rest, my pay would total roughly $1,100 for the fourteen months I was there. A dollar in 1944 is worth about

$15 now (it probably is more than that; I bought my first home in California for $8,000, gasoline was about twenty cents a gallon, and my weekly salary was $75), but let's be generous and say $10, so that is $11,000. Add to this compound interest for fifty-eight years at a minimal 3 percent per year, and you end up with about $70,000–90,000.

And let's get something clear. This isn't charity—it's compensation. It has nothing to do with what the ex-slave is making now, what he is going to do with it, or whether he really needs it. It is just wages that were stolen, not paid, diverted to the corporate coffers.

There is also the matter of my father's death. He collapsed on his way to work. The rest of the column kept on going and I just saw him being taken away, on a handcart. He was placed in a so-called hospital barracks for people who were dying. There was no medicine, no food, no water. Once a day a handcart would take away the corpses to be dumped in a mass grave outside the camp, but before that, a man who had been a distinguished dentist in the normal world before the war came in to pull the gold teeth from the cadavers' mouths. I came back from work while Dad was still alive. I said goodbye to him and I think he understood. And then he was gone. I have no idea how to calculate the value of my dad's life.

So, after California abolished the statute of limitations in such cases, I and about forty other former Holzmann slaves in California found a lawyer who was willing to sue Holzmann for compensation.

Naturally, the SOBs resisted. Powerful, expensive lawyers did everything they could to beat us, to tire us out, to prolong the process so that time would catch up with us and we would be gone. The SOBs don't mind spending money—my money, our money—on hiring lawyers who specialize in obfuscation, using long, complex words on extra-long pages of heavy paper that no one ever reads more than once. These lawyers can explain the difference between "compensation" and "restitution," between "confiscation" and "seizure," or between "forced" and "slave" labor. The SOBs like that. The more time is spent on conversations, explanations, definitions, and clarifications, the more time is used up and eventually, like I said, we will all be dead and very quiet.

The SOBs are powerful. They are rich and influential. They expect to win and they are winning so far. What hurts is that throughout, from one court to the next, from one appeal to another, they had the support of my government. Apparently the White House and the State Department decided that justice meant less than appeasement of the German corporations. The government stepped in on behalf of the Germans, spending taxpayer money—your money, my money—to defend the slave owners. State Department experts during the Clinton administration testified that "lawsuits by former slave laborers would be tantamount to interference with the foreign policy of the United States." There was expert testimony on the expiration of statutes of limitations on claims by former slaves, the unconstitutional usurpation of powers by states like California, and much more gobbledygook. The point is that we kept losing. And another thing happened more recently. Several Jewish organizations appointed themselves as representatives of me and my fellow slaves and began negotiating with Germany on the final resolution of all claims. A German Foundation was created (the "Remembrance, Responsibility, and the Future" Foundation, to be exact) in which German slave owners were going to deposit $5 billion as final compensation for all claims in perpetuity. There was jubilation all around. Hands were shaken, champagne was poured, Foggy Bottom bureaucrats breathed a sigh of relief that this bothersome irritation was resolved, and lawyers and Jewish organizations salivated at the prospect of the millions that will be paid out in legal fees, grants, and all the rest. It seems that in the end, all valid claimants will receive about $7,500 each. And then there will be "legal peace," now and forever.

I am bothered. I never authorized any Jewish organization to negotiate for my father or me. There are, of course, some ex-slaves who gladly accepted the agreement—and they have the right to do so. There are others, like myself, who object. We want direct confrontation and compensation to be decided in court, on our behalf, by a jury of our peers. This opportunity now appears to have been eliminated by my government's decision and by that of the self-appointed Jewish *makhers* ("big shots").

And here are a few interesting footnotes on my personal SOB, the Philipp Holzmann A.G.

Just a little over three years ago, on April 13, 2001, to be exact, the business section of the *New York Times* ran a story under the heading "Global Conspiracy on Construction Bids Defrauded U.S." I don't know what prompted me to read it. It sounded boring, but I read on.

The gist of the *Times* article was that a unit of ABB Ltd., described as a "Swiss engineering giant," admitted to being part of a conspiracy that lasted over seven years. The participants rigged the bidding for projects in Egypt that were to be paid by the U.S. Agency for International Development. As a result, America paid out a few hundred million dollars more than it should have. The article didn't indicate the total amount involved, but it mentions contract #29 for $135 million and contract #20 for $107 million. We can reasonably assume that there were at least twenty-nine similar contracts; at about $100 million each, the total would be about $3 billion.

There were at least six other international companies involved, joined together in the cause of cheating the U.S. taxpayer. They were American or American subsidiaries of European concerns. They called themselves the "Frankfurt Group" because some of the largest participants were based in Frankfurt, Germany.

And here is where it gets personal for me. One of the largest participants, who had already pleaded guilty in August 2000, was J.A. Jones Construction of Charlotte, North Carolina, itself a subsidiary of Philipp Holzmann A.G. of Frankfurt, Germany. The article said that a fine was imposed and paid but it didn't say how much it was. An Internet search wasn't really productive: it suggested that Holzmann and its subsidiary admitted culpability—but not guilt (?)—and paid something in the neighborhood of $35 million in fines. In case you think that this is all, relax. The story now branches out in another direction altogether. Recently, a national monument was erected in Washington to honor the GIs of World War II. And guess which construction company got the $56 million contract to build the memorial? Give up? Too absurd? No, it isn't.

It is the Tompkins Builders of Washington, D.C., which is wholly owned by the J.A. Jones Construction Co., a subsidiary of J.A. Jones Inc., of Charlotte, North Carolina, that was bought in 1979 by Phillip Holzmann A.G.

In the interest of fairness, here is additional information from a J.A. Jones statement in response to the fuss I made when I found out about all this. They say that J.A. Jones has also built nine American military bases that trained U.S. troops during World War II, as well as two hundred Liberty-class warships. It also built the Washington Mall Reflecting Pool, the White House West Wing, and the East Wing of the National Gallery. "Anyone who questions the patriotism of J.A. Jones Construction Co., its employees, and our historical commitment to a free world is misguided and misinformed," says company president John D. Bond III.

Still, I find it disconcerting that a monument to dead American soldiers should be built by a company owned by a corporation that tried so very hard to help Hitler manufacture the weapons that killed them. But, of course, I am probably not seeing the big picture and am not aware of the complexities that are so obvious to the true professionals who work behind the scenes.

And now, as they say, to something completely different. A slightly different cast of SOBs who won't give me my money.

The word "insurance" implies trust, security, and someone who will look out for you when disaster strikes or if, God forbid, a loved one has passed away. After all, if you can't trust your insurance company, whom can you trust?

Well, actually, it all depends on geography. If your life was insured by a European insurance company, your heirs' chances of collecting on it are somewhere between hell freezing over and pigs flying. That is, of course, if the deceased insured was a Jew during the Holocaust and died without a death certificate issued by the authorities, who were too busy murdering Jews to bother about paperwork.

Let me tell you about my dad. He had a name before he became #82192. In Lithuanian, he was Mykolas Frumkinas. In Russian, which we spoke at home, he was Nikolay Grigorievich Frumkin, but his friends called him Kolya and, of course, to me he was Papa—Daddy. Strangers called him, in the East European fashion, Engineer Frumkin because he had an engineering degree from a major German university, but he never worked as an engineer.

My dad was an automobile dealer. He sold Harley Davidson and Triumph motorcycles, Willy's Overland automobiles, SKF Swedish ball bearings, and even German NSU motor scooters. He traveled widely—every year my mother and he would go to France or England or even to the World Fair in New York in 1936, and they would always bring me presents.

When my parents didn't want me to understand them, they spoke French. My mother had graduated from the Sorbonne and we subscribed to the French newspaper *Paris Soir* in the days before the Soviets annexed Lithuania and took away my father's business. The Soviets didn't take away his name though. That came later.

All this is just for background, just to show that my father was an educated, sophisticated man. Now here's the point. It is inconceivable that a man like my Papa, a cosmopolitan businessman, would not have provided for his family in case something happened to him. It is absurd to assume that he didn't have a life insurance policy. I am convinced that he did, but I can't prove it.

In 1944, my father lost his name. He became #82192 at the KZ Dachau, Arbeitslager Kaufering #1. The death of inmate #82192 was duly recorded in German archives on April 7, 1945—twenty days before I was liberated, stopped being #82191, and went back to being Simon Frumkin.

Fifty-eight years have passed since then. A few years ago the world suddenly realized that European insurance companies had been holding on to hundreds of thousands of unredeemed insurance policies on the lives of Jews who died when the Nazis ruled Europe. The companies refused to pay anyone. Even the few who recovered the actual policies were told that a death certificate was needed, or some other silly and cruel excuse.

In 1999, there was actual pressure—primarily from California, which enacted a law requiring any insurer doing business in the state to disclose information about any policies sold in Europe from 1920 to 1945. The European thieves in business suits who stole the Jewish life insurance premiums reacted, but not by opening their files and showing the lists of the insured Jews. No, they did the same thing the slave owners did; they hired expensive lawyers and went to court. After the cases dragged on and on, in June 2002, the U.S. Supreme Court overturned the California law, ruling 5 to 4 that the state was improperly interfering with the conduct of foreign affairs. Really? Hiding the names of insured and murdered Jews influenced our foreign policy?

An exception was the major Italian company, Assicurazioni Generali, but what they did was much more sneaky. In 1990 they turned over to the Israeli Holocaust museum, Yad Vashem, a list of several hundred thousand names of owners of life insurance policies in Eastern Europe in the 1930s. Generali then took out ads in Israeli papers bragging about what a good and ethical company it was. I even have a picture from the June 4, 1999, edition of the *Jerusalem Post* showing Bobby Brown, the advisor to then Prime Minister Benjamin Netanyahu, beaming on camera as he showed off a computer disk purportedly containing "a hundred thousand names and information of wartime Generali insurance policies issued in Eastern Europe before W.W.II." Initially we were told that the list had three hundred thousand names and that Yad Vashem had to sign a confidentiality agreement not to reveal the names to anyone. About a year later, the numbers on the still-secret list shrank to just one hundred thousand names and we were told that Yad Vashem had to examine the list, sort the list, isolate the Jewish names, and then make it available. There were also many conflicting explanations and excuses as to why the list couldn't be published—unpaid computer processing bills, incompatible computer programs—but the upshot is that now, four years later, apparently somewhere around thirty thousand names have been revealed. Or maybe not.

There were other developments as well. By the year 2000, the Europeans were getting very annoyed by all the fuss and came up with a brilliant scheme. They would create an international commission that would have authority and decision-making power in the matter of all these claims of dead Jews. The insurance companies would be members of the commission and would hire the respected and influential retired U.S. Secretary of State Lawrence Eagleburger to run it. They would then invite insurance commissioners from several states to be members of the commission. It would have a very impressive name: International Commission of Holocaust Era Insurance Claims, usually referred to as ICHEIC. Eagleburger would be receiving a yearly salary of $360,000 from the insurance companies, and the headquarters would be in London, far away from all those pesky survivors.

The insurance SOBs were apparently aware of the old proverb, "He who pays the piper picks the tune." In this case, the piper surely pleased those who paid for the tune. During congressional hearings in September 2002—after almost three years of work—Eagleburger acknowledged that ICHEIC had spent $56 million on overhead, salaries, travel, and all the rest while offering only $35 million to settle claims by qualified claimants with "acceptable" proof. Much—maybe most—of these offers were actually rejected by the claimants. An example is a friend of mine who is one of the few claimants who has an actual paper policy, for $2,000, issued in 1936. It should have been paid in 1945! Generali, the insurer, who had refused to even acknowledge it for thirty years, has finally admitted that the policy is valid and offered to pay $5,000 as a settlement in full. Apparently the formula devised by ICHEIC, and accepted by all concerned, is that a 1936 U.S. dollar is worth somewhere around two dollars in 2002! I guess ICHEIC hasn't heard of inflation or interest.

Generali admitted that it has in its files about one hundred thousand names of unpaid Holocaust-era life insurance policyholders. So far it has refused to publish them on the ICHEIC website.

Generali is big, rich, and very smart. So far it has been able to keep the money it stole. The expenses it has incurred so far are minuscule compared to the money it owes. And here, too, it has the cooperation of the U.S. government and its judiciary in acknowledging ICHEIC—created, financed, and controlled by the insurance SOBs—as the only legitimate body to rule, decide, and control Holocaust-era insurance claims.

But control of ICHEIC wasn't good enough for another major player: Allianz A.G., a major German company with branches in the United States and owner of Fireman's Fund, a major American insurer. Remember the German Foundation that gave the slave owners a chance to get rid of all claims once and for all in the German Slave Labor Settlement? After the German corporations were given a promise of "legal peace," Allianz decided that it too wanted to play. It took very little effort to join them— after all, it too was German, a corporation, and a major target of survivor claims. So, just like that, Allianz was accepted into the Foundation, the only member that wasn't actually accused of using slave labor, just of stealing the slaves' money. Allianz is now free and clear of all further responsibility, cannot be sued by insurance policy holders, and can continue making a lot of money in Europe and the United States.

I don't know if my father's insurance policy was issued by Allianz. There is little hope that I will ever find out. The way things are, even if I had proof, I wouldn't be able to collect anything. My government has promised "legal peace" to the slave owners, to the insurance cheats, to those who made their fortunes out of the war and the Holocaust.

Still, I want to see those lists. I am sure that my father's name appears on one of them. I am also sure that tens of thousands of others whose parents or grandparents perished will find their relatives on those lists.

Hitler took away my father's name and gave him a number. The insurance companies took it away again. It isn't on any revealed lists and they pretend that he never existed. I want them to acknowledge that he lived, that he died, and that the way he died matters to his son and to the grandchildren he never knew.

Part II

The Bank Litigation

A Litigator's Postscript to the Swiss Banks and Holocaust Litigation Settlements

How Justice Was Served

Melvyn I. Weiss

Through the collaborative and tenacious efforts of U.S. class action attorneys, the governments of the United States, Germany, Israel, Poland, the Czech Republic, Ukraine, Belarus, and Russia, Jewish and human rights organizations, survivors of the Holocaust, and those who had been forced and slave laborers, settlements were reached amounting to more than $8 billion, resolving a series of Nazi victims' economic claims, their demands for compensation having largely been ignored for more than fifty years. At issue were dormant Swiss, French, Austrian, and British bank accounts confiscated from Jews during the Nazi occupation of Europe, looted real and personal property, unpaid insurance policies, and the Nazi use of uncompensated slave and forced labor.

For many observers, the two main focuses of the cases generally referred to as the Holocaust litigation were the restitution of property seized by the Nazis and their allies, and compensation for forced and slave labor. From my perspective, the focus was as much, if not more, on the postwar failure of the banking, industrial, and governmental beneficiaries of that conduct to acknowledge what they had done, to intentionally obfuscate their responsibilities, and to continue to take advantage of their profiteering even after the atrocities had ended.

The Class Actions against the Swiss Banks

Accusations that the allegedly neutral Swiss and their banks had collaborated with the Nazi regime and profiteered from its World War II dealings with it surfaced soon after the war. Even as the financial dealings between the Swiss banks and the Nazi regime gradually came to light in the first decades after World War II, Holocaust survivors and heirs of Holocaust victims were unable to recover funds they or their relatives had deposited for safekeeping in Swiss bank accounts. During the Nazi era, the Swiss banks had, in an attempt to increase their deposits from Europe's Jews, encouraged European Jews under imminent threat of Nazi persecution to open numbered bank accounts in Swiss banks with the promise that numbered accounts would be unidentifiable to the Nazis and their assets would thus be protected from Nazi confiscation. It was only after the Swiss banks cases were settled that those rightful owners of Swiss bank accounts and safe deposit boxes could successfully assert claims and receive their deposited assets. At the same time, it was only in the midst of the litigation that the Swiss private banks and the government-directed Swiss National Bank acknowledged their wartime financial complicity with the Nazis. Following the war, and until the lawsuits, Swiss bankers, their professional organizations, and the Swiss National Bank persistently sought to conceal both their complicity with the Third Reich (they had, in many cases, simply when requested and with no legal authority, transferred Jewish-owned assets to the German central bank) and their illicit retention of bank accounts owned by Jewish Holocaust victims.[1]

The Swiss banks litigation began in 1996, when class actions were filed against several Swiss banks in the U.S. District Court for the Eastern District of New York. Later, the Swiss National Bank was sued in the federal court in Washington, D.C. The banks were accused of collaborating with the Nazi regime by knowingly trading "Nazi gold" (gold stolen by the Nazis from treasuries of conquered nations and individuals), laundering Nazi seized ("looted") assets, and profiteering from slave and forced labor.[2] The lawsuits further accused Swiss banks of concealing the true nature and scope of their unlawful conduct during and after the Holocaust. The heart of the suits, however, were claims against private Swiss banks for participating in an unlawful scheme to retain Holocaust victims' assets voluntarily deposited in Swiss bank accounts and safe deposit boxes for safekeeping in anticipation of and during World War II.

I was honored to have been asked, by a group of plaintiffs' lawyers, to be part of the leadership of this historic effort to seek justice against the Swiss banks for Holocaust-related claims that had remained unresolved more than half a century after the war's end. As a member of the Plaintiffs' Executive Committee,[3] and one of three designated negotiators for the survivors' interests, I saw clearly that the effort would be tremendously complex legally, and surrounded by highly emotionally charged confrontations between the victims and defendants.

The 1996 litigation and the negotiations beginning in 1998 resulted in a global settlement, signed on January 26, 1999. The political and diplomatic pressure stimulated by the World Jewish Congress and Senator Alfonse D'Amato, assisted by the U.S. government, who were represented by Stuart Eizenstat, and the Hevesi Commission, a coalition of state and local government finance officers formed by New York City comptroller Alan Hevesi, which together threatened financial and regulatory sanctions, substantially augmented the unyielding and very difficult legal efforts of the plaintiffs' attorneys to reach a favorable settlement with the Swiss banks.

According to the settlement agreement, the Swiss banks' contribution of $1.25 billion would resolve all outstanding financial obligations against all Swiss entities and the Swiss government arising from Holocaust-era Swiss dormant accounts, Switzerland's closing its borders to refugees fleeing Nazi-controlled territories, Swiss laundering of slave labor proceeds, World War II forced labor for Swiss companies, and the laundering of assets stolen by the Nazis.

The settlement was unprecedented; after more than half a century of nonaction, elderly Holocaust survivors were able to obtain assets their families had deposited in Swiss banks for safekeeping, a trust those banks had intentionally broken by holding the proceeds until after the settlement. To date, the settlement has distributed hundreds of millions of dollars of prewar and wartime deposits to their rightful owners, and compensation has been provided to the remaining members of the ever decreasing generation of victims of Nazi slave and forced labor worldwide (for German and Swiss companies respectively), victims fleeing Nazi persecution denied entry into Switzerland, and individuals whose assets Swiss banks laundered. Another significant aspect of the settlement is the explicit inclusion and recognition of non-Jewish victims of the Nazis, specifically Sinti and Roma, the physically and mentally disabled, and homosexuals persecuted by the Nazis.

The Solomonic job of allocating the recovery was agreed to be left to the discretion of Chief Judge Edward R. Korman (United States District Court for the Eastern District of New York). Judge Korman elected to hold public hearings, in Israel and the United States, inviting all interested parties to participate. After several days of hearings, Judge Korman appointed a Special Master, Judah Gribetz, the highly respected former deputy mayor of the city of New York, to recommend a plan of allocation. Notices of the hearings were distributed throughout the world in multiple languages. Jewish organizations, led by the Conference on Jewish Material Claims against Germany, were staffed to assist interested parties in understanding the process and to explain their future rights.

A significant aspect of the Swiss banks litigation is the resulting historical research and documentation about Swiss complicity with the Nazi regime and their postwar unlawful behavior. Reports by the Volcker Committee and the Bergier Commission, and the one accompanying Special Master Gribetz's allocation recommendations, along with one preexisting report by Stuart Eizenstat and the survivor records assembled by the Claims Resolution Tribunal in connection with the administration of the claims process, comprise the most comprehensive analysis to date of the Swiss and their banks' World War II activities and postwar breaches of trust.

Given the strong moral issues underlying the litigation, most of the attorneys, including myself, litigated the Swiss banks case pro bono.

The Class Actions against German Industry

The cases against German industry opened contentiously and legalistically. Shortly after the first complaints against German companies' for their World War II use of slave and forced labor were filed (in March 1998), twelve of Germany's leading companies, all defendants in our suits, consistent with their past practice of insisting they had done nothing wrong, formed the German Foundation Initiative, an ad hoc initiative designed to circumvent the lawsuits by seeking the assistance of the U.S. and German governments to force a diplomatic resolution to all claims. Of note is that the German government's response was markedly different from that of the Swiss government. The German government actively participated in the resolution process; the Swiss government refused to engage at all.

Of particular concern to German industry was the highly negative publicity surrounding the cases that threatened, they believed, their U.S. business interests. They hoped that the establishment of a central foundation that would compensate a select group of the remaining members of the dying generation of victims, approved by the two governments, would put a quick end to the negative publicity, or at least minimize it, until the lawsuits were resolved. What was far from clear at the time was how intensively the German and to a lesser extent the U.S. media would continue to investigate and report on Germany's widespread use of slave labor during World War II.

The victims, of course, were well aware of the extent of Germany's and its industrial entities' World War II use of forced and slave labor, and that they had been bypassed by earlier compensation programs—a matter of great irritation in victims' circles since the end of the war. Early attempts by Germany's former slaves to seek compensation, either from the German government or its industry, had been thwarted by German courts since the 1950s.[4] The highest German court held that claims by non-German victims were nonjusticiable pursuant to somewhat ambiguous language in the 1952 London Agreement on German External Debt, promulgated to permit the German economy to reconstitute itself after the war and create a bulwark against Soviet expansion into Western Europe. German courts have thus consistently held that that agreement prescribed a moratorium on victims' claims against either Germany or its industrial entities until the Allies executed a peace treaty with Germany, a formality that has still not been achieved. What precipitated the U.S. slave labor litigation were two German district court decisions in 1997. Two principled German courts had, after six years of litigation, held that at least for the purposes of the moratorium imposed by the London Debt Agreement, the 1990 German Reunification Treaty constituted the peace treaty required by that agreement, ending the moratorium on victims' claims. Those long-hoped-for decisions formed the basis for my firm's filing, in early March 1998, the first of what ultimately ended up being approximately thirty lawsuits against industrial entities, both German and American (those with German subsidiaries), that had used slave and forced labor during World War II. The suits were filed in the district of New Jersey, the first one against Ford Motor Company and its German subsidiary, Ford Werke. We alleged the Ford Motor Company controlled Ford Werke well into the war, violating the Trading with the Enemy Act. Under Ford Motor Company's control, Ford Werke produced Blitz trucks for the German military even after Germany's 1939 invasion of Poland. Two Ford Motor Company executives, including Edsel Ford, continued to serve on Ford Werke's Board of Directors.

Six months after our first case was filed, the first of approximately seventy similar lawsuits began to be filed by other law firms. Shortly thereafter, in February 1999, multilateral negotiations began, alternating between Washington, D.C., and Germany, first in Bonn and then, once the German government moved to Berlin, in Berlin.[5]

The negotiating sessions that took place in the U.S. and German Departments of State had a United Nations–like atmosphere. The negotiations were simultaneously translated, as needed, into five languages. Eight nations' government representatives, ten or more representatives of German industry, nongovernmental victims' organizations, and the U.S. lawyers participated in the negotiations. The American lawyers were clearly the group most intent on obtaining a significant recovery. Approximately one year later, under the auspices of the German and U.S. governments, a settlement was reached. During the negotiations, it became clear that most of the surviving victims had worked for companies that no longer existed. Therefore, with the assistance of the German and U.S. governments, we converted the negotiations into ones seeking a global resolution of the lawsuits.

As in the Swiss banks cases, emotions ran high, and the result was, as Rabbi Israel Miller of the Conference on Jewish Material Claims against Germany noted, "a small measure of justice." The payment only partially recompensed the material debt, being a pittance compared to the value of what was forcibly taken. The settlement also contained a statement of moral responsibility (the first on behalf of the German government) by President Johannes Rau.

Answering the Criticism

Inevitably, revisiting the financial aspects of World War II's horrors, particularly when dealing in a sterile and relatively emotionless legal environment and especially when magnified by broad media coverage, triggered a host of criticisms. These included harsh and pointed reactions by survivors and their heirs, who view economic compensation as unseemly and morally denigrating. That subset of survivors feels that since it is impossible to provide anything resembling compensation commensurate to the loss and suffering, accepting any amount at all would attach an unacceptably low value to their suffering. Most survivors, however, responded positively. Not only were they most grateful for the financial aspects of the settlements; they were also pleased with German President Johannes Rau's December 1999 apology to the Third Reich's victims, and the worldwide media attention focused on their suffering. Both were direct results of the litigation. Former slave laborer Elly Gross, in a letter to me expressing her deep gratitude for the effort made to prosecute these past wrongs, observed that it "remind[ed] the world how hate and prejudice creates destruction" and that the litigation "reminded everyone of the forgotten past when millions were wiped out."[6]

One of the most troubling criticisms was voiced by Norman Finkelstein, a Jewish American author and son of Holocaust survivors. In his highly controversial book *The Holocaust Industry*, Finkelstein accused the "Jewish-American establishment" of exploiting the Holocaust remembrance.[7] Finkelstein argues that the various litigations constituted a "Holocaust industry," an enterprise established by lawyers to "extort" billions of dollars from the Swiss banks and others in the name of, Finkelstein alleges, nonexistent, or at least far, far fewer "needy Holocaust victims" than actually exist. The so-called Holocaust industry, alleges Finkelstein, has shrunk the moral stature of the victims' martyrdom, as has the inclusion of a subcategory of supposed victims, people, Finkelstein argues (without plausibility or evidence), who could not have been victims at all. Finkelstein further maintains that the "Holocaust industry" is a greater threat to the memory of the Holocaust than are Holocaust deniers. In making these assertions, ironically, Finkelstein relies on the arguments of Holocaust deniers regarding the number of victims.

Finkelstein's claims received overwhelming condemnation,[8] most notably by Professor Israel Gutman, formerly chief historian of Yad Vashem, Israel's Holocaust museum and research institute, who said that Finkelstein's book "takes a serious subject and distorts it for improper purposes" and should be considered "nothing more than an anti-Semitic lampoon."[9] Similarly, Hans Momsen, the highly regarded German history professor, described Finkelstein's book as "most trivial . . . appeal[ing] to easily aroused anti-Semitic prejudices."[10]

Finkelstein's characterization of the Swiss banks litigation as an "extortion" serving the personal, political, and financial motivations of what he refers to as "the Jewish-American establishment" gravely misses the essential moral value that formed the heart of these processes.

Specifically, the financial component of the Holocaust litigation is but one dimension; it does not encapsulate the significance of the achievement to Holocaust survivors, both Jews and non-Jews, and, more generally, to civil society. To me and those whom I represented, the settlement primarily represents the malefactors' acknowledgment of their wrongdoing both during and after World War II, and their profit-motivated complicity with the Nazi regime. Basic notions of justice and morality required that victims be compensated as soon as possible, not five decades later. The same applies to their acknowledgment of wrongdoing.

That view has been seconded by others. Referring to the American-led international compensation campaign, Elie Wiesel wrote that "it is not really about the money. . . . In a deeper sense, it is about something infinitely more important and more meaningful; *it is about the ethical value and weight of memory.*"

The long, costly legal battle and the ensuing settlement agreement with the Swiss banks, and later with the other European defendants, also were denounced on the grounds that they primarily served Jewish interests. Critics viciously—and inaccurately—portrayed the historic effort leading to the resolution of Holocaust-era claims as an entirely Jewish enterprise. Such critics rely on the fact that the public and legal campaign against those entities that, for profit, were complicit with the Nazis was primarily led by prominent Jewish organizations and leaders to argue that that campaign promoted only Jewish interests. However, the vast majority of the settlements' beneficiaries—80 to 90 percent of the 1.7 million people compensated—were non-Jews. Although the Jews were among the most severely persecuted Nazi victims, many non-Jews fell victim to that same horrific conduct and were, quite appropriately, included in the settlements.

Seeking to further denounce the moral legitimacy of the $1.25 billion settlement agreement with the Swiss banks and the approximately $6 billion payment from the German and Austrian interests, critics also argue that the settlements provide woefully inadequate monetary compensation to Holocaust survivors.[11] From my perspective, trying to draw a connection between the moral legitimacy of the settlements and normative judgments about monetary adequacy is a misplaced effort that underestimates the true value of the litigations' achievements and their long-term implications. The unavoidable truth is that no remedy can compensate Holocaust victims for the horrors of their losses and suffering. Echoing the imperfection of legal remedies, Elie Wiesel asks, "Who can give . . . [the] books I purchased with my pocket money in my childhood . . . back to me? Who will give me back the *tephilin* of my father and my grandfather?"[12]

In that vein, I would suggest that even though literal corrective justice is clearly beyond our reach, the historic legal and public campaign not only acknowledged the victims' suffering; it also actually hurt the defendants' pocketbooks and led the perpetrators to acknowledge their wartime misdeeds, thus offering Holocaust survivors some emotional closure. This accomplishment cannot be overestimated. The psychological value of having your own representative seek to hold malefactors accountable is incalculable in terms of monetary value. To many others who subscribe to the teachings of a civilized society, the reinforcement of the belief that human values can be achieved by the rule of law is monumentally important. It also lends credence to the notion that individual liberty—including the respect of property rights—is not an unrealistic ideal.

Legal Fees

There was some criticism that lawyers took fees in cases filed after the ones against the Swiss banks. Those fees amounted to 1.25 percent of the German settlement, including expenses—far below the market value of the services provided. According to Stuart Eizenstat,

> It was the American lawyers, through the lawsuits they brought in U.S. courts, who placed the long-forgotten wrongs by German companies during the Nazi era on the international agenda. It was their research and their work which highlighted these old injustices and forced us to confront them. Without question, we would not be here without them.[13]

The Legacy for the Future

In retrospect, the litigation against Swiss banks, German industry, and others reinforces my strong belief in the precious role of the American legal system as a significant cornerstone of modern society. The ability of elderly Holocaust survivors to access the justice system to seek a legal remedy for wrongs committed more than a half-century ago demonstrates the vital role of America's legal system in protecting and, indeed, safeguarding human rights and the rule of law.

The class action device that was employed—Rule Twenty-Three of the Federal Rules of Civil Procedure—is a unique feature of the American legal system and has proven to provide a powerful litigation mechanism for those unable to litigate individually. Equipped with class action lawsuits, a team of willing plaintiffs' attorneys, devoting their financial and intellectual capital, was able to help achieve what governments, world organizations, human rights activists, and foreign legal systems had failed to achieve since the end of World War II.

The message here is clear. Against this backdrop, any attempt to constrict access to the American court system, or otherwise limit the efficacy and vitality of the class action device should be resisted as an attack on a cornerstone of America's greatness. Time and again it is shown that a strong legal system and unimpaired citizens' access to justice—along with goodwill and empathy for human suffering—are the fundamental elements of freedom and liberty. Some of the great cases of the past half-century were class actions; they achieved desegregation and resolved a myriad of challenges to discriminatory practices, reapportionment, consumer protection, safety, and the environment.[14] Unless individuals within a society have the tools to stand up against the powers of the state and those who dominate through the use of power and wealth, the risk to liberty and justice for all is too great. Various forms of racial, ethnic, gender, age, and disability discrimination would go on unchecked, marketplace fraud would be more pervasive, and more toxic substances would still be in our midst if citizen access to the justice system was restricted. Indeed, the absence of the class action device in both Germany and Switzerland, along with a number of other procedural impediments existing in those countries and in most civil law systems, were significant, in reality insurmountable, hurdles to victims seeking recompense in any court system other than that of the United States.

Shortly after the 1990 German reunification, a small number of concentration camp survivors filed suit in German courts, asserting claims for having labored as slaves during World War II. The claims ultimately were subsumed by the U.S. class actions, but only after six years of ponderous and technical analysis of their claims in German courts. Of the twenty-one victims that filed claims in Germany, sixteen were dismissed on the specious grounds that they had received other forms of compensation in the past. Even if the cases had been pursued to completion, they would not have had precedential value for other victims or provided a blueprint for subsequent claims. More significantly, had those victims lost, under the fee-shifting rules in Europe, they could have been liable to the German companies and government for their legal defense costs. These and other procedural hurdles made suit in Germany, and similarly Switzerland, impracticable. The availability of lawyers willing and able to represent novel and uncertain claims that were likely to be attacked by a series of procedural defenses, who would serve on a contingency basis and who are not required to follow the European rules requiring payment pursuant to an official fee schedule, is another feature of American law unavailable to plaintiffs in Europe. The availability of contingency fee arrangements in the United States permits victims unwilling or unable to finance valid challenges to large entities to shift the risk to able and capable lawyers.

Speaking for myself and most of my colleagues, all of whom provided legal services pro bono or under a contingency fee arrangement, this incredibly high-risk undertaking against a group of the most powerful economic entities in Europe was pursued without any thought of economic gain but out of a sense of recognition of the underlying humanity of "the cause." The legal battle against the Swiss banks, and later against German and Austrian industry and banks and the French banks, was not only just but also served a noble human cause and produced a worthy legal legacy.

NOTES

1. Switzerland has no escheat laws, so Swiss banks were able to keep their illicitly retained assets.

2. "Slave labor" used in the context of the Holocaust litigation came to mean labor performed in settings in which the lifespan of the laborer was measured in months. "Forced labor" in that context designated labor performed for minimal or no pay and under force, but by those for whom the traditional economics of slavery still applied, namely, it was intended that the victims would survive and continue to perform labor for their captors. *See* Benjamin B. Ferencz, *Less Than Slaves* (2002).

3. Constituted of Michael Hausfeld, Robert Swift, and myself. Judge Korman later appointed Prof. Burt Neuborne as special counsel.

4. In his seminal book on the subject of Germany's World War II slave laborers' attempts to obtain compensation, Benjamin Ferencz details the early cases brought before German courts. *See* Ferencz, *Less Than Slaves.*

5. Ironically, the very first use of the new German State Department, the Reichsbank during World War II, was for these negotiating sessions.

6. See Elly Gross, *Storm against the Innocents: Holocaust Memories and Other Stories* (2003), 114.

7. Norman Finkelstein, *The Holocaust Industry: Reflections on the Exploitation of Jewish Suffering* (2000).

8. *See e.g.* Katherine Klinger, "Reflections on Finkelstein," *Jewish Quarterly* (Autumn 2000).

9. *See* Yair Sheleg, "The Finkelstein Polemic," *Ha'aretz Magazine,* March 30, 2001.

10. Id.

11. *See e.g.* Steven Greenhouse, "Capping the Cost of Atrocity: Survivor of Nazi Experiments Says $8,000 Isn't Enough," *New York Times,* November 19, 2003, B1.

12. See "Foreword" by Elie Wiesel in Stuart E. Eizenstat, *Imperfect Justice* (2003).

13. Stuart E. Eizenstat, "Address at the 12th and Concluding Plenary on the German Foundation Berlin, Germany," July 17, 2000.

14. *See generally* Arthur R. Miller, *Of Frankenstein Monsters and Shining Knights: Myth, Reality, and the "Class Action" Problem,* 92 Harv. L. Rev. 664 (1979).

Chapter 9

Rewriting the Holocaust History
of the Swiss Banks
A Growing Scandal

Edward R. Korman

The impetus for my contributing an essay to this collection stems from what I see as an unfortunately common misrepresentation of the historical record concerning the activities of the Swiss banks before, during, and in the aftermath of World War II with regard to bank accounts and other assets deposited with the banks for safekeeping by their Jewish customers during the Nazi era.

My first public response to the false record being created was a lengthy opinion published in February 2004 (*In re Holocaust Victim Assets Litigation*, 302 F. Supp. 2d 59, E.D.N.Y. 2004), superseded by a slightly modified opinion (at 319 F. Supp. 2d 301), issued in June 2004. My opinion came in response to a myriad of statements by the Swiss banks and aimed to expose the banks' three "Big Lies": (1) that they never engaged in "systematic document destruction" and therefore should not be assigned blame for any difficulty we are having in distribution of the settlement funds; (2) that during the Nazi era, they did not engage in widespread forced transfers of customers' assets to the Nazis; and (3) that the allegations that they engaged in massive destruction of Nazi-era bank records in the post-war era "are incorrect and could be characterized as malicious in light of specific conclusions to the contrary in the ICEP and Bergier Reports."[1] As I stated in that opinion, "These statements continually distort and obscure the truth."[2]

In painting a false picture, however, the Swiss banks were not without their allies. In September 2000, the respected Jewish monthly *Commentary* published an article entitled "Holocaust Reparations—A Growing

Scandal?"[3] by Gabriel Schoenfeld. In June 2004, I wrote to Mr. Schoenfeld, setting out in detail how his analysis of the class action litigation against the Swiss banks needed correction. In my seventeen-page letter, I made Mr. Schoenfeld aware of some of the actual history of the Swiss banks' behavior as set out in my court opinion.

Unfortunately, *Commentary*'s editors chose not to publish a correction. At most, they were willing to publish a highly eviscerated version of my letter. I declined their offer, since such an abbreviated version could not faithfully correct the misleading factual assertions made by Mr. Schoenfeld.

This volume provides an opportunity to set out the accurate facts as well as to respond specifically to some of the misstatements and erroneous assertions in the Schoenfeld article.

In his article, Schoenfeld seems to conclude that the Swiss banks' behavior with respect to deposited assets during and after the Holocaust was excusable and does not warrant a lawsuit. He states, for example, that "the offending behavior was evidently limited to a relatively small number of banks and is not of recent vintage."[4] He also writes that "with the dormant bank accounts, the Volcker Committee's authoritative report clearly refutes the accusation that the Swiss bankers engaged in widespread and systematic larceny."[5] Thus, Schoenfeld concludes, the Volcker Committee has revealed "the suspect nature of a good number of the claims for compensation that have been streaming in ever since this issue was highlighted in the 1990's."[6]

Each of these statements is the result of a misreading of historical accounts or of a premature rush to judgment, and each serves to whitewash decades of improper behavior by Swiss banks. Schoenfeld's conclusions may have in part been affected by the unavailability in September 2000 of certain historical evidence and reporting that has since come to light. In particular, he lacked the final report of the Bergier Commission, which employed historians, researchers, and economists to examine the role of Switzerland and its financial center during the Nazi era.[7] Nevertheless, *Commentary*'s failure to address these sources upon my drawing them to its attention is telling.

The central claim of the class action plaintiffs was that the Swiss banks either improperly transferred the plaintiffs' assets to the Nazis or otherwise withheld them through stonewalling or document destruction. Schoenfeld concedes that the Volcker Committee found a far higher number of accounts possibly belonging to Nazi victims than the Swiss banks had previously identified. And he concedes that "[t]he disparity is overwhelmingly the result of sheer bad faith on the part of the Swiss."[8] But he then proceeds to write,

> On the other hand, the offending behavior was evidently limited to a relatively small number of banks and is not of recent vintage. Rather, it "took place years ago in a particularly difficult period with different banking standards." Significantly, the Volcker commission uncovered *no* evidence of "organized discrimination against the accounts of victims of Nazi persecution" or "concerted efforts to divert the funds of victims of Nazi persecution." Although many records could not be located, this could not be attributed "to systematic or widespread and deliberate alteration or destruction of bank-account records for the purpose of obliterating the history of the accounts of these victims." Indeed, in a stunning conclusion completely contrary to the picture drawn by the World Jewish Congress and the Western media, the commission reports "many cases" in which banks "actively sought out missing account holders or their heirs, including Holocaust victims, and paid the account balances of dormant accounts to the proper parties."[9]

As an initial matter, Schoenfeld's unquestioning reliance on statements by the Volcker Committee report is misplaced. The Volcker Committee was comprised of accountants. The accountants were not seeking historical truth; they were trying to efficiently identify bank accounts that may have once been held by victims of the Holocaust. Moreover, the accountants had long-term and ongoing relationships with the banks that they hoped would continue. While the accounting firms employed were probably the only ones capable of undertaking the enormous task they faced, the effect of this conflict on the audit cannot be measured. And this was not the only problem. The Swiss Bankers Association (SBA) had appointed three of the seven members on the Volcker Committee. A unanimous statement required compromises. The Volcker Committee's findings should not be ignored—indeed, when read in context they actually reveal a great deal more than Schoenfeld suggests—but more reliance should be placed on the historical conclusions of the Bergier Commission. With these clarifications as a backdrop, I will address and refute Schoenfeld's points in order.

First is Schoenfeld's suggestion that the banks' behavior should not be the subject of a class action lawsuit because it is "limited to a small number of banks." I do not know how Schoenfeld came to this conclusion.

What I do know is that the two defendants in the Swiss banks litigation, Credit Suisse and UBS, were repeatedly cited by the Volcker Committee and later the Bergier Commission as examples of banks that engaged in the sort of improper behavior that forms the basis of the lawsuit. Indeed, 87 percent of the accounts identified by the Volcker Committee as probably or possibly belonging to Jews were held by these two banks. Moreover, these two banks (while arguably a "limited number") through acquisitions and mergers now contain more than 40 percent of all bank accounts open or opened in Switzerland during the Nazi era. Thus, Schoenfeld's suggestion that this behavior was "limited to a small number of banks," even if true, would be wholly irrelevant.

Second is Schoenfeld's claim that the banks' behavior should be excused because it is "not of recent vintage" or because it "took place years ago in a particularly difficult period with different banking standards." Much of the behavior at issue here—particularly the banks' refusal to pay account proceeds to proper parties through stonewalling and document destruction in the postwar period—continued until the onset of the class action lawsuits. While I will discuss bank stonewalling and document destruction at greater length below, the suggestion that this behavior is "not of recent vintage" or occurred "in a particularly difficult period" is simply incorrect. The other relevant behavior—forced transfers of account proceeds to the Nazis—also cannot be so casually excused as having occurred "in a particularly difficult period" of a different "vintage."

The Bergier Commission found that throughout the Nazi era the banks chose to place their own perceived economic self-interest ahead of their customers' as a matter of policy. Time and time again, banks completed transfer orders that they knew were requested only because of Nazi persecution, and that they suspected were not in their customers' best interests. An example that reflects the concerted policy of the Swiss banks is described by the Bergier Commission as follows:

> After overrunning Poland in September 1939, the new ruling [Nazi] power endeavoured to acquire Polish assets deposited in Switzerland. As early as 20 November 1939, the Polish bank Lodzer Industrieller GmbH asked Credit Suisse to transfer assets deposited with it to an account at the German Reichsbank in Berlin. The bank saw a fundamental problem in this procedure and asked its legal affairs department to examine the matter. The latter recommended not complying with the request since the customer's signature had most likely been obtained under duress by the occupying authori-

ties. . . . The legal affairs department also pointed out that for Poland, German foreign exchange regulations represented a war measure taken by an occupying force and that Switzerland had not yet recognized the new political situation. *Managing Director Peter Vieli subsequently discussed the issue with Rudolf Speich, his counterpart at the Swiss Bank Corporation.* The latter contacted the Reichsbank, which agreed that in view of the unclear constitutional situation in Poland, Swiss banks were not obliged to comply with requests from German administrators (*Reichskommissäre*). Nevertheless, according to a file note "the directors of the Reichsbank and Dr. Speich were of the opinion that duly signed requests from customers for their assets held in Switzerland to be transferred to an account with the Reichsbank must be executed since absolutely no justification could be found for not doing so." *Although there were legal and moral objections to transferring the funds, the consideration that they "still had important interests in Germany, and should avoid friction and unpleasantness whenever possible" prevailed at CS [Credit Suisse].* They complied with the request and opted for the principle of carrying out legally signed orders even when they were not received directly from customers, but via the Reichsbank in Berlin. Their comportment in Poland was in this respect typical of how the banks dealt with the assets of Nazi victims: *as a rule, they complied with transfer orders from foreign customers without properly checking whether the signatures they bore had been obtained under duress by the Nazi authorities and whether the orders were in fact in the customer's interest.*[10]

The two major banks in this example (Credit Suisse and Swiss Banking Corporation) consulted with one another and *together* decided to disregard the legal advice of Credit Suisse's legal department. It is possible to imagine situations where a bank's decision to order a forced transfer would have been morally justified as a way to protect a client's life, but that was clearly not the case for these banks. These banks did not decide to order forced transfers because they thought doing so would serve their clients well during the "difficult period"—they did so to "avoid friction and unpleasantness" with their business interests in Germany. Unpleasantness for their clients was not even a consideration.

Even during this "particularly difficult period" of a different "vintage," Swiss courts recognized that these forced transfers were illegal under Swiss law.[11] Moreover, neither the law nor banking standards have ever changed on this subject: it has always been improper for a fiduciary to comply with a request known to be made under duress. Nevertheless, as

Bergier Commission member Helen Junz explained, "Although there are documented cases where banks acted to safeguard clients' assets—by moving them to numbered accounts or into other-named accounts—current evidence shows that *the cases in which accounts were released predominated.*"[12] Independent researchers Barbara Bonhage, Hanspeter Lussy, and Marc Perrenoud "estimate that in this way the major banks released some SF 200 million worth of deposits and securities to the German banks and/or the Reichsbank."[13] Using the Claims Resolution Tribunal's conservative conversion rate, this sum—just for the forced conversions—would equal over $1.7 billion today, greater than the $1.25 billion global settlement reached by the Swiss banks.

Again, the banks had a choice. They could have chosen to adhere to their fiduciary obligation and refused to honor transfers requested under duress. They could have frozen customer assets or otherwise blocked transfers as a matter of policy. Their failure to do so is revealing. As study number 15 prepared for the Bergier Commission explained,

> [P]ublic opinion would have likely welcomed a freeze of German and Austrian assets in 1933 and 1938, respectively, and because [Swiss] courts hindered the forced transfers when they were called in to decide such cases, it is very hard to understand today why Swiss politicians and banks did not vehemently take steps against the implementation of the German laws. . . .[14]

It is less "hard to understand" when one considers the premium banks placed on "avoid[ing] friction and unpleasantness" with their interests in Nazi Germany. The banks can certainly attempt to defend their Nazi-era decisions, but blithely stating that it was a "particularly difficult period" is insufficient.

Third is Schoenfeld's claim that the Volcker Committee found "*no evidence*" that the lack of account records can be attributed "to systematic or widespread and deliberate alteration or destruction of bank-account records *for the purpose of obliterating the history of the accounts of these victims.*"[15] While this statement is a proper quotation from the Volcker Committee report, it is an artfully crafted statement that ignores more insightful facts. Before I delve into what the Volcker Committee in fact found, it is important that I clarify the incentives the banks had for stonewalling and then destroying countless bank records.

Swiss banks were aware of the fact that they had made improper transfers during the Nazi era and that they could be held liable if they released information. After the war, many surviving account holders or their heirs approached the banks seeking information about accounts, often with valid legal claims. The banks, which had improperly transferred the funds in the accounts to the Nazis, were afraid that they would be called to account for the breach of their fiduciary duties.[16] Equally important, the problem was not disappearing. "Although assets transferred to the Third Reich were left out of the inventory of unclaimed assets of Nazi victims in Swiss banks, they were nevertheless part of the restitution claims" that had been filed against the banks.[17]

Additionally, the banks received a direct economic benefit from their silence. The Volcker Committee found that "the problems with dormant accounts appear to be partly a byproduct of the absence of a Swiss escheat law dealing with unclaimed property in banks."[18] "Unlike other countries (such as the United States) where dormant assets are transferred to state governments, in Switzerland dormant assets remain indefinitely with the banks."[19] If no one claimed the assets in an account (or if a bank simply refused to comply with a claim) a Swiss bank could keep the money. The Bergier Report summarized the troubling result:

> The banks lost nothing if the dormancy persisted; on the contrary, the monies entrusted to them that affected the balance sheet continued to improve their interest balance—particularly as the banks usually stopped paying interest on the dormant accounts.[20]

Last, the banks anticipated an indirect economic benefit from stonewalling. Before the war, the Swiss banks had been seen as an attractive repository because of their commitment to secrecy and "private property rights." Many bank officials anticipated that steadfast devotion to secrecy would be critical as they went forward. The ironic result is that the banks turned on Nazi victims on the basis of the very same principles that had previously led the Nazi victims to turn to the banks.[21] Helen Junz explains the situation as follows:

> The banks quickly realized that post-war political developments were bringing new opportunities to the field of asset management. . . . [They] perceived that hewing to their commitment to bank secrecy and protection against cross border compliance with tax and foreign currency regulations of other countries would give them a further material advantage. Compared with the cold-war generated new client potential, the Holocaust survivor

clientele held no interest—on the contrary. Basic policies, though not enunciated as such, thus generally aimed—of course with some exceptions —to ignore this clientele.[22]

Or, as put differently by the Bergier Commission, "[t]op executives in the banks . . . assumed that they would enhance their appeal to new customer segments by a resolute defence of banking secrecy."[23]

In the face of these incentives, the Swiss banks stonewalled as a matter of course. Because claimants typically lacked information as to the exact location or nature of the items deposited, the banks could routinely "entrench themselves behind banking secrecy" and cite the claimant's inability to sufficiently document a legal entitlement as a reason to deny payment.[24] Where the claimants had precise information, the banks turned to still more deceitful tactics. As explained in the Bergier Report, "A situation was reached where even death certificates were being demanded for people who had been killed in the [concentration] camps."[25] It is thus not surprising that

> [t]he unwillingness of the Swiss financial institutions in the immediate post-war period to find the legal owners of unclaimed assets or to support rightful claimants in their search, constitutes the main point of criticism of the banks' behavior, already tainted by certain dubious decisions and questionable attitudes in the period between January 1933 and May 1945.[26]

To illustrate what was probably the most common method of stonewalling, I turn first to a poignant example provided by an award made in the claims process to the heirs of Prof. Dr. Albert Uffenheimer, who at one time had a bank account at the Zurich branch of Credit Suisse.[27] Born in 1876, Dr. Uffenheimer lived in Germany at the time of Hitler's rise. He remained there until 1938, when he fled to England. His wife remained in Germany. In December 1938, bank records show that Dr. Uffenheimer contacted his bank from London and instructed it to pay out the assets in his account (securities valued at SF 3,000) to the Constance, Germany, branch of the Deutsche Bank. The bank complied with the request.

Passing over the complicated moral question of whether completing this transfer was proper or improper, I turn to the far clearer issue of the bank's postwar conduct. The bank received a letter dated May 11, 1949, on behalf of Dr. Uffenheimer's widow requesting information regarding the account. It responded with a letter that stated,

In response to your query of 11 May 1949, we must unfortunately inform you that, pursuant to Swiss legal requirements regarding banking secrecy, we cannot provide information about activities that pertain to the business dealings of our customers during their lifetime, not even to their heirs. In addition, we draw your attention to the fact that the activities referred to in your letter happened more than ten years ago, while we are only obligated to preserve our correspondence for ten years.[28]

This response was not simply a form letter. Indeed, an internal memorandum from the bank's legal department, dated May 17, 1949, reveals how considered a strategy it was. The memorandum indicates that the bank knew it had transferred Dr. Uffenheimer's securities to the Deutsche Bank. It quotes Dr. Uffenheimer's request, which explained that he was making the request pursuant to an order from a German finance minister who threatened that noncompliance would be penalized. With his wife still in Germany, Dr. Uffenheimer had agreed to make the request. The bank's memorandum correctly reasoned that "from this correspondence it follows that Professor Uffenheimer was forced by the German authorities to hand over his assets deposited with us to the Deutsche Bank."[29] What is troubling is that the memorandum then concludes, "*for these reasons,* we are careful about providing information and withhold information. If necessary, we should rely on the fact that, since then, more than ten years have passed, so that we no longer today are obligated to preserve this correspondence."[30] Precisely because the bank was aware that it had acted in a way that could expose it to liability, the bank refused to divulge information. This stonewalling, which prevented Dr. Uffenheimer's heirs from gaining restitution, was the principal basis for the Claims Resolution Tribunal's award.

In 1950, the general director of Union Bank of Switzerland and former secretary of the SBA stated that "the best solution" would be "never to mention the entire affair [of forced transfers] again."[31] He was apparently not the only Swiss bank official to hold this view. The Bergier Commission made the following discovery:

In May 1954, the legal representatives of the big banks coordinated their response to heirs so that the banks would have at their disposal a concerted mechanism for deflecting any kind of enquiry. They agreed not to provide further information on transactions dating back more than ten years under any circumstances, and to refer to the statutory obligation to keep files for only ten years, even if their records would have allowed them to provide the information.[32]

The most noteworthy aspect of this Bergier Commission finding may be the fact that it was such a collective decision by the banks. The banks, as a matter of policy, refused to disclose information regarding dormant accounts, even when they had it. It is no surprise that the letter received by Dr. Uffenheimer's representative matched the major banks' agreed-upon language almost exactly.

Again, this stonewalling policy was a specific response to victims of the Holocaust. The Volcker Committee quotes from a 1969 letter it found in the records of one of Switzerland's large commercial banks on the procedures to be followed for responding to claims of Jewish account holders and their heirs whose assets were transferred to Germany in the 1930s:

> [I]n the case of inquiries about Jewish clients whose assets had to be transferred on their instructions to Germany during the 1930s, or with regard to inquiries received from their heirs, we have always responded that we could not supply the requested information as we are only obliged to retain ledgers and correspondence for a period of 10 years.

The Volcker Report comments,

> The legal department recognized that because the transfer orders were made under duress, the risk existed that the bank might be liable to restore the accounts to the rightful owners. However, the legal department noted that claims by non-Jewish German nationals were not considered a liability, which suggests that the bank treated inquiries from Jewish customers differently from those received by non-Jewish German nationals. [33]

This passage refutes Schoenfeld's suggestion, and that of the Volcker Committee itself, that the Volcker Committee had found "no evidence" of "organized discrimination against the accounts of victims of Nazi persecution."[34]

The banks also resorted to stonewalling in the face of broad-based efforts to uncover assets of Nazi victims. The Volcker Report states, "[T]he banks and their Association lobbied against legislation that would have required publication of the names of such so called 'heirless assets accounts,' legislation that if enacted and implemented, would have obviated the ICEP investigation and the controversy of the last 30 years."[35] Indeed, in order to thwart such legislation, the Swiss Bankers Association encouraged Swiss banks to underreport the number of such accounts in a 1956 survey. "'A meager result from the survey,'" it said, "'will doubtless contribute to the resolution of this matter [the proposed legislation] in our favor.'"[36] The banks adhered to the SBA's recommendation: "For instance, Swiss Bank Corporation (Schweizerischer Bankverein, SBV) indicated in 1956 that it could not state 'with certainty' that it had such accounts but there were 13 cases (with a total value of 82,000 francs) where this was probable."[37] Given what the Volcker Committee was able to find forty years later, these estimates were clearly nothing more than a lie.

When external pressure forced Switzerland in 1962 to adopt the Registration Decree, which was "meant to provide a genuine solution [to] the problem that had remained unresolved throughout the 1950s," the banks again put forth "concerted resistance."[38] This time the banks did not vigorously resist the law's passage; rather, they completely frustrated its implementation. Pursuant to the Registration Decree, banks were obliged to "report any assets whose last-known owners were foreign nationals or stateless persons of whom nothing had been heard since 9 May 1945 and who were known or presumed to have been victims of racial, religious or political persecution."[39] "A total of 46 banks reported 739 accounts containing a sum total of 6,194,000 francs."[40] They declined to report accounts of people who died after May 9, 1945 (even where one customer had died in the Dachau concentration camp on May 13, 1945), accounts held in the name of a trustee, and accounts where the account holder's name was arguably not Jewish.[41] "In short, a whole raft of measures was adopted with the aim of deliberately minimising the results of the investigation."[42] And again, this raft of measures was not adopted by isolated banks in isolated situations—it was a collective decision to deceive by the Swiss Banking Association that delayed justice in some cases for several decades, but in most cases indefinitely.

It is important to reiterate that the Swiss banks' devotion to secrecy and their repeated acts of stonewalling were not based on principles—they were profit driven. Put differently, "the banks' rhetorical efforts to uphold the existing 'legal system,' guarantee the [v]iability of the law and protect 'property rights' on the basis of banking secrecy" were merely that—rhetoric.[43] As the Bergier Commission found, "it is apparent that the claims of surviving Holocaust victims were usually rejected under the *pretext* of banking secrecy and a clear preference for continuity in private law. Over the many years of such rejections, a large number of accounts were reduced to zero or almost [zero]."[44] Where economics counseled against upholding secrecy, private law, and property rights, however, the banks were quick to abandon their supposedly entrenched values.

A particularly telling example of profits being placed above "banking secrecy" is the secret postwar deals reached by the Swiss with Poland and Hungary to loot unclaimed accounts belonging to Holocaust victims. "[T]he primary aim of [these deals] was to favour Swiss interests in the wake of nationalisation of assets in Poland and Hungary."[45] Historian Gerhard Weinberg explained the deal with Poland as follows:

> [I]n 1949 the Swiss government signed a secret agreement with the Communist government of Poland under which the Swiss government with the agreement of the regime in Warsaw located the accounts in Swiss financial institutions of those Polish citizens who had been murdered and who either had no heirs or whose heirs had been stonewalled. The proceeds of this looting operation were then paid over to Swiss citizens who had claims on Poland arising out of the nationalization and/or confiscation of their property in Communist Poland.[46]

The deal with Hungary was similar in operation.[47] What is most striking about these secret agreements is that, as the Bergier Commission pointed out, "[s]urprisingly, it was now apparently possible to conduct an internal investigation so that a list of dormant accounts relating to these countries could be drawn up."[48] Indeed, "[n]either private property rights nor banking secrecy had been a barrier to the release of these assets."[49] Dr. Weinberg explained,

> [A]ccounts which previously have been announced in diplomatic negotiations as either not existing or incapable of being located, and which have been withheld from the heirs either for those reasons or because the heirs cannot produce documents acceptable to the financial institutions, can suddenly be identified, their contents removed, and legal title to the assets transferred to Swiss citizens whose claims against Poland or Hungary might hinder future profitable Swiss trade with those countries.[50]

While stonewalling was generally an effective way for the Swiss banks to insulate themselves from liability and benefit economically, wholesale destruction of records was even more successful. Document destruction is probably the most contentious subject regarding the banks' behavior in the postwar period, and it is naturally the subject on which it is the most difficult to obtain information. As noted at the outset, there are records pertaining to 4,100,166 accounts out of an estimated 6,858,116 accounts open or opened between 1933 and 1945. Of those 4.1 million accounts for which some record exists, it is quite common to find nothing more than a customer registry card. Records of account activity or closing documents are rare. The findings of the Bergier Commission and Volcker Committee help explain why records are so often lacking.

The Swiss banks generally complied with Swiss law on record keeping, but this is precisely the ruse. The Swiss Code of Obligations requires only that banks keep correspondence and accounting records for a period of ten years, regardless of whether an account is open or closed.[51] If the banks could stonewall for ten years, then they could "legally" destroy the very documents that might answer claimants' questions. This is precisely what they did. Banks "regularly and systematically" destroyed material that was ten years old.[52] In some banks, the document destruction was annual, in some it was semiannual, and in some it was simply intermittent. But it happened across the board. And thus the banks destroyed countless records that might have been critical in explaining their Nazi-era actions with respect to accounts once held by Nazi victims. Schoenfeld claimed that the Volcker Committee found "*no* evidence" that the lack of account records can be attributed "to systematic or widespread and deliberate alteration or destruction of bank-account records *for the purpose of obliterating the history of the accounts of these victims.*"[53] But the qualification—which was surely the result of lengthy negotiations among the members of the Volcker Committee—renders this statement irrelevant. The destruction was part of the banks' ordinary course of business, and it was massive.

The Volcker Committee explained how unexceptional this practice of document destruction was for the banks. Banks "did not retain lists of records destroyed in the normal course of business and in accordance with Swiss law."[54] "Therefore, large quantities of documents [from banks] relating to accounts from the Relevant Period have been destroyed in the normal course of business without record."[55] This reveals the critical issue— the banks made no effort to save relevant documents, despite the fact that they knew Nazi victims and their representatives were clamoring for them.

Even given the banks' policy of destroying decade-old records, some records of dormant but still open accounts (the most recent ten years' worth) would presumably have survived. In the case of large dormant accounts, banks would often "manage the assets in the interest of customers about whom no further information was available."[56] The banks could use these accounts to generate substantial commissions and fees, and records would persist. In the case of small dormant accounts, however, the banks devised ways to eliminate the accounts altogether, and then eliminate all record of them. For instance, the banks would continue to charge activity fees on dormant, non-interest-bearing accounts, and when claimants would request that the bank perform a search for their account, the bank would charge high search fees. The search fees could reach twenty-five francs in the 1950s, 250 francs in the 1960s, and 750 francs by the 1980s.[57] "The practice of opening safes and selling assets to pay for the cost of hiring the safe also is documented for that period."[58] The Bergier Commission summarized the effect of such fees:

> Because dormant accounts often contained small amounts, these fees frequently exceeded the value of the assets being sought and, together with the routinely charged administrative or other costs, reduced them substantially. . . . Due to the deduction of such fees, unclaimed accounts, deposits and safe-deposit boxes could also disappear in the space of a few decades.[59]

Once accounts were closed, "all traces of individual accounts disappeared because banks could destroy all records relating to customers whose accounts had been closed out after a ten-year archiving period."[60]

This practice of routine document destruction and account erasure not only flourished in the immediate postwar period; it continued until the Bergier Commission and ICEP were established in 1996. Indeed, in the 1980s, the Union Bank of Switzerland issued instructions on how to close accounts: "The closure is to be effected by charging as many fees, expenses, etc. for different services to the accounts as to wipe out any balances they contain."[61]

In any event, one might assume that the Federal Decree of 1996, which commanded that all documents from the relevant period be preserved, would have put an end to the Swiss banks' destruction of records. This has apparently not been the case. Though the rate of destruction has undoubtedly slowed greatly, the Volcker Committee and the Bergier Commission still found that certain banks have engaged in destruction of relevant materials since 1996. The Bergier Commission cites one notorious example.[62] In early 1997, night watchman Christoph Meili exposed an attempt by Union Bank of Switzerland to destroy potentially relevant documents. The bank, for its part, then "initiated proceedings against the night-watchman, who was accused of having breached bank secrecy."[63] The Volcker Committee also addressed this incident and noted that despite increased scrutiny, the bank was caught on three subsequent occasions having approved the destruction of potentially relevant records where destruction was clearly barred by the Federal Decree.[64]

Ultimately, it is impossible to know how common such incidents were or what relevant documents were destroyed. What we do know is that for 40 percent of bank accounts open or opened in Switzerland between 1933 and 1945, there is no record at all, and for the rest, there is often no more than a customer registry card.

In short, what the Volcker Committee *did find*, and what the Bergier Commission confirmed, is that banks "regularly and systematically" destroyed documents that were over ten years old, as technically permitted by Swiss law.[65] However the banks' motives for destruction are described, their motives are wholly irrelevant to the question of whether the banks committed wholesale destruction of documents that they knew would have allowed Nazi victims and their heirs to locate accounts on which they had claims.

The critical fact is that the Swiss banks did not comport with basic notions of equity. There is a principle in the law of evidence called "spoliation." The doctrine of spoliation instructs that if a party destroys evidence that it knows to be relevant to a legal claim (whether or not that legal claim has yet been raised in court), and if that party is ever brought into court for that legal claim, an adverse inference can be drawn against the party that destroyed the evidence. In other words, the law assumes that the destroyed evidence was harmful to the destroyer. For over half a century the Swiss banks destroyed evidence they knew to be relevant to legitimate claims that were being made by account holders and their heirs. The banks knew that, if substantiated through documentation, these claims would expose the banks to liability. The fact that the destruction may not have violated Swiss law—which was not amended to accommodate the claims of heirs of account holders whom the Swiss knew were slaughtered in the Holocaust and who could not make a successful claim if records were destroyed—is nothing more than a sad commentary on the manner in which the banks were permitted to operate.

Finally, Schoenfeld's last point was the suggestion that in "many cases" the banks "actively sought out missing account holders or their heirs" and paid account proceeds to proper parties. Even assuming that "many" is an accurate description of the number of times the banks sought out missing account holders or their heirs, this is not a defense of the banks' behavior. The Volcker Committee investigated 254 banks. Not every bank was deceptive in every instance. What is striking, and what is relevant, is that as a matter of policy, Swiss banks repeatedly put up a conscious wall of silence in the face of claims by victims of Nazi persecution and their heirs.

Schoenfeld's article similarly whitewashes the root causes of the Swiss banks' actions during and after the Nazi era. He writes,

> [T]he root cause of the problem . . . lay less in cupidity (though there was that, too) than in the underlying legal framework of the Swiss banking system. One pillar of that framework was, and remains, the secrecy rules that were adopted in the 1930's, ironically enough in large measure to protect the assets of persecuted German Jews. . . . A second and no less important pillar was the absence of an escheat provision that would, as in most other countries, mandate the transfer of unclaimed banking assets to the state after a specified period of inactivity.[66]

As an initial matter, Swiss banking secrecy laws were not passed "in large measure to protect the assets of persecuted German Jews." The head of the Legal Service at the Swiss Federal Banking Commission recently explained,

> Contrary to the legend, a desire to safeguard the assets of Jewish refugees was not the reason for instituting protection of banking secrecy under criminal law. The real origin lay in the measures which began to be taken in 1931 by German customs and inland revenue offices on the basis of general currency regulations. These provisions became more stringent following the seizure of power by the Nazis in 1933 and the adoption of racial laws etc. Jewish assets were therefore not the origin but, or so at least one hopes, the first beneficiaries of the protection of banking secrecy in criminal.[67]

More importantly, Schoenfeld is wrong to separate the two attributes of Swiss law he references—banking secrecy and the lack of an escheat provision—from the Swiss banks' cupidity. While the Volcker Committee, in its apparent search for unanimous conclusions, similarly avoided connecting banking secrecy or the lack of an escheat provision to the Swiss banks' greed, that is no excuse for not recognizing the obvious. These two "pillars" simply allowed the banks to profit from their greed. Indeed, if the Swiss secrecy laws and the lack of an escheat provision opened the door to fiduciary violations, it was the greed of Swiss banks that drove them through.

Again, "Swiss banking secrecy" is not some holy grail that stands apart from financial motives. It was a concerted policy decision to which the Swiss banks referred when it benefited them (attracting depositors in the 1930s and turning away claimants in the postwar period) and that the Swiss banks abandoned when it harmed them (in their deals with Poland and Hungary).

Schoenfeld concludes that

[a]lthough [the Swiss banks] clearly harbored their share of miscreants, for the most part their dereliction, characteristic of bankers, lay in applying the ordinary rules of procedure to an extraordinary situation. Thus, what can be said of them as a whole is that they failed to rise to the occasion, *and* that they made no systematic effort, until challenged, to resolve a glaring scandal.[68]

But again, this gives the banks too much credit. The banks did not merely make "no systematic effort" "to resolve a glaring scandal"; they actively covered it up. In 1956, the Swiss banks made a concerted effort to minimize the results of surveys that had sought information about accounts possibly belonging to Holocaust victims so as to prevent legislation that would have begun to resolve the "glaring scandal." And for decades thereafter, they destroyed documents that also could have resolved the scandal. Even were we to pass over these facts and accept Schoenfeld's statement, by otherwise "applying the ordinary rules of procedure to an extraordinary situation," the banks time and time again violated their fiduciary duty to account holders and destroyed documentation to cover up their tracks. Whatever their motives and whatever their moral culpability, their actions gave rise to legal liability. This is the central premise of the class action litigation against the Swiss banks, and it rests on a strong foundation.

Part of Schoenfeld's motive in writing the article appears to have been his statement that "[t]o reprove Swiss neutrality from an office in Washington five decades after the fact, without considering the alternative and what it would have entailed, is to indulge in the worst kind of armchair moralizing."[69] Whether "armchair moralizing" is a valid concern with regard to some reparations efforts, it is not applicable to the Swiss bank litigation. The class action against the Swiss banks is based on continuing conduct and rests principally on the notion that a bank is a fiduciary to its account holders. If a bank complied with a transfer request made under duress, that bank is legally liable for the transfer. If a bank failed to pay the proceeds of an account to the account holder or its heirs, that bank is legally liable. These facts have nothing to do with the morality of Swiss behavior during the war. Nor are they altered by the fact that five decades have passed, a period when the banks continued to violate their fiduciary duties through stonewalling and the destruction of relevant documents.

NOTES

1. Response of Defendants UBS AG and Credit Suisse Group to Special Master's Interim Report and to Declaration of Burt Neuborne, dated December 16, 2003, at 14.

2. 319 F. Supp. 2d at 303.

3. Gabriel Schoenfeld, Holocaust Reparations: A Growing Scandal? *Commentary*, September 2000.

4. Schoenfeld, at 32.

5. Id. at 33. The Volcker Committee, formally known as the Independent Committee of Eminent Persons and also sometimes referred to by its acronym, ICEP, was formed by the Swiss Bankers Association in May 1996 to audit the Holocaust-era records of Swiss banks to determine the extent of dormant accounts held by the banks. Paul Volcker, former head of the U.S. Federal Reserve Bank, was tapped to head the committee.

6. Id.

7. In December 1996, the Swiss government created a nine-member historical body to assess the role of Switzerland during World War II. The commission was headed by Swiss historian Jean-François Bergier and consisted of a multinational panel of historians.

8. Schoenfeld, at 31.

9. Id. at 32.

10. Final Report of the Independent Commission of Experts, Switzerland—Second World War, 276–77, available at http://www.uek.ch (emphases added) (footnote omitted) (hereinafter "Bergier Report").

11. Id. at 276 (finding that when opponents of forced transfers had been able to take legal action in Switzerland, the requests made by the Nazi authorities were rejected by the judges and the blocked assets were deposited with the court.)

12. Helen B. Junz, Bergier Commission: Analysis of Swiss Bank Behavior, at 2 (emphasis added), *reproduced in In re Holocaust Victim Assets Litigation,* 302 F. Supp. 2d 59 (E.D.N.Y. 2004).

13. Id. (citing UEK study, no. 15, *Nachrichtenlose Vermögen bei Schweizer Banken*).

14. UEK study, no. 15, *Nachrichtenlose Vermögen bei Schweizer Banken,* at 166.

15. Schoenfeld, at 32 (emphasis added).

16. *See e.g.* Albers v. Credit Suisse, 67 N.Y.S. 2d 239, 244 (N.Y. City Ct. 1946) (holding Credit Suisse liable for transferring a client's assets to a German bank pursuant to the client's orders because "above all it knew that the plaintiff was not likely of his free will to transfer property of his located in Switzerland to a bank in German territory controlled by the German government").

17. Bergier Report, at 443.

18. Volcker Report, at 45, *available at* http://www.icep-iaep.org (hereinafter "Volcker Report").

19. Id.

20. Bergier Report, at 449.

21. Volcker Report, at 48.

22. Junz, at 4.

23. Bergier Report, at 457.

24. Bergier Report, at 449.

25. Id.

26. Id. at 277.

27. *See* CRT Awards, Group XXXVII, award no. 40, *available at* www.crt-ii.org.

28. Id.

29. Id.

30. Id. (emphasis added).

31. Bergier Report, at 445–46.

32. Id. at 446 (emphasis added).

33. Volcker Report, Annex 5, at 83 (emphasis added).

34. Schoenfeld, at 32; Volcker Report, at 13.

35. Volcker Report, at 48.

36. Volcker Report, Annex 5 ¶ 37 (quoting a letter from the Swiss Bankers Association to its board members, dated June 7, 1956).

37. Bergier Report, at 451.

38. Id. at 451.

39. Id. at 452.

40. Id. at 453.

41. Id. at 454.

42. Id.

43. Id. at 448.

44. Id. at 455 (emphasis added).

45. Id. at 450.

46. *Swiss Banks and Nazi Gold: Hearings before the House Comm. on Banking and Financial Servs.*, 105th Cong. (June 25, 1997) (statement of Gerhard L. Weinberg).

47. *See* Special Master's Proposed Plan of Allocation and Distribution of Settlement Proceeds, G-32 n.94 (hereafter "Proposed Plan") (citing Gerhard L. Weinberg, German Wartime Plans and Policies Regarding Neutral Nations, statement before American Historical Association, January 10, 1998 [hereafter "Weinberg, AHA Statement"]).

48. Bergier Report, at 450.

49. Id. at 451.

50. Proposed Plan, at G-33 n.94 (quoting Weinberg, AHA Statement, at 3–4).

51. Volcker Report, Annex 7 ¶ 3.

52. Id., Annex 7 ¶ 11.

53. Schoenfeld, at 32 (emphasis added).

54. Id.

55. Id. at Annex 7 ¶ 22.

56. Bergier Report, at 455; *see* Junz, at 5.

57. Bergier Report, at 446.

58. Junz, at 3.

59. Bergier Report, at 446.

60. Id. at 447.

61. Bergier Report, at 447.

62. Bergier Report, at 40–41.

63. Id. at 41.

64. Volcker Report, Annex 7 ¶¶ 27–34.

65. Volcker Report, at Annex 7 ¶ 11.

66. Schoenfeld, at 32.

67. Urs Zulauf, Banking Secrecy and the Publication of Dormant Accounts, at ¶ 32 (translated from German text, Nobel, *Aktuelle Rechtsprobleme des Finanz-und Börsenplatzes Schweiz, Bem* [1998]).

68. Schoenfeld, at 32 (emphasis added).

69. Schoenfeld, at 31.

Chapter 10

The French Holocaust-Era Claims Process

Eric Freedman and Richard Weisberg

Introduction

This essay addresses the present-day consequences of the expropriation, or spoliation, of Jewish assets that preceded extermination, as seen in the French government's attempts at restitution or indemnification. It provides an overview of the current situation regarding the French Holocaust-era claims process, and may be considered a follow-up to the analysis of the French bank settlement as described by Bazyler and Eizenstat in their treatises on Holocaust restitution.[1]

We shall first summarize the French restitution process, which integrates, but is not limited to, the French-American Washington Accords of 2001. We shall then give an update on current developments, with a view to evaluating the process in a way we hope is critically constructive.

The French-American Washington Accords of 2001

We begin with a historical summary and a recognition that, in fact, France and the United States appear to have two slightly varying historical accounts of events leading up to the French restitution settlements.

France dates the beginning of the restitution movement to President Jacques Chirac's speech of July 16, 1995, in which he accepted the responsibility of France in its deportation of Jews by the Vichy régime during the Occupation. This then led to the creation in 1997 of the historical fact-finding Mattéoli Commission, whose task was to examine wartime spoliation and restitution.

The Mattéoli Commission issued two interim reports, published in December 1997 and February 1999. The second report included a proposal to

135

create an indemnification commission to deal with financial wrongs not hitherto addressed. The proposal rejected global indemnification (based on the Swiss or German model) in favor of an individual claims process. Specifically, the Mattéoli Commission "proposed the creation of a body that would examine individual claims from victims of anti-Semitic legislation passed during the Occupation." The French government accepted this recommendation and such a body, known as the Drai Commission, was established by a decree of September 10, 1999.

The third and final thirteen-volume, 3,000-page report of the Mattéoli Commission, published in April 2000, made nineteen recommendations, including three on individual restitution and two on banking and insurance matters.[2]

The final report detailed both the enormous extent of Vichy "legalized" spoliation against Jews in wartime France, in which no economic sector was left untouched (apart from mining or fisheries), and also the extent of postwar attempts at restitution. In order to remove all supposed "Jewish influence" from the French economy, between 1941 and 1944 approximately sixty thousand companies had been "Aryanized," the Vichy term for expropriating companies owned by Jews. These included companies of all sizes and values, from small tailoring workshops to department stores and industrial companies. By the mid-1950s, approximately thirty thousand of these had been restored to their former owners.

In addition, the Mattéoli Commission listed approximately eighty-six thousand bank and share accounts of Jewish account holders that were either blocked or seized in the Occupied Zone as of the end of December 1941. Twenty percent of these were company accounts. There is still no consensus about how many of these accounts were restituted after the war, or the value of the amounts restored. At the very least, there remains a "grey zone" for approximately 30 percent of these accounts, whose fate after the war remains unknown.

Unfortunately, the final report failed to fully examine spoliation against Jews in some critical sectors of the French economy during Occupation, including the stock exchange, public notaries, the cinema, and geographical areas other than Paris, such as the Southern Zone (Lyons, Montpellier, Marseilles). As a result, the famous claim of the Mattéoli Commission's final report that 90 percent of the assets spoliated were returned after the war refers only to the reimbursement of taxes by the Treasury and not to the number or the value of all restored assets, whose estimates vary widely. These taxes of varying percentages (5 and 10 percent) were in fact obligatory contributions to the Vichy state regularly made from or rather removed from "Jewish" accounts of over ten thousand francs.

Of course, there had indeed been postwar restitution efforts, and had President De Gaulle's postwar legislation been completely applied to financial institutions, including their illicit profiteering, there may well have been less need for the current indemnification by the Drai Commission of the blocked or seized bank accounts. However, it is also true that postwar legislation, in addition to being time barred, also excluded non-French citizens or approximately 150,000 Jews living in France on the eve of the Occupation, many of whom had earlier fled to France for safety from lands previously occupied by Nazi Germany.

In the United States, the historiography of the French restitution process begins with the class action lawsuits filed against Swiss banks in 1996 and 1997, which directly led to similar class action suits being filed against French and other banks implicated in wartime spoliation in France. From the U.S. point of view, another important step leading to the restitution process was the hearing conducted on French bank spoliation by the U.S. House of Representatives Committee on Banking and Financial Services, held in September 1999, coincidentally less than a week after the creation of the Drai Commission.[3] That same month, New York City comptroller Alan Hevesi added the French bank matter to his Executive Monitoring Committee's work of reviewing the progress of the various Holocaust restitution claims.

In the U.S. version of the French restitution story, the lawsuits and the political actions taken in the United States by federal and state officials are generally credited with influencing the Mattéoli Commission to include French banks in its purview of spoliation activities, and with bringing pressure to bear on the French banks for a settlement.

A critical event in the U.S. story was the decision in August 2000 by the federal judge overseeing the litigation to reject the French banks' motion to dismiss the lawsuits, which was supported by the French government. By the time of this decision, two of the banks sued (Barclays and J.P. Morgan) had already moved to settle.[4]

The French banks and Chase Manhattan Bank filed a motion to delay discovery, which was refused on December 21, 2000. At that time, the Drai Commission had already been in existence for over a year, and, without any form of publicity or communication, had already received around fifteen hundred claims for seized or looted property, although it did not give separate consideration for bank claims.

The French banks and the French government then turned their efforts toward formulating a diplomatic rather than a judicial solution, with the goal of obtaining complete legal peace from the litigation and full closure of the claims against them. The banks' and the French government's shift to diplomacy led to negotiations between the parties, conducted in Paris and Washington and arbitrated by U.S. under secretary of the treasury, Stuart Eizenstat.[5] The diplomatic negotiations concluded in the French-American Accords, signed in Washington on January 18, 2001 (the "Washington Accords"). The Washington Accords essentially substituted mass class action litigation in favor of acceptance by all parties of individual bank-related claims to be processed by the Drai Commission and paid out from funds contributed by the French banks.

Two fund categories were established, a renewable $50 million "Fund A" for provable, that is documented, "hard" bank claims, and a capped $22.5 million for presupposed but nondocumented "soft" claims justified by a good faith affidavit. At the end of the claims process, any unpaid funds from "Fund A" are to be returned to the banks, whereas any unpaid funds from "Fund B" are to go to the French Shoah Foundation, to be used for Holocaust remembrance and education. Each "Fund B" claim receives an initial sum of fifteen hundred dollars followed by a further payment of the same amount.

The Claims Process of the Drai Commission

The Drai Commission, acting pursuant to the Washington Accords, published its first progress report in March 2001 and began to deal with bank claim recommendations separately as of June 2001. Professor Richard Weisberg, representing the plaintiffs' lawyers, was appointed to an oversight committee of five members on Fund B, the other four members representing the U.S. State Department and the French Foreign Ministry. The Simon Wiesenthal Centre Europe,[6] based in Paris, has been given access to the bank account database (originally created by the Mattéoli Commission for its own historical sampling purposes) in order to assist claimants, and the Centre appointed Eric Freedman as research consultant to the Drai Commission. Unfortunately, the French government refused to publish the database of the eighty-six thousand spoliated accounts, citing French privacy laws as a barrier.[7]

Worldwide notices of the claims process pursuant to the Accords were not published in the press until September 2001, and specific bank claims did not really begin flowing into the commission before the beginning of 2002, one year after the Accords were signed and two years after the Drai Commission's creation.

What is the nature of the Drai Commission and how does it work? It is a French government administrative commission whose specific aim is to compensate victims of spoliation perpetrated because of the Occupation-era antisemitic legislation. It has no power to return the actual property taken or to order the return of that property.[8] Although it is not formally a judicial body, most of the commission members who deliberate and recommend on claims are French judges, aided by magistrates, archivists, historians, and researchers. The commission deals only with individual claims concerning material or financial spoliation, including the forced seizure of companies; looting of equipment, apartments, and furniture; seizure and sale of other valuables; and blocked and nonrestituted bank and share accounts. It does not award compensation for any physical or moral suffering, or for loss of life. Furthermore, loss of earnings or pension rights are not indemnified, whereas, in some cases, loss of property rental income is compensated. The commission's "jurisprudence" is developed on a case-by-case analysis.

The administrative procedure is essentially conducted in four main stages:

1. Claim submission through a questionnaire and any pertinent documents. The deadline for affidavit submission concerning nonproven bank accounts, to be indemnified by Fund B, closed in January 2003. This means that any current bank claims must be justified either by the claimant's own documentation or by the commission's research. Such "proven" accounts are indemnified through Fund A. There is no deadline as yet for these provable accounts. Currently, approximately forty claims arrive each month at the Commission's offices in Paris.
2. Verification of any prior indemnification and archival research, conducted in Berlin and in various Parisian and regional archives.
3. Synthesis, assessment, and proposals in a report prepared by a "rapporteur" who is otherwise a full-time magistrate. The rapporteur usually, but not always, discusses the nature of his/her report and

proposals with the claimant. The claimant or the claimant's representative may be given access to the full report and file.

4. Commission hearing and recommendation. The hearing is not open to the public nor is it recorded, although a session secretary takes notes. The claim report is read aloud before a three-member commission panel by the rapporteur. The claimant, if present, may then make any comments on the claim and may include biographical elements beyond the specific claim in question, so that the commission also hears the human dimension of the claim. The claimant may be represented at the hearing. A French government representative may also be present and give his/her analysis on the report. Whether bank representatives should continue to be present, usually to argue that the claim should be rejected, continues to be a debatable point between the U.S lawyers and the commission's practice, since no specific procedures concerning the participation of the banks in the hearing are outlined in the Washington Accords. At the end of the commission hearing, the recommendation decisions are made in camera, and the claimant is informed in writing of the recommendation in a matter of weeks, although there may be a delay in the eventual claim payment of up to six months or more. Currently, approximately fifty claims are heard per week.

Analysis of the Claims Process

We begin with the commission's own statistics. These show, at the end of November 2004, 14,069 registered claims, of which 7,074 were bank claims. The total number of all payout recommendations is 13,705, of which 6,498 were bank claims. There remain, therefore, only 576 bank claims still to be adjudicated, plus the approximately twenty new bank claims that arrive each month. It is important to note that although the affidavit deadline was reached in January 2003, the claims process for bank assets is still open.

A closer analysis shows that the total number of all Fund A payment recommendations is only 2,244, which represents only 2.6 percent of the 86,000 blocked accounts. Of this total, only 559 were proven accounts of over 10,000 francs (1941 value), and 1,685 were proven accounts of less than 10,000 francs, usually, but not always, post office savings accounts, paid out from both Fund A and Fund B.

As of end September 2004, Fund A payout figures were around $2 million, which represents only 4 percent of the Fund A initial uncapped total of $50 million. One of the reasons why Fund A is so underused is because so-called high-value company accounts and shares (those designated as being over 10,000 francs in 1941) are excluded from indemnification by the banks, according to the commission's "jurisprudence." The total number of all Fund B payment recommendations is 3,393, which refers to nonproven accounts of any magnitude, according to affidavit. The most typical affidavit states that the claimant has reason to believe that named family members had bank accounts spoliated in France during the war and not restored after the war. As of September 30, 2004, Fund B payout figures were around $17 million, and given the previously noted linkage of Funds A and B, it is highly probable that—unlike with Fund A—the capped total of $22.5 million will be reached.

Concerning other material claims, 7,207 had been paid out by the end of November 2004. Company expropriation is included among material claims, but there may also be company bank accounts and shares involved. Usually, but not always, these are high value accounts of over 10,000 francs, which, as stated above, are not considered by the commission to be bank claims, and so their indemnification, if any, is integrated into the material claims proposal and recommendation. Such bank accounts or shares may have been "administered" by a Vichy state–appointed Administrateur Provisoire, and so the current French state considers indemnity to be its responsibility and not that of the banks who allowed such spoliation in the first place.

This distinction created by the Drai Commission between types of spoliated bank accounts is not part of the Washington Accords, since the Accords do not differentiate between individual and company accounts or administered and nonadministered accounts. Rather, the Accords contemplate compensation for a provable account so long as there is no clear proof that there has been prior indemnification for the spoliation. For this reason, the U.S. lawyers representing the interests of the claimants have contended that all of the provable spoliated accounts should be indemnified from Fund A. The commission, however, has not yet accepted this position.

Individualization is a positive feature of the process, as each claimant is dealt with on a case-by-case basis. Unfortunately, there is a long wait between claim submission and eventual indemnification, averaging today approximately three years. The commission tries to give priority to the aged (those over eighty years old), the sick, and the needy, but dealing with individual claims and research inevitably leads to delays. All along the claims process—which encompasses questionnaire filling, file registration, archival research responses, report writing by the rapporteurs, planning for hearings, payment recommendations, and actual payouts—there are delays.

Could long delays have been avoided with better planning? One of the alternatives that might have led to a speedier payment (or at least partial payment) to claimants is the application of the Fund B process to Fund A claims. A claimant making a Fund A claim would receive a minimal payment after a brief claim review, pending further detailed research and a subsequent higher remainder payment. Unfortunately, this has never been done.

As we already mentioned, we are not dealing with actual restitution of assets but with compensation, and thus evaluation of the spoliated assets is considered important. In order to calculate current values, the commission uses the French government statistics office (INSEE) indicator of the purchasing power value of the French franc in 1938 and in 1941 in relation to today's Euro.[9] No compound interest or investment calculations are made. This was a purely technical decision and, although well established by now, continues to give rise to discussion between the U.S. lawyers and the commission.

Considering the current low payout from Fund A for proven bank accounts, it may well be that now is the time to publish the list of eighty-six thousand blocked accounts, especially given that Yad Vashem has now put online its three-million-name database of Holocaust victims, which includes Serge Klarsfeld's list of seventy-six thousand Jews deported from France. Furthermore, the 87,000-name list of shot or deported French Resistance members (of whom 50 percent survived) has recently been published.

The French government, however, is resisting this move on privacy grounds. Why privacy laws in France do not apply to former Resistance victims (as all their names have now been published, deceased and surviving) but do apply to spoliation victims (most of whom are by now deceased) is never made clear. The French government's current answer is that "religious" discrimination led to the spoliation, and that France today cannot publish lists linked to mention of religion. However, the list of eighty-six thousand blocked accounts can be published without mention of religion, only of spoliation. Moreover, presupposing that most, if not all, spoliated account holders are now deceased, the list can be published legally since French privacy laws do not apply to the dead.

The role of the banks remains an ongoing problem, since they are given an opportunity to rebut any claim, which they do not hesitate to use. In so doing, they usually assert in writing that the claim should not be paid because there had been "reactivation" of the account after the war or, at the least, an opportunity for account access when the accounts were "unblocked" in 1944. This is, of course, disingenuous, since it misses the point of the banks' initial legal responsibility for blocking accounts of their Jewish account holders between 1941 and 1944, for which they should pay, not to mention the still nonrestored accounts that the banks have held on to for sixty years, enriching themselves as a result. Proof of wartime spoliation and valuation of the assets is hard enough but unfortunately is made more difficult by sometimes ongoing refusal and rejection by the banks, after sixty years of obfuscation and enrichment. Fortunately, the commission does not always accede to the banks' rejections.

Conclusion

Spoliation is a war crime without a time bar, unrecognized for too long. The French Holocaust-era claims process has been slow and, at times, less than fully equitable. For us as insiders, seeing this first hand has often been frustrating. We would wish that by now the process had been concluded and the funds allocated to compensate for wartime spoliation had been fully distributed. We are mindful, however, of the fact that an ongoing claims process does exist and is slowly moving to a conclusion. This signifies a momentous victory for those trying to right some of the enormous financial wrongs committed against the Jews in wartime France.

NOTES

1. *See* Michael J. Bazyler, *Holocaust Justice: The Battle for Restitution in America's Courts* (2003), 172–201; Stuart E. Eizenstat, *Imperfect Justice: Looted Assets, Slave Labor, and the Unfinished Business of World War II* (2003), 315–37.

2. *Available at* www.ladocfrancaise.gouv.fr.

3. One of us testified at the hearings. *See* Testimony of Professor Richard Weisberg, *World War II Assets of Holocaust Victims,* U.S. House of Representatives

Committee on Banking and Financial Services, September 14, 1999, *available at* www.house.gov.banking/91499rhw.htm.

4. Barclays had agreed on a settlement of $3.6 million in July 1999 and J.P. Morgan concluded a settlement of $2.75 million in September 2000.

5. *See* Eizenstat, *supra* note 1, at 315–37 (*op. cit.*).

6. Directed by Dr. Shimon Samuels, and assisted by Alex Uberti. Their office shepherds claimants, personally receives and assists them, and greatly helped the authors with regular updates and overall technical support.

7. However, while the list of eighty-six thousand accounts has not been published, the general sources used by the Mattéoli Commission to create its bank data were part of the archives of the Occupation-era, Vichy-instituted Commissariat Général aux Questions Juives (CGQJ), deposited and now publicly available in the French National Archives (Collection AJ.38) in Paris. Parts of Collection AJ.38 have been microfilmed and are also publicly available in the U.S. National Archives and Records Administration, in Washington D.C.

8. Details on the Drai Commission may be found on its website, http://www.civs.gouv.fr.

9. See the INSEE website at www.insee.fr.

Chapter 11

The French Bank Holocaust Settlement

Shimon Samuels

The domino process of World War II looted assets restitution research, negotiation, and claims was a lever for the settlement of historical accounts. Media and judicial pressure demanded transparency, and combatants and neutrals established national archival commissions to investigate banks, insurance companies, museums, and private property records. The restitution campaign shook to the core national myths of World War II neutrality and resistance, calling human behavior into question and disestablishing collective memories.

Throughout the 1980s and 1990s, as director of the Simon Wiesenthal Centre in Paris, I had sought to draw a connection between the lessons of the Holocaust and the contemporary Jewish condition in Europe so as to illustrate that what starts with the Jews inevitably impacts society generally.

The 1980s ended dramatically, with the fall of both the Berlin Wall and communism, which initiated the opening of World War II archives across Eastern Europe and stimulated an imperative to transparency that moved ever westwards. By 1995, the fiftieth anniversary of the war's conclusion, the spotlight was on research findings that challenged accepted collective memories and that might afford a final measure of justice to the disappearing Holocaust generation.

Just as the name Wiesenthal had been associated with bringing war criminals to justice as part of an evolving jurisprudence on genocide, so the increasingly accessible evidence of the greatest theft in history inspired the Wiesenthal Centre to contribute to an expanding moral pedagogy on spoliation, loot, and restitution.

Taking its lead from the biblical injunction "in the fiftieth year . . . thou shalt restitute . . . to each his property" (Leviticus 25:10), the centre's Paris office dredged French archives on the stolen gold trail, seeking points of convergence along the escape routes of Nazi war criminals.

The focus shifted to unpaid insurance policies and led us to Winterthur Versicherung (now part of Credit Suisse) as cosponsor for our 1997 Geneva conference on "Looted Property and Restitution: The Moral Responsibility to History." This path-breaking gathering convened in the context of the Swiss bank Holocaust account investigation, which unleashed a torrent of nationalist and antisemitic invective.

With public attention on the Swiss bank drama, the Wiesenthal Centre began to focus on French banking. The monies from victims' accounts had not disappeared; they had just remained in the wrong hands. The banks were guilty of "unjust enrichment." As in all restitution issues, we stressed the paper trail, i.e., the opening of all archives to reputable external auditors, professional document "archeologists," and historians of the Holocaust—in legal parlance, this was our commitment to "discovery."

In the half-century since the war, banks had presented a variety of excuses for nonpayment of Holocaust-era claims:

- inadequate documentation (a death certificate was often demanded);
- nationalization of assets;
- disappeared archives;
- pre-merger negotiations were subject to public pressure demanding transparency; and
- following a merger or acquisition, paper trails were lost and accountability blurred.

Throughout this period, the banking industry's response to survivor claims was, at best, bad public relations and, otherwise, deliberate theft—a fact borne out by the accumulating evidence of evasion as policy. It was apparent that only the glare of publicity and the application of international leverage could achieve justice against banking delinquency.

In 1998, I saw a brief article in the *New York Times* in regard to an Anna Zajdenberg, who was to launch legal measures in order to recover her family's looted Paris bank accounts. As my name at birth was Zeidenberg, I was intrigued and called her. We met some weeks later in New York in the company of her class action lawyers.

On my return to Paris, I began broadcasting on the French Jewish radio about the suit and eventually received some two hundred queries about how to enter the class. When the class action lawyers visited Paris, press meetings were organized for them at the Wiesenthal Centre. They were invited to speak at the Yom HaTorah (Holocaust Remembrance), an event held every four years in Le Bourget and attended by over forty thousand Parisian Jews. By then, we were receiving three to four claims against French banks per day from Australia to Chile, Israel to South Africa, as the story reached the international media. Following a blessing from Chief Rabbi Sitruk, the lawyers and claimants addressed the crowd, to the chagrin of French Jewish establishment figures, who publicly chastised me as "a traitor serving avaricious American lawyers."

Though the Centre Simon Wiesenthal—France is a French organization, registered under the Law of 1901 with its own board and over one thousand members, it is, of course, also part of the international constellation of the Simon Wiesenthal Centre headquartered in Los Angeles.

Since there is no global Jewish consensus, European Jewish leaders often differ in nuance from their transatlantic brethren, sometimes expressing their national viewpoint. Thus, President Jacques Chirac's 1995 acknowledgement of French culpability for Vichy had the Jewish establishment elated at the successive apologies for collaboration expressed by the church, the police, the lawyers, the medical profession, and others.

Prominent figures in the French Jewish community enthusiastically endorsed the collaborators' mea culpa the alternative to material restitution or compensation, contending that a bitter claims process would poison these reconciliation initiatives, tarnish the memory of the victims, and unleash another antisemitic backlash.

This policy of discretion for some, a culture of denial for others, was repeated three years later with the outbreak of antisemitic violence in those Paris suburbs heavily populated by Jews and Arabs, related to events in the Middle East. The community leaders, for over a year, joined the French government, the police, and the media in rejecting the gravity of events taking place a few miles away. The issues of restitution in the late 1990s and antisemitic attacks from September 2000 led the Wiesenthal Centre to receive the angry phone calls of the French Jewish street, demanding "an American approach."

It was too late for a banker's apology, which was, anyway, unlikely ever to come. Growing numbers of putative claimants now sought to join the class action suit.

As honorary president of the Europe-Israel Forum (a businessmen's club), I arranged for the visiting American lawyers to debate with Roger Cukierman, the current president of CRIF (the Representative Council of

French Jewry), at a forum breakfast. The audience sided with the U.S. suit, and the following day Cukierman called me to seek advice on how to work together. Meanwhile, I was publicizing the case in my travels from Santiago to Archangel, from meetings with UNIFANE (Union of French and North African Immigrants) in Israel to Johannesburg, and was receiving increasing numbers of claims. With the Alien Torts action, elderly and infirm plaintiffs were arriving at my office, though we had never practiced an "open door policy."

The federal court held a preliminary hearing in Brooklyn in August 1999, under Judge Sterling Johnson. I flew in, by invitation of plaintiffs' counsel. Each side was given fifteen minutes, with the French banks' attorneys seeking dismissal. Plaintiffs' counsel spoke some ten minutes on the history of Vichy, succeeded by four minutes of technical-legal points on "sovereign immunity." Johnson had, that morning, already dismissed five cases (most against American Airlines). We were the sixth, and he was clearly dozing! I approached the bench and gave him a short handwritten note: "I arrived from Paris yesterday and am returning tonight. I have a message from seventy-one claimants in France; please give me just thirty seconds." Johnson said, "I give you forty-five." I then took out of an envelope seventy-one handwritten depositions and said, "Your Honor, this case is a human story and here is its face, the spindly handwriting of frail survivors. Please do not betray them." Johnson said, "I want your statement in my chambers by four o'clock." I responded, "By four, I will be leaving for the airport; you will have it by two o'clock."

A defense counsel for the French banks listed in the suit appealed to the judge, saying, "We had no advance knowledge of this hostile witness and wish to respond." (Remember, he was there to dismiss!) Johnson replied, "Don't worry; you'll have plenty of opportunity to respond." Some eight or nine survivors in the court ran to embrace me, as I, emotionally, felt a part of jurisprudential history in the making. We rushed to plaintiff counsel's office to type and courier my statement to the judge.

A month later, a former president of French Jewry sent an affidavit to the court. Made public, it attacked the Simon Wiesenthal Centre and myself by name as "American interlopers in French affairs." Our centre continued to be deeply absorbed in the case, especially in both Paris and Washington as U.S. deputy state secretary, Stuart Eizenstat, shuttled between the plaintiffs' counsel and ourselves, on the one hand, and the French banks' representatives on the other. Participating in the 18 January

2001 State Department signing ceremony of the Franco-American Settlement was a moment of unprecedented satisfaction.

The tale of the claims process, the Drai Commission, and the United States–France Governmental Oversight Committee is more exhaustively addressed by other contributors to this volume. Suffice it to say that the Wiesenthal Centre was, under an accord with the French prime minister's office, the primary research and advisory facilitator for claimants. The centre had also lobbied for an extension of the claims procedure deadline in view of the French government's nine-month delay in announcing the very existence of the settlement.

Success has many parents, while failure is an orphan. So, too, the community leaders, for whom a bankers' apology would have been adequate, were forced to respond to the indignation of the people in the street, who demanded justice concretized by material claims. Some feared a resurgence of antisemitism related to the restitution campaign. Others saw such expression as one more excuse for well-rooted Jew hatred that had justified over fifty years of theft.

The restitution campaign that closed the twentieth century has contributed to an evolving jurisprudence on human rights and war crimes regarding loot and spoils. Drawing lessons from its exposure provides an expansion of a moral pedagogy, for this issue is not exclusive to Jewish claimants. As so often in history, the treatment of Jews is a moral barometer that can serve as a measure of societal well-being and an early warning system for more universal scourges. During Kabila's march on Kinshasa, Congo, CNN financial analyst Myron Kandell wryly commented that "it took a Holocaust banking scandal to prise open Mobutu's Swiss accounts."

Thus, the spoliation of Jewish property, both during and after the war, as a serious violation of human rights, provides lessons for jurists in their treatment of war crimes and crimes against humanity in other theaters of genocidal behavior. The Holocaust, in its focus on the total extermination of the Jews, is not only primus inter pares among genocides but also a benchmark for the atrocities wrought upon *all* the victims of Nazism, and for current and future excesses in man's inhumanity.

The restitution campaign experience must primarily focus upon the moral dimension, and by the exposure of truths lance a long-festering boil. The cleansing of this wound can be an act of catharsis for the collaborator, an end to lip service for the bystander, a rejection of denial of responsibility for the perpetrator, added armament against the Holocaust revisionist, and a final accounting for the victims—both Jewish and non-Jewish—and their heirs.

Did the restitution process match the hopes of our campaign? The pressure to conclude negotiations by 19 January 2001—the departure of the Clinton administration—left open too many questions. I had watched admiringly as Stuart Eizenstat indefatigably shuttled between our room and that of the French bankers and their government representatives in the final negotiations.

The deal was done and signed in the State Department ceremony of 18 January without having addressed such key issues as the following:

- For the evaluation coefficient of a 1941 franc in 2002, the banks adopted an exchange of one looted franc at 1.7 current francs and any interest was rejected out of hand.
- The "soft claims" based upon affidavits were never paid out automatically, as had been intended in the settlement, but were adjudicated only after lengthy investigation.
- The French authorities delayed the global advertising campaign of the settlement by nine months, and then announced it sparingly in only a few publications over the Jewish high holidays of 2002, when many people would have been away from home.
- The adjudication process was often a "star chamber" in which the adjudicating officials humiliatingly interrogated plaintiffs and remorselessly cut down evaluations of their claims, usually in the presence of arrogant representatives of the defendant banks.

Though it is impossible to determine the percentage of potential claimants reached, or the degree to which restitution has been equitable, the process now arrives at its conclusion, leaving very mixed feelings.

Fund A (established to pay out the claims of a database of some eighty thousand named and numbered accounts) was a dismal failure. Of a revolving credit of $50 million, only $2 million has been restituted. The planned scandalous return to the French banks of the remaining $48 million plus interest carries the echo of the bankers at the Eizenstat negotiations shuttle, who confidently predicted that "all possible claimants have perished."

On the other hand, Fund B (set up to pay "soft claims" at a derisory rate of $3,000 per family, based upon affidavit) was an apparent success. Of $22 million, over $17 million has been paid out. The remaining $3 million, plus interest, is to go to the $600 million Foundation for the Memory of the Shoah, a French Jewish foundation endowed by the banks under pressure of the government, ironically, as an attempt to forestall the U.S. class action suits.

Apprehensions that the claims process would result in expressions of antisemitism are, in today's climate of Jew hatred in France, as absurd in hindsight as 1942 arguments that the bombing of rail lines to the death camps would have exacerbated German antisemitism.

So that we may draw the appropriate lessons from the restitution process, a full study of its disappointments, failures, and irregularities is now vital. If looting in the context of genocide might be viewed as a crime against humanity, then the denial or obfuscation of restitution should be defined as complicity.

The Hebrew scripture condemns both the murderer and the thief in stating, "*Gam ratsachta, vegam yarashta*" ("You have both murdered and inherited"). The sense of the text is that the act of murder has been compounded by the looting of the victims' property.

The story of the French bank settlement ends without apology and with a very qualified measure of justice.

Chapter 12

Unholy Profits
Holocaust Restitution and the Vatican Bank

Lee Boyd

Introduction

In August 2000, tens of thousands of Ukrainian and Jewish Holocaust survivors and their heirs sued the Vatican Bank and the Order of Franciscans for restitution of expropriated funds stolen by the Ustasha—the Nazi regime in the former Yugoslavia. The case was filed on the heels of large settlements in the Swiss, French, German, and Austrian bank cases brokered in large part by Stuart Eizenstat at the U.S. State Department. Indeed, in 1998, Eizenstat had called for the opening of Croatian, Serbian, and Vatican archives so that a full accounting could be made of the fate of the Ustasha treasury.

The restitution claims alleged were for unjust enrichment, and conversion of the funds that were looted and expropriated from the victims of the Nazi-directed Ustasha.[1] The complaint asserted that these assets had been transferred from the Ustasha treasury to the Vatican Bank through the efforts of the Franciscan monks who held high positions in the Ustasha government. In short, the plaintiffs alleged that the Vatican accepted, stole, and profited from the assets looted by Ustasha during its reign of terror.

Like the defendant banks in the earlier cases, the Vatican Bank and the Franciscans filed motions to dismiss the claims on similar grounds: foreign sovereign immunity, political question doctrine, comity of nations, lack of standing, lack of personal jurisdiction, and statute of limitations.[2]

However, unlike the European banks, the Vatican Bank did not offer to enter into settlement negotiations or to establish a voluntary relief fund for Holocaust victims. In a strategy similar to Japan's in the Holocaust restitution cases brought against Japanese companies, the Vatican refused negotiations. However, unlike Japan, the Vatican had never been a party to postwar treaties whose terms were found to bar claims against Japanese companies. The Vatican stands alone as the only defendant in Holocaust restitution cases that has offered no postwar compromise for its participation in the mass theft committed by the Nazis.

I was asked to consult on the case when a motion to dismiss was pending. The judge limited the oral argument to the sole issue of why the political question doctrine did not bar plaintiffs' claims, and eighteen months later, in January 2003, the district court dismissed all claims against all defendants on that ground.[3] Knowing that many of the plaintiff survivors were aging and might not live to see resolution of the case or receive any compensation, I began drafting the appeal to the Ninth Circuit Court of Appeals.[4]

The Dismissal: Are Political Cases Political Questions?

The political question doctrine is a justiciability doctrine, like standing, that requires judicial abstention in all cases that present questions reserved to the political branches by the Constitution. *Baker v. Carr*[5] set forth six factors that, if presented by the issues in the case, would require dismissal.

The district court's dismissal of the *Alperin* case was based on two of these factors. The court found first that the claims of the Holocaust victims for "war reparations" were textually committed to the executive branch in its constitutional exercise of foreign affairs powers.[6] Second, the court reasoned that there were no "judicially manageable standards" for the court given the distance in time and location from the events of World War II.[7]

The court relied heavily on two Holocaust restitution cases that were dismissed on political question grounds in 1999 by district courts in New Jersey: *Iwanowa v. Ford Motor Co.* and *Burger-Fischer v. DeGussa AG.*[8] Both cases were among several filed in New Jersey by the plaintiffs' lawyers in the Holocaust restitution case against the Swiss banks and against German companies that used slave labor to supply the Nazi death camps during the Holocaust.[9]

However, the New Jersey dismissals were strongly criticized by scholars, the bench, and even the State Department.[10] Scholars argued that *Iwanowa* and *Burger-Fischer* were wrongly decided because the U.S. postwar treaties with Germany governed the issue of whether the claims were barred.[11] Treaty interpretation is always within the purview of the judicial branch, not a political question reserved to the executive.

But *Alperin* was a very different case from both *Iwanowa* and *Burger-Fischer.* First, the Vatican was not a party to postwar reparations treaties that would require judicial interpretation to determine if private party claims were barred.[12] Second, the *Alperin* plaintiffs sued a foreign bank for expropriation of funds stolen by, and laundered for, the Nazi regime.

Yet the defendants argued, and the district court agreed, that since there were no treaties barring the claims brought by the *Alperin* plaintiffs, the claims were best left to the reparations negotiations then being conducted by the State Department.[13] What the district court did not take into account, however, was that such government negotiations were commenced in prior instances only as a result of the class action suits brought by lawyers on behalf of Holocaust survivors—and involved only the parties to those cases.[14]

Moreover, the State Department's negotiation efforts were always in collaboration with the courts and the lawyers on both sides to mediate a settlement of the claims in favor of compensating the victims. When determining that the *Alperin* plaintiffs' war reparations claims were committed solely to the executive branch for state-to-state negotiation, the district court did not consider the historical policy of the executive to encourage restitution through settlement of class action claims before the courts.[15]

In fact, the executive's foreign policy would hardly be compromised by judicial resolution of the *Alperin* plaintiffs' claims when the State Department had actively endorsed judicial settlement in favor of plaintiffs in all previous Holocaust restitution cases. Even after I contacted the State Department to apprise them of the *Alperin* case and to request intervention, it remained on the sidelines. This silence is telling in light of the department's historical lack of hesitation to file Statements of Interest or to intervene in other Holocaust-era cases to protect its interests.[16]

Finally, the district court in *Alperin* did not consider Congress's endorsement of the adjudication of Holocaust-era claims by courts. The Foreign Sovereign Immunities Act of 1976 (FSIA) granted jurisdiction to the federal courts to decide whether sovereigns and their instrumentalities —like the Vatican Bank—could be sued.[17] Indeed, in *Republic of Austria v. Altmann,* the Supreme Court held that the FSIA was to be applied retroactively to allow subject matter jurisdiction for Holocaust-era claims.[18] While the *Altmann* plaintiff sought to recover specific property stolen by the Nazis and expropriated by the Austrian national museum, the fact that the Supreme Court held that the FSIA was to be applied to Holocaust-era conduct is directly applicable to the viability of the *Alperin* case.

Not only does *Altmann* evidence political branch endorsement of the judicial resolution of Holocaust restitution claims brought against a state instrumentality, but it is important for another reason. Justiciability doctrines, like standing and political question, that address the judiciary's constitutional power to entertain claims are routinely addressed *sua sponte*.[19] However, in *Altmann,* the Supreme Court remanded the claims without considering or even mentioning the political question doctrine.[20] This omission by the Court did not escape notice by the Ninth Circuit panel that heard the *Alperin* appeal on October 7, 2004.

Accordingly, by failing to consider the tandem effort by the three coordinate branches in resolving Holocaust restitution claims in favor of recovery and justice for the plaintiffs, the district court wrongly found that the restitution claims brought in *Alperin* were exclusively reserved for the executive branch. While the conduct of foreign affairs is reserved to the political branches, neither the Vatican Bank nor the executive branch itself presented any evidence showing that U.S. foreign policy would be compromised if the court adjudicated the claims.

A second, more subtle misapplication of the political question doctrine was the district court's finding that there were no judicially manageable standards by which the court could adjudicate the *Alperin* plaintiffs' claims. This factor of the *Baker* analysis is aimed at barring the courts from deciding issues that call for policy judgments of the type typically reserved for governmental decision making.[21] The doctrine is grounded in the separation of powers and is based on the notion that courts simply do not have the expertise to pass upon the wisdom of uniquely governmental decisions, such as reviewing national defense policy,[22] or choosing appropriate impeachment procedures.[23] As long as the court is able to apply rules of decision arising under basic principles of law—in this case, tort law and international law for the claims of restitution, conversion, unjust enrichment, and violations of the law of nations—the *Baker* analysis does not apply.

But the district court in *Alperin* misinterpreted the meaning of "manageable standards." Rather than considering whether resolution of the claims would require the court to pass on the wisdom of some policy judgment made by the executive branch, the district court found that there were too many parties and too many documents from too long ago for a court to manage the voluminous discovery and resolution of claims.[24]

In support of its conclusion, the court cited *Kelberine v. Societe Internationale, Etc.,*[25] a D.C. Circuit Court of Appeals case from 1965.[26] *Kelberine* is an example of one of a few early failed attempts by Holocaust victims to bring restitution claims in American courts. The case was dismissed at a time when judicial power was far less expansive, given that Federal Rule of Civil Procedure Twenty-Three providing for class action suits was adopted in 1966, one year after the *Kelberine* decision.[27] Under Rule 23, manageability issues in complex cases like *Alperin* are routinely considered in a motion for class action certification. Since 1966, the federal courts have handled many complicated class actions, involving multiple parties and a vast number of documents and discovery.[28] Accordingly, grafting the manageability analysis for the propriety of maintaining a class into the analysis of the political question doctrine, which was designed to protect the constitutional separation of powers, was both logically and legally incorrect.

The dismissal on political question grounds was legally flawed, albeit politically expedient. No doubt the politically charged context of the case would be daunting to many courts. However, U.S. courts have routinely adjudicated political cases, including many that deal with wartime and even the Holocaust. As the *Baker* case points out, political cases do not necessarily make political questions.[29]

Alperin in Context: The Case for Judicial Remedies in Political Cases

The court's desire to abdicate its judicial power so as not to be seen as a threat to the executive branch's ability to maneuver in foreign relations reflects a larger struggle present in human rights litigation. The Holocaust restitution cases of the 1990s spurred the filing of several non-Holocaust-related human rights cases against private companies on theories based on even wider circles of complicity. Several recent human rights cases evidence a judicial uneasiness with this "new plaintiff's diplomacy" resulting from human rights litigation that is interwoven with foreign policy issues.[30] In these cases, the courts either dismiss the cases in deference to past executive decisions, or cry out to the political branches for deliverance from this type of litigation.

In *Republic of Austria v. Altmann,*[31] a Holocaust restitution case brought against the Austrian national museum to recover looted art work, the Supreme Court upheld subject matter jurisdiction under the FSIA but explicitly called for the executive branch to file Statements of Interest in cases where its foreign policy interests were implicated.[32] The Court was clear that such statements "might well be entitled to deference" by the courts in determining the propriety of exercising jurisdiction.[33]

This judicial request for assistance from the executive branch was repeated three weeks later in *Sosa v. Alvarez-Machain*.[34] *Alvarez-Machain* was the first Supreme Court review of a human rights case brought under the Alien Tort Statute for violations of international norms.[35] In holding that the statute provided jurisdiction for a limited number of international law claims—the most egregious and most widely recognized human rights abuses—the Court again cautioned the courts to defer to executive branch Statements of Interest in such cases.[36]

Accordingly, the *Alperin* court's decision to abdicate jurisdiction in favor of the political branches resolving the claims represents the pervasive reticence of the courts to assume full responsibility for deciding human rights claims that involve complicated foreign policy issues.

Nevertheless, there are several arguments against judicial abdication to the political branches in resolving human rights claims that reflect the Holocaust-restitution model. First, judicial remedies provide a more appropriate response to an alleged human rights injury. Judicial remedies are far more tailored to addressing the specific injuries of both individual plaintiffs and groups. Whereas in civil litigation the remedy must fit the proven offense, politically negotiated settlements of postwar or postconflict claims involving mass atrocities focus not on injuries to the victims but on state responsibility.

Secondly, judicial resolution of these claims allows the victims, both individually and as a group, to have a cathartic "voice" in telling the historical story of abuse. State-to-state–negotiated war reparations discharge state responsibility and provide no platform for individual victims to participate in the process of justice and reconciliation.[37]

Finally, in the broader regime of accountability for grave human rights crimes, courts play a critical role in implementing the rule of law.[38] Judicial resolution of past injustices in both domestic and international courts is oftentimes more effective in ending the historical impunity that human rights abusers have enjoyed than negotiated settlements between states. This is especially true given that state and political interests often conflict with the need to provide justice to individuals that the state itself has injured.

Accordingly, while a certain degree of deference may be owed to the coordinate political branches under legal formulae such as the political question doctrine, courts are well within their constitutional power to heed the presumption in favor of exercising jurisdiction—even in political cases.[39]

Postscript

On April 18, 2005, the day Benedict XVI was appointed the new pope of the Catholic Church, the Ninth Circuit Court of Appeals issued an opinion reversing in part the decision of the district court dismissing the lawsuit against the Vatican Bank and the other defendants. The Ninth Circuit, in a 2-1 decision, recognized that the Holocaust survivors' claims for stolen property in *Alperin*[40] were not barred by the political question doctrine, the sole ground upon which the trial judge dismissed the lawsuit. The dissenting judge's vitriolic critique of the majority's decision to overturn the dismissal and send the case back to the district judge as "nothing less than the creation without legislation of a World Court and international tribunal with breathtaking and limitless jurisdiction to entertain the World's failures" evidences the gravity of the victory for the plaintiffs.[41]

Whether the Vatican will abide by the new pope's promise of openness and dialogue and voluntarily open its archives to shed light on the alleged transfers of money from the Ustasha remains to be seen. One would hope that Benedict XVI will encourage dialogue with the plaintiffs in order to reach a settlement of the Holocaust survivors' sixty-year-old claims. Moreover, the plaintiffs hope that the Vatican Bank will now reconsider its assertion that the lower court still has no jurisdiction in the case and drop its other arguments for dismissal, such as lack of jurisdiction under the Foreign Sovereign Immunities Act or expiration of the statute of limitations. The Ninth Circuit detailed the massive "hurdles" that plaintiffs still face on remand to the district court, indicating that their victory may be pyrrhic after all.[42]

Indeed, there are other indicators that the *Alperin* plaintiffs' battle for justice may drag on for years. As of this writing, the Vatican Bank has filed a petition for a rehearing *en banc* before the Ninth Circuit, asking that a larger panel of judges review the majority decision of the three-judge panel, hoping to capitalize on the divide between those U.S. judges that would endorse a judicial role in redressing legal wrongs regardless of the international context and those that succumb to the magnetic pull toward dismissing such claims on political question grounds.

Knowing the battles that face us and the long delays that the elderly survivors must endure, the plaintiffs' lawyers have once again contacted the U.S. State Department, as well as other individuals, to help broker a settlement similar to the recent settlement brokered in the Hungarian Gold Train litigation. Even the Ninth Circuit struggled to understand the executive branch's silence, expressing despair that, with so much seemingly at stake, the president had chosen to stay on the sidelines and suggesting that it was not too late to weigh in.[43] As the majority opined, "[I]n the landscape before us, this lawsuit is the only game in town with respect to claimed looting and profiteering by the Vatican Bank."[44] Now that the possibility of recovery has been resurrected for the Holocaust survivors, a settlement would be the surest route to winning the game for justice for the aging victims.

NOTES

1. Alperin v. Vatican Bank, 242 F. Supp. 2d 686, 688 (N.D. Cal. 2003); *see also* Third Amended Class Action Complaint, *Alperin* (No. C99-4941). Later, Serbian plaintiffs were added, and another defendant was named—the Croatian Liberation Movement.

2. *Alperin*, 242 F. Supp. 2d at 689; *In re* Holocaust Victim Assets Litig., 105 F. Supp. 2d 142 (E.D.N.Y. 2000); Bodner v. Banque Paribas, 114 F. Supp. 2d 124 (E.D.N.Y. 2000).

3. *Alperin*, 242 F. Supp. 2d at 686.

4. Brief for Appellants at 20–21, *Alperin* (No. 03-15208) (available at 2003 WL 22767874) (9th Cir. argued Oct. 7, 2004).

5. Baker v. Carr, 369 U.S. 186, 217 (1962).

6. *Alperin*, 242 F. Supp. 2d at 690–92.

7. *Id.* at 692–95.

8. *Id.* at 690–95.

9. Deutsch v. Turner, 324 F.3d 692, 712–13 (9th Cir. 2003).

10. *See, e.g.,* Stuart E. Eizenstat, *Imperfect Justice: Looted Assets, Slave Labor, and the Unfinished Business of World War II* (Public Affairs 2003), 245–47.

11. *See, e.g.,* K. Lee Boyd, *Are Human Rights Political Questions?* 53 Rutgers L. Rev. 277 (Winter 2001): 290–98; Michael J. Bazyler, *Nuremberg in America: Litigating the Holocaust in United States Courts,* 34 U. Rich. L. Rev. 1 (March 2000), 209–32.

12. *See* Burger-Fischer v. Degussa AG, 65 F. Supp. 2d 248, 265–72 (1998).

13. *Alperin*, 242 F. Supp. 2d at 692.

14. *German Defs. Litig.*, 129 F. Supp. 2d 373, 378–80 (S.D.N.Y. 2000).

15. Brief for Appellants at 20–21, Alperin (No. 03-15208) (available at 2003 WL 22767874) (9th Cir. argued Oct. 7, 2004).

16. *See, e.g., In re* Nazi Era Cases against German Defs. Litig., 129 F. Supp. 2d 370 (D.N.J. 2001); Hwang Geum Joo v. Japan, 172 F. Supp. 2d 52 (D.D.C. 2001).

17. 28 U.S.C. § 1602 (2004).

18. Republic of Austria v. Altmann, 124 S. Ct. 2240, 2247 (2004).

19. *See* United States v. More, 3 Cranch 159, 172 (1805).

20. *Altmann,* 124 S. Ct. at 2255–56.

21. Japan Whaling Ass'n v. Am. Cetacean Soc'y, 478 U.S. 221, 230 (1986); Northrop Corp. v. McDonnell Douglas Corp., 705 F.2d 1030, 1047 (9th Cir. 1983); Koohi v. United States, 976 F.2d 1328, 1331–32 (9th Cir. 1992).

22. *See* No GWEN Alliance of Lane County, Inc. v. Aldridge, 855 F.2d 1380 (9th Cir. 1988).

23. *See* Nixon v. United States, 506 U.S. 224 (1993).

24. *Alperin,* 242 F. Supp. 2d at 695.

25. Kelberine v. Societe Internationale, 363 F.2d 989 (D.C. Cir. 1965).

26. *Alperin,* 242 F. Supp. 2d at 693.

27. Fed. R. Civ. P. 23; Manual for Complex Litigation, Fourth, § 21 (p. 243).

28. *See, e.g., In re* Holocaust Victim Assets Litig., 225 F.3d 191 (2d Cir. 2000); Hilao v. Estate of Marcos, 103 F.3d 767 (9th Cir. 1996); *In re* Copley Pharm., Inc., 161 F.R.D. 456 (D. Wyo. 1995); Cimino v. Raymark Indus., Inc., 751 F. Supp. 649 (E.D. Tex. 1990).

29. *See Baker,* 369 U.S. at 211.

30. Anne-Marie Slaughter and David Bosco, *Plaintiff's Diplomacy,* 79 For. Aff. 102 (2000).

31. *Altmann,* 124 S. Ct. at 2240.

32. *Id.* at 2255.

33. *Id.*

34. Sosa v. Alvarez-Machain, 124 S. Ct. 2739 (2004).

35. 28 U.S.C. § 1350 (2004).

36. *Alvarez-Machain,* 124 S. Ct. at 2766 n.21.

37. Boyd, at 301; *see also* Dinah Shelton, *Remedies in International Human Rights Law* (1999), 77–79.

38. Shelton, at 68–80.

39. *See* Alfred Dunhill of London, Inc. v. Republic of Cuba, 425 U.S. 682, 700 n.14 (1976).

40. *See* Alperin v. Vatican Bank, — F.3d — (9th Cir. 2005); 2005 WL 878603 (9th Cir. (Cal.)).

41. *Id.* at 29 (Trott, J., dissenting).

42. *Id.* at 13.

43. *Id.* at 17.

44. *Id.* at 17–18, 20.

Part III

The Slave Labor Litigation

Chapter 13

Where Morality Meets Money

Gideon Taylor

Holocaust-era reparations is truly the place where morality meets money. The amount of money handled by the Conference on Jewish Material Claims Against Germany (Claims Conference) is, by any standard, large. As a result of negotiations by the Claims Conference since 1952, more than half a million victims of persecution by the Nazis have received close to $60 billion.[1]

Yet Holocaust-era compensation and restitution is about much more than money. It is also about justice, history, law, politics, and social work. It is about those who are entitled and about those who need help. It is about responsibility and about fairness.

As Israeli Prime Minister David Ben-Gurion wrote in a 1952 letter to Nahum Goldmann, founder of the Claims Conference,

> For the first time in the history of the Jewish people, oppressed and plundered for hundreds of years in all countries of the Old World, the oppressor and plunderer has had to hand back some of the spoil and pay collective compensation for part of the material losses.[2]

Half a century later, Israeli Prime Minister Ariel Sharon used the fiftieth anniversary of the 1951 founding of the Claims Conference to note that it "has been at the forefront of the struggle for justice for Holocaust survivors in Israel and around the world."[3] On the same occasion, U.S. president George W. Bush commended the Claims Conference "on your efforts to use the memory of the past to create justice in the present."[4]

Our society has a tendency to measure many complicated concepts in primarily financial terms. At the Claims Conference, we deal with one of the greatest moral challenges to humanity in the last centuries—the

Holocaust—and seek to translate the quest for justice into one of the most basic forms of human interchange—money.

The task of the Claims Conference is, by definition, impossible. The struggle to reconcile the irreconcilable goes back to the origins of the Claims Conference. Following efforts by Jewish leaders and the State of Israel, Chancellor Konrad Adenauer of West Germany addressed the German Parliament on September 27, 1951:

> Unspeakable crimes were perpetrated in the name of the German people which impose upon them the obligation to make moral and material amends, both as regards the individual damage which Jews have suffered and as regards Jewish property for which there are no longer individual claimants.[5]

The newly formed Claims Conference, while welcoming the statement of the chancellor and making clear that it supported the concept of claims for compensation and restitution, issued a public statement after its first meeting:

> Crimes of the nature and magnitude perpetrated by Nazi Germany against Jews cannot be expiated by any measure of material reparations. No indemnity, however large, can make good the destruction of human life and cultural values or atone for the agony of the men, women and children, tortured or put to death by every inhuman device.[6]

Some opposed the idea of any Holocaust reparations. Rabbi Isaac Lewin of Agudath Yisrael took the position that the offer of the chancellor to commence negotiations should be immediately rejected. At the initial meeting of the Claims Conference, he cited the Bible: "Ye shall not take ransom for the life of a murderer that is guilty of death (Numbers 35:31)."[7]

In Israel, the opposition was even more vehement. Angry demonstrators gathered outside the Knesset, Israel's parliament, and hurled stones as legislators inside gathered to debate the issue. The police responded and hundreds were injured.[8] Menachem Begin, a future prime minister of Israel, spoke to the huge crowd against accepting reparations: "That blood which was poured out in German concentration camps gave us courage to rise and overthrow the British. . . . How shall we face the world after trading that blood for marks?"[9]

Still, the Luxembourg Agreements of 1952, consisting of an agreement between the German Federal Republic and the State of Israel, and a parallel agreement between the German Federal Republic and the Claims Conference, ultimately came to be accepted.

In retrospect, these agreements were truly remarkable in concept. In addition to the large financial sums that were paid to Israel and that continue to be paid to Holocaust survivors, the agreements paved the way for the postwar relationship of Germany with the State of Israel and with the Jewish people.[10]

I have lost count of the number of times in the course of my work at the Claims Conference when I have sat at negotiations, a meeting, or a briefing and started with the words "It's not about the money," only to continue with an explanation as to why this or that particular group of survivors needed to be included in a particular program, which inevitably results in the question "Well, how much does it cost?"

Is the mantra "it's not about the money" really true?

It is a question that the Claims Conference faces every day. How does one take issues of justice and morality and translate them into dollars and cents? Is Holocaust restitution demeaning the memory of the Holocaust? Are the moral issues getting lost?

But what is the alternative? To agree that too much time has elapsed since these events took place? To abandon these claims? To say that survivors who have fallen through the cracks unfortunately just missed their chance?

The German Foundation agreement, which arose in 2000 out of negotiations for compensation payments for former slave and forced laborers, is, together with its implementing legislation, one hundred pages long.[11] The agreement is of tremendous financial and legal significance. The Claims Conference has distributed some $1 billion arising from it. Yet, perhaps the two most significant documents are not part of the formal materials. Their significance goes well beyond their legal status or their financial importance.

The first document emerged from a small meeting on November 16, 1999, in Berlin while the main negotiations dragged on. Rabbi Israel Singer, then chairman of the Negotiating Committee of the Claims Conference, and I had requested a meeting with the president of Germany.[12] In postwar Germany the office of the president is a position of tremendous moral authority and Johannes Rau, whose father was a preacher, had maintained the tradition of using the presidency as a forum for addressing important issues of morality and justice.

As we sat in a corner of the elegant reception room in his official residence, Schloss Bellevue, President Rau listened sympathetically to our request. We explained our concern: that if an agreement were reached, it would be perceived publicly as just another financial settlement. We told him that any agreement that dealt only with money would be of limited significance for the Jewish world. We asked that the president accompany any agreement with a statement that addressed issues of morality and responsibility. He agreed.

Just one month later we were back in Berlin and the agreement was finally reached. That afternoon we returned to Schloss Bellevue. The room was silent and the mood solemn. In front of a simple podium was a battery of television cameras and journalists from the world's media.

In a statement that took just a few minutes to read, the president spoke of the history of those terrible times. He said,

> At the time, many companies profited from the victims of forced labor. . . .
>
> [B]oth government and business accept the shared responsibility and moral duty arising from the injustices of the past.
>
> We all know that no amount of money can truly compensate the victims of crime. We all know that the suffering inflicted upon millions of women and men cannot be undone. . . .
>
> This compensation comes too late for all of those who lost their lives back then, just as it is for all those who have died in the intervening years. . . .
>
> I know that for many it is not really money that matters. What they want is for their suffering to be recognized as suffering and for the injustice done to them to be named injustice.
>
> I pay tribute to all those who were subjected to slave and forced labor under German rule and, in the name of the German people, beg forgiveness. We will not forget their suffering.[13]

There are Holocaust survivors who believe that the moral issues are more important than the financial ones and those who believe that they are less important. Regardless, the historical record now includes President Rau's powerful statement, which for the first time acknowledges that German industry was not an innocent party during those terrible times, but an active participant in the death and destruction that was the Holocaust.

The second document, of equal importance, is not an elegant statement publicly addressing issues of responsibility and morality. It is instead a rather dry and technical letter issued during the negotiations by a mid-level official in the German Ministry of Finance.

The agreement envisaged "legal peace" for German companies in U.S. courts, but a far more important issue for the Claims Conference and survivors was the issue of the effect of the German Foundation agreement on future negotiations with the German government.

Early in the negotiations regarding slave and forced labor, some on the German side took the position that if an agreement were reached this would mean *schlusstrich,* or closure. After this, there would be no more claims for Holocaust compensation against the German government. We indicated that we could not accept such a position. Ultimately, the German position was withdrawn. This led to the letter, which noted that the Claims Conference had open issues with Germany and confirmed that "the Foundation legislation will not impede such discussions in any way."[14]

Certainly, this letter was important for ongoing negotiation efforts with Germany on Holocaust compensation. Indeed, since the German Foundation agreement was signed, the Claims Conference successfully negotiated the inclusion of thousands of additional survivors into the Article 2 program, which pays quarterly pensions.[15] And these negotiations continue.

However, for the Claims Conference, the letter was of importance well beyond its financial significance. There may be "legal peace" in courts for German industry. But this simple letter effectively acknowledged that there can never be "closure" with the German government. The German government is the legal successor to the Third Reich. There have been various forms of "closure" or "legal peace" with Switzerland, with other European countries, and with German industry, but there cannot be closure with the successor to the entity that was responsible for the Holocaust. As long as there is one Holocaust survivor alive, we do not believe that such closure can be granted.

One of the key elements of Holocaust-era compensation is that it is fundamentally symbolic. No amount of money can ever make up for what happened. During the negotiations in the 1950s the Germans used the term "*Wiedergutmachung*" (which, translated literally, means "making whole"). We do not. Nor is the word "compensation" a satisfactory one; we use it as shorthand to describe payments to individuals that are in some way related to their suffering in the Holocaust.

In the negotiations regarding former slave laborers, there were suggestions by some to have a scale of payments for the survivors according to how long they were in a concentration camp. Ultimately the Claims

Conference approach was that, as any payment could be no more than symbolic, every person who had been in a concentration camp or ghetto should receive an equal amount.[16] As one survivor graphically put it, "To be in Auschwitz for one day was like a lifetime."

Holocaust-era compensation is about absolute justice and yet it is also about compromise. "Time is our greatest enemy," "the enemy of the good is the perfect," "the clock is ticking." The clichés are no less true for being clichés. As the German Foundation negotiations dragged on and the discussions continued, the question was raised whether to fight for more, or settle now.[17]

What do the survivors want? Our negotiating team, composed primarily of Holocaust survivors, themselves constantly grappled with these issues. Yet at our offices hundreds of survivors called daily to ask, "When will I finally get a payment? Will it be during my lifetime?"

When the founders of the Claims Conference first came together in 1951, they discussed what the name of the organization should be. After much debate they inserted the word "material" into an already unwieldy name: the organization would be called the Conference on Jewish *Material* Claims Against Germany.[18] They wanted to emphasize that negotiations regarding material compensation would never replace the moral challenges posed by the Holocaust. And half a century later, that remains the position of the Claims Conference.

Perhaps the reality is that Holocaust compensation and restitution is not about the money and it is about the money. It may on occasion cloud the important lessons of the Holocaust, yet it can also be a vehicle for educating a wider public. At the end of day, it has helped many hundreds of thousands of Holocaust survivors around the world to live out the remainder of their lives with a little more dignity than they might otherwise have had. It ultimately represents a measure of justice—no more, no less.

NOTES

1. Major Direct Compensation Programs for Jewish Victims of Nazi Persecution, http://www.claimscon.org. For a comprehensive history of the Claims Conference and of Holocaust compensation programs, *see* Nana Sagi, *German Reparations: A History of the Negotiations* (Dafna Alon, trans., Magnes Press, 1980), 33; Ronald Zweig, *German Reparations and the Jewish World: A History of the Claims Conference,* 2d ed. (2001); Angelika Timm, *Jewish Claims against East Germany* (Central European University Press, 1997); *History of the Claims Conference: A*

Chronology, 1951–2001 (2001) (hereinafter "*Chronology*"); *In Re Holocaust Victims Assets Litigation (Swiss Banks) Special Master's Proposal,* Sept. 11, 2000, Annex E; Karen Heilig, "From the Luxembourg Agreement to Today: Representing a People," *Berkeley Journal of International Law,* Vol. 20, No. 1 (2002); Menachem Z. Rosensaft and Joana D. Rosensaft, "A Measure of Justice: The Early History of German-Jewish Reparations," *Leo Baeck Institute Occasional Paper #4, 2003. See also* Saul Kagan, "The Claims Conference and the Communities," *Exchange* (1965), the author of which is one of the giants in the history of Holocaust-era restitution and compensation.

2. *Chronology,* 14.

3. Id. 4.

4. Id. 5.

5. Id. 6.

6. Id. 8.

7. Zweig, 30.

8. Sagi, 81.

9. John Authers and Richard Wolffe, *The Victims' Fortune: Inside the Epic Battle over the Debts of the Holocaust* (HarperCollins Publishers, 2002), 378.

10. Sagi, 202–4.

11. For details of the German Foundation "Remembrance, Responsibility, and the Future" *see* http://usembassy.de/policy/holocaust/index.htm. *See also*: Stuart E. Eizenstat, *Imperfect Justice: Looted Assets, Slave Labor, and the Unfinished Business of World War II* (Public Affairs, 2003), the author of which has played a pivotal role in the restitution process since 1995; Authers and Wolffe; Michael J. Bazyler, *Holocaust Justice: The Battle for Restitution in America's Courts* (New York University Press, 2003).

12. Joan Gralla, "Jewish Groups to Meet Germany's Rau on Holocaust," Reuters, Nov. 15, 1999.

13. Statement by German President Johannes Rau, Dec. 17, 1999 (translation).

14. Letter from German Federal Ministry of Finance to Dr. Karl Brozik, Claims Conference Representative in Germany, July 3, 2000.

15. Conference on Jewish Material Claims Against Germany, Inc., Annual Report 2001, 26; Annual Report 2002, 21. Annual Report 2003, 27.

16. Claims Conference Position Paper, June 15, 1999.

17. "We not only want to see a measure of justice achieved but we want those who suffered indescribable horrors to be alive to see that a new generation in a new century has not forgotten them." Testimony of Gideon Taylor, Hearing before the Committee on Banking and Financial Services, U.S. House of Representatives, Restitution of Holocaust Assets, Feb. 9, 2000.

18. Zweig, 31.

Chapter 14

The Negotiations on Compensation for Nazi Forced Laborers

Otto Graf Lambsdorff

The project of payments to Nazi forced laborers was and is a moral and historical challenge for the German government and for German industry. It involved numerous legal and economic issues that I had to master in three years of arduous negotiations.

The Historical Background

Foreign laborers, especially agricultural workers from Poland and Russia, had been traditionally employed in Germany since well before the First World War. But, the demand for labor during World War II far surpassed the possibilities of voluntary recruitment. The Nazi government, thus, resorted to pressure, coercion, and, finally, brutal force. For example, of twenty-seven thousand foreign workers in the armament sector in May 1942, only forty-two participated voluntarily. In 1944, the number of foreign workers peaked at a quarter of the overall work force in Germany: 7.6 million. Approximately half of the agricultural and arms factories work force were foreigners. More than half of these foreign workers came from the Soviet Union.

Due to growing pressure caused by the absence of German workers who were serving in Hitler's armies, the SS abandoned their intention of making Germany *judenrein,* "clean of Jews." Concentration camp inmates were hauled back from the East with the declared intention of working them to death. Inmates were also being used for "lucrative" ends: the SS rented them to German industry, just as the Army rented POWs for daily fees, guaranteeing their replacement in case of failure or death.

The Postwar Period

Restitution of property and compensation to victims of the Nazi-regime began immediately after Germany's surrender. However, compensation for forced labor was expressly excluded.

The German government refused requests for compensation for forced labor—the moral validity of which were never denied—for two political reasons. First, compensation for the illegal employment of civilians from occupied territories was, and is, considered a reparation issue under public international law. Germany has already delivered much more in reparations than the Allies ever contemplated in Potsdam and thereafter. Moreover, German territories were handed over to Russia and Poland, dismantled industries and products were similarly delivered, and German POWs were kept by the Soviet Union as a free work force for almost a decade.

The second reason compensation for forced labor was excluded related to the Cold War. Germany was not willing to pay billions of dollars in hard currency to people living in the Soviet Union and its satellite states. In addition, East Germany also flatly denied any legal or moral responsibility, thus demonstrating a high degree of hypocrisy.

The German Unification

After the wall fell and the Iron Curtain collapsed, German perceptions started to change. In the early nineties, Chancellor Helmut Kohl financed reconciliation foundations for the purposes of compensation. Foundations were established in Warsaw, Kiev, Moscow, and Minsk, making DM 1.5 billion available. However, these foundations took over ten years to finish their task, and much money was squandered along the way.

At that time, according to their own statistics, the foundations compensated roughly 1.5 million people living in the former Soviet Union and Poland, most of whom were former forced laborers. The average payment was one thousand Deutschmarks. However, a typical former forced laborer who did not suffer from any additional disablement received approximately half of that amount.

In the process of establishing the Foundation "Remembrance, Responsibility, and the Future" ("the Foundation"), the German government decided to partner with the reconciliation foundations and the German-Czech Future Fund, but to subject the new foundation to stricter controls than had been applied in the past. The reason for the partnership was quite simple: the established foundations already possessed files on many applicants that could save many from the ordeal of revisiting the past and assembling the documentation required by the new Foundation.

The payments of the foundations, and similar steps taken by other Eastern countries, put the subject of compensation to rest once and for all in the eyes of many Germans. However, some—first the young Green party, and later the Social Democrats—favored a second step, this time financed predominantly by German industry.

Some German industries concluded their own compensation agreements with the Claims Conference, or set up independent compensation. However, these schemes principally addressed so-called slave laborers only (former concentration camp inmates).

Class Action Lawsuits in the United States

The legal claims raised against German companies greatly increased the latter's willingness to engage in serious talks about compensation for forced labor. In March 1998, the New York lawyer Melvyn Weiss filed a suit against prominent German industries active in the United States, and against Ford Motor Company. Three months later leading German industries called upon Chancellor-elect Gerhard Schröder to assist them in stemming an ever increasing flood of court cases.

It is important to underscore that none of these lawsuits, either in Germany or elsewhere in the world, was won by any claimant in the past decades. But German companies had reason to be afraid of the damage done to their corporate reputation and their standing in the United States. In addition, they were vulnerable to all kinds of attacks by state legislators and regulators.

This situation threatened not only German companies but also German-American economic and political relations. Both governments, therefore, had to act.

The Beginning of the Negotiations

On February 16, 1999, the German chancellor and the chief executives of twelve leading German corporations issued a joint statement outlining their commitment to addressing the twin issues of moral and historical responsibility, as well as a lasting and all-embracing legal peace for German industries in the United States. The federal chancellor dispatched his aide, Federal Minister Bodo Hombach, to the White House to seek U.S. government assistance. President Clinton designated Under Secretary of State Stuart Eizenstat to assume this task. German industry nominated Dr. Manfred Gentz, chief financial officer and board member of Daimler-Chrysler, to coordinate their efforts and to act as their spokesman. Without Gentz's considerable weight and efforts, the Foundation Initiative would undoubtedly not have been so successful.

The German-American negotiations were initiated in March 1999. In July 1999, Chancellor Schröder asked me to act as his personal representative in the negotiations leading to the establishment of the Foundation and to cochair these negotiations with Eizenstat.

By the time I came on board, three basic decisions had already been made. First, the decision was made to address not only the issue of forced labor but also property claims and life insurance policies. This decision was justified by three arguments: (1) claims against banks were also being based on forced labor, alleging that these banks directly or indirectly benefited from it; (2) German industry wanted an all-embracing legal peace and not an introductory first step; (3) necessary funds could not be raised without massive support by German industry and banks.

The second decision was to combine the private and public compensation schemes into one fund. This decision was made after it became known that a very high percentage of forced laborers had been employed —or rather used—by the public sector of the Third Reich.

I have always defended the decision to finance three-quarters of the Foundation by the public sector. It was not only the direct employment of forced labor in the public sector that brought us to that conclusion but also the fact that a large part of the labor force was recruited—or, to be more accurate, in many cases apprehended—by the German police and army and subjected to draconian and racist laws in order to replace German workers employed in Hitler's armies. This put the bulk of moral responsibility on the German government that represented Germany in succession to the Third Reich.

The third decision was to extend the bilateral government-to-government negotiations by including the leading plaintiffs' lawyers, as well as representatives of states and organizations directly involved. At our twelve plenary sessions roughly one hundred persons sat around the table headed by Mr. Eizenstat and myself: German industry led by Dr. Gentz and company lawyers; government representatives from Israel, Russia, Poland, the Czech Republic, Belarus, and Ukraine; the Claims Conference representatives; and a dozen U.S. plaintiffs' lawyers. That such a circle could reach consensus is in my mind close to a miracle.

The Major Challenges of the Negotiations

Three major hurdles had to be overcome in order for a successful conclusion of the negotiations to be achieved. Stuart Eizenstat and I were determined to succeed because there was no alternative.

1) The Capital of the Foundation

First, from the beginning of negotiations through December 17, 1999, the talks centered around the Foundation's capital, the "capped amount," which was to cover all claims from the Nazi era and World War II against the German industry. This issue, in particular, brought us to the brink of failure.

From the beginning we recognized that no price could be attached to a human life, a lost youth, years of work stolen, and assaults on human dignity. So, there could not be any *Wiedergutmachung*, as compensation is called in German.

Instead we asked, "What is a dignified amount on an individual scale?" We could only discuss this issue seriously if we had an idea of the number of survivors. Professor Lutz Niethammer took it upon himself to consult representatives of the partner countries and the Claims Conference in order to calculate raw figures. His calculated results were accepted by all as a political basis for negotiation.

On the other side stood an equally unknown factor, namely, the willingness of thousands of German enterprises to participate in an endeavor that could not be based on individual guilt and responsibility. At that point we were too optimistic and underestimated the reluctance of many companies. When the Foundation Initiative asked for April 2000 as a deadline for compensation, they did not know that it would take more than a year and considerable sacrifice on the part of the founding members to honor the obligations assumed in December 1999.

We had, by December, gone a long and arduous way from the early summer of 1999, when the negotiations started with a vague offer of DM 1.3 billion on the German side and a $23 billion demand on the other side. But with the direct intervention of Chancellor Schröder and President Clinton, we were able to settle at DM 10 billion.

From the beginning, however, we knew that the whole exercise was not merely about money. It was a process of collective and painful learning, which brought to light many sensitivities and deep wounds on both sides. It was, therefore, with a united feeling of relief that we listened to the historic speech of President Johannes Rau in December 1999 in front of survivors and the negotiation partners following agreement on the Foundation's capital:

> We all know that no amount of money can really compensate the victims of crime. We all know that the suffering inflicted upon millions of women and men cannot be undone. I know that for many [survivors] it is not really money that matters. What they want is for their suffering to be recognized as suffering and for the injustice done to them to be named injustice. I pay tribute to all those who were subjected to forced or slave labor under German rule and, in the name of the German people, beg forgiveness.

2) The Allocation of Funds

The second decision was the allocation of funds among the five Eastern European partners, the Claims Conference, the International Organization for Migration, and the International Commission on Holocaust-Era Insurance Claims (ICHEIC). This part of the negotiations took place on March 23, 2000.

At the beginning, we were facing a difficult situation. Who could broker amounts among sovereign nations, all of which suffered under the Nazi regime?

Under these circumstances it was of vital importance that Poland, led by the then Polish ambassador to Germany, Dr. Jerzy Kranz, took the lead and established a consensus among the five Eastern European partners. These figures could not be accepted as absolute amounts; they were accepted instead as relative proportions.

After the compensation for slave and forced labor fell into place, we still had to agree on the issue of property while at the same time defending the

Future Fund—an endowment designed to finance in perpetuity projects designed to combat racial prejudice and xenophobia. We did not succeed completely on either front.

It proved to be an especially arduous task to combine the expectations attached to Mr. Eagleburger's ICHEIC with the Foundation. We were reasonably sure that open insurance policies underwritten by German insurance companies that were not paid or compensated after the war did not exceed some DM 10 to 30 million, while the administration set up by the ICHEIC consumed a multiple of that amount, with additional expenses still under negotiation.

On the other hand, the Future Fund, originally intended to take up half of the Foundation's capital, dwindled down to DM 1 billion and, finally, DM 700 million. But nevertheless the expected yearly earnings from accruing interest will form a solid basis for the financing of projects in the field of youth exchange, Holocaust education, and other related topics.

3) Legal Peace

The third and final part of the negotiations was dedicated to the materialization of an all-embracing and enduring legal peace for German industries against claims arising from the Nazi era and World War II, as promised by President Clinton to Chancellor Schröder in a 1999 letter.

Considering the independence of the American judiciary on the one hand, and the class action system on the other, this was by no means easy to achieve.

We excluded two options quickly. First, we excluded an international treaty on compensation, which would have basically been a bilateral or multilateral reparation agreement. Such a treaty would not have had the slightest chance of being ratified by the U.S. Senate. Also, from the German perspective, the prospect of the renewal of international reparation agreements—a second "London Conference" akin to the earlier one convened in 1922 to address German war reparations following World War I —was clearly incompatible with the German position more than fifty years after the Second World War in a changed political world.

The second possibility, a class action settlement, was also excluded for a number of reasons: (1) the example of the Swiss bank settlement, where money began to flow only three years after the agreement, had been hardly edifying; (2) such a settlement presupposed at least the possibility of an existing legal claim, a notion excluded by Germany for a number of reasons under international and national law—the statute of limitations being one of them; (3) a class action settlement would have put the whole Foundation, largely financed by German taxpayers' money, under the supervision of an American judge—a notion incompatible with any idea of German sovereignty.

A) THE STATEMENT OF INTEREST BY THE U.S. GOVERNMENT

The breakthrough option—a Statement of Interest filed by the U.S. government—owes much to the brilliance of the American counsel of the Foundation Initiative, Mr. Roger Witten, and also to the creativity on the part of U.S. government lawyers from the Department of Justice and Department of State.

However, at two moments during our talks even the considerable political weight of Stuart Eizenstat and his principal aide, Ambassador J. D. Bindenagel, was not sufficient to overcome the resistance of the Department of Justice. The German chancellery had to go back to the White House to seek a political decision. It was only at this highest level that the necessary steps could be taken.

In the meantime, the U.S. government filed Statements of Interest in a number of cases that were accepted by judges all over the United States. We were convinced that this precedent would serve as an effective deterrent to any future lawyer who considers basing another individual or collective suit on facts already covered by the Foundation.

It took a full ten months after the German and the U.S. governments signed an executive agreement in Berlin on July 17, 2000, to reach this place. The first two months were spent in an uphill fight, mainly with the Department of Justice translating the obligations assumed by the United States into a Statement of Interest. The U.S. government had to tread the fine line between supporting the dismissals, by stating that the dismissal of all pending lawsuits was in the interest of U.S. foreign policy, and risking actions by the class action lawyers addressing their claims against the U.S. government because this Statement of Interest might constitute a breach of the property rights of U.S. citizens.

B) THE JUDGES

The other half of the problem was the judicial branch itself. The multi-district litigation (MDL) panel refused to consolidate all sixty actions against German industry in July 2000 and did not want to reconsider that decision. Thus, we had to deal with a number of judges. The legal peace, once expected in summer 2000, seemed to be out of reach.

Two judges, Judge William Bassler of New Jersey and Judge Michael Mukasey of New York, were helpful in dismissing the labor and the insurance cases, respectively. But the Bundestag, which had reserved for itself the last word on satisfactory legal peace, could not make a decision before the bank cases before Judge Shirley Kram were dismissed. In the months that followed, everybody was under terrible strain—well aware that 1 percent of the forced laborers was dying every month.

Initially, Judge Kram refused voluntary dismissal twice and plaintiffs and defendants had to go to the court with their joint request. But she remained steadfast in her refusal to dismiss the cases. Finally, after the successful appeals decision by the Second Circuit, Judge Kram reacted expeditiously in dismissing the consolidated bank cases on May 21, 2001. In reaction to this, on May 30, 2001, the German Bundestag ordered the Foundation to begin making payments to the partner organizations. Within days, former forced laborers were receiving the payments they had long been waiting for.

Achievements

By the end of 2003, a little more than three years after the establishment of the "Remembrance, Responsibility, and the Future" Foundation, more than 1.5 million elderly former slave and forced laborers (out of approximately 1.7 million who will receive a payment), living today in eighty different countries, have received the first installment of their payments. These payments total approximately $3 billion.[1] Eight hundred million dollars went to 135,000 Jewish survivors, $819 million to 443,000 people living in Poland, $642 million to 462,000 victims in the Ukraine, $233 million to 128,000 people living in Belarus, $819 million to 198,000 people living in Russia, $198 million to 75,000 people living in the Czech Republic, and $168 million to 60,000 survivors in the rest of the world.

Second, as of 2004 installments have already started in the Czech Republic, Poland, and Belarus. Other countries will follow soon. Therefore, the payments are most likely to be completed by all partner organizations in 2005.

Roughly $124 million was transferred to the International Commission on Holocaust Era Insurance Claims (ICHEIC) for insurance claims and ICHEIC costs. ICHEIC received another $217 million for its humanitarian fund.

Once the payments to slave and forced laborers are concluded, the Foundation organs, trustees, and executive directors will find themselves left with the perpetual task of administering the Future Fund.

As for the all-embracing and enduring legal peace for German industries, as reaffirmed in the German-American agreement, the results remain unsatisfactory. As of 2004 some lawsuits based on forced labor and "Aryanization" are still pending. Threats of discriminatory state laws covering insurance claims are still in the air, in spite of the final agreement reached among the Foundation, ICHEIC, and the German insurance industry on October 16, 2002.

Outlook

Overall, we have reached most of our goals and can be satisfied, not with ourselves, but with the fact that the victims will receive their material compensation, thus laying to rest a difficult legacy that had been left aside for decades. Eventually, the work of the Foundation, ably led by Dr. Jansen, a former company manager, will bring the chapter to financial closure.

We know there can never be moral closure. The public debate in Germany during the past four years has reopened a painful chapter in our history, the history of slave and forced labor. The message of stolen youth, wasted years, and exploitation has been taken up by many Germans. They are willing to take their individual pasts, the dark heritage of their living quarters, or their industrial companies into their own hands. In some cases, they have even gone back to visit the dismal places in Eastern Europe where the former forced laborers now live, or invited them back to their working place, this time as free citizens.

Even in the home countries of the former forced laborers, tides have changed. When they returned home, many were suspected of collaboration with the Hitler regime and treated accordingly. Now for the first time, it is publicly recognized that they too were victims of the Hitler regime. This I think is the best windfall of our work.

I returned my mandate to Chancellor Gerhard Schröder in August 2002. It was personal motivation that made me respond to the call of the German chancellor, long after my retirement and my withdrawal from active politics. I not only made friends on this road, but I do not regret having thus rendered a last and hopefully lasting service to my country.

NOTES

1. Exchange rate €/US$ of December 8, 2003.

Chapter 15

German Economy and the Foundation Initiative

An Act of Solidarity for Victims of National Socialism

Lothar Ulsamer

In recent decades German companies have assumed historical and moral responsibility for their cooperation with the Nazi regime during the Second World War. Initially this sense of responsibility was expressed on an individual basis. Later it was expressed on a larger scale, with more than sixty-five hundred companies contributing to the German Economy Foundation Initiative "Remembrance, Responsibility, and the Future" (hereafter "Foundation Initiative") in a major gesture of reconciliation. Numerous companies founded after the war participated in this effort as well, thus placing it on a broader footing and making it possible to provide financial compensation to former forced laborers who worked for companies that no longer exist today.

Needless to say, the initiators of the Foundation Initiative were well aware that there is nothing that can compensate for the horrors that were perpetrated by the Nazi regime and have remained indelibly imprinted in the minds not only of the victims but also of many people in Germany as well as in other nations. Nonetheless, it is a significant fact that a large number of companies have assumed historical and moral responsibility for their involvement in economic activities that caused suffering to many people during the Nazi dictatorship. It has been important in ethical terms to make this gesture to those victims still alive. The gesture also helps to raise the level of our credibility when we talk to others about social and political responsibility in our era. Carlo Schmid, one of the fathers of the postwar German constitution and someone who strongly advocated reconciliation with Israel, Poland, Russia, and France, said, "No nation can shape its future meaningfully without a solid knowledge of its own history."[1] The same applies to industrial companies.

The Foundation Initiative was created in the 1990s. Its purpose was to pave the way for the establishment of a foundation that would provide humanitarian aid for former forced laborers and other victims who suffered damage to their physical or financial well-being as a result of activities pursued by industrial companies during the Nazi regime. From the outset the Foundation Initiative also strongly advocated the creation of a Future Fund that would be dedicated to the funding of projects that promote human rights and international understanding. At the same time, for the companies involved and for German industry as a whole it was important to create an environment, particularly in the United States, in which they would be secure from legal attacks based on claims going back to the Nazi era and the Second World War. It was felt that long, drawn-out legal disputes should be avoided in order to ensure that the process of making payments to victims could begin as soon as possible and to prevent such disputes from posing a continuous threat to the German economy and to its image in the various countries concerned.

Changed Level of Awareness

For a variety of reasons, the question of providing compensation for former forced laborers became a subject of public attention in the 1990s. The 2 + 4 Treaties of 1990 had not only made the reunification of Germany possible; they were also seen as taking the place of a peace treaty that was never concluded with Germany after 1945. It had been decided in the postwar years to postpone a decision on the possibility of providing compensation for forced labor until such time as a peace treaty could be concluded.

With the end of the Cold War and the disappearance of the Iron Curtain, the lack of justice for the victims of Nazi crimes who were living in Central and Eastern Europe became more evident. Up until then the victims living in these countries had received only about 1 percent of the compensation payments made by Germany, amounting to well above DM 100 billion. There was a change in the level of awareness of this matter both at the government level and in industry. A number of U.S. attorneys recognized the opportunities this situation held out for them and found a number of Nazi-era victims in Central and Eastern Europe who were willing to file suits.

In addition to the abovementioned factors that drew renewed public attention to the subject of forced labor during the Nazi regime, there was a further and, in my view, much more important factor involved. Many former forced laborers I talked to emphasized that the suffering they were subjected to is something that should not be forgotten. Their primary interest, however, was not that of ensuring that the horrors of National Socialism will be remembered. Instead, they urged that we not be fixed on the past but rather derive lessons from the past for the present and the future. It became evident in conversations with victims that for most of them this was their main interest. Every conversation with victims who experienced those times is of concern to us. Every personal destiny counts.

Reconciliation Rather Than Confrontation

Originally there were twelve and then, later, seventeen companies in the Foundation Initiative. They went on to recruit other companies as providers of financial contributions. The process of collecting the money needed for the desired foundation was only one of the tasks pursued by the Foundation Initiative. Parallel to this there was a need to conduct a series of complex international negotiations. The Foundation Initiative remained a loosely structured group, comparable to a civic initiative, and it remained focused on the objective of finding a positive solution both for the victims and for German companies.

Provocative media appearances on the part of U.S. plaintiffs' attorneys, fomented by parts of the German media and certain survivor organizations, at times created the impression that the negotiations were bound to end up in fierce confrontation. The Foundation Initiative, working together with a large number of the other negotiating partners, made a significant contribution towards toning down the conflict. Over time, the attitudes of many of those involved in the negotiations changed, and there was an increase in mutual understanding of interests and feelings. It soon became clear that a positive outcome could be achieved only if all the participants showed goodwill in approaching the task of finding a solution.

This is not to say that the negotiations did not go through phases of conflict. Indeed, considerable effort had to be expended to smooth over these bumps in the road.

The difficulties encountered in the negotiations derived not only from the nature of the matters being discussed but also from the fact that so many different parties were involved in them. In many cases there were more than a hundred people seated at the negotiating table. They included representatives of the governments of the United States, Israel, Poland, the Czech Republic, Russia, Belarus, Ukraine, and Germany, alongside representatives of the Conference on Jewish Material Claims Against Germany, U.S. plaintiffs' attorneys, as well as representatives of the Foundation Initiative. The goal was to reach an agreement not only on the overall sum involved but also on how the money was to be divided among the former forced workers and other persons who suffered damage to their physical or financial well-being. There was a need to agree on eligibility criteria for applicants in the various categories. Humanitarian funds provided in remembrance of victims who died were to supplement the funds that had been earmarked for living victims. The precondition established for initiating the payment process was the conclusion of a comprehensive legal peace for German companies. The Foundation Initiative was always aware of the need to conclude the negotiations quickly in order to help as many of the surviving victims as possible.

There was a change in awareness not only on the part of the persons actively involved in the negotiating process but also on the part of the companies and persons involved in the Foundation Initiative. This effect extended far beyond the group of direct participants and included companies that had initially decided against making a financial contribution to the Foundation. The issue of forced labor in the Nazi era gained increasing attention in the general public. This was important in that it helped people to confront a part of their own history. The Foundation Initiative had always considered it important to use its powers of persuasion to win other companies over to its point of view and get them to support the Foundation. It decided not to "blacklist" companies who chose not to contribute. The character of a voluntary fund-raising campaign was retained despite the fact that it was not always easy to secure the necessary funds. The Foundation Initiative also wanted to avoid creating new aversions or evoking old prejudices as a result of trying to pressure companies into joining.

Rapid Payment

The negotiating partners agreed on an overall total of DM 10 billion. This amount was subsequently confirmed by President Bill Clinton and by Chancellor Gerhard Schröder. Half of the total amount (plus DM 100 million in interest) was to be paid by the Foundation Initiative and the other half by the German federal government. After intensive collection efforts the Foundation Initiative paid its half in full to the Foundation "Remembrance, Responsibility, and the Future."

From the beginning it was of great importance for the Foundation Initiative that the payments made be distributed as rapidly and comprehensively as possible to the victims. The Foundation began transferring funds to its partner organizations for distribution to the victims on June 15, 2001. These partner organizations are responsible for processing applications submitted in their respective countries by specific groups of victims and for making payments to individual victims. Up to June 15, 2005, more than 4 billion euros had been transferred to partner organizations for distribution to some 1.6 million eligible recipients.

During the process of collecting money from companies who had pledged contributions, the question was repeatedly asked whether the money being provided would actually find its way to the eligible victims. On the one hand, there was a need to ensure that these humanitarian payments to the victims were made as rapidly and efficiently as possible. On the other, there was a need to avoid possible misappropriation of funds by unmeritorious persons at the expense of the victims.

The close cooperation that exists between the partner organizations and the Foundation, together with auditing teams who carry out spot checks, is ensuring that everything possible is being done to rule out any improper use of the money.

Legal Peace

In the course of a public debate regarding the activities of the Foundation Initiative, various groups criticized the mixing of moral and legal issues. On closer examination it would seem that the solution of the legal problems that existed has done just as much to bring about a better relationship between the parties as the morally motivated provision of money for humanitarian assistance. As far as the companies are concerned, there were no legal reasons for making these payments, a position firmly established also by the German government on the basis of the comprehensive compensation legislation and payments made after the war. The focus was thus on moral reasons. A perception of historical responsibility led to these payments being made on humanitarian grounds.

It was clear to the representatives of the companies and to the representatives of the governments involved that all the suits pending against German companies would have to be dismissed in order not to endanger the whole process of reconciliation and the relationship between Germany and other countries, particularly the United States. It is safe to say that the primary intention of U.S. attorneys was not necessarily to obtain court decisions in the suits they filed. They wanted to draw public attention to their cases and the courtroom was to serve as a media platform for getting their message out. With all this in mind it is easy to understand why the German and U.S. governments got involved, bringing in high-level chief negotiators, i.e., Stuart Eizenstat and Bodo Hombach, later succeeded by Count Otto Lambsdorff. The negotiating delegation representing German industry was led by Manfred Gentz. A political solution was needed, and this was something the companies could not and did not want to resist. A way had to be found to avoid having a negative impact on political and economic relations with the United States as well as with other countries.

The negotiations resulted in the signing of the Berlin Agreements on July 17, 2000. On their basis the German parliament passed legislation to establish the Foundation. On May 30, 2001, the parliament further passed a resolution confirming that a sufficient level of legal security had been attained for German companies, particularly in the United States. Following this resolution the Foundation Initiative decided it could begin to transfer the funds it had pledged to the Foundation. Under the Berlin Agreements it would not have been required to do so until all suits pending against German companies in the United States had been dismissed by the courts or voluntarily withdrawn. The Foundation Initiative decided, however, to expedite the process of getting financial assistance to the victims.

The kind of legal peace granted to German companies in the United States includes protection against lawsuits as well as against unjustified administrative and legislative interventions. On this basis the Foundation Initiative continues to work for the dismissal of suits pending in U.S. courts against German companies in connection with the Nazi era and the

Second World War. In so doing the Foundation Initiative has been supported by the German and U.S. governments. Specifically, in the Berlin Agreements the U.S. government agreed to intervene in any suits brought against German companies relating to the Nazi era and the Second World War and to file a Statement of Interest with the courts that it would be in the foreign policy interest of the United States for the cases to be dismissed and for the Foundation to be the exclusive forum for resolving such claims.

It has been very disappointing and frustrating for the Foundation Initiative and the German companies to see U.S. attorneys file new suits in the United States after the signing of the Berlin Agreements, despite the fact that by signing these agreements many of them promised to work towards achieving legal peace. Thus far, however, the filing of Statements of Interest has been successfully used to dismiss several cases against German companies.

Fight for Human Rights

The remembrance of past crimes is intended to increase public sensitivity for events in today's world, precisely what many of the victims of past crimes have called for. We need to react sensitively to initial signs of discrimination and see them as antidemocratic tendencies. Repression usually begins gradually and once the barriers erected by democracy, the rule of law, and human rights have been broken down, it becomes increasingly difficult to prevent disaster. The Holocaust Museum in Washington shows in impressive manner the descent into violence that ultimately led to the horrible crimes committed during the Nazi era. Photographic and written documents make it clear that the Germans waited too long after human rights violations became evident. The exhibition "Jews in Berlin" shown at the New Synagogue Foundation in Berlin traced the introduction of discriminatory practices that finally led to the total denial of rights to Jewish citizens. Early signs, such as prohibiting bakeries from selling cakes to Jews, signaled impending danger of far more ominous measures. The introduction of each of these discriminatory measures was just another step down the road to a repressive and dehumanized society. With each step it became more and more difficult to stop the spread of Nazi terror into all areas of life.

Mindful of this historical background, the Foundation Initiative sought from the outset to create a Future Fund within the framework of the Foundation "Remembrance, Responsibility, and the Future." After much resistance it was finally possible to gain acceptance for the establishment of the fund "Remembrance and the Future" (named Future Fund in public), the purpose of which is to improve international understanding, to protect human rights, and to contribute towards peace in the world.

Increased contact among people of different countries, religions, and cultures will help to promote international understanding. The intention is to have young people from different countries work together in projects wherever possible. For example, experience from Poland, Israel, and Germany could lead to fruitful discussions and the initiation of learning processes on all sides. With its projects the Future Fund wants to achieve a higher level of sensitivity to and protection of human rights. Activities that will lead to the building and strengthening of civil society structures can be supported in this context. The focus must be on the implementation of theoretical strategies in practical work. Political extremists and their movements must be counteracted early on and with great resolve in all regions of the world. The promotion of moral courage among citizens is important so that antidemocratic tendencies will encounter strong resistance on a broad front.

The Future Fund has taken up its work and is providing support for humanitarian projects as well as meetings with surviving witnesses of Nazi-era crimes. A number of scholarship programs have been created. A funding program entitled "History and Human Rights" is intended to contribute towards the strengthening of human rights and international understanding.

Learning from the Past

National Socialism was a singular phenomenon. But criminal regimes, dictatorships, and repression exist in a wide variety of forms. Large numbers of persons who were forced laborers under the Nazi regime experienced this sad fact after the war when, upon returning home, they were arrested and imprisoned by a communist dictator. These unfortunate people were the victims of two dictatorships. The lesson for us is that we need to work to promote respect for human rights everywhere in the world. The objective of the Future Fund is not to make the past something we can forget or to crowd it out with other topics. The objective is to understand the relevance of the past for the present. We need to learn lessons from history so that we can shape a common future.

NOTES

1. "Ohne solide Kenntnis seiner Geschichte kann kein Volk seine Zukunft gestalten." Carlo Schmid: Erinnerungen, dritter Band der Gesammelten Werke (Collected Works, Vol. 3, Remembrance), Bern, München, Wien 1979, S. 855.

Chapter 16

Processing of Claims for Slave and Forced Labor

Expediency versus Accuracy?

Roland Bank

The program of awarding payments to victims of slave and forced labor as well as other National Socialist injustice through the Foundation "Remembrance, Responsibility, and the Future" has been carried out from the outset under intense time pressure: more than fifty-five years after the end of World War II, the victims are very old and any delay in the procedures inevitably would mean the gesture of compensation would reach fewer of its addressees. As a consequence, it was repeatedly emphasized during the course of international negotiations and the drafting of the German law establishing the Foundation (hereinafter "Foundation Law") that procedures for determining eligibility must be nonbureaucratic and expedient. On the other hand, there has always been pressure to make sure awards are exclusively made to those persons fulfilling the criteria of eligibility and that there are no misdirected payments. This pressure partially goes back to German public opinion after some bad experiences with global payments to certain Eastern European states during the 1990s that partly disappeared into unknown channels. The pressure has also been kept up by victims groups who have been keen on sharing the limited amount of money only with persons actually eligible for an award under the criteria established by the Foundation Law. Therefore, one of the fundamental challenges to the program—both for its drafters and for everybody involved in putting it into practice—has been to strike a fair balance between the conflicting aims of accuracy and expediency.

Three aspects have proven to be of crucial importance in reconciling expediency and accuracy: (1) the Foundation's solution determines eligibility along general criteria rather than trying to differentiate according to the individual fate suffered; (2) relaxed standards of proof have been applied in order to speed up procedures and to alleviate problems of proof; and, (3) certain review procedures aim at detecting both systematic as well as individual ,mistakes thereby assuring a satisfactory degree of accuracy.

Generalized Approach versus Case-by-Case Approach

The individual fates addressed by the Foundation solution vary enormously. The situations range from slave labor performed by detainees in SS concentration camps to work in a gardening company or in agriculture. It includes situations in which people were deported several thousand kilometers from their home as well as those involving people who were forced to work but allowed to sleep at home. The Foundation Law addresses this huge variety of historical exploitation and persecution with three categories of eligibility:[1]

- slave labor in concentration camps, ghettos, or comparably atrocious situations taking place in other places of confinement;
- forced labor under severe and discriminating living conditions or detention carried out after deportation from the home state;
- an "opening clause" for other National Socialist injustice involving either forced labor, deportation, or detention (e.g., forced labor in agriculture), with criteria for eligibility determined by the partner organizations resolving applications.

Eligibility under one of these categories triggers a lump-sum payment, the amount of which was specified in the course of the international negotiations: for the first category a payment of up to fifteen thousand Deutschmarks was foreseen whereas situations falling under the other two categories qualify for a payment of up to five thousand Deutschmarks. Application of these broad categories allows for both working and living conditions to be evaluated in a generalized manner. Moreover, the duration of the confinement was excluded from consideration, as was the damage to health or professional career. Consequently, there is, for instance, no differentiation between a person who was detained for a few days in a concentration camp and another person who survived the horrors of several concentration camps over a period of several years. In both cases, under the German Foundation Law the lump sum compensated will be fifteen thousand Deutschmarks.

The only instrument for differentiation within each of these legal categories is the possibility of defining subcategories. With the exception of cases of confinement in concentration camps or ghettos, the Foundation Law entitles partner organizations to establish subcategories in which they may establish different compensation amounts according to the severity of treatment experienced by the victim. While at first sight this may seem to open the door for an evaluation of individualized criteria, it must be kept in mind that the power given to partner organizations pertains to *categorizing* different situations within the ambit of one category. In practice, partner organizations often established subcategories in which the maximum sum for cases of detention in specific places of confinement or for the entire category is lower. On the other hand, within the respective opening clauses, as defined by the partner organizations, a considerable diversification among the various subcategories has been established. However, partner organizations have sought to avoid more individualized criteria of differentiation, such as the harshness or duration of the work or the severity of living conditions. Even if these were the criteria intended by the drafters of the Foundation Law, such criteria are extremely difficult to prove after some sixty years have elapsed since the events under consideration. Moreover, going into more detail about the suffering would have been contrary to the general objective of an expeditious processing of applications.

In sum, the general solution favors broad categories over a detailed individual review of the damage suffered. The latter approach would have allowed for more individual justice to be done, but would have consumed an enormous amount of time in light of the 2.5 million applications that had to be examined. But this broad measure was necessary not only in order to speed up proceedings but also in order to avoid evidentiary problems that could lead to erroneous decisions. Frequently, the exact time spent in one or another camp or under certain working conditions can no longer be easily established. Consequently, given the age of the victims, increasing individual justice by a more thorough evaluation of the individual suffering might have resulted in a decrease of the overall justice pursued with the program, which sought to provide this gesture of reconciliation to as many victims as possible while they were still alive.

Standards of Proof

The standards of proof applied clearly have an impact on the conflict between accuracy and expediency: strict standards of proof in this area may increase accuracy to some extent whereas more relaxed standards increase expediency.

The fundamental objective of the standard of proof developed by international agreements is that in order to establish that an applicant satisfies the criteria for eligibility, his or her claim must be credible. In the German Foundation Law, a priority is given to documentary evidence; only in the absence of such evidence is the standard of credibility applied.[2]

One approach that is taken with a view to establishing credibility is an overall assessment of each application based on all the evidence submitted, including the written personal statement of the applicant, historical research on a specific situation, and archival research for individual proof. However, a thorough evaluation requires an individual review and therefore is time consuming. In a number of cases, this may be the only way to help an applicant if he or she cannot present any documents that meet the eligibility criteria. On a broader scale, the standard of credibility permits broad presumptions based on historical experience that apply to a larger number of applications. Ample use has been made of such presumptions under the German law. For instance, it is presumed that all persons who were detained in a concentration camp or a ghetto were forced to work. Therefore, every applicant who can show that he or she was detained in one of these places does not need to provide any independent proof with regard to forced labor. Similarly, with persons who could establish that they were deported from their home state in Eastern Europe to the German Reich or occupied territory, it is presumed that they were forced to work. This presumption is based on the historical knowledge that this was the typical fate suffered by deportees from Eastern Europe. Moreover, the credibility approach permits schematic acceptance of certain documents as sufficient proof of a certain element and thereby guarantees a high output of decisions.

Moreover, it may even be doubted that relaxed standards of proof decrease accuracy. Given the time that has elapsed since the events, it may be regarded as a rule rather than the exception that applicants do not have any documentation about their fate at the time in question. Although there may be good documentation in the archives of the International

Tracing Service, in memorial institutions of certain former concentration camps, in museums, or in national archives, there are still a considerable number of claimants who do not appear in any archival documentation. To insist on documentation as the standard of proof required for eligibility, therefore, would mean that an important number of actual victims would not qualify for a positive decision. Therefore, even if the likelihood of historically accurate positive decisions may be better if documents are required, the probability of historically false rejections would be higher. In the particular context of the Foundation, which addresses situations of more than five decades ago, the percentage of decisions that do not coincide with the historical truth is therefore probably lower with the use of a relaxed standard of proof.

Control and Complaints Procedures

As a measure for increasing accuracy, decisions taken by partner organizations on individual claims are audited by the German Foundation and are subject to appeals procedures, which may be initiated by the applicant.

In order to allow for an audit by the German Foundation, partner organizations submit lists of cases decided to the German Foundation, which will then carry out an accuracy check on a selected number of cases before payments are finally processed. Decisions rejecting applications are reviewed in a similar way. This allows the German Foundation to detect eventual systematic problems in the processing of applications by a partner organization and, by and large, guarantees that the criteria of the Foundation Law are observed. With the help of this system, problems can largely be avoided or be quickly resolved. Moreover, the auditing has served to contribute to a fine tuning of the interpretation of the Foundation Law in a unified manner throughout the seven partner organizations.

For errors pertaining to individual cases, all applicants have the opportunity to submit appeals against decisions, addressing them to an independent body established as an annex to the organization responsible for processing the application.

Usually, appeals procedures do not delay the process with regard to other applications, as long as only a relatively small number of cases are brought to the appeals bodies. Therefore, appeals could be seen as a proper way to increase accuracy without diminishing expediency. However, there was a certain danger that a large number of pending appeals could delay the payment of a second installment. The Foundation Law established a system of distributing payments in two installments; the second of these installments is subject to a pro rata system that allows for the sharing of a predefined sum between eligible applicants if the resources allocated to the partner organization are insufficient to provide for the full amount foreseen. The negative effects of this construction have been mitigated to some extent by the fund proceeding with the payments of the second installment if a reserve of 5 percent of the overall allocation made to the responsible partner organization is sufficient to cover the appeals cases.[3] Expediency in appeals procedures has been upheld as an important goal, and in practice, problems of this sort seem to have been avoided.

Conclusion

Balancing individual justice and a contribution to general justice for the large majority of victims is a very difficult task. It seems, however, that the rules of the international agreements leading to the adoption of the Foundation Law and the implementation of those rules provide for an appropriate solution by emphasizing those factors that are useful for expediting the processing of claims while guaranteeing the necessary level of accuracy within the system.

It is worth noting that Germany has long-standing experiences with a completely contrary approach: the Federal Law on Compensation (*Bundesentschädigungsgesetz*) addresses harm suffered at the hands of the National Socialist regime because of persecution for reasons of political opinion, race, religious belief, or conscience. This law has provided for compensatory payments to victims who suffered damages to life, body, health, freedom, property, or assets. Both the intensity of persecution as well as the amount of damage suffered were evaluated in great detail according to a highly complicated set of rules by administrative authorities whose decisions were subject to scrutiny by the courts. In the application of this case-by-case approach, some two million claims submitted by roughly one million applicants were positively decided whereas 1.2 million claims were rejected.[4]

Processing of these claims and especially legal disputes in courts continued for several decades.

When the Foundation solution was adopted, there was no doubt that the urgent need for expediency required very different rules. After so many years had elapsed since the events, it would have been impossible to allow for more differentiation of the individual suffering without significantly prolonging the process and producing insurmountable problems with regard to proof. Given the advanced age of the victims, a decisive emphasis on the simplification of criteria was necessary so that some 2.5 million applications could be processed expeditiously. It could be argued that the solution adopted for the Foundation goes far in the direction of generalizing historical situations for the purpose of establishing categories of eligibility and thereby oversimplifies the diversity of individual fates. However, in practice, more than four years after the adoption of the Foundation solution, only one of the partner organizations responsible for processing claims is close to finalizing its payments, while the finalization of the entire program will take at least two more years.[5]

This may serve to illustrate that the drafters of the Foundation solution did just enough to avoid the establishment of another long-term project and to provide instead a suitable framework for reaching as many survivors as possible with this gesture of reconciliation.

NOTES

1. Foundation Law, § 11, ¶ 1.
2. Foundation Law, § 11, ¶ 2.
3. German Foundation Law, § 9, ¶ 9.
4. Numbers provided in H. G. Hockerts, *Wiedergutmachung in Deutschland: Eine historische Bilanz, 1945–2000* (Reparation in Germany: A Historical Balance, 1945–2000) *in* K. Doehring, *Jahrhundertschuld, Jahrhundertsühne* (A Century's Guilt, a Century's Expiation) (2001), 107 *et. seq.*
5. Situation in late 2004.

Chapter 17

Corporate Profits and the Holocaust

A Dissent from the Monetary Argument

Peter Hayes

Much of life often seems to be a matter of "two steps forward, one step back." The quest for compensation to victims of the Holocaust certainly has made great strides forward in the last decade. Billions of dollars have been extracted from the German and Austrian states and from European financial and industrial enterprises for the benefit of living survivors and, in some cases, their descendants. Along with these successes have come enormous increases in information about the complicity of officially neutral countries during World War II and of firms in the Axis or Axis-occupied nations. Italian, French, German, Swiss, and Austrian commissions have compiled multivolume accounts that delve exhaustively into such matters, and many well-known German corporations have granted historians unprecedented and unrestricted opportunities to scrutinize their records and publish the resulting analyses.[1] All who care about the victims of National Socialism and about putting the memory of the Holocaust to use for humankind have ample reason for satisfaction with much of what the clamor for full disclosure and justice has achieved.

Now that these victories have been won, however, the time has come to take stock of the collateral damage. For in this battle, as in most, emotion often has ruled the day. The result has been considerable harm to the cause of accurate historical understanding. In particular, the popular fixation on personal and corporate profits as a cause and consequence of the cruelties inflicted on European Jews strikes me as misplaced and misleading. Moreover, lawyers' insistence upon "disgorgement" of supposed earnings from exploitation as the appropriate form of compensation is both practically and morally problematic. The historical record indicates that persecution often did not redound greatly or lastingly to the material benefit of German enterprises, primarily because (1) the Nazi state contrived to take the bulk of what it extorted from Jews, including the proceeds of their labor, for its own purposes and (2) Hitler's war destroyed most of the gains firms obtained. Because basing claims for restitution on putative profits amounts to arguing from an often phantom premise, both lawyers and scholars need to find a sounder index of corporate liability for the Holocaust if we are to have any hope of the restitution settlements acting as meaningful precedents in the future.

I came to my thoughts on these subjects over the past six years, in the course of researching and writing a book on the German Gold and Silver Separation Institute (now known as Degussa, the acronym for the original German name).[2] In particular, I explored that enterprise's participation in four dimensions of Nazi criminality: (1) takeovers of some twenty-five pieces of Jewish-owned property through so-called Aryanization; (2) the refining, storing, and disbursing on commission of gold, silver, and platinum extorted or otherwise stolen in Germany and occupied Europe, including from Jews, indeed in some case from their corpses; (3) the exploitation of some six to ten thousand foreign, usually forced, laborers by the firm and its principal subsidiaries between 1940 and 1945, along with some three to four thousand camp and ghetto inmates (sometimes called "slave" laborers), of whom about 40 percent were Jews; and (4) the distribution, via a subsidiary called Degesch, of Zyklon B, the pesticide infamously used to asphyxiate about one million people at Auschwitz and Majdanek.

As I worked, I kept encountering a surprising discrepancy between my expectations and my evidence. On the one hand, many plaintiffs' lawyers in class action suits against German corporations were alleging something that seemed quite likely—that participation in the persecution of the Jews had been immensely profitable to German industry—and something that seemed at least plausible as a result—that a significant proportion of that industry's postwar prosperity is traceable to the plundering of the Jews. On the other hand, no one seemed to have strong statistics to back up these suppositions, and Degussa's records appeared to tell a very different story. I could trace a great deal of that corporation's earnings in the Nazi period and of its economic strength afterwards to the company's embrace of the Third Reich's policies of autarky and armament. From 1933 to 1944, Degussa's annual sales almost doubled, its total published assets almost tripled, and its cash reserves almost quadrupled. In 1946, after deductions for all of the firm's known losses as a result of the war (equal to almost $500 million today), Degussa was still worth three times as much as in 1925. Since the great bulk of the increases in sales and profits occurred after 1933 and stemmed from products the Nazis favored, there can be no doubt that Degussa's postwar prosperity *did* rest in substantial measure on money and know-how gained by cooperating with Hitlerian economics and aggression. I also could trace some of the firm's postwar earning power to several of the Aryanizations it conducted, but only to ones for which it also made substantial compensation or restitution payments after the war.

However, I could trace very little of Degussa's wealth during or after the Nazi period to its most glaring acts of complicity. Probably seven tons of Zyklon B were used at Auschwitz and Majdanek to kill people during the period 1942–44, for which the purchase price came to only about thirty-five thousand Reichsmarks (equal to some $140,000 today). Sixty percent of this sum went to the manufacturer and the retailer, neither of which belonged to Degussa. The remaining 40 percent, which is to say fourteen thousand Reichsmarks, was the Degesch subsidiary's cut as the patent holder on the substance, before deductions for overhead and taxes. Degussa's share of the residue would have been 42.5 percent, corresponding to its shareholding. In other words, even if all fourteen thousand Reichsmarks in revenue were turned into distributed profits, Degussa's earnings on killing over one million people would have come to 5,950 Reichsmarks or approximately $23,800 today. Even when one considers all Degesch's sales to the SS as a whole from 1942 to 1945 (approximately eighty-five tons of Zyklon B, primarily used to fumigate the organization's own barracks and those at concentration camps), Degussa's total resulting dividend cannot have exceeded 72,250 Reichsmarks or $289,000 in present-day U.S. currency.

Or, consider the proceeds on precious metals plundered from Jews and routed through Degussa's refineries, storehouses, and distribution offices. Two sets of numerical information exist on this. The first concerns the so-called *Judenmetallaktion* (Jew metal action) of 1938–39. During this vicious program, Jews in Germany, Austria, and the Sudetenland were compelled to surrender nearly all their possessions containing gold, silver, and platinum to the state-owned pawnshops and given rudimentary compensation, most of which the Nazi regime later confiscated one way or another. Degussa processed some seventy-two metric tons of the 130 metric tons of silver that the Reich had melted down as a result of these inflows (i.e., almost 56 percent) and some 1.2 of the 1.5 metric tons of gold (80 percent). By my calculations, the refining, holding, and resale fees that the firm earned from the Nazi state in this operation came to about 490,000 Reichsmarks or nearly $2 million today. But the profits were much less because of discounted smelting rates and storage fees for the government, coming to only about sixty thousand Reichsmarks or $240,000 today. Moreover, the sales and profits were not additional to what Degussa otherwise would have earned. For every ounce of Jewish gold and silver received by Degussa during the action, the government reduced the firm's other allocations in this completely state-rationed industry by the same amount.

As for what Degussa made from the gold and silver extracted from Jews all over Europe after World War II began, the data are more fragmentary. We may be reasonably sure that the total quantity of gold plundered by the Nazis during World War II reached 487 metric tons, of which the bulk came from state reserves and national banks and only about seventy-three metric tons from private firms and individuals. The surviving sources also warrant the strong inference that nearly all the gold and half the silver Degussa produced during the war years stemmed from plundered materials, that as much as 15 percent of the gold (five tons) and 5 percent (ninety tons) of the silver probably came from Jews, and that the firm's gross profits from all plundered metals were 14.6 million Reichsmarks and from those taken from Jews 1.97 million, which is to say $58.4 million and $7.9 million today. These are substantial sums, but again there is a complication. The victorious Allies seized without compensation at the end of the war precious metals from Degussa worth $16–20 million in today's values, one-third of the company's overall gains on theft, more than twice as much as what it reaped from the robbing of Jews. Finally, Degussa's gains at Jews' expense were relatively unimportant to the firm's long-term fortunes. The 1.97 million Reichsmarks in gross profits on metals taken from Jews came to 6.2 percent of what Degussa's precious metals division earned over the same period, and just over 1 percent of what the corporation did.

But, what of the proceeds of slave labor? The corporation used such individuals—defined as people whom it did not pay but for whom it paid the SS or a camp or ghetto administration—at four known installations: on the assembly lines at two gas mask factories of Degussa's wholly owned Auergesellschaft subsidiary at Oranienburg and Guben, both near Berlin;

on the construction site of a new, massive Central Works at Fürstenberg an der Oder (today called Eisenhüttenstadt); and on both building and operating a new carbon black factory at Gleiwitz that belonged to another Degussa offshoot, the Deutsche Gasrusswerke, in which Degussa held half the shares. At the Auergesellschaft factories, the slave laborers consisted of around twenty-five hundred mostly Slavic women from the Ravensbrück concentration camp, and they worked for some eight to ten months between the summer of 1944 and the end of the war. At Fürstenberg, the laborers were two hundred Jewish men from the Lodz ghetto, who arrived in late February 1942 and were transferred elsewhere about seven months later. At Gleiwitz, the number of laborers exploited was larger (fifteen hundred to two thousand), the duration longer (almost three years, from February 1942 to January 1945), and their origins different (nearly all were Jews, at first from Western Europe, then mostly from Upper Silesia, and finally from all points of the compass via Auschwitz). We do not know how many of the people at Fürstenberg died there or as a result. At the Auer plants, the toll appears to have been about three hundred. At Gleiwitz, my best estimate is that perhaps six hundred expired on the site or after being put in the infirmary, then shipped to Auschwitz.

Although each site clearly was the scene of criminal exploitation of human beings, none of the sites ultimately earned their owners a cent. The Auergesellschaft became so deeply indebted while struggling to keep up with the Reich's demand for gas masks that Degussa had recovered by 1944 only half of what it paid for the firm ten years earlier. Moreover, the subsidiary's plants were leveled by Allied bombers in early 1945; the Russians then captured and confiscated the company's cash reserves. In the end, the firm's ruins had to be almost completely written off, since they fell largely in the Soviet occupation zone. Fürstenberg was never finished and produced only a small quantity of formaldehyde in 1944. The plant represented a net loss of 25 million Reichsmarks to Degussa, since it too ended up in the German Democratic Republic. Gleiwitz was completed three months before being conquered by the Red Army, but had an accumulated operating loss at the time of 3 million Reichsmarks. Moreover, the construction had eaten up 11 million Reichsmarks in profits from a sister factory. Even had the installation not fallen to Poland in 1945, it would have been worthless to Degussa as a result of technological innovations a few months earlier that rendered it superfluous.

In this connection, I discovered something that is even more surprising:

so-called slave labor was relatively cheap to Degussa only when the workers, as in the case of the women at Oranienburg, Guben, and Gleiwitz,
were used on production lines. Because most women could adapt to the
work, it proceeded indoors and was not physically debilitating, and the
charges for them (e.g., fees to the SS, outlays for barracks and guards) were
a great deal less than wages for German male workers (and slightly less
than for German female ones), such slave laborers offered, in principle,
cost advantages. But matters were significantly different concerning the
far more numerous male slave laborers put to work on construction, for
which they were generally ill prepared, where the work was dangerous and
exhausting, and where corresponding German workers would have cost
the firms little, if any, more money than they paid out for barracks and
guards as well as to the SS for the inmates. In short, slave labor was not
always profitable even in the short run; its economic attraction was usually
availability, not price. Amidst the general German labor shortage, one
took the workers one could get, then tried to make doing so pay somehow.

   In other words, the more I explored Degussa's history under the Nazis,
the more I thought the firm had engaged in acts that extinguished or
gravely damaged the lives of many and for which it clearly "owed" at least
the survivors something, but that it had not made much money directly
from any of these deeds—indeed, it probably, in the aggregate, lost some. I
came to the conclusion that the contribution of the Holocaust to the prof-
itability of Degussa was not direct or immediate, but indirect and delayed.
Degussa processed metals seized from Jews, sold a pesticide used as poison
gas, and exploited slave labor to make products the regime wanted because performing such in-themselves-unlucrative tasks would protect its
market positions and might lead to more remunerative favors. Cooperation regarding plundered precious metals, for example, clearly smoothed
Degussa's path to government-authorized sales monopolies on various sil-
ver-based products during World War II. Asking no questions about the
SS's use of small quantities of Zyklon B produced quasi-official allocative
responsibilities for Degesch's leader, and thus enabled him to sell every
kilogram the company could make and to feel like a big shot. Accepting
slave laborers on Auer's assembly lines and the Fürstenberg and Gleiwitz
building sites was a way of proving that the firm was ready to do what had
to be done and thus should be, respectively, spared a government investigation of problems with its gas mask production, allowed to build its big
but militarily not very important Central Works, and permitted to retain
its monopoly on carbon black production. Yes, in the end, complicity was

about the money, but not simply about it, and not about the money derived from the Jews per se, at least in Degussa's case.

All that said, clearly the German state and firms like Degussa engaged in manifestly criminal activity, even by the standards of their own day. That is why many individuals and organizations recently have taken up the task that the U.S. government shirked after World War II, namely, extracting some recompense for those who suffered. We can hardly be surprised that lawyers in class action suits resorted to familiar legal concepts (conspiracy, profiteering, disgorgement) to deal with this challenge. Hyping the image of companies living high off the hog from monies stolen from helpless victims promised an enormous moral edge in court, and no other approach to computing corporate liability offered the prospect of comparably large settlements. How well the approach ultimately worked is open to question, however. If I understand the main settlements correctly, all were deals worked out in negotiations among plaintiffs, suspect firms, Jewish community organizations, and government representatives, not direct court judgments. And all produced financial obligations for the participating corporations that bear no discernable relationship to what each actually did in Nazi Germany or earned by virtue of doing so, as well as payouts to survivors that seldom approximate adequate compensation for what they lost. In other words, the argument from profits served as a club, not a measuring stick, and it was, at best, partially successful. In retrospect, it is hard to imagine how things could have been otherwise, since the American judicial system predictably shrank from the consequences of exacting retribution from German industry for nearly the same reasons that American strategists and occupation authorities did in the late 1940s, namely, the substantial harm that such a course would do to the economic and political interests of the United States.[3]

Still, "negotiated justice" is better than nothing, just as convicting Al Capone of income tax evasion was preferable to not punishing him at all.[4]

Now that incomplete compensation has been obtained from many complicit corporations, I hope we can stop distorting the historical realities. One of these is that few enterprises, German or otherwise, grew rich from the Holocaust. There are exceptions, but the general pattern is of criminal deeds and marginal, mostly fleeting gains. Perhaps if we talk less in the future about disgorgement of largely fictitious profits on extreme human suffering, we can talk more about finding a way for domestic and international courts to assess appropriate recompense for what really mattered: heartbreakingly huge and irreparable losses.

NOTES

1. See especially Harold James, *The Deutsche Bank and the Nazi Economic War against the Jews* (New York: Cambridge University Press, 2001); Gerald D. Feldman, *Allianz and the German Insurance Business, 1933–1945* (New York: Cambridge University Press, 2001); Stephan Lindner, *Inside I.G. Farben: Hoechst in the Third Reich* (New York: Cambridge University Press, 2005); and, for a good overview, Oliver Rathkolb, ed., *Revisiting the National Socialist Legacy* (Innsbruck: Studien Verlag, 2002).

2. Peter Hayes, *From Cooperation to Complicity: Degussa in the Third Reich* (New York: Cambridge University Press, 2004).

3. *See,* for example, Burger-Fischer v. Degussa AG, Civil Action No. 98-3958 (D.N.J, Sept. 10, 1999); and Vogel v. Degussa AG, Civil Action No. 98-5019, (D.N.J, Sept. 10, 1999). Judgments by Dickinson R. Debevoise.

4. The quoted phrase is from Elazar Barkan, *The Guilt of Nations* (New York: Norton, 2000).

Chapter 18

It's Not about the Money

A Survivor's Perspective on the German Foundation Initiative

Roman Kent

For more than two years—from the beginning of the German Foundation Initiative in 1998 to 2000—I was intimately involved in the intense negotiations with German government and German industry regarding compensation for survivors who had been slave or forced laborers during the Nazi era. Originally, the meetings were held in Bonn, but they were subsequently moved to Berlin, the new capital of a unified Germany.

Beside myself, the Jewish lay leadership delegation consisted of two additional survivors, Ben Meed and Noah Flug; and the staff of the Claims Conference was represented primarily by Gideon Taylor, Saul Kagan, Karl Brozik, and Karen Heilig. The negotiating team of the Claims Conference was chaired by Dr. Israel Singer. We were also accompanied by attorneys Stanley Chesley and Jean Geoppinger, who served as our legal advisors on a pro bono basis. The Israeli delegation was headed by Bobby Brown.

The Germans gave these negotiations an elaborate name. As if "German Foundation Initiative" was not enough, the foundation they eventually established to effectuate the settlement was called "Remembrance, Responsibility, and the Future." How ironic it was for the Germans to include the words "initiative," "remembrance," and "responsibility" in the heading of the negotiations when in fact the question of accountability was forced upon the Germans by demands of survivors linked to economic and legal actions, including class action suits. The "initiative" was about sixty years late!

As the negotiations progressed, it became clear in my mind why the German government and German industry chose to establish the Foundation and negotiate with us, namely, former Jewish slave laborers, as well as Eastern European governments representing primarily thousands of forced laborers. Facing survivors' demands and class action suits, Germany's objective was to create legal closure for outstanding problems and issues arising from the Nazi era. During the talks, it soon became evident from the sentiments expressed by representatives of German industry, headed by Dr. Manfred Gentz (the chief financial officer of DaimlerChrysler) and the representative of German government, Otto Graf Lambsdorff, that it was essential for the Germans to settle these matters once and for all. It was obvious that Germany sought to create goodwill not only with the United States but also with the Eastern European countries since they had now become an important and substantial market for German goods.

With time, I also realized that the basis for these negotiations on the part of the Germans, as well as the great majority of class action lawyers, was not founded on moral and humanitarian purposes. It was strictly business. For the Germans it was legal closure; for the lawyers who had filed the class action lawsuits against the German companies, it was millions of dollars in fees. In spite of this, I saw the prospect of utilizing the opportunity at hand to bring some relief to needy survivors in Eastern European countries as well as Jewish Holocaust survivors throughout the world.

In addition, from a historical point of view, there was something more important to be gained. The negotiations would bring official exposure and acknowledgment of the evil acts perpetrated by Germans against humankind. They would prove the direct, large-scale involvement of German industry at large. Thus the negotiations would show beyond a shadow of a doubt that not only Hitler and the Nazis were responsible for the atrocities, as the Germans wanted the world to believe, but the totality of the German nation was also responsible.

Unlike a usual legal case that consists only of two parties, namely, a defendant and a plaintiff, these negotiations became much more complicated because of the number of parties involved. The first party was the German government and German industry with their respective lawyers; the second party was Eastern European countries with their representatives and their attorneys; the third party was the representatives of the Jewish organizations under the umbrella of the Claims Conference; and the fourth party consisted of scores of class action attorneys. With each party having a different agenda and interests, the negotiations were difficult, to say the least. As the negotiations dragged on, it became more and more obvious to all parties that the German government, particularly German industry, literally wanted to resolve the matter for "peanuts." On the other hand, the opposite extreme was expressed by the rapacious lawyers who demanded exorbitant amounts of money to justify their anticipated multi-billion-dollar settlements. Sadly, the only legitimate voices representing morality and ethics in these negotiations were ours, the survivors'. In fact, in witnessing the situation unfolding before us, with the full approval of the survivors on the negotiating team, I put on the table two conditions that would not be subject to negotiation, and without which no agreement would be accepted by us.

1. There must be a full and sincere apology on the part of German government and German industry for the crimes they committed during the Holocaust.
2. Slave and forced laborers will be referred to only by name; under no circumstances will they be denoted by numbers as we were referred to in the concentration camps.

The negotiations were chaired by high-ranking representatives of the U.S. and German governments. Representing the American side was Stuart Eizenstat, deputy secretary of the Treasury. On the German side was Minister Bodo Hombach, later replaced by Otto Graf Lambsdorff, representing Chancellor Gerhard Schroeder. I developed a good rapport with Minister Hombach and was indeed sorry when he was replaced by Otto Lambsdorff. To my mind, Mr. Lambsdorff's attitude brought a completely different atmosphere to the negotiations, one that was more antagonistic and confrontational. One of the most difficult meetings, if not the most difficult, occurred when a well-known German historian, Professor Lutz Niethammer, was called in to express his opinion and provide statistical information about the slave labor situation prevailing in German industry during the Holocaust. To me, his testimony was more than distasteful. The way I understood his testimony, we, the Jewish slave workers, should be thankful that German industry employed us, since at least this employment afforded us ninety days' grace time before we were condemned to die through "Tod Durch Arbeit," the bestial "death through work" program devised by the Germans.

This was the one and only time when I really lost my temper during negotiations. In my opinion, the German motto "death through work" was the most brutal form of exploitation of human beings, including slavery, ever undertaken by humankind.

An additional complication we faced was brought about by the fact that the Jewish side and the class action lawyers negotiated primarily on behalf of slave laborers, and the Eastern European countries and their lawyers negotiated primarily for forced laborers (who were not in concentration camps), with the exception of attorney Michael Hausfeld, who somehow had both slave and forced laborers as clients.

The situation came to a head when negotiations with the Germans were going to result in one lump-sum payment to be divided among all categories. The Eastern European governments and their lawyers wanted to distribute the same amount of money for forced laborers as was to be provided for slave laborers. In effect, they preferred that there be no distinction between slave and forced labor.

Our point was a strong one, and I believe totally valid and just. It was more than imperative that a distinction be made between forced and slave labor. It was the Jewish slave laborer who was actually condemned to death, and maybe only 10 percent or so survived the inhuman conditions prevailing in the concentration camps. On the other hand, the forced laborers did not experience as severe treatment, and practically all survived. Thus, we claimed that a ratio of compensation must be established to differentiate between slave and forced labor and to acknowledge the inhuman conditions suffered by the farmer.

The situation at hand totally divided the Jewish and Eastern European sides, and it soon became a critical issue. When this topic came to a head at the first negotiating meeting in the U.S. Embassy in Berlin, I approached Stuart Eizenstat with an idea that only delegates should meet face to face, without lawyers being present. I asked Mr. Eizenstat to start the proceedings on this basis, and he agreed. When Mr. Eizenstat asked that all lawyers and individuals who were not actual members of delegations leave the room, I noticed that there was still an attorney present in the Polish delegation, Michael Hausfeld.

I brought this to Mr. Eizenstat's attention, and he did ask Mr. Hausfeld to leave. At that point, Mr. Hausfeld had a hushed discussion with the Polish delegation. When their talk concluded, the head of the Polish contingent stated that Mr. Hausfeld was now an official member of the delegation, and as such, he could remain in the room.

I did not approve of this but had no recourse. I then addressed the Eastern European delegation directly:

We Jews were the main victims of the Nazi regime, simply for being Jewish, as evidenced by the six million of us who perished. It is equally true that each of your countries also became victims of the Nazi regime, and millions of you perished as well.

Thus, in a way, both of us were victims of the Nazis. As such, I want to state clearly and emphatically that we, the Jewish survivors, will not be a party to a fight between us, both victims of Nazism, while the Germans throw some scraps with the intent to divide us and then sit laughing on the sidelines as they watch us fight.

At this moment, I cannot say definitely what the situation is in Russia, the Ukraine, and the other Eastern European countries. However, I can say what is happening in Poland, since I have received copies of articles appearing in Polish newspapers which are clearly anti-Semitic in nature and contrary to the actual facts. You, the Polish delegation, must be aware of the articles to which I refer that plainly indicate Jews are grabbing billions of dollars in compensation from the Germans.

Therefore, I address you, the Polish delegation, and ask how dare you let these factual lies exist? It should be your moral obligation to defend the truth of the situation! Shame on you when you know that only approximately 25 percent of the money in question would be distributed to Jews, while the balance will be divided among gentiles.

Furthermore, it is we, the Jewish side, who stated that there be no distinction between Polish and Jewish slave laborers or Polish and Jewish forced laborers. Also, it is we, the Jewish side, who spearheaded the fight for some semblance of justice. If we in this room do not harmoniously make the distinction between forced and slave labor, we are not worthy of being part of the negotiating team.

I was immediately supported on this issue by Israel Singer, and I strongly believe that this issue was diffused by the above statements. Regretfully, the same subject was indirectly addressed again later by Mr. Hausfeld, who, representing the Eastern European countries, wanted a larger share of money for the majority of his clients, the forced laborers.

As I perceived it, in order to accomplish this, Mr. Hausfeld subtly tried to equalize slave and forced labor by placing a slash between them in some of the documents he presented at the meeting. Considering whom he represented, I did not hesitate to chastise him for this. I also felt that Mr. Hausfeld had a conflict of interest in representing two different classes of clients, the slave laborers and the forced laborers, both of which were seeking the largest amount for themselves from a limited pool of available funds.

Incidents such as this are indicative of the problems we survivors faced in defending and protecting the sacred memory of the six million who perished.

Inevitably, fights ensued between the lawyers and the Germans. At issue was the total cost of the settlement, and the fixed assignment of money for each category and country. We survivors feared that such infighting would ultimately leave a lasting impression that all the survivors were interested in was money. During these meetings, I could not help but see most of the lawyers as vultures, sitting atop tree branches just waiting for their spoils. In retrospect, we survivors actually had three adversaries to contend with —the Germans, the Eastern Europeans with their insistence on a larger share for the forced laborers, and the lawyers.

The one calming force prevailing throughout these tedious, lengthy negotiations was the presence of Stuart Eizenstat. When presented with totally opposing points of view, he was always instrumental in bringing the issue to a more positive, less confrontational conclusion.

On one occasion, and one occasion only, I did see Mr. Eizenstat "blow a fuse." This happened at what was supposed to have been a closed negotiation meeting, just between the German and Jewish sides. Mr. Lambsdorff and Dr. Gentz opened the meeting by telling us that they were presenting us with a "take it or leave it" offer, and therefore no further negotiations would be needed.

This infuriated Mr. Eizenstat, and he shouted angrily, "To hear this, we did not have to travel from the United States to Germany for negotiations, when, in fact, you are telling us that there will be no negotiations." The Germans were taken aback. They did not expect such an explosion from the always calm Mr. Eizenstat. At that point, Gentz and Lambsdorff privately consulted with each other, and shortly thereafter, the negotiations continued.

Eventually, the negotiations reached a stage where to me they seemed like a "three-ring circus." This situation created the need to finalize the agreement without delay, and Mr. Lambsdorff lost no time in seizing the opportunity to attempt to include some new issues in the scope of the agreement. He now wanted to incorporate closure for matters concerning German insurance, an issue that had not been discussed previously and that had no place in the slave and forced labor agreement.

To put it bluntly, I did not take kindly to his proposal. As far as I was concerned, insurance and even banking problems had nothing to do with slave and forced labor issues. I voiced my opinion that for us to agree to include insurance companies in our agreement would be totally uncalled for and a mistake.

This was particularly true in view of the fact that the International Commission on Holocaust-Era Insurance Claims (ICHEIC) had previously been established, and Allianz, the largest German insurance company, was a signatory to ICHEIC. As a member of ICHEIC, Allianz would have to adhere to the rules and regulations of the commission and be held accountable to it, rather than to this new entity the Germans were in the process of creating that had nothing to do with insurance.

Unfortunately, I stood alone, and my position did not prevail. This was largely due to the fact that Mr. Lambsdorff loudly stated that if the German insurance companies were not included in the Foundation agreement, he could not provide the DM 10 billion to which the German government agreed. Sadly, this position was supported by Stuart Eizenstat and by the lawyers.

Thus, with great fanfare, the agreement providing some measure of compensation to slave and forced laborers for the work they performed during the Holocaust was signed. To emphasize the importance of the agreement, an official ceremony was staged in the Presidential Palace in Berlin on December 17, 1999.

On this momentous occasion, President Johannes Rau officially and solemnly acknowledged the guilt of the Germans during the Holocaust when he stated the following: "I know that for many it is not really money that matters. What they [survivors] want is for their suffering to be recognized as suffering, and for the injustices done to them to be named injustices. I pay tribute to all who were subjected to slave and forced labor under German rule and, in the name of the German people, beg forgiveness."

There I stood in the Presidential Palace, visualizing my life sixty years earlier in the ghetto and concentration camps. Thinking back and reliving this horrific time of my life, I felt compelled to reply to President Rau's statement. Here are excerpts from my reply:

From the very beginning, we survivors fought for and stressed the moral issues and tragedies of the Holocaust, not only for us as Jews but for the world at large. Even today the unimaginable damage caused by the Holocaust cannot be fully comprehended. One and a half million Jewish children were killed; no, not killed, brutally murdered.

Sixty years ago, I, too, was a child. I was one of the few who survived. Thus, the moral issues and historical justice are what we survivors fought for.

The remarks that have been made here today, and the ones made by you, President Rau, justify the efforts we have made concerning morality, and morality only. . . .

The official signing of the agreement took place in Berlin on July 17, 2000. Under the circumstances, I don't know if one can really call it a privilege and honor, but rather a duty and obligation, that I was asked to attend the signing and represent the community of Jewish Holocaust survivors. Thus, it fell upon me to make a closing statement in the name of survivors, parts of which I share with you now:

As I stand here today, there are two very painful questions in my mind. . . . Why did the Holocaust happen, and secondly, why did it take until the year 2000 to officially recognize the "death through work" bestiality and establish the Foundation?

Let me, a survivor, a slave laborer condemned to "death through work" by the Germans, share with you my simple explanations. The Holocaust is the most tragic example of what can happen when prejudice and hate reign and people follow. By people, I do not mean just the Nazis, soldiers, or guards in the concentration camps. I mean the engineers, the draftsmen, the doctors, the chemists, the scientists, the businessmen, the politicians, and yes the lawyers who legalized it . . . all of whom devoted their energies to create the most efficient means of mass destruction of the Jewish community.

As to the Foundation, well, why call it "initiative" when in actuality the need for accountability for slave and forced labor, both Jewish and non-Jewish, was brought about by the recent demands of survivors linked with economic and legal issues. But to my way of thinking, it was possible to establish the Foundation because in a way Germany entered a new era . . . an era when the new generation born after the war realized the magnitude of the destruction brought forth by their forefathers and understood that Auschwitz, Treblinka and "death through work" acquired a meaning of their own since they represent evil, the worst that mankind can offer.

This Foundation, approved by approximately 90 percent of the Bundestag, is the conscience of the new generation. Yes, it was enacted sixty years late and is only a token gesture to financially compensate the slave and forced labor. But it is the moral recognition for past wrongs, and we survivors take it as such. I and the other survivors associated with the negotiations did not speak about money. How could we? The lives of one and a half million Jewish children are priceless. We will never equate morality and ethics in terms of dollars and cents. We only stress morality; this is our sacred duty. . . .

I have hope that you, the new German generation, by this acknowledgment of your moral responsibility will follow in our footsteps. If the Foundation is to have any meaning for the future, the terrible lesson of the Holocaust must be understood in your land and throughout the world so that the Holocaust can never happen again to us or to any other people.

When I completed my remarks, a great round of spontaneous applause brought me back to the paradox of the present reality. After all, I was standing in a historic building that had been the former headquarters of the Reichsbank (the Nazi central bank) during the war. This was the very same bank that was responsible for the gold transactions involving melting of gold teeth, rings, and other miscellaneous jewelry of the victims. I felt utterly drained. With perspiration flowing from my body, I was suddenly surrounded and embraced by a number of friends and dignitaries, both members of the delegation as well as Germans. At that moment, I did not fully understand whether this outpouring of attention was due to my having happened to be the last speaker, or to the fact that my remarks made such an emotional and meaningful impression on the audience. I hoped that it was the latter.

There I was, one lone survivor speaking, with the responsibility of representing the six million Jews who were murdered during the Holocaust as well as the small percentage of us who survived. I knew that I and the other survivors who participated in these negotiations stood steadfast in our determination to make these negotiations more than just a fight with the Germans, who basically had legal closure in mind. In essence, I was more than serene that we had accomplished almost the impossible. For President Rau in the Presidential Palace, and the Bundestag (the German parliament) in its preamble documenting the establishment of the German Foundation, at long last finally acknowledged "the moral and historical responsibility for the injustices that had been committed under German rule."

Mentally, my participation in the German Foundation Initiative was very difficult to endure. What brought me some solace, however, was knowing that tens of thousands of survivors received a small form of justice, imperfect as it was, toward the end of their lives. After all, in the long run, the monetary settlement, so reluctantly given by the German government and German industry, will become merely a footnote in history. However, the meaningful words of President Rau and those inscribed by the Bundestag will live forever as a moral victory. Thus, with such admission of guilt on behalf of the entire German population, history had now been accurately documented.

Chapter 19

Germany's Reexamination of Its Past through the Lens of the Holocaust Litigation

Deborah Sturman

Those familiar with Germany in 1996, when the Holocaust litigation began, would agree that it was no surprise that most Germans experienced some *schadenfreude* at seeing the Swiss and their banks brought to task for their World War II activities. The Swiss litigation provided at least a momentary diversion from Germany's decades-long introspection about the horror and evil that is its own World War II history. The diversion was all but forgotten less than two years later, in March 1998, when Germany's former World War II slave laborers filed suit in U.S. courts against Germany's largest and most respected corporations, seeking compensation for having been brutally exploited by them during the war.

The slave labor and accompanying litigation concerning the "Aryanization," or wartime theft, of Jewish property, were front page news in Germany from the moment of their inception until they were resolved two years later by the establishment in 2000 of the settlement foundation "Remembrance, Responsibility, and the Future" ("the Foundation"). There are a number of reasons why Holocaust litigation in U.S. courts produced such an intense interest among the German public. Not only was there a real fear that the cases would have potentially meaningful economic consequences on German industry; there was also a moral fear that made Germany's industry, government, and media struggle with the issues raised and memories stirred by the cases.

The combination of the highly sensitive issues that were the subject of the claims and the fact that they were heard by American courts (which most Germans viewed as wildly unpredictable) helped sensationalize the coverage. The cases precipitated a nationwide discussion about the wide-spread use of slave labor during World War II (virtually every business and most farms had used slave labor), the practice of "Aryanization," and, most profoundly, that "ordinary" Germans both participated in the development and execution of those policies and derived their benefits. That debate helped shatter the widely accepted myth that only a small number of senior Nazis bore responsibility for the crimes of the Third Reich.

The slave labor litigation descended on a Germany that to this day continues to be deeply troubled and gripped by World War II and the Holocaust. In many ways, World War II is a centrifugal force around which much of German public life rotates. Public discourse about the Nazis and World War II has always been intense and continuous, but most delicate topics, such as the involvement of the "ordinary" German, that is, the vast majority of the German (and Austrian) people, in both the prosecution of the war and the crimes committed against the victims of the Holocaust were for decades painstakingly avoided. Similarly, Germany's foreign affairs are carefully designed to avoid igniting still smoldering foreign sensitivities. Before sending troops to Bosnia in 1997, for example, German foreign minister Klaus Kinkel quietly made sure that the Allies would not object to Germany sending its troops outside its borders for the first time since World War II. Once NATO agreed to the deployment, Kinkel proudly hailed NATO's consent as signaling the end of Germany's "special role" as a country held back by its Nazi past.

Public discourse about the war has carefully distinguished between "ordinary (World War II–era) Germans," who, it is believed, cannot be held accountable, and the handful of recognized "Nazis" who, so the argument goes, bear all responsibility. Hitler's closest collaborators are, more often than not, depicted as not quite real or human. They are frequently portrayed as extraordinary symbols of wickedness, which relieves others of responsibility for the evildoers' conduct. Only relatively recently have broad segments of the German public, inspired by Hannah Arendt's examination of the "banality of evil,"[1] begun to examine Nazi leaders as real human beings,[2] and only recently has there been a corresponding public examination of "ordinary" Germans' roles in the war and the Holocaust.

The class actions brought to the fore that the participation or, at least, the acquiescence of "ordinary" Germans—now Germany's elderly—was an integral element of the operation of the Third Reich. They also brought to public awareness the charge that the successor generations' inheritance was derived, at least in part, from profits accrued through the use of slave labor and "Aryanization."

The views of Germans about World War II and the Holocaust generally fall into three generational categories. The elderly, who were participants in the war, generally agree that they acquiesced in the activities of the Nazis and helped them do what they wanted. They tend to say, however, that they did not realize the enormous implications of what they were doing, nor, most of them allege, were they aware of just how genocidal the regime was that they served. They are more likely to focus on their inability to have affected or controlled wartime events ("I was following orders"). Their children, mostly in their fifties and sixties, place the blame squarely on "the Nazis," the ill-defined, very small group of Hitler's ringleaders who allegedly were solely responsible. The most recent generation tends to take a less defensive view, accepting the fact that World War II and the Holocaust could not have taken place without widespread public support. That view occasionally, but disturbingly, takes the tack that the widespread support of Hitler was justified, for any number of reasons: the unfairness of the Treaty of Versailles, Stalin's supposed planned attack on Germany, or the Jews' alleged undue wealth, to name a few.

These positions are very difficult to accept. For while there was some resistance, the Germans not only elected Hitler, but they also supported his actions. The German armed forces, for reasons that seemed valid to them at the time, overran Poland and committed genocide on the Slavs, largely because they were thoroughly convinced of Aryan racial superiority. Moreover, the Holocaust required massive civilian and military cooperation. It was impossible to live in Germany between 1933 and 1945 and not witness the mistreatment of the Jews, the seizure of their property, and their deportation to "labor camps," even if the details of the gas chambers were not widely known until late in the war.

Although average Germans' discomfort with their World War II history decisively influences public discourse and Germany's foreign (and to some extent, domestic) policy, the German willingness to defend against war-related accusations and to obscure reminders of the period increases from generation to generation, as the chronological distance from the war grows and the numbers of Germans who actually witnessed it steadily decreases. As the war becomes ever more distant, Germans become more readily willing to disregard (or at least consider resolved) the crimes of the war and the Holocaust and instead focus on the Allies' wartime and postwar excesses. Complaints about the bombing of Dresden, the abuse of German women by Soviet soldiers, the late repatriation of West Geman POWs (some were held in Russian gulags through the mid-1950s), and the postwar expulsion of German nationals from Silesia and the Sudetes (areas lost to Germany at World War II's end) have, in recent years, increased markedly in frequency and volume.

Concurrent with the Holocaust litigation's approaching settlement in 1999, public discussion about German wartime suffering began to appear more frequently in the German media, something that would have been unthinkable even a few years earlier. The German public began to vocalize demands for compensation for, among others, German POWs who had labored as slaves in Siberian gulags. Those demands appeared in various forms, for example, in letters to the editors of German newspapers. Demands for restitution of land that now belongs to Poland and the Czech Republic were made by Germany's "refugee" organizations, organizations of Germans who had been expelled from the Sudetes and Silesia after the war.

By 2001, "refugee" organizations that had existed since the end of the war started to make headlines, became more forceful, and were suddenly viewed more seriously by the public. At that point, their demands were no longer considered quaint and hopeless; they came to be seen as realistic, not only because the fall of the Iron Curtain made property restitution in the East possible but also because of a growing sense of the inherent justness of their claims, which, incidentally, contributed significantly to the souring of relations between Germany and Poland and the Czech Republic, then European Union candidates.

In 2001 and 2002, novels and histories about the suffering of German refugees at the end of the war and the Allies' devastating bombing raids became bestsellers. Germany's Nobel Prize–winning novelist Günter Grass wrote the highly acclaimed novel *Crabwalk,* depicting the war's traumatic effect on three generations of a German family. Questions such as "what about German suffering?" became pervasive, more so than at any time since the early 1950s.

Thus, as the Holocaust litigation and the discussion precipitated by it were coming to an end, many Germans hopefully concluded that the establishment of the Foundation would, once and for all, put an end to World War II victims' demands and permit the discussion of German suffering to begin in earnest. The law enacting the Foundation referred to its funding as the "final" payment. What was meant to refer to a final economic payment was widely accepted as also including the last moral installment to Germany's World War II victims. Implicit (and at times explicit) was the understanding that they (the Jews) had gotten enough. This evolution in the discussion of shameful wartime events was fueled in part by the realization that the chapter on World War II restitution was being closed, forever, and the book on German losses probably would be closed correspondingly, unless vocal demands were made to keep that side of the ledger open.[3] The need to achieve a sense of finality with the demands of the victims was driven in part by the desire of the generation born during and shortly after the war to be able to address their own traumas and experiences, or indeed, even to openly mourn their own wartime dead.[4]

The public sentiment that enough had been said about (and paid for) Jewish suffering was illustrated by an unexpected and, in context, wholly gratuitous statement by the highly regarded German intellectual and novelist Martin Walser. When accepting the German book dealers association's 1998 "Peace Prize" in the midst of the slave labor debate, Walser, whose writing had never involved World War II or the Holocaust, surprisingly announced that the Jews (it was understood) should no longer use Auschwitz "as an always available means of intimidation or as a moral cudgel"[5] against the Germans. The slave labor debate thus appeared to have touched a sensitive nerve, instigating a months-long public debate between Walser and the late Ignatz Bubis, head of the Central Council of Jews in Germany, a ghetto and concentration camp survivor. That sentiment had been heard before, for example, in the 1980s, when minister president of Bavaria Franz Josef Strauss once publicly proclaimed that "a nation that has built an economy as strong as ours has a right not to hear about Auschwitz anymore."

Incidents like this were only possible given the generational shifts in attitudes towards the war. With each successive generation having a less personal relationship to, or first-hand knowledge of, the war and its participants, Germany's willingness to assume either moral or economic responsibility towards the victims has declined. It should come as no surprise, therefore, that the term *"Vergangenheitsbewältigung"* (coming to terms with the past, a not too subtle reference to World War II) was recently nominated as the most beautiful word in the German language. It says much about Germany's successful postwar introspection that a process once too painful to contemplate is now a subject of celebration.

Among the underlying causes of the visceral public response to the

Holocaust litigation was that it brought three very delicate subjects squarely into the spotlight.

First, with the collapse of the Berlin Wall, West Germany (with four times the population of East Germany) controlled the reunited nation's cash and productivity, and thus, the future of East Germany. West Germany became the center of all authority over East Germany. Its government had a moral legitimacy that the East Germans' government did not have, and it was the strength of the West German economy that permitted the absorption of and provision of welfare to the bankrupt East Germany. West German regulators demanded the professional reeducation of former East Germans (somewhat controversially), and the West German media took it upon itself to reeducate East Germans about World War II and communism. (The East German party line had been that its president, Erich Honecker, and his functionaries were heroes of antifascism, having liberated Germany from the Nazis. In the East, the Berlin Wall was the "Anti-Fascist Protection Wall.") West Germany's moral authority permitted it to provide the East Germans with, in addition to a government and legal system, its accepted historical view of World War II, namely, that a discrete number of Nazi functionaries were solely responsible for the horrors and evils of the Third Reich.

West Germany asserted its moral authority, rather heavy-handedly, by criminally prosecuting leading East German functionaries and politicians. One such case was against Erich Mielke, East Germany's much feared and widely despised minister for State Security, the secret service of East Germany, from 1957 through the fall of the Berlin Wall. In 1931, Mielke, as a young Communist, had shot and killed two Nazi Party functionaries. Mielke was heralded as a hero of antifascism in East Germany. Sixty-two years later, after the collapse of East Germany, the West Germans charged Mielke with, among other things, the 1931 murders.[6] He was imprisoned in West Berlin until the age of eighty-seven, when his failing health and descent into senility (he reportedly spent hours on end talking on an unconnected telephone in his cell) prevented continuation of the proceedings against him.

To this churning and somewhat unstable environment was added the stimulant of the Holocaust litigation. The lawsuits' internationally disseminated accusations that West Germany and its industry had both profiteered from slave labor and Aryanization and avoided responsibility for doing so for over fifty years threatened to shake the foundation of the West's assumed moral authority.

Second, as the litigation alleged, and reports such as the Volcker Report on the Swiss banks' illegitimate World War II activities confirmed, World War II was big business, and for fifty years, German industry had been able to keep and reinvest massive amounts of seized assets and profits accrued from the use of slave labor. Although the Allies had briefly taken control of Germany's assets in the first years after the war, the political exigencies of the Cold War resulted in the 1952 London Agreement on German External Debt and certain other treaties that quickly restored control of the assets to German industry and protected it from victims' claims. With that, Germany and its industry were able to begin peacetime production with state-of-the-art factories, a tight web of industrial relationships, and no threat of liability to the laborers that had helped make that possible. Their claims had been quietly swept under the rug of larger geopolitical issues.

Fortunes amassed through slave labor and Aryanization were among the fundamental elements that allowed Germany to become the political and economic power it quickly became. Volkswagen's headquarters and main factory, still in use today, for example, were built almost entirely by slave labor. Not only was slave labor instrumental in maintaining wartime industrial productivity; it also permitted extensive investment in production machinery that was dragged to safety from Allied bombings (at great cost in slaves' lives) to *Autobahn* tunnels and underground factories (dug and built by concentration camp prisoners). Apart from these direct material benefits, the economy of West Germany also derived significant indirect benefits from the massive modernization in management and production methods that had been achieved during the wartime experiences, as well as by the tight web of business relationships created by the war effort. These were among the most important legacies of Hitler's *Volksgemeinschaft,* the racially pure community of "Aryans." The 1950s economic miracle, of which postwar Germans are so proud, was thus deeply rooted in benefits accrued during the war, largely through universally condemned practices.

Finally, Germany's local and national importance had become threatened by the post–Iron Curtain regional reconfiguration. With the Iron Curtain gone, and the Soviet satellites having regained their place as independent countries, the demands for economic compensation could have threatened Germany's thus far successful efforts at keeping its Eastern World War II victims at bay. Compensation paid (by the German government, never before by industry) to the Third Reich's victims amounted to only a small fraction of the profits made through slave labor and Aryanization. Given the postwar collapse of the German government and the uncertainties of the early years of occupation, no one expected full restitution to all of Germany's victims. Nonetheless, successful Holocaust litigation in the United States would include demands by Eastern Europeans. The only practical judicial forum in which Eastern Europeans could bring suit, given the virtually insurmountable procedural and economic hurdles that exist in Europe's civil law systems, was the United States. Moral and political pressure from Eastern Europe was escalating. If the demands made in the United States were indeed successful, Germany would have been pressed to provide meaningful compensation to the newly independent Soviet satellites.

Given the dangers posed by the litigation, German industry, with the full support of its government, deployed its full media and diplomatic power to crush the lawsuits, something the German Industrial Foundation Initiative (an organization formed by twelve leading German corporations to circumvent the lawsuits after the first suits were filed) hoped to achieve quickly and decisively. The possible emergence in U.S. courts of successful lawsuits brought by German industry's victims threatened to become a significant economic challenge, certainly the largest facing German industry in terms of demands for restitution since the formation of the federal republic in 1949. The lawsuits demanded compensation for labor performed, restitution of bank accounts and unpaid insurance policies, and full restoration of stolen property, along with whatever interest had accrued over fifty years. Since earlier restitution programs were largely limited to German real estate (there was never compensation paid for any property, real or other, located outside of Germany) and only provided modest compensation to a limited number of people for injuries sustained in concentration camps, the demands, if successful, could have amounted to enormous sums of money.

That explains why German industry fought back with all its might. Since disparagement of the victims was hardly acceptable (although there was some denouncement of the Jewish victims' "never ending demand for money"), the American lawyers and their lawsuits became the central focus of German industry and the German government's wrath. It became a battle between adversarial goliaths. Each had a strategy. Germany and its representative industrialists were determined to put an end to all legal claims and in a way that they, and not the American lawyers, wanted. The

American lawyers and their clients, for their part, were equally determined not to allow an entirely diplomatic resolution that was likely to end in wholly unsatisfactory compensation to the victims and would fail to reflect the moral, economic, and emotional concerns of the victims.

Settlement negotiations commenced under the auspices of the German and U.S. governments, shortly after the establishment of the "Foundation Initiative," which hoped that its unilateral promise to compensate a limited number of World War II slave laborers would create the basis for a wholly diplomatic solution, without the participation of the American lawyers and their clients. The American lawyers nonetheless were invited to participate in the negotiations, and became the wild card in them. When two New Jersey district courts dismissed the first two slave labor cases, the Germans naturally thought they had escaped the worst. But the massive ad campaign, with its pointed reminders of the ugliness of the Third Reich, initiated by my colleague Mel Weiss, caused more trouble for the Germans, as did the uncertainty presented by the appeals of the dismissed cases. German industry was not out of the woods yet.

In the end, the compensation offered to the Holocaust victims by the Foundation, which settled the lawsuits, is in sharp contrast to the economic value provided by the slave laborers' involuntary efforts, and even in sharper contrast to the value of the misappropriated property. The assertion made even before the late 1990s litigation, that Germany already had adequately compensated its victims, has always has been wide of the mark, as is the assertion that the compensation provided by the Foundation was satisfactory. In fact, before receiving the payments made by the Foundation, most of Germany's World War II slave laborers had received no compensation at all. Equally bizarre is German industry's claim that its contributions were substantial. German industry not only received massive tax breaks (approximately 40 percent of industry's contributions were fully deductible and were awarded well before they were made), but, we were told, those payments amounted on average to 0.01 percent of a company's annual revenue, hardly noticeable on the bottom line. The seventeen large corporations that negotiated on behalf of German industry have never provided an accounting for their contributions to the Foundation. One can only surmise that of the approximately $2.5 billion German industry agreed to raise, only a fraction was paid by Germany's largest and most culpable corporations. A portion of German industry's contribution was paid by well-meaning individual contributors, who presumably did not realize that their contributions were being directed not to compensate former slave laborers but to subsidizing German industry's contribution to the Foundation.

Viewed positively, the Holocaust litigation did provide some compensation to the victims, gave rise to the first apology to the victims of Nazi persecution by a leading German statesman,[7] and significantly promoted Germany's postwar introspection. By shedding light on German industry's wartime conduct and obliging people to face the reality of the profiteering that was the inevitable byproduct of slave labor and Aryanization, it contributed to Germany's ongoing catharsis, perhaps helping it come closer to a conclusion. For the survivors' and succeeding generations, the litigation also afforded a modicum of satisfaction, both financial and in terms of the "Remembrance" referred to in the foundation's name.

Irrespective of the existing difficulty most Germans have in facing the crimes of the Third Reich, it is not too soon to show Germans some magnanimity. They must, however, not be allowed to sanitize—still less forget —their World War II history. Germans must always remember that their nation, inventor of the printing press, famous for its music, literature, art, science, and industry, committed the Holocaust, the atrocity that remains the defining evil of the modern age. The Germans should continue to be challenged about their nation's zealous participation in those crimes, but not constantly castigated. The significance of the Holocaust to Germany must go beyond *Vergangenheitsbewältigung* (coming to terms with its past). The Germans must ultimately be able to embrace, as has the Western world, the impetus that the Holocaust has provided for some of the most important political and ethical decisions taken since.

NOTES

1. Hannah Arendt used the term "banality of evil" in describing Adolf Eichmann's 1961 trial for genocide in Jerusalem. Her thesis is that participants in genocide would, more often than not, represent an ordinary cross-section of people, most of whom would successfully pass any standard set of psychological screening tests. See Hannah Arendt, *Eichmann in Jerusalem: A Report on the Banality of Evil* (1993).

2. Germany had, as early as the 1960s, produced a number of courageous historians and institutions, including the Institut für Zeitgeschichte, led by Professor Martin Broszat, which wrote expert opinions for Holocaust victims' use in German courts. The 1980s gave rise to historians such as Ulrich Herbert and Norbert

Frei, who researched the average German's role in World War II. Nevertheless, it took the Holocaust litigation to bring their work to broad public attention.

3. Germany has always provided generous pensions to its World War II veterans, their widows, and even Lithuanians who supported the war effort, irrespective of their degree of culpability. The pensions are considerably more generous than any pension received by Holocaust survivors, whose eligibility for compensation requires that they both survived at least twelve months in a concentration camp (where life expectancy averaged around six months) or eighteen months in a ghetto (with similarly reduced life expectancy rates) and suffered a measurable disability. Generous land grant plans were also established to aid German refugees from Silesia and the Sudetes.

4. It was only in 2004 that Chancellor Gerhard Schröder visited his father's wartime grave in Romania.

5. Book Dealers Peace Prize 1998, Martin Walser. Acceptance Speech.

6. Mielke's 1993 prosecution for the 1931 murders followed four years of unsuccessful attempts by the West Germans to prosecute Mielke for a number of more recent events for which he was probably culpable.

7. As part of the ceremony commemorating the Berlin Accords, President Rau offered Germany's first formal apology to its World War II victims.

Chapter 20

Austria Confronts Her Past

Hannah Lessing and Fiorentina Azizi

Introduction

To understand Austria's attempts to confront her past and face responsibility for acts of persecution perpetrated during the Nationalist Socialist regime, we need first to ask whether compensation measures are an integral part of this process and, more specifically, what the meaning of "compensation" could possibly be in this context. In fact, a legal and an ethical interpretation could be given to the idea of compensation. The legal definition seems ready at hand: restitution or monetary reparation given to the victims and their heirs. On the other hand, it seems very difficult to give any ethical definition. Terms come to mind like "recovery of dignity," "freedom," and "identity." Turning away from the individual, another aspect of this ethical answer most likely will include a quest for historical truth and acknowledgment of moral responsibility.

This essay aims to discuss these various aspects of compensation in the context of Austria's recognition of its wartime past.

Historical Background

For a long time, Austria has given only a legal answer about her role during World War II. From the point of view of international law as well as national politics, Austria heavily relied on the Moscow Declaration. In that declaration, the governments of the United Kingdom, the Soviet Union, and the United States agreed in 1943—well before the war ended—on a formula stating that Austria was the first country to fall victim to Hitler's aggression. As an occupied country of Nazi Germany liberated by the Allies, Austria after the war could not be held legally responsible for the wrongful acts carried out by the Nazi regime of the German Reich on Austrian territory. Nevertheless, Austria did enact a series of measures immediately after the war for the return of property taken from those persecuted during the Nazi years. Article 26 of the Austrian State Treaty of 1955, restoring Austria's independence, subsequently codified Austria's obligation to restitution "in so far as such action has not already been taken."

Very roughly, three phases can be discerned with regard to the legal restitution and compensation measures in Austria after 1945. The first phase in 1945–46 can principally be seen as a phase of registration, administration, and declaration of looted assets. The second phase, lasting from 1946 until 1976, encompasses the restitution and compensation measures taken during the Allied occupation of Austria, the State Treaty of 1955 establishing Austria's independence, and the Cold War. The third phase can be situated from the end of the 1980s to the present day and encompasses the presidential election campaign in 1986, which sparked a new discussion on Austria's culpability during the war.

In the wake of this new political era of confrontation with the past, Austria has left behind her purely legal interpretation of compensation for the victims and, in view of a more ethical interpretation, has started to assume her part of the moral responsibility in the crimes perpetrated by the Nazi regime. As a result, new compensation laws have been enacted, covering for the first time groups of victims previously ignored, such as persons accused of "asociality," homosexuals, and physically or mentally handicapped persons, as well as categories of property insufficiently compensated during the earlier phases.

Moral Obligations

We now consider the ethical questions behind the issue of compensation. In fact, there is the moral obligation to compensate. As Professor Adolf Arndt, one of the great German legal theoreticians and himself a victim of Nazi persecution, phrased it,

> The orders of the National Socialist rulers did not constitute the justice of that time, but the injustice of that time, and the injustice, nothing else, is the reason for any right to compensation. . . . Compensation is therefore necessary for us all, in order for us to become honest to ourselves again, and to allow those injured by the injustice to reconcile with their people and their State.

Achieving compensation that goes beyond strictly monetary reparation requires a quest for the historical truth and a broad acknowledgment of responsibility. This concept has been reflected in international standards relating to reparation and in particular in the UN-based Basic Principles and Guidelines on the Right to a Remedy and Reparation for Victims of Violations of International Human Rights and Humanitarian Law. These principles include, as one form of reparation, the necessity for satisfaction, i.e. verification of the facts and full and public disclosure of the truth, as well as the need for an apology, including public acknowledgment of the facts and acceptance of responsibility.

Until recently, many Austrians knew very little about the dark side of their country's history. During the last two decades, the Austrian public has started to confront the unspeakable crimes of the Nazis as well as the role that the people of Austria played within the Nazi system. In this context, one needs to mention that the notion of "collective guilt," although seldom mentioned, was somehow always present. Former chancellor of Austria Franz Vranitzky clarified this position: "We have always felt and still feel that the connotation of 'collective guilt' does not apply to Austria. But we do acknowledge collective responsibility, the responsibility of each and every one of us to remember and to seek justice."

At the same time, it is recognized that initiatives to comprehensively research Austria's past during the era of National Socialism are an essential part of assuming the collective responsibility to remember. In order to gain knowledge of historical facts related to assets looted by the Nazis, as well as facts about the restitution of property after the war, the Austrian government established in 1998 an independent Historical Commission, which included both Austrian and non-Austrian members.[1] The Commission intended to study all aspects of "Aryanization," as well as the state's postwar efforts to make restitution to the victims of the Nazi persecution. The Commission acted as a purely investigative body, whose findings formed the basis for later negotiations on restitution.

The National Fund

The other side of this ethical interpretation of compensation and, more generally, the acknowledgment of a collective responsibility by the Austrian government, as described above, meant that a new and sensitive approach towards the victims themselves had to be sought.

On the occasion of the Republic of Austria's fiftieth anniversary, the Austrian parliament, the National Council (Nationalrat) adopted, on June 1, 1995, a federal law establishing the National Fund of the Republic of Austria for Victims of National Socialism ("National Fund").[2] Heinz Fischer, former president of the Austrian parliament and chairperson of the Board of Trustees of the National Fund, declared that "the establishment of the National Fund should represent the recognition of our moral joint responsibility and the wrong inflicted on humanity in Austria by Nazism, and recognise that special help should be given to the victims, recognizing the fact however that the suffering can in no way be 'repaired.'"

As we were soon to see, special help was desperately needed. Victims of National Socialism, over the years, had grown to believe that no one was interested in them or their families' fates. The National Fund worked hard to approach and connect with survivors. At the center of the National Fund's outreach endeavors stands the individual: the person who has suffered, the person who was driven from his or her home in Austria, the person who survived the hell of the concentration camps, the person who lost all his or her loved ones, and those who define their very existence by having lived through that inferno. More than twenty thousand people came personally to the office of the National Fund over the last nine years seeking assistance. Some of them told their story—the fate of their family and friends —for the first time. Many of them had their first encounter with representatives of an Austrian governmental institution willing to listen to them.

Next to our goal of building bridges, we distributed material help. The National Fund has administered the payment of a symbolic lump sum of ATS 70,000 (approximately $5,000) to victims of National Socialism. Since 1995, more than €150 million has been paid out to more than 29,400 individuals in seventy countries worldwide.

In accordance with its underlying legislation, the National Fund also subsidizes projects that benefit victims of National Socialism, as well as conducting scholarly research on National Socialism and the fates of its victims. Legislation passed in 1998 also allowed the National Fund to administer monies transferred to it from the International Nazi Persecutee Relief Fund. These funds are earmarked not only for individual payments to Holocaust survivors in need but also for projects providing aid and support to victims or communities that suffered severe persecution through National Socialism.

The subsidized projects can be divided into five main groups: (1) *projects providing physical and psychiatric care to Holocaust survivors*; (2) *projects supporting the activities of Jewish communities,* including assistance with food, medical care, and blankets for the winter in such towns as Czernowitz, where most of Ukraine's forty-five hundred Holocaust survivors presently reside; (3) *projects of commemoration,* such as the erection of a memorial in Birkenieki Forest on the eastern outskirt of Riga, Latvia, where over forty thousand Jews, some four thousand of Austrian origin, were shot and buried in mass graves between 1941 and 1944; (4) *educational projects,* such as the publication by a secondary school in Vienna of the biographies of 104 Jewish pupils who had been expelled from this school; and (5) *projects conducting scholarly research into the Nazi period in Austria,* such as support for an electronic database of those who were murdered that is being compiled by the Documentation Center of Austrian Resistance.

The Joint Statement of 2001 and the Creation of the General Settlement Fund

The discussions by neighboring European countries on the issue of restitution and class action lawsuits filed in American courts against Austrian companies led Austria to search for adequate measures both to provide compensation for assets plundered from Nazi victims and to make up for the gaps and deficiencies in the previous restitution and compensation measures.

In May 2000, Ambassador Ernst Sucharipa was appointed Special Envoy for Restitution Issues. After eight months of intensive negotiations with the United States, represented by his counterpart Stuart Eizenstat, and representatives of the Conference on Jewish Material Claims against Germany, the Austrian Jewish community, Austrian companies, and plaintiffs' attorneys, an agreement was reached in Washington, D.C., on January 17, 2001, and adopted by the Austrian government on January 23, 2001. The Joint Statement confirming the Agreement provided for three new measures to benefit victims of National Socialism: immediate compensation for survivors, the establishment of a General Settlement Fund (GSF) to comprehensively resolve open questions of compensation for Nazi victims, and an improved social benefits legislation package for survivors.

Due to the National Fund's successful work with the complex issue of compensation since 1995, it was given the task of implementing and administering the "immediate compensation for survivors." On the other hand, the Agreement also provided that two organs of the National Fund, that is, its Board of Trustees and the Secretary General, would at the same time function as organs of the newly established GSF. Moreover, the two Funds rely to a large extent on the same secretariat for the administration of their respective tasks.

Immediate Compensation for Survivors under the National Fund

Following the Joint Statement in Washington, the Austrian government in March 2001 made a $150 million contribution to the National Fund for the purpose of compensating for losses of apartment and small business leases, household property, and personal valuables and effects. This amount is currently being distributed to surviving victims of National Socialism originating from or having lived in Austria, with each eligible survivor receiving $7,000. Unlike the previous payment made by the National Fund, which was meant as a symbolic gesture of recognition to the victims, this new payment, although also a lump sum, is a specific and final compensation in the abovementioned categories of property.

It should be noted that not every survivor previously recognized as a victim by the National Fund also suffered such material losses and that payments can only be made if such a loss has been made plausible along relaxed standards of proof. The National Fund, through its own team of historians, also undertakes research in the Austrian archives to substantiate the claims.

Since April 2001, when payments under the January 2001 agreement commenced, more than $143 million has been paid out to more than 20,500 individuals in sixty-five countries worldwide.

Moreover, the National Fund Law provides that after the processing of all applications, the remaining amount of the allocated $150 million will be distributed in equal parts among all persons entitled to benefits or their heirs, respectively. As a result, in October 2004, the National Fund began distribution of an additional payment of €1,000 to every person who previously received the lump-sum payment of $7,000. More than sixteen hundred such payments have already been made.

The General Settlement Fund

The GSF was established in order "to acknowledge, through voluntary payments, the moral responsibility for losses and damages inflicted upon Jewish citizens and other victims of National Socialism as a result of or in connection with the National Socialist Regime." For this purpose, the GSF will be endowed with an amount of $210 million, paid out on the basis of the decisions taken by an independent Claims Committee, which consists of one member chosen by the government of the United States, one selected by the Austrian federal government, and the chairperson chosen by the two members. The individual payments will not be in the form of a lump sum, as in the case of the compensation for apartment leases, but will depend on the extent of the losses claimed by each applicant. The total sum will be divided among the claims that have been substantiated, on a pro rata basis. Payments can therefore only be made after the Claims Committee has reviewed all submitted applications.

Applications can be filed by victims of the National Socialist regime, their heirs, or victims' communal organizations. Compensation will be provided for several categories of losses, including liquidated businesses; real property; bank accounts, assets, bonds, and mortgages; moveable property; insurance policies; professional and educational losses; as well as other losses and damages. The GSF, conceived to "comprehensively resolve open questions of compensation" for Nazi victims, therefore encompasses a much broader field of application than the National Fund. Unlike the restriction providing for payments by the National Fund to be made only to survivors (this is true both for the symbolic first payment as well as for the more recent payments of $7,000 and €1,000), the GSF law also entitles heirs of victims and communal organizations to apply for compensation.

Due to the legal prerequisites of the GSF law, the process of compensation itself differs in many ways from the procedure before the National Fund. In particular, the compensation payment will be dependent on the substantiation of a specific loss. The GSF law, however, by allowing for relaxed standards of proof, does reflect the fact that applicants often lack documentation. Moreover, the GSF's own team of historians, on the basis of the information contained in each application form, is conducting standardized research in several Austrian archives to concretize the claims and to determine whether any prior restitution was made.

Until the end of the application deadline on May 28, 2003, more than nineteen thousand applications were received by the GSF from applicants in seventy-four countries.

It needs to be stressed, though, that payments under the GSF ultimately depend on the outcome of litigation in the United States. Under the Agreement of January 17, 2001, and the Austrian legislation of January 21, 2001, the $210 million endowment of the GSF is dependent on legal closure, that is, the dismissal of all lawsuits against Austria or Austrian companies arising out of or related to the National Socialist era or World War II, pending before U.S. courts as of June 30, 2001. (The $7,000 lump-sum payment and the €1,000 additional payment were specifically not linked to legal closure, so that an immediate payment could be made to survivors.) At the moment, however, two such lawsuits are still pending before courts in the United States. Since this is preventing legal closure, the GSF cannot be endowed with the provided funds and no payments can be made until these lawsuits are dismissed.

Arbitration Panel for In Rem Restitution of Publicly Owned Property

Some of the real property taken from victims of National Socialism during the war is now in public hands. For this reason, an independent Arbitration Panel was established with the GSF to review applications for in rem restitution of both real estate and buildings owned by the Republic of Austria on January 17, 2001. Moreover, the City of Vienna and the Austrian provinces of Upper Austria, Carinthia, Salzburg, Lower Austria, Vorarlberg, Burgenland, and Styria have decided to accept recommendations of the Arbitration Panel for in rem restitution of their publicly owned property. Unlike the Claims Committee, the Arbitration Panel (also composed of three members, one chosen by the U.S. government, one selected by the Austrian government, and a chairperson chosen by the two members) can recommend the actual restitution of such property, or an award of a comparable property, to the competent federal minister.

Although the structure of the proceedings before the Arbitration Panel reflects some elements of international arbitration, neither the Republic of Austria nor any of the provinces are parties to the proceedings before the Panel. They are, however, allowed to submit a statement to the Panel. The

Rules of Procedure of the Arbitration Panel also establish that the Panel will support the applicants in providing additional information to complete an application, if necessary. In fact, extensive research has been undertaken by the historians of the GSF for every single case filed for in rem restitution.

The filing period for lodging applications with the Arbitration Panel, extended until December 31, 2004, was still open at the time of writing. By that time, around seventy potentially substantiated applications had been filed and eight decisions issued by the Arbitration Panel.[3] One should note, however, that recommendations of the Arbitration Panel can only be executed by the competent federal minister once legal closure has been achieved. In other words, property recommended for restitution can therefore only be returned once the abovementioned class actions pending before U.S. courts have been dismissed.

Impact on Austrian Society

After reviewing these mostly legal measures aimed at confronting a terrible past, let us finally focus on their potential impact on Austrian society as a whole. What impacts have the National Fund and the GSF had on the victims' community, on the one hand, and on the general public in Austria, on the other? It is important to note that both measures were holistic in their approach. The National Fund in particular focused specifically on the actual victims and was meant as a measure of financial support to the surviving victims, most of whom are elderly and often in financial need. At the same time, as we have seen, both funds aimed and are aiming at more than mere financial compensation. As discussed, such monetary compensation can always only be a part of coming to terms with the past and a connection with the victims. Through those personal contacts established by the two funds with over thirty thousand survivors worldwide, a new culture has emerged in Austria in dealing with Nazi victims. For many victims the National Fund gave them a new esteem and a sense of respect that they had found missing from the official Austria for too long. Their life stories are now not only honored but also, with their consent, published to reach an ever wider audience. For the first time, the victims and their personal fates have become the very center of the efforts made by Austria to confront her past. One can therefore say that the first impact of these two recent compensation measures has been a repositioning towards those who had suffered from Nazi persecution, not least towards those groups not previously recognized as victims, such as, among others, persons with a physical or mental handicap. In this way, the National Fund and the GSF have functioned as a catalyst for a reappraisal of the past.

On the other hand, within the realm of these two funds, the role of the general public in Austria was not reduced to one of mere financial contributor. The creation of the two funds sparked a broad public debate about Austria's wartime role and the participation of ordinary Austrians in the crimes of the Nazi regime. In this way, awareness has been raised within the Austrian public and, not least through the funding of the National Fund and the GSF, responsibility has been acknowledged.

Moreover, next to the individual payments made to the victims and their heirs, the projects subsidized by the National Fund have contributed in several ways, as described above, to keeping alive the memory of those murdered and to assisting the survivors.

In parallel with these most recent (compensation) measures of the National Fund and the GSF, many other measures, which cannot all be mentioned here, have strongly influenced the way the Austrian general public faces its past. Most importantly, a national Holocaust Memorial Day and the teaching of the Holocaust as an integral part of the school curriculum have reshaped the public perception and knowledge of the Nazi crimes in Austria. Such measures have decisively contributed to dismissing the picture Austria had of itself as the first victim of Hitler's aggression and to encouraging Austria to assume responsibility for the crimes perpetrated during the Nazi regime.

Conclusion

As a final set of remarks, let us look at the other side of this process, beyond the measures taken by the state. We would like to pay tribute to those survivors who, after all they went through, are prepared to assist a society that chased and humiliated them to overcome its xenophobia, anti-Semitism, and intolerance towards minorities in general. In particular, Holocaust survivors who visit schools to convey their experiences, and thereby open the eyes of young people to a past of injustice, are making a critical contribution to present-day Austrian society. For the sake of all future generations, their knowledge and their stories are also safeguarded through written publications and recordings as oral history tapes, which keeps their memories alive forever. And, with every passing year, more young people take over the survivors' legacy, marching side by side with survivors through the Mauthausen concentration camp during the annual gatherings commemorating its liberation and leading the path to a future of tolerance and understanding.

NOTES

1. *Historikerkommission der Republik Österreich,* available at www.historiker kommission.gv.at.

2. The text of all laws relevant to the functioning of the National Fund and the GSF (including the criteria for eligibility), as well as the rules of procedure mentioned in this essay, are available at www.nationalfonds.org.

3. The decisions can be found under www.nationalfonds.org/decisions.

Part IV

The Insurance Litigation

Chapter 21

Holocaust-Era Insurance Claims
Legislative, Judicial, and Executive Remedies

Lawrence Kill and Linda Gerstel

Introduction

One may have assumed that of all the Holocaust class action litigation, the class action concerning failure to pay Holocaust survivors and their heirs the proceeds of insurance policies should have been resolved swiftly.[1] However, the litigation concerning Holocaust insurance policies has been interminable. While the creation of the International Commission for Holocaust-Era Insurance Claims (ICHEIC), an alternative to litigation, was probably begun with an abundance of good intentions, it had the effect of slowing down the litigation process and setting up an administrative nightmare.

I. The Judicial Front

The first class action complaint seeking the proceeds of unpaid Holocaust-era insurance policies from European insurance companies, *Cornell v. Assicurazioni Generali S.p.A. et al.*, was filed in the spring of 1997. Shortly thereafter, multiple class actions and individual actions were filed in various state and federal courts. The cases were consolidated in the Southern District of New York in Manhattan before Judge Michael B. Mukasey (hereafter, the "Consolidated New York Proceedings"). Publicly, some insurance company defendants responded by promising internal investigations designed to evaluate the claims. At the same time, the companies filed motions to dismiss the claims, challenging the jurisdiction of American courts to handle this litigation. Aside from two peripheral defendants whose motions to dismiss were granted, the issue of personal jurisdiction was rendered academic as a result of a global settlement entered into with, among others, Germany, the United States, and class action lawyers. The settlement became a model for additional settlements by the United States with business enterprises in Austria and France (hereafter, the "executive agreements").

By the summer of 2000, only one insurance company defendant, Assicurazioni Generali S.p.A. ("Generali"), remained after the majority of others settled their claims under the executive agreements. Since Generali was an Italian insurance company and not a party to any executive agreement, it filed a motion seeking to dismiss lawsuits against it on the basis of *forum non conveniens*. In 2002, Judge Mukasey denied Generali's motion to dismiss, finding that neither ICHEIC nor the European venues provided an adequate alternative forum. Mukasey also held that the forum selection clauses in the prewar insurance policies that called for suit in various European forums were not enforceable.[2]

Two months later, on November 11, 2002, Generali filed a new round of motions seeking to dismiss the Consolidated New York Proceedings cases on the grounds that (1) the claims are governed by European law, which would bar such claims under statutes of limitations and (2) the claims are barred under the U.S. Constitution's foreign affairs power and the political question doctrine. These motions remained undecided for over two years. While the decision was under judicial consideration, the Consolidated New York Proceedings were dormant. As a result, the majority of the efforts to promote some relief concerning Holocaust-era claims took place in the regulatory legislative and executive arenas.

II. The Regulatory/Legislative Front

The class action lawsuits acted as a wake-up call to the U.S. state insurance regulators. Under the auspices of the National Association of Insurance Commissioners (NAIC), hearings were held in several cities in the United States to gather testimony about the experience of Holocaust survivors in their efforts to file claims on unpaid insurance policies. The hearings also became a forum for the insurance companies to explain their defense, i.e., difficulties of obtaining death certificates and policy information by claimants, lack of records, and the nationalization of the insurance industry by communist governments in Eastern Europe following World War II.

As a result of the lawsuits and the attention the issue was receiving from insurance commissioners, legislation addressing Holocaust insurance was being introduced and enacted both on the state and the federal levels.[3] The wording of the legislation, the requirements, and the sanctions differed from state to state. Some statutes contained reporting requirements; others eased burdens of proof and extended statutes of limitations. For example, the California statute at issue in *Garamendi* required each insurer to report to the insurance commissioner with regard to how many Holocaust-era policies it has issued, the names of the policyholders, the current status of policy, and the names of the beneficiaries, and it directed the insurance commissioner to place the information in a central public registry.[4] Adjusting the rules of evidence and the statute of limitations provided for in these statutes would allow the Holocaust claimants to overcome the greatest hurdles to proving their claims. Different state commissioners approached the Holocaust-era insurance issue with varying degrees of interest and commitment. States such as California attached a high priority to these claims even at the expense of disappointing the significant business interests of the insurance companies.

It became abundantly clear, therefore, that any insurance company that was doing business in the United States and desired to continue doing business in the United States had to grapple, at the very least, with the American insurance regulators and demonstrate that the company was attempting to address the issue. On August 25, 1998, faced with litigation and legislation, six major European insurance companies[5] signed a nonbinding Memorandum of Understanding (MOU) with certain Jewish nongovernmental organizations (NGOs), the State of Israel, and certain U.S. state insurance regulators. It was no surprise that the six insurance companies that joined ICHEIC sold insurance in the United States and were subject to the state regulators' authority. The MOU was, in effect, a nonbinding "agreement to agree" on a framework for resolving claims. While it guaranteed a measure of financial commitment, any insurance company could withdraw from the agreement with no legal consequences. While the regulators had input, the insurance companies were the driving force behind the implementation of the guidelines that ICHEIC would follow. The agreement became a spectacular public relations success since it allowed the insurance companies to publicly announce that they were committed philosophically to resolving the claims.

ICHEIC was thereby created with the twin goals of providing (1) a swift track for resolving claims and (2) relaxed levels of evidentiary proof.

Despite the terms of the MOU, up until the very end of the claims filing period the insurance companies continued to resist, on the basis of European data protection laws,[6] releasing the names of the policyholders. As of September 2003, only 52,175 of the 519,009 names posted on ICHEIC's website came from the companies themselves. The publication of the remaining names was the result of investigation of government sources and ICHEIC's independent archival research. The companies succeeded in limiting the number of claims and their potential liability by refusing to provide potential claimants with information they needed to file claims. Many of the claims of individuals whose relative's name appeared on lists were denied with inadequate explanation. There was no advocate overseeing the insurance companies' implementation of ICHEIC rules so as to insure the success of the matching process. Many individual claimants relied upon the perseverance of their state's regulators to perform the follow-through necessary to process their claims. The dedication of personnel from insurance commissioners' offices clearly varied on a state-by-state basis.

ICHEIC had an encouraging precedent, an organization formed by Swiss banks to resolve claims on dormant bank accounts. The Swiss had gained credibility by recruiting an eminent American chairman: Paul Volcker, former chairman of the Federal Reserve. The insurers picked Lawrence Eagleburger, who was, for a brief period, secretary of state under George H. W. Bush. Under the federal court's auspices, Volcker promoted an independent investigation of the banks, and the federal judge administering the Swiss banks settlement approved a plan of distribution. In contrast, the insurance companies never agreed to an independent investigation of their records, nor to have rules for payment approved by a court. Instead, the process is private, beginning with a submission of claims to the insurance companies, which determine both validity and value on the basis of ICHEIC guidelines. Although an appeals process exists, it, too, is a private procedure. In the words of Judge Mukasey, ICHEIC was (and continues to be) a "company store."[7]

While battles continued to be waged in the courts and executive agreements were in the process of being negotiated, ICHEIC acted as a "back door" to resolving claims swiftly. As of September 17, 2004, ICHEIC had received 79,732 eligible claims, with only 5.5 percent of all claims (4,492) receiving offers, totaling between $70 and $90 million. At the same time, 61 percent of all claims were still waiting to be processed.[8]

III. The Executive Front

In the fall of 1998, in response to additional class action lawsuits against German banking institutions for looting and confiscation of assets and against other sectors of German industry for slave and forced labor claims, negotiations began for the creation of a foundation funded by German corporations and the Republic of Germany for the benefit of certain victims of National Socialism.

Among the elements of the Foundation Agreement was the granting of "legal peace" for German companies through which fifty-five lawsuits in U.S. courts against several hundred German companies were consolidated and dismissed. Since the settlement was not a typical class action settlement, which would usually take the form of a class action release, "legal peace" was to be achieved by plaintiffs' voluntary discontinuance of such actions and to be supported by the U.S. Justice Department's filing of "Statements of Interest" in which the United States declared that it was in the foreign policy interests of the United States that all Holocaust-related claims against German enterprises be resolved exclusively through the Foundation (the "Statements of Interest"). Similarly, any pending or additional Holocaust-related lawsuits against German companies not voluntarily discontinued would be met by the filing of such a Statement of Interest declaring "that dismissal of the suit would be in the foreign policy interests of the United States Government, and recommending dismissal on any valid legal ground."[9] In addition, the U.S. agreed to take "all appropriate steps to oppose state and local actions against German companies arising out of the Nazi-era claims in the United States that threaten to undermine the legal peace we seek."[10]

Over the initial objections of class action lawyers, ICHEIC was included in the framework of the executive agreement to resolve insurance claims against German insurance companies. Ultimately, the class action lawyers agreed to this framework for three reasons. First, the claims against German insurance companies were subject to additional defenses not available to non-German companies, i.e., the West German government had already made payments to certain policyholders under previous German legislation reparation programs. The German government was adamant that the executive agreement should not dismantle German reparation legislation. Second, many of the German insurance companies had few contacts in the United States, and so personal jurisdiction may have been difficult, if not impossible, to obtain against them. Without jurisdiction, U.S. courts were incapable of providing any judicial remedy to Holocaust survivors.[11] In effect, by conceding to an ICHEIC framework with all of its warts and blemishes, the executive agreement provided for extraterritorial reach to those German insurance companies that would not have been subject to any U.S. judicial remedy. Finally, in the fall of 1999, two federal judges in New Jersey issued decisions dismissing litigation against German companies in Holocaust class action slave labor and looted assets cases.[12] The class action lawyers felt that with the Foundation provision of a framework for claims resolutions through ICHEIC, they had spun gold out of straw in view of jurisdictional hurdles, the New Jersey decisions, the defenses of previous reparation payments, and in some cases complete absence of records of Holocaust-era policies for German insurance companies whose warehouses had been bombed by the Allies in the 1940s.

The German Foundation pact has served as a model for similar agreements with Austria and France.[13] However, these piecemeal executive agreements with different countries did not act to resolve all Holocaust-era claims. Left standing at the altar was Generali. In some respects it is ironic that Generali still faced multiple lawsuits while other defendants settled claims through the executive agreement. Early in the litigation, Generali was one of the first insurance companies to discuss settlement with the class action lawyers. In August 1998, a settlement for $100 million was reached and presented for approval to Judge Mukasey. Under that settlement, plaintiffs and the judge would have had a role in the claims evaluation committee and a humanitarian fund committee, and no humanitarian funds would be distributed until all claimants had been paid. Most significant, the insurance companies would not be the sole arbiters of valuation guidelines and approval of claims. Shortly following class counsels' and Senator Alfonse D'Amato's presentation of the settlement to Judge Mukasey, the state insurance regulators began to criticize the $100 million settlement figure as insufficient. Their real reason was that they wanted their imprimatur over any settlement. Generali's board of directors also was reluctant to approve the settlement, since it would not insulate Generali from the wrath of the insurance regulators and the potential penalties that new state insurance laws could impose upon Generali. While the regulators continued to belittle the amount of the settlement, and were singlehandedly responsible for derailing it, in 2000 ICHEIC, the NGOs, and the State of Israel approved the same monetary deal with Generali, i.e., $100 million, behind the closed doors of ICHEIC. Unlike in the first $100 million deal, however, individual claimants in this latter settlement had to share the settlement proceeds with NGOs and foot the uncontrollable ICHEIC administrative costs. The latter settlement also lacked adequate transparency in the procedure used to evaluate and approve claims. As a result, unhappy claimants, failing to obtain a fair resolution of their claims out of this $100 million settlement, continued to file lawsuits against Generali.

IV. The U.S. Supreme Court's Garamendi *Decision*

The state and federal efforts to resolve the insurance claims culminated in the June 23, 2003, decision of the Supreme Court in *Garamendi* that invalidated California's Holocaust Victims Relief Act (HVIRA). The HVIRA required foreign carriers doing insurance business in California to disclose information[14] about unpaid Holocaust-era insurance policies or face the possibility of losing their licenses to sell insurance in California. The petitioner insurance companies filed suit challenging the HVIRA's constitutionality. In a 5-4 decision, the Court ruled against California, finding that indeed its law conflicted with the right of the federal government to determine foreign policy. The Court held that in enacting HVIRA and thereby forcing European insurance companies to reveal their Holocaust-era insurance records as the price of doing business in the state, California seeks to use "an iron fist [against the insurance companies] where the President has consistently chosen kid gloves."[15] Indeed, the class action lawyers alternated at times between the use of iron fists and kid gloves. Where it was clear that personal jurisdiction could not be obtained over certain German and Austrian companies, the executive agreements that the lawyers helped to conclude provided the framework for relief outside the judicial system. The class action lawyers went along with the executive agreements in lieu of litigation because they realized that kid gloves were the only real alternative in such instances. The judicial system in fact was unlikely to be able to deliver any remedy to claimants of those companies no longer in business or lacking jurisdictional contacts with the United States. Indeed, a number of insurance companies that took part in the funding of the German Foundation would not join ICHEIC because the absence of any significant U.S. business left them immune to the media pressure and unmotivated by any "economic benefit." The kid gloves approach also benefited those policyholders who bought policies from European insurance companies that went defunct and other companies whose successor liability was difficult, if not impossible, to trace. ICHEIC's guidelines provided some relief to these policyholders who would have had no recourse in the court system.[16]

The iron fist approach, however, seemed more appropriate against an insurance company like Generali. First, Generali was a major marketer of insurance policies during the Holocaust period. Second, Generali does significant business in the United States, and therefore jurisdiction against it was not questionable.[17] In light of its significant business dealings in the United States, Generali felt the economic pressure and regulatory pressure to "behave well." Third, and perhaps most significantly, Generali had most of its Holocaust-era policies stored intact in a warehouse in Trieste, Italy.

V. The Federal District Court's Remand Decision

Following the *Garamendi* decision, Generali supplemented its still pending motion to dismiss by arguing that the decision lent further support for an outright dismissal of the Consolidated New York Proceedings. Clearly, the legislation at issue in California and examined in *Garamendi* did not distinguish between companies that had participated in the German Foundation and those companies whose governments did not enter into such executive agreements with the United States government. Generali relied on statements that supported ICHEIC as the exclusive forum made by sub-cabinet-level U.S. officials in connection with the implementation of the German Foundation Agreement. By exporting these statements of support for ICHEIC in the context of the Foundation Agreement, Generali claimed it was entitled to immunity from litigation. The plaintiffs argued that Generali ignored the fact that the Supreme Court in *Garamendi* viewed as critical the fact that there were executive agreements among sovereigns, i.e., the United States, Germany, France, and Austria, which purported to settle claims on a nation-to-nation level.

On October 14, 2004, Judge Mukasey ruled on Generali's dismissal motion by granting the motion. This ruling dealt the final blow to the remaining Holocaust survivors and their heirs who had lawsuits pending against Generali. In his opinion, Judge Mukasey dismissed these remaining lawsuits on the ground that the cases interfered with the foreign policy preference set by the president to resolve Holocaust-era insurance claims through ICHEIC ("*Generali II*").[18] While Judge Mukasey had, in an earlier opinion, recognized the infirmities of the ICHEIC mechanism for resolving these Holocaust claims, in the post-Garamendi period he now ruled that such claims should be dismissed in favor of the infirm ICHEIC mechanism. Mukasey recognized that although there was no separate Executive Agreement with Italy, the *Garamendi* ruling nevertheless strongly implies that the executive policy "need not be formally embodied in an executive agreement in order for the policy to have an effect judicially."[19] In effect, this ruling allowed Generali a "free ride" by allowing it to hang on to the coattails of the German Foundation Agreement, despite the fact that neither the company nor Italy were signatory parties to that agreement. Mukasey also refused to infer any executive policy from the silence or failure of the government of the United States to submit a Statement of Interest requesting the court to dismiss claims against Generali. The judge noted that this sort of inferential reasoning by the court is a "perilous enterprise."[20] Following *Garamendi*, a door had been left open to allow litigation against insurance companies, such as Generali, not covered by any executive agreement. Judge Mukasey's ruling in *Generali II* effectively closed that door.

Conclusion

The experience of the Holocaust litigation reveals that each of the remedies and paths toward achieving some relief for Holocaust survivors has offered benefits and disadvantages. The lesson from the Holocaust-era insurance cases is that a judicial remedy may at times be appropriate while at other times is unavailable or, at best, uncertain. The executive branch provided an alternative solution to those instances where judicial resolutions were imperfect and, in some cases, nonexistent. The class action lawyers recognized this reality and agreed, on a country-by-country basis, to create a framework for resolving claims through executive agreements.

The legislative branch—at both the federal and state levels—sought also to assist the Holocaust litigation by enacting favorable legislation that was designed to (1) provide access to information on policies; (2) ease burdens of proof; and (3) extend statutes of limitations. The state regulators' response to the litigation—the creation of the voluntary ICHEIC solution—initially promised a quick resolution, albeit through an imperfect model.

The dedication of the state insurance regulators to resolution of Holocaust-era insurance claims varied from state to state. The state insurance commissioners in California[21] and Washington[22] made efforts to address the shortcomings of ICHEIC by suggesting reforms for more accountability.[23] The office of the California state insurance commissioner acted as a constant thorn in ICHEIC's side by publishing regular progress reports and by its participation in the *Garamendi* litigation.

At the federal legislative level, the U.S. House of Representatives' Reform Committee held two hearings during which it critically examined ICHEIC's shortcomings.[24] Congress members on the committee, like the California and Washington State insurance regulators, offered concrete suggestions on how to make ICHEIC more effective.

Suggestions on how to improve ICHEIC, however, often fell on deaf ears. Moreover, since ICHEIC was providing relief to some claimants, there was also little motivation for Judge Mukasey to allow the litigation to move forward. By failing to rule for almost two years on whether U.S. courts have jurisdiction over the Generali litigation, Mukasey stopped the litigation process in its tracks. His indecision, however, did have one positive effect. The failure of the Court to decide the jurisdiction question in the *Generali* litigation resulted in continued pressure on Generali to cooperate with ICHEIC. His issuance of *Generali II* removed that pressure. The *Generali II* decision was issued only after the time to submit claims under ICHEIC had passed and when the push to provide further funding for ICHEIC had ceased. It is unlikely, therefore, that ICHEIC's funding will be renewed following *Generali II* since there is no longer a judicial hammer hanging over ICHEIC. The pending class action lawsuits placed enormous pressure on Generali and other insurance companies to come up with a solution to resolve claims through ICHEIC. Once the driving impetus to participate in ICHEIC disappeared, so too would any further commitment to ICHEIC by the European insurance companies.

The creation of ICHEIC was a great idea that, unfortunately, failed in its implementation and execution. The loss ultimately was borne by Holocaust survivors or their heirs, since it denied these Holocaust-era insurance claimants complete access to policyholder lists. The ICHEIC model was "reduced" to a paradigm in which the insurance companies were the final arbiters of the validity of claims. The final decision was stamped with the ICHEIC "good housekeeping seal of approval." In short, the legal remedies, whether legislative, judicial, or executive, were, at best, incomplete. The inability of the three branches—judicial, legislative/regulatory, and executive—to work together was perhaps the main reason why the implementation and execution of the ICHEIC solution to the problem of unpaid Holocaust-era insurance policies failed.

NOTES

1. The authors are grateful to Leslie Tick, Esq., senior staff counsel of the Department of Insurance of California, for reviewing drafts of this essay and for being an exemplar of the efforts made to arrive at a solution to provide a remedy for claimants with Holocaust-era insurance claims.

2. *In re Assicurazioni Generali, S.p.A. Holocaust Ins. Litig.*, 228 F. Supp. 2d 348, 355–58 (S.D.N.Y. 2002), *reh'g denied*, No. MDL 1374, 2003 WL 145545 (S.D.N.Y. Jan. 21, 2003) (hereinafter "*Generali I*").

3. *See, e.g.*, Holocaust Victims Relief Act (HVIRA), Cal. Ins. Code § 13800–13807 (West 1999); N.Y. Holocaust Victims Ins. Act of 1998 (HVIA) 2 N.Y. Ins. Law § 2701 (McKinney 2000); "Holocaust Victims Relief Act," General Ins. Powers Minn. Stat. § 60A 0530 (2000); The Holocaust Victims Insurance Act, Fla. Stat. ch. 626.9543 (1998); Holocaust Victims Insurance Relief Act, Wash. Rev. Code § 48.104 (1999).

4. Other California statutes extended the statute of limitations for filing claims (Cal. Civ. Proc. Code § 354.5) and provided for suspension of licenses of insurance companies who had not paid on valid claims (Cal. Ins. Code § 790.15)

5. Allianz Lebensversicherungs AG, AXA of France, Basler Lebenversicherungs, Gesellschaft, Winterthur, Zurich of Switzerland, and Generali of Italy. Basler later withdrew from the ICHEIC. In May 2000, the member companies of the Dutch Insurance Association joined the commission. ICHEIC subsequently signed additional agreements relating to German, Belgian, and Austrian insurance companies.

6. Washington 2004 Report, at 21.

7. *Generali I*, at 356.

8. Washington 2004 Report, at 3.

9. 39 Int'l Legal Materials, at 1304.

10. 39 Int'l Legal Materials, at 1300.

11. In fact, the decisions of Judge Mukasey in the summer of 2000 dismissing two defendants on personal jurisdiction grounds left the door open for more unfavorable jurisdictional rulings with regard to other German insurance companies.

12. *See Burger-Fischer v. DeGussa AG*, 65 F. Supp. 2d 248 (D.N.J. 1999); *Iwanowa v. Ford Motor Co.*, 67 F. Supp. 2d 424 (D.N.J. 1999).

13. *See, e.g.*, Agreement between the Austrian Federal Government and the Government of the United States of America concerning the Austrian Fund, *Reconciliation, Peace, and Cooperation*, 40 Int'l Legal Materials 523 (2001).

14. The reporting statutes would provide beneficiaries of those policies with

two pieces of information crucial to the pursuit of a settlement: the possible existence of a claim and which company may have issued the policy.

15. *Garamendi*, 123 S. Ct. at 2378.

16. Under ICHEIC guidelines providing for humanitarian payments, approximately $2.3 million in offers were made to individuals with claims for companies in Eastern Europe that were nationalized or liquidated or where there is no formal successor company. *See* ICHEIC Quarterly Report, 20 (Oct. 2004).

17. In fact, Generali was the only insurance company, other than Zurich, that did not even attempt to challenge personal jurisdiction.

18. *In re Assicurazioni Generali*, 2004 WL 2311298.

19. *Generali II*, at 8.

20. *Generali II*, at 9.

21. The California Department of Insurance Holocaust website (www.insurance.ca.gov/docs/fs-holocaust.htm) provides policyholder lists from insurers who complied with HVIRA prior to the litigation.

22. The Washington State Office of the Insurance Commissioner lists several links to lists of Holocaust-era policyholders (www.insurance.wa.gov).

23. *See* Washington 2004 Report.

24. *See* Committee on Government Reform (http://reform.house.gov).

Chapter 22

The Road to Compensation of
Life Insurance Policies
The Foundation Law and ICHEIC

Kai Hennig

When the law creating the "Remembrance, Responsibility, and Future" Foundation ("the Foundation") entered into force on August 12, 2000, the way was paved not only for payments to former forced laborers under the National Socialist regime but also for settling individual claims on unpaid Holocaust-era German insurance policies. German insurance companies contributed approximately DM 600 million of the DM 10 billion paid to the Foundation. According to the Foundation Law, the handling of unpaid insurance claims stemming from the Nazi era will be carried out by the International Commission on Holocaust-Era Insurance Claims (ICHEIC). This essay briefly summarizes the payment of claims related to German insurance policies under the auspices of ICHEIC.

ICHEIC was founded in 1998 for the purpose of establishing an international procedure for processing unpaid insurance policies held by victims of the Nazi regime.

The members of ICHEIC signed a Memorandum of Understanding (MOU) in which they agreed to voluntarily pursue the goal of resolving the insurance claims of Holocaust victims. The signatory companies are required to cover the expenses of ICHEIC and are subject to an intensive auditing process.

Because membership in ICHEIC is voluntary, and no signatory insurance company is required to pay any claim that is attributable to a non-MOU signatory, this agreement did not ensure the all-embracing legal peace that German companies were seeking. It was therefore necessary to include ICHEIC and the compensation of unpaid life insurance policies in the German Foundation Law.

The executive agreement between the German and U.S. governments concerning the Foundation stipulates in Article 1(4),

> The Federal Republic of Germany agrees that insurance claims that come within the scope of the current claims handling procedures adopted by . . . [ICHEIC] and are made against German insurance companies shall be processed by the companies and the German Insurance Association on the basis of such procedures and on the basis of additional claims handling procedures that may be agreed among the Foundation, ICHEIC, and the German Insurance Association.

The Trilateral Agreement

1) The Negotiations

Therefore, Article 1(4) required the conclusion of a Trilateral Agreement among the Foundation, the German Insurance Association (GDV) and ICHEIC in order to stipulate the procedures for application processing and payment.

In the beginning, the negotiations started only between the GDV and ICHEIC. When these talks ended in a stalemate, the Foundation, which held the capital, mediated the dispute. From that point on, incremental progress was achieved and after almost two years of negotiations, an agreement was finally reached in October 2002. Immediately after the signing, the entire sum of 281 million euros was transferred to ICHEIC.[1]

At the beginning of the talks, no one could possibly imagine that we would end up with a voluminous document consisting of one main agreement and eleven annexes. Negotiations were very difficult, foremost because of the complexity of the problems to be addressed. But the difficulties transcended mere complexity of issues. The deep mistrust by plaintiff organizations towards the German insurance companies overshadowed the entire negotiations and made it difficult but necessary to negotiate all eventualities. This mistrust had its roots not only in the horrible crimes against the victims during the Nazi era but also in the suspicion that for decades the insurance industry had been sitting on assets that belonged to Holocaust victims. In stark contrast, the German insurance market was and remains convinced that practically all open insurance policies of the National Socialist era were compensated in the extensive compensation efforts of Germany during the 1950s and 1960s.

The mistrust was nurtured especially in the United States, where there continued to be reports of hundreds of thousands of eligible persons with billions in unpaid policies. During the negotiations, the German insurance companies could do very little to dispel these suspicions. They could neither present any figures as to how many of the approximately six hundred thousand Jews in the German Reich[2] had a life insurance policy, nor could they give any statistics as to how many unpaid life insurance policies were compensated in the 1950s and 1960s.

During implementation of the agreement, however, figures became clearer. The agreed provisions and procedures under the Trilateral Agreement proved the suspicions wrong. According to its own statistics, ICHEIC received approximately eighty thousand claims and enquiries regarding life insurance policies, of which only approximately twenty-four thousand related to the German insurance market.

2) The Contents of the Trilateral Agreement

In order to understand the complexity of the compensation of unpaid life insurance policies, it is necessary to get an overview of the main points of the Trilateral Agreement.

SCOPE OF THE AGREEMENT

The agreement serves to determine the criteria used to compensate for insurance policies unpaid or confiscated by German insurance companies during the time of National Socialism (1933–1945). For this purpose, ICHEIC has been provided with 102 million euros by the Foundation to cover compensation payments, with any residual funds to be transferred to an ICHEIC Humanitarian Fund. Additionally, ICHEIC received 179 million euros in humanitarian payments by the Foundation for use in the Humanitarian Fund.

PREREQUISITES FOR AN ELIGIBLE CLAIM

A life insurance policy is eligible for compensation if (1) a German insurance company issued the policy; (2) it was in force between January

1920 and May 1945; and (3) it has become due. Furthermore, it should not have been previously paid and should not have been the subject of a former compensation process.

A claimant can be (1) the policy beneficiary or his or her heir; (2) the policyholder or his or her heir; or (3) the insured person or his or her heir. In addition, the policy beneficiary, the policyholder, or the insured person must be a Holocaust victim according to the definition in the agreement.

In order to establish a claim, the companies and ICHEIC utilize relaxed standards of proof for establishing that a life insurance policy existed. However, the insurance companies are entitled to use the same relaxed standards when establishing that the insurance sum was already paid in a regular manner. The companies and ICHEIC also utilize specific rules for succession to determine whose heir is entitled to the insurance claim. Principally, a wide-ranging line of succession to specific rights and obligations is possible, so that in almost all cases an entitled applicant can be found.

DISTRIBUTION OF FUNDS

Payments will be made out of a so-called claims fund and will be distributed to pay for administrative overheads between 2001 and 2005, claims approved by German insurance companies, and claims settled by German insurance companies prior to the agreement. Any residual funds will be transferred to the ICHEIC Humanitarian Fund to pay for claims against unknown insurance companies.

LEGAL PEACE

ICHEIC will use its best efforts to achieve an all-embracing legal and administrative peace for German insurance companies in the United States. The agreement constitutes a final settlement among the three parties. With limited exceptions relating to audits and monitoring, the agreement supersedes any legal agreements between ICHEIC and German insurance companies.

A claimant who accepts the offer of an insurance company has to sign a declaration that he or she waives any further claims regarding the insurance policy.

3) The Jewish Policyholders Project

Another aspect of the Trilateral Agreement that has engendered significant interest relates to the Jewish Policyholders Project. During the whole course of negotiations, there was always one particular demand from the Jewish side that was their greatest concern. They demanded that the insurance companies open their archives so that possible policyholders who may have a claim can be identified. According to their understanding, only the publication of the list would ensure that all possible claimants who are to a large extent successors or heirs of the original policyholder or beneficiary would become aware of a potential claim. The insurance companies, on the other hand, were not willing to give uncontrolled access to their archives due to confidentiality agreements and German data protection laws.

The compromise that was found was the establishment of a special agreement among the GDV, ICHEIC, and the Foundation on the publication of a list of possible insurance policyholders who later became Holocaust victims. The aim of the parties to this agreement was to compile and publish a list of Jewish policyholders during the relevant period who had a life insurance policy with a German insurance company.

The German insurance companies committed themselves to compiling a list of all the German policyholders (including also non-Jewish policyholders) from 1920 to 1945, insofar as this data was available on electronic databases. This compilation was monitored by the German Federal Financial Supervisory Authority and contains some 8.5 million names.

The Foundation assumed responsibility for compiling a list on an electronic database of Jewish residents in Germany between 1933 and 1945. Such a list did not previously exist. The Federal Archive took on the task of coordinating the generation of this list using the 1939 census as its starting point and continuing with hundreds of additional sources. The Federal Archive was advised by and assisted in selecting its sources by an Advisory Group. The Advisory Group was made up of representatives from ICHEIC, Yad Vashem, the German insurance companies, the Land Archive Berlin, Jewish organizations, selected international archive experts, and the Foundation. The Federal Archive and the Advisory Group then coordinated the results of their extensive research, putting together a collection containing a total of 2.5 million names. Of course, since the data was compiled from nearly a hundred different sources, it contains many duplicate entries. Most historians estimate that there were between 550,000 and 650,000 Jewish residents in the German Reich at that time.

The aim was to match this database with the generated list of all policyholders (German, Jewish, and non-Jewish policyholders—8.5 million names), thereby obtaining a list of possible Jewish policyholders.

The experts agreed that it was not absolutely necessary to remove duplicate entries for the purpose of compiling a list of Jewish policyholders, since only the matched names from the companies' list would be published.

The matching was completed successfully and resulted in a list containing some 360,000 names of possible Jewish policyholders. The list was published in April 2003 on ICHEIC's website. It is important to notice that the list does not distinguish between names of people who have already received compensation and those who have not. Nevertheless, it allowed descendants of Holocaust victims to check whether a relative had a life insurance policy with a German company, thus enabling compensation claims to be submitted.

The Implementation of the Trilateral Agreement

1) Examination, Prefinancing, and Disbursal Procedure

In the months following the signing of the agreement, the Foundation, together with ICHEIC and the GDV, had to work out a detailed financing system.

Since ICHEIC already had the funds, it was necessary to develop a disbursal procedure. Thus, an implementation guideline was required that both protects the interests of ICHEIC, in particular its equity, and also protects the legitimate interest of the companies, particularly in having a procedure that is final and conclusive.

It proved to be extremely difficult to draft such guidelines at first, as the companies and ICHEIC took the same critical and suspicious attitude in shaping these details as they had taken in previous negotiations.

On March 25, 2003, the compromise proposal, submitted by the Foundation, was accepted by both sides, which meant companies were now able to make offers to eligible claimants. The claimants have up to four months to accept these offers or to lodge an appeal.

2) Claims Status and Payment Status

The filing period ended December 31, 2003. Claimants, who already had a claims form, could send in their application until March 31, 2004. According to ICHEIC information, it has received approximately 120,000 general applications. These include enquiries, unnamed claims, and named claims. Named claims are applications in which the claimant names a company. Unnamed claims are applications that do not name a company. There are also files mentioning only inquiry status, including vague and general inquiries.

Of the approximate 125,000 general applications received by ICHEIC, approximately forty thousand are ineligible for the ICHEIC claims process. These ineligible claims consist of applications for pensions or applications from countries without private insurance companies (e.g., Russia). That means ICHEIC received a total of about eighty-five thousand applications and/or requests concerning compensation of life insurance policies. These cases have to be processed with the cooperation of German and other European insurance companies. Of all the claims, approximately twenty-nine thousand are named and fifty-six thousand are unnamed.

Thus far, of all ICHEIC claims, approximately 5,570 offers have been made to claimants amounting to $87 million in compensation, with 8,140 claims declined by companies.

3) Claims Status and Payment Status under the Trilateral Agreement

Out of the eighty-five thousand claims, fifty-nine thousand refer to claimants and insurance policies from other European countries, mainly in Central and Eastern Europe. Thus, at present there are approximately twenty-six thousand applications relating to possible insurance policies issued in Germany. The publication of the list of possible Jewish policyholders did not result in any significant increase in applications. Of the twenty-six thousand, approximately four thousand are for named claims, and approximately twenty-two thousand are for unnamed claims.

Named claims are sent to the German federal filing agency—Bundeszentralkartei (BZK), which forwards applications to the appropriate state compensation office. The state compensation offices keep records showing whether or not a certain policy has already been paid out or compensated, especially during the compensation procedures in the 1950s and 1960s.

Any named insurance company in the claim meanwhile checks its own archive to find out whether the policy was paid in the past. If these investigations are negative, the company makes a compensation offer to the claimant according to the valuation guidelines of the Trilateral Agreement. Due to this complicated but necessary procedure, payments are made once a month. So far approximately twenty-three hundred claimants received under the Trilateral Agreement compensation payments totaling $21.9 million. So far, approximately twenty-six hundred claimants were rejected by the companies, either because compensation had already been paid or because respective eligibility could not be proven despite the relaxed standards of proof under the Trilateral Agreement.

With respect to twenty-two thousand unnamed claims, approximately seventy German companies are presently examining their archives to see whether or not an insurance policy was taken out with their company. All twenty-two thousand unnamed claims will be examined by each of these companies. Should no policy be found, the application cannot be processed within the scope of the Trilateral Agreement's compensation procedure and is returned to ICHEIC. If a policy is found by one of the companies, the unnamed claim becomes a named claim and is integrated into the agreed procedures. So far, out of the first five thousand unnamed claims examined by the companies, approximately twelve hundred could be converted into a named claim.

4) Humanitarian Payments by ICHEIC on Unnamed Claims

A final component of compensation relates to outstanding unnamed claims. According to the MOU of 1998, it is possible to have a humanitarian payment for unnamed claims.[3]

Consequently, ICHEIC addressed the possibility of a humanitarian payment for those applications. For ICHEIC, questions arose as to the amount of payments that should be made and the evidentiary requirements necessary for cases under this category that otherwise cannot be proven under the relaxed standards of proof. In order to answer these questions, ICHEIC had set up a working group chaired by Sandy Berger, the former foreign and national security policy adviser of U.S. President Clinton.

So far, sixteen thousand claimants who could present so-called anecdotal evidence for their claim to the working group received each $1,000 as a humanitarian payment. A second payment for several thousand further claims is currently being processed.

Outlook

According to current estimates, it will take until the end of 2005 to decide on all claims, and up to summer 2006 to finalize all appeals proceedings.

On the one hand, the three parties to the Trilateral Agreement concur that while the processing and payment procedure is certainly difficult and takes time, it is working well. However, it has be-come obvious that excessive expectations regarding uncompensated policies and the amounts that have to be paid are unjustified.

This dilemma is one of the main reasons why the compensation process is under constant observation and harsh criticism, especially in the United States.

Assertive, clear, and open public relations efforts of all parties involved are necessary to counter false expectations and provide the utmost transparency to the process. Through this kind of information the compensation process will gain more credibility, and this increased credibility will, in a wider sense, secure legal peace.

The complicated process and payment procedure is a political and technical administrative challenge that requires a continuously high level of attention and political reinforcement until all claims have been processed. The Foundation will do its utmost to secure the success of this part of the Foundation Law and its effort to bring this chapter of restitution to a satisfying closure.

NOTES

1. The entire amount is broken down to €102 million for the claims fund and €179 million for the humanitarian fund.

2. The period of the German Reich extended from 1933 to 1945.

3. The Trilateral Agreement refers to this regulation in section 7, paragraph 2.

Chapter 23

ICHEIC

Excellent Concept but Inept Implementation

Sidney Zabludoff

Holocaust survivors and their heirs seeking justice through the settlement of their insurance claims have once again fallen victim; this time the culprit is inept governance and poor management by those charged with helping them. Making matters worse is the failure of insurance companies to fully honor their initial pledges of cooperation and to "expeditiously address the issue of unpaid insurance policies," as the ICHEIC charter states.

The International Commission of Holocaust-Era Insurance Claims (ICHEIC) got off to a promising start when cooperation among its members initially led to a credible system to meet the unpaid life insurance claims from the Holocaust era. But the implementation of this effort was seriously flawed by inept management and governance. Instead of the envisaged two-year endeavor, the process will take at least nine years and has been constantly plagued by justified complaints. As a result, ICHEIC's reputation has sagged badly, and the idea of resolving issues through an agreement among the parties to a dispute has suffered a major setback. Upon completing its tasks, ICHEIC will have paid claimants and provided for humanitarian funds an amount equivalent to only about 3 percent of the 1998 unpaid amount of life insurance policies outstanding fro the Holocaust era. This percentage does not even come close to achieving "rough justice." ICHEIC also has done nothing to handle non–life insurance claims, such as those resulting from the enormous destruction of Jewish property during Kristallnacht in November 1938.

The Successful First Period

ICHEIC was a good idea. Born in 1998 during a resurgence of interest in restoring assets lost during the Holocaust to survivors or their heirs, ICHEIC brought together insurance companies, U.S. state regulators, and Jewish organizations (including the State of Israel) in a nongovernmental organization. Its aim was to quickly reimburse unpaid insurance policies from the Holocaust era in a manner that avoided the problems of ongoing restitution efforts such as the cumbersome nature of government agreements, high costs, and prolonged class action suits.

During ICHEIC's first two years, extensive cooperation among the three parties led to the development of the needed framework for the effort. Five European insurance companies participated: Allianz, AXA, Generali, Winterthur, and Zurich. The companies pledged to meet the cost of ICHEIC's operation, pay claims quickly, and contribute to a humanitarian fund to account for the many Holocaust-era policies that all sides recognized would remain unpaid. The cooperative negotiations and compromises by the three parties in various committees created a system of rules allowing relaxed standards of proof and a means to value unpaid policies at current prices. Lawrence Eagleburger, a former secretary of state, was named ICHEIC chairman.

All parties realized that after more than sixty years and the horrors of the Holocaust, few surviving policyholders or their heirs still had documents indicating the existence of a policy. With the acceptance of claims, this fact became abundantly clear. Only about a third of the claimants were able to name the company with which the policyholder was insured and only 5 percent could provide evidence (policy, premium notice, etc.) that a policy existed. Thus, from the beginning it was recognized that considerable emphasis had to be placed on obtaining policy information from company records and government archives, and on publishing the names of the policyholders.

Little or No Performance Progress during the Second Period

Cooperation faded and the companies' financial pledges evaporated between February 2000, when claims were first accepted, and October 2002. At the same time, the claims process got bogged down in uncertainty and errors. Such initial processing deficiencies are not abnormal, especially in cases like this one where the effort is groundbreaking. Moreover, ICHEIC failed to put in place during this period a system to ensure that offers and denials made by the companies followed ICHEIC rules. These problems were clearly pinpointed by several critical reviews (including U.S. congressional hearings in November 2001).[1] But ICHEIC management of claims processing, conducted by an office in London, failed to make the necessary and obvious corrections. Moreover, the London office provided little oversight of the sole contractor that had been hired to handle the processing of claims.

It was no wonder, given the inadequacies of the ICHEIC system and the slowness of the companies to handle claims, that the chorus of complaints from claimants and those assisting them grew dramatically and the reputation of ICHEIC sagged. There were numerous highly disparaging newspaper articles. For example, the *Financial Times* of January 25, 2002, explained that "[b]oth governments [U.S. and German] admitted the system of settling claims was failing"[2] while the *Baltimore Sun* in a July 14, 2002, editorial based on reports by one of the paper's investigative journalists concluded, "ICHEIC is in need of immediate and deep reform."[3]

At a strategic level, there was also a management failure. No effort was made to present an overall view of how the various elements of the ICHEIC should proceed and be integrated in terms of priorities, timing, and costs. For example, it was obvious that it was necessary to move quickly to have companies publish names of Holocaust-era policyholders so that potential claims could be filed. But this effort never received the priority that was needed and in fact by the December 31, 2003, deadline for filing claims the companies had published few policyholder names, except in the case of Germany.

A major stumbling block was the management of the London office. Its head and deputy chairman of ICHEIC, Geoffrey Fitchew, insisted that ICHEIC's role was simply that of a "post office" that sends claims to the companies for decision. Although ICHEIC Washington stated numerous times that that was not the case, the London office failed to significantly alter its course of action. When combined with other problems, such as the failure to address unforeseen issues, the result was an expanding number of unresolved system errors that persist to this date.

ICHEIC's inept governance made conditions worse. Not only did this situation impair the management of ICHEIC, but it also created a corrosive atmosphere. Except for occasional decisions on some issues by the chairman, the effort drifted in disarray. The effective committee structure of the earlier period was essentially disbanded. Rather than a consensus-building process on which the ICHEIC charter was built, the major decisions were made by the chairman on the basis of input from the head of the London operations and his discussions with those ICHEIC members the chairman felt necessary to communicate with. Such actions may have been effective in terms of secret diplomacy but caused dissension within ICHEIC and undermined public confidence.

Another major culprit was the long, drawn-out negotiations required to reach an accord with the German Foundation for "Remembrance, Responsibility, and the Future" (German Foundation) on how to handle all insurance claims for Jews living in Germany during the Holocaust era. Many of the ICHEIC-stipulated rules were not accepted by the ICHEIC member companies, who waited to see the outcome of the German agreement. In all, through the second period, the ICHEIC chairman did little to correct the problems, the companies' performance in handling claims was lackadaisical at best, most state regulators lost interest, and the Jewish participants essentially put up with the difficulties, seeing no alternative.

Raised Expectations Frustrated by Little Progress in Third Period

With the signing of an agreement between ICHEIC and the German Foundation in October 2002, it was hoped that the claims process would be reinvigorated. Despite the delays in reaching the agreement and numerous difficult compromises, there were clear benefits. All German claims were considered rather than just those from the participating ICHEIC company members, a list of Jewish policyholders in Germany was published, and ICHEIC received the necessary funds to sustain its operations. This additional money made up for the amount the participating companies had originally pledged and then reneged on.

These hopeful expectations were strengthened when in July 2002 a chief operating officer (COO) was hired to tackle the ongoing problems. But progress has either been slow, minimal, or nonexistent in terms of the many key claims-processing issues. The one important step forward was putting in place after more than three years of promises a scheme to verify that claims processed by the companies follow ICHEIC rules. The effectiveness of the verification system, however, still remains unclear as errors and questions persist. Moreover, no system was put in place to clarify and codify the many outstanding issues.

During the same period, ICHEIC published on its website a list of some 350,000 possible Jewish life insurance policyholders in Germany from the Holocaust era. This effective effort was not handled by the COO but by committees made up of representatives of the ICHEIC participants, its staff, and the German Foundation. Their cooperation was reminiscent of the first ICHEIC period.

The German agreement had a major flaw, however. The German government insisted that the ICHEIC calculate the current value of policies using the same minimal payout system used to pay claimants in the postwar period, with interest only from 1969. The outcome was offers averaging about $1,000 per policy. After years of negotiations on this issue, the German Foundation in October 2002 agreed to pay a minimum of $3,000 per policy for those who perished during the Holocaust and $4,000 for those who survived. But even with these improvements, German payments are still only about 15 percent of the reasonable benchmark system of determining current value. As a result, the average payment for German policies is less than half of the already discounted East European policies that resulted from a compromise with the insurance companies who initially argued they were not responsible for East European policies because of the communist nationalization of their firms.

Meanwhile, the lack of cooperative overall governance persisted. There continued to be no committee or any other system to bring together the three ICHEIC parties to address outstanding issues. Those decisions that were made were made in a haphazard fashion by Chairman Eagleburger or the COO, with minimal consultation with ICHEIC members. In most cases, discussion was with only those who agreed with them. One outlandish example was the COO simply declaring that there were no outstanding valuation issues. Indeed, a veil of secrecy as to what steps were or were not being taken descended over the ICHEIC effort.

As the magazine *The Economist* said in an August 2, 2003, editorial, "If ICHEIC fails to improve its performance and quickly, by demonstrating greater independence, acting more openly and paying claims faster, then those who have not yet filed a claim may choose to go directly to the law. That would hardly help insurers or claimants to resolve this issue speedily."[4] It must be added that the same is true of those who have already filed claims.

Late Attempts to Respond to Long-Standing Problems in Stage Four

To resolve the governance and management crises, the Jewish group met immediately before the October 2003 ICHEIC meeting and decided on corrective actions that should be undertaken urgently. These included the reestablishment of the committee system, the appointment of an ombudsman to handle the numerous complaints from claimants, and the development of a program designed to accelerate the handling of claims by the companies. At the ICHEIC meeting, it was decided to discuss and move ahead with these steps.

In all cases, through mid-April 2004, ICHEIC did almost nothing. The pace of handling claims did not change significantly and the ombudsman effort never materialized. After a six-month delay, the chairman finally initiated an Operating Committee to discuss long-standing issues but for the most part appointed only those who would not challenge his views. Through 2004, the Operations Committee rarely met and only a few of the many outstanding issues were addressed. Thus, little was done to make up for the protracted time and money poorly spent as well as the disregard of claimant interests that resulted from years of faulty management and governance. At this point the two parties (the Jewish group and the state regulators) that could make a difference seem to have been worn down by years of inaction, discord, and a turnover of participants that has undercut institutional memory.

ICHEIC management meanwhile increasingly stifled criticism by relying strictly on those who do not raise concerns and by ostracizing those with legitimate questions. Most distressing was the removal from office of Dale Franklin, the chief of staff of the Washington office, who was the only one within ICHEIC management who diligently worked to overcome the long-standing problems.

The ICHEIC meeting in April 2004 reiterated its hopes of closing down ICHEIC by year's end. This goal was not achieved. Moreover, with minor exceptions the companies belonging to ICHEIC (outside of Germany) had not made available their list of names of Holocaust-era policyholders even for use in the internal matching process. Little effort has been undertaken to handle non–life insurance policies as pledged in ICHEIC's initial charter. It seems that the policy of ICHEIC chairman and the COO is to close the effort as soon as possible and declare victory.

California's insurance commissioner, John Garamendi, and an ICHEIC commissioner, in a June 8, 2004, letter to ICHEIC Chairman Eagleburger tried to persuade him to take appropriate action to right ICHEIC's problems. The response was a rambling public relations defense that showed that the chairman and his staff did not even know the facts. For example, in his June 11, 2004, response to Commissioner Garamendi's suggestion that ICHEIC's Valuation Committee (which consists of all ICHEIC parties) should meet to deal with inconsistencies in interpreting the rules and unforeseen issues, Chairman Eagleburger stated that these rules were finalized on October 16, 2002, when the agreement with the German Foundation was signed. He went on to say, "These are, in effect, contractual obligations. As such they cannot be unilaterally set aside. That may be the way you do business in California but it would be my definition of truly amateurish."[5]

Chairman Eagleburger obviously did not read or does not understand the agreement he signed with the German Foundation. That agreement stated, "The parties shall endeavor in good faith to resolve any dispute in relation to the interpretation or application of this Agreement amicably by negotiations between the parties."[6] These words were purposely inserted into the agreement in order to finalize it, its creators being cognizant that many issues had not been resolved and others could arise in interpreting the agreement.

At the November 16, 2004, ICHEIC meeting, a key issue was the completion of the claims processing. It was now hoped that this task would be concluded by the end of 2005 with appeals and audits finished by mid-2006.[7] This compares with the initial planned ICHEIC closure date of late 2002, later postponed to the end of 2004. Even the completion goal set at the November 2004 meeting will be difficult to accomplish considering that only 43 percent of eligible claims had been processed by companies as of April 15, 2005 (according to statistics at www.ICHEIC.org).

Achieving the completion goal has been made even more questionable by the termination "with cause" of the Israeli-based Generali Trust Fund (GTF) that had been handling the processing of Generali claims, which account for most ICHEIC claims.[8] At the November 16 meeting, it still remained unclear whether the processing of these claims would be taken over by Generali headquarters in Italy or by a new organization established in Israel.

Although Chairman Eagleburger in his termination letter tried to place the blame on the GTF, this was clearly another ICHEIC management malfunction. Since signing a contract with the GTF in April 2001, ICHEIC has failed to provide adequate oversight despite the fact that it had been told from the start that GTF's labor power was inadequate. Moreover, U.S. state regulators continuously pointed out the many GTF processing errors and the problems created by GTF's insistence that it follow Israeli law rather than ICHEIC rules in regard to documents required of claimants, such as those that link heirs to policyholders.

By the time ICHEIC completes its task, it will probably have paid some $150 million to claimants and some $300 million for humanitarian purposes to account for the many unpaid policies for which no claim was filed or the claimant lacked sufficient information. This total of $450 million is only about 3 percent of the $15 billion (in 2003 values) conservative estimate of the face value of Holocaust-era life insurance policies that remained unpaid immediately before the start of ICHEIC. Little or nothing will be paid to account for the sizable losses incurred under nonlife policies.

The heart of ICHEIC's problem is a common human flaw. Those with a political bent often are successful in fostering good ideas by drawing people together and effectively balancing conflicting interests. But they often lack the skills, patience, and interest to deal with day-to-day governance and management. This was ICHEIC's story.

NOTES

1. *See* website of House Reform Committee, www.democrats.reform.house.gov/investigation.asp?Issue=Holocaust-Era+insurance+restitution.

2. Richard Wolffe, "Belief Wanes in Holocaust Insurance Process," *Financial Times*, 25 Jan. 2002.

3. Editorial, "The Holocaust Endures," *Baltimore Sun*, 14 July 2002.

4. "Holocaust and Insurance: Too Late, Too Slow, Too Expensive," *Economist*, 2 Aug. 2003.

5. www.ICHEIC.org.

6. Agreement concerning Holocaust Era Claims between ICHEIC and the German Foundation for "Remembrance, Responsibility, and the Future," section 11(3). www.ICHEIC.org.

7. Presentation: Meeting of ICHEIC, Washington, D.C., 16 Nov. 2004, www.ICHEIC.org.

8. Letter from Chairman Eagleburger to ICHEIC Commissioners, Alternates and Observers, 1 Nov. 2004.

Part V

The Looted Art Litigation

Chapter 24

The Holocaust Claims Processing Office
New York State's Approach to Resolving Holocaust-Era Art Claims

Monica S. Dugot

> Ismar Littmann was my grandfather. I never got to know him. Ismar Littmann committed suicide in 1934, when the world as he knew it was crashing down around him. Within five years of his death, his family home was abandoned, his children had fled Germany for different continents, his wife escaped to England, and his life's treasure, his art collection, had disappeared: lost, looted, confiscated, stolen. . . . What a tragedy that his collection was dispersed, and that his reputation as a great collector was never recognized or acknowledged. I am therefore so grateful . . . to the museums that have already willingly come forward in Emden, Cologne and Berlin, to return pieces from our family collection and to connect Ismar Littmann's name to the ownership. . . . We are only one family looking for our heritage; there are many others. And there's still so much left to be done.
> —Jane Lerner, granddaughter of Dr. Ismar Littmann

And there's still so much left to be done. These closing remarks by Jane Lerner, the daughter of Dr. Ismar Littmann's eldest daughter, Eva, at a ceremony in New York in February 2001 celebrating the return of Alexander Kanoldt's *Olevano,* summarize the situation in which the art world finds itself. For all the hard work that has gone into researching Nazi-era art looting and clarifying the provenance of many items and collections, there is much that remains to be done.

The event at which Jane Lerner spoke was both celebration and commemoration. *Olevano* was part of a large collection originally owned by Dr. Littmann, a prominent attorney, art collector, and supporter of the arts, in prewar Breslau, Silesia, and Poland. With the Nazis' rise to power, Dr. Littmann suffered considerable personal and professional persecution that led to his suicide in 1934. His family was forced to liquidate his art collection shortly thereafter. Part of his collection of almost six thousand paintings and drawings was sold at auction while many other pieces of the collection were simply confiscated. *Olevano,* which had hung in the National Gallery in Berlin since 1951, was recovered as part of a Holocaust-era settlement arranged by the New York State Banking Department's Holocaust Claims Processing Office (HCPO).

The Littmann claim was one of the very first art claims filed with the HCPO. Still, many elements of this early claim are echoed in subsequent claims filed by owners and heirs seeking to recover their collections lost or looted during the Nazi era. Since the Littmann heirs filed their claim, the HCPO has received more than 120 claims from individuals in nine countries and eighteen states seeking the location and return of a total of approximately twenty-five thousand objects, ranging from relatively minor objects to major works of art.

How does a state bank regulatory agency find itself involved with art restitution issues? For the HCPO, it was a natural outgrowth of the office's original mandate. Established in 1997 by Governor George E. Pataki, the HCPO was originally intended to provide assistance to Holocaust survivors, or their heirs, seeking to recover assets deposited in Swiss banks. The office's mission quickly expanded to meet the real needs of its constituents and by late 1997 the HCPO found itself working to assist claimants seeking to recover assets held in other European banks, proceeds from Holocaust-era insurance policies, as well as lost, looted, or stolen art. This was done not merely to simplify the claims process for claimants but also to address banking and insurance claims in their entirety. After all, some bank claims referenced art stored in safe deposit boxes; similarly, insurance claims were filed relating to insured art objects stolen during World War II. Thus, the HCPO found itself developing an expertise in art-restitution issues.

Over the last six years, the HCPO has been effective in resolving a number of art disputes, ranging from a painting in a North Carolina museum to paintings discovered in European collections and auction houses, providing evidence that just resolution of Holocaust-era art claims is possible, although it takes time, perseverance, and diverse skills. The HCPO has been an especially valuable advocate for claimants whose paintings have been found in public institutions; for claimants whose looted paintings ended up in a financial institution; for claimants seeking to recover sizable collections; for claimants seeking to recover paintings of low monetary value; for claimants with well-documented claims; and for claimants with limited resources.

The HCPO's successes in investigating and locating these items is due to a dedicated team of professionals with a broad range of skills who can draw on their legal, historical, economic, and linguistic backgrounds. The team secures documentation so as to strengthen and bolster claims. The multifaceted aspect of the office is the key to successful restitution: it is not uncommon for an art claim to include three languages, if not more, depending on where the family lived before the war, the exact circumstances of the painting's confiscation, and the place where the painting might have been subsequently sold. In addition, the research necessary to secure restitution is not limited to one area, such as art-historical research; the circumstances of the seizure make these cases as much a part of social, business, and economic history as art history. Knowing how they were seized, how they might have been resold, and how they might have entered any of thousands of collections around the world provides critical clues to tracking a work of art.

Holocaust-era provenance research is a time-consuming task. Often this is due to the paucity of published and accessible provenance information. The Nazis looted across the board and many of the paintings they seized were not limited to the much reported museum-quality seizures for Hitler's "Führer Museum" in Linz, Austria. On the contrary, they also took ordinary middle-class collections as well—second-tier paintings, tapestries, decorative arts, and antiquities. For many of these items, the art-historical literature is not particularly deep, making restitution work difficult and labor intensive. Furthermore, the information needed to resolve a case is usually in more than one place. Prewar collections, such as the Littmann collection, have not survived intact; they have been dispersed and consequently items can and do surface anywhere, which presents considerable logistical challenges. Successful location of items sought by Holocaust survivors and return of these to this aging population or its heirs is only possible through coordinated research and restitution efforts.

Given that each art claim involves a specific and identifiable object, art claims have been resolved on a case-by-case basis. Because looted art claims have not been funneled into a large process or commission and have not been part of the global litigation settlements reached with Switzerland, Germany, France, and Austria, many of these claims, once filed with the HCPO, are directly within the control of the HCPO, from the beginning of the process to its resolution. This is important in that it differs substantially from the more "wholesale approach" on the bank and insurance front, where Holocaust-era asset litigation resulted in the establishment of claims processes and tribunals set up to resolve claims. In the area of Swiss bank and insurance claims, for example, the HCPO is dependent on outside entities such as the Swiss Claims Resolution Tribunal and the International Commission on Holocaust-Era Insurance Claims. Thus, despite a significant amount of success, the HCPO has run into frustrating delays in the resolution of a number of these claims.

In contrast, because the HCPO handles art claims independently of any overarching process or commission, it is able to be creative in coming up with fair and swift solutions. This is not to suggest that it resolves art claims in isolation. Most often, complex provenance research needs to be done in cooperation with any entity that seems likely to have pertinent information. It is a fact that most claimants do not come to the HCPO bearing detailed provenance information; indeed, sometimes the evidence of ownership is a dim childhood recollection of having seen a painting in a parent's dining room.

That being said, one voice or source is rarely enough to prove a claim: experience has shown that proper research and ultimately fair resolution of Holocaust-era art claims requires collecting the most detailed and accurate information possible, including working with museums and archivists, as well as with all other participants in the sale and transfer of artwork. Wherever possible, the HCPO has endeavored to cooperate with all such groups and individuals.

Still, in addition to research, close attention to what the individual claimants have to say is vital. They hold the most critical pieces of the puzzle. Often, the resolution of Holocaust-era claims turns on the quality and degree of a claimant's documentation. It is important to note, however, that less information does not necessarily result in a less compelling case, just one that may be—and often is—more difficult to adjudicate.

As the HCPO endeavors to resolve claims, one of the ground rules has been that all means of restitution outside the court system are explored. The HCPO team has come to rely heavily on urging disparate parties to cooperate. Where cooperation among parties exists, claims can be presented clearly and convincingly—while the current generation of claimants is still alive—to secure closure on an issue that has remained unresolved for far too long.

Experience with lawsuits filed in the United States has shown that litigation is not the most productive avenue for reaching fair and appropriate solutions with regard to artwork looted during the Nazi era. First, it is very costly. Attorneys' fees can easily exceed the monetary value of the works involved. Second, the legal process can be an emotionally wrenching and public affair. Moreover, litigation results in resolutions that are unpredictable, often cash driven, and anything but amicable. To date the HCPO has avoided litigation by promoting a climate of cooperation. The HCPO has been aided on this front by new protocols and policies concerning art restitution matters in Europe, the existence of the Washington Conference Principles on Nazi-Confiscated Art, the American Association of Museums' and the Association of Art Museum Directors' ethical guidelines and principles regarding Nazi-era spoliation of art, and the Holocaust Victims Redress Act, Public Law No. 105-158, 112 Stat. 15 (1998), which calls on all governments to take action to ensure that artworks confiscated by the Nazis be returned to their rightful owners. The guidelines exert strong moral pressure and reflect a spirit of fairness. They also encourage institutions to provide provenance information and, importantly, to clarify that institutions may elect to waive certain available defenses in order to achieve equitable and appropriate resolutions of claims.

Because of its success in providing a centralized venue for Holocaust survivors, their heirs, and the heirs of Holocaust victims over the years, the HCPO has become a recognized authority on matters relating to Holocaust-era losses, compensation, and restitution. The office has been able to leverage this unique position, as well as its position as an office within the New York State Banking Department, to exert pressure on other entities such as state-funded museums and financial institutions, thereby making these entities more responsive to claimants.

Claims where the HCPO has been particularly successful in achieving fair resolution include instances where the painting being sought has been found in a public or government-funded museum. Paintings that are located in public institutions provide the HCPO, a state agency, with a unique opportunity to engage in both intergovernmental and intragovernmental dialogue. For example, three paintings, Lucas Cranach the Elder's *Madonna and Child in a Landscape* in the North Carolina Museum of Art, Lesser Ury's *The Seamstress* in the New Gallery in Linz, and Corneille de

Lyon's *Portrait of Jean d'Albon* in the Virginia Museum of Fine Arts were located in public collections. *The Seamstress,* which had been owned by a German businessman and sold under duress in 1941, was located in an Austrian municipal collection and was returned to the grandson of the original owner. In the second case, *Madonna and Child in a Landscape,* owned by an Austrian industrialist and seized by the Nazis, turned up in a public collection in North Carolina. *Portrait of Jean d'Albon,* in turn, had been owned by the collector Julius Priester, who lived in Vienna, Austria. As a result of Nazi persecution, Mr. Priester fled to Mexico in 1938 and the *Portrait* and other paintings were seized by the Gestapo in 1944 from the Max Fohr depot. The *Portrait* was ultimately found in Virginia in early 2004.

These three families had been trying to locate the collections and achieve the return of individual paintings since the end of World War II. Before they filed claims with the HCPO, these restitution attempts only led to enormous amounts of paper. However, when these papers were compiled correctly and read in context, they made very compelling cases. In all cases the HCPO found that approaching the three museums directly, sharing all information available, and fostering a reasoned dialogue among the parties was enormously successful. The preponderance of the evidence, along with this approach, led the museums to acknowledge the rightful ownership of the claimants without undue expense or delay.

The HCPO has been able to successfully use its leverage to resolve a number of art claims for the heirs of Dr. Littmann. In the matter of Kanoldt's *Olevano,* the HCPO urged the Conference on Jewish Material Claims against Germany ("Claims Conference") to withdraw its claim to the painting so that the National Gallery in Berlin could return *Olevano* to its rightful owners. The Claims Conference had filed a universal claim for the Littmann collection in 1998, an action that succeeded in preserving the legal rights of the Littmann heirs. *Olevano,* together with roughly one thousand works from the Littmann collection, had been sold at the Berlin auction house Max Perl on February 26 and 27, 1935. Also in this same sale was Lovis Corinth's *Portrait of Charlotte Corinth,* another painting from the Littmann collection that the HCPO was able to recover from the Hamburgische Landesbank, a financial institution in Germany. After being sold at Max Perl, *Portrait of Charlotte Corinth* arrived at the National Gallery in Berlin, from which a Berlin art dealer acquired it in 1940. In subsequent years, the painting changed hands on at least three occasions, ultimately arriving at the Hamburgische Landesbank, which held the painting as collateral for a loan. When the borrower defaulted, the bank put the painting up for sale. As an office within the state banking regulatory agency, the HCPO was able to work closely with the Hamburgische Landesbank and promptly secure the return of the painting to the Littmann family.

Indeed, the Littmann claim serves to illustrate why and how the HCPO has been effective in resolving looted art claims and what is critical for the successful resolution of Holocaust-era art claims. The claim demonstrates that the willingness to coordinate and cooperate with various groups is as essential as is the need to remain focused and to doggedly pursue each and every claim, regardless of the monetary value of the art in question. Because the HCPO charges no fee to pursue claims nor is its service contingent upon a percentage of claimants' restitution awards, the HCPO can pursue a claim regardless of the value of the object. Thus, there is no ulterior motive or internal conflict of interest. The value the HCPO brings to the table is that the office does not only depend on recovery of the object for successful resolution of a claim; successful resolution can be formal acknowledgment to the claimant by the current holder that a painting was wrongfully taken from the claimant or his or her family. Success can also simply be achieving closure for a claimant by showing the claimant that the painting believed to have belonged to a grandparent and consequently looted could not have been the one being sought given that it had been in continuous ownership by another family for over a hundred years.

Not driven by the need to make a profit, the HCPO can seek solutions that are in the best interest of the claimant. Other for-profit organizations, lawyers, and even certain not-for-profit groups do not necessarily have the luxury of pursuing a claim for a painting where the expenses exceed the actual value of the painting. The HCPO has therefore been able to take on a number of art claims that would have nowhere else to go. These claims are by no means less important and deserve attention.

For example, the HCPO was effective in recovering four objects seized or looted from the Littmann collection precisely because of its ability to focus on all objects in the collection, not only those of very high value, thus pursuing the claim in its entirety. Like so many others, Ismar Littmann's collection is comprised of works that range from being very valuable to those whose value is largely sentimental. To illustrate, last summer, again assisted by the HCPO, the heirs of Ismar Littmann recovered Lucien Adrion's *La Procession,* which had been put up for auction at Villa Grisebach by the Friedrich Ebert Stiftung in Germany. Although the painting has enormous emotional significance to the heirs, it is not monetarily valuable. *La Procession* now hangs in the home of Ruth Haller, Ismar Littman's youngest daughter, in Israel.

Of Littmann's four children, only Ruth Haller remains alive. Now in her eighties, assisted by her husband Chaim, she continues to search for her father's vast collection in an effort to piece together her lost family history and legacy, and to ensure that his significant collection, consisting largely of German expressionist works, finally receives the recognition it deserves.

As to how to resolve these cases fairly, guidelines and principles actually exist but the key lies in the quality of documentation. If a case is well documented, it is often difficult to do better than the HCPO. This has been the HCPO's experience in a number of cases, which include *Madonna and Child in a Landscape, The Seamstress,* and *Olevano.* Claims are often difficult to resolve because what is most often lacking is specific provenance information and archival documentation such as Nazi seizure documents and shipping records. The reality is that few Holocaust-era looted art cases are as well documented as the claim for *Madonna and Child in a Landscape,* and even after much research has been done, gaps in provenance still remain.

Although such claims are more challenging, the HCPO has been able to facilitate amicable agreements between claimants and institutions even where gaps in the provenance still remained. Emil Nolde's *Bauernhof* was owned by Heinrich and Elizabeth Bamberger of Frankfurt am Main in Germany prior to World War II. In 1938, Mrs. Bamberger, by then a widow, was forced to register all of her property with the Nazi authorities. She fled Germany in 1940, leaving her property behind with the cantor of her synagogue. During the war, the painting ended up in the hands of Wilhelm Schumann, an art dealer and member of the Nazi Party. The painting subsequently changed hands several times over the years, eventually ending up in 1984 in the Kunsthalle in Emden in Germany as a bequest from the Henri Nannen Foundation.

Although the HCPO researched the claim extensively, a small gap in the painting's provenance remained. Nonetheless, an amicable settlement was achieved, leaving *Bauernhof* in the Kunsthalle, exhibited with its proper provenance and referencing the former prewar ownership of the claimant's family.

The HCPO is able to assist claimants who have limited resources, but without easy access to certain data, the HCPO has been at times limited in the assistance it can provide.

While it is unrealistic to expect that all relevant information be made publicly available anytime soon, important steps towards accomplishing this goal continue to be made. More and more public and private databases are now available online. These new developments are both important and eminently helpful as the HCPO continues to assist claimants in locating and recovering their objects.

Art restitution is a painful exercise for everyone involved and requires creative thinking by all parties and a willingness to craft solutions that at first glance may appear highly unusual. At the same time it is critical to remember that there is nothing "usual" about the events that have led us to this task. Museums and private and public collections find themselves at times faced with doing something that is not part and parcel of the normal course of business, namely "de-accessioning" treasured items. The art market as a whole finds itself suffering from the effects of uncertainty, and claimants find themselves having to relive traumatic events that took place more than a half-century ago. Moreover, while the successful return of a family treasure is a joyous and momentous occasion worth celebrating, it is also a bittersweet reminder of other painful losses. Perhaps this was best expressed by the heirs of Philipp von Gomperz, who, after being told that the North Carolina Museum of Art had decided to return *Madonna and Child in a Landscape,* responded, "If only Father had lived long enough to see this!"

The HCPO has been a steadfast advocate for Holocaust survivors, their heirs, and the heirs of those who perished, assisting individuals of all backgrounds to achieve some measure of justice in the resolution of their claims. The HCPO's experience shows that the restitution process can be less complicated and painful if conducted by means of an honest, reasoned, respectful dialogue, and in a spirit of cooperation that sets out to avoid the rancor so often part and parcel of litigation. Its steadfast commitment to these ground rules stems from the belief that survivors and heirs should not be traumatized anew through their recovery efforts. Moreover, the HCPO's philosophy is based on the recognition that it is in all our interests to arrive at fair and just resolution of these claims so that we may achieve closure for claimants, the current holders, and future generations alike.

Chapter 25

Portrait of Wally

The U.S. Government's Role in Recovering
Holocaust Looted Art

Howard N. Spiegler

In 1999, a magistrate judge, acting in response to a request by the U.S. Government, issued a seizure warrant for a portrait by the noted Austrian artist Egon Schiele. The work was on loan to the Museum of Modern Art in New York ("MoMA") from the Leopold Museum in Vienna as part of a major Schiele exhibition. Although the other works in the show had been allowed to go to their next destination when the exhibition ended in early 1998, the portrait, a haunting depiction of Schiele's mistress Wally Neuzil entitled *Portrait of Wally*, had been subpoenaed by New York State authorities and became the centerpiece of a civil forfeiture action brought by the federal government. The case, *U.S. v. Portrait of Wally* (or simply "the Schiele Case," as it also known), has gained symbolic importance as one of the cornerstones of the contemporary movement to restore artworks looted by the Nazis to their former owners or their heirs.

This case has also generated much controversy. While many see it as an important step in the efforts to correct a small portion of the innumerable injustices perpetrated by Nazi Germany, others view it as an attempt by the U.S. Government to insert itself unnecessarily into a private dispute over property rights in a work of art. Still others view it as a threat to the long-standing cooperation among museums in the United States, their foreign counterparts, and private individuals that has permitted loans of important artworks to this country for exhibition. As a member of the law firm representing the Estate of Lea Bondi Jaray (generally referred to as "Lea Bondi"), who is acknowledged by all sides to the litigation to have been the painting's owner before World War II, I would like to address some of the controversy that has arisen since the lawsuit's inception and to respond to the arguments that have been raised against it. Before doing so, however, I will recount the basic facts for those who may not be familiar with them. Because of my involvement in the case, I will limit my discussion to facts that are already "on the record," i.e., those that were alleged in the Government's Third Verified Complaint.[1]

In the late 1930s, after Nazi Germany's annexation of Austria, Lea Bondi, a well-known Jewish art dealer, was forced to sell her gallery to a Nazi art dealer named Friedrich Welz pursuant to recently adopted "Aryanization" laws in Austria prohibiting Jewish business ownership. *Portrait of Wally,* however, was in Bondi's private collection, which she kept in her apartment. Shortly before Bondi and her husband fled to England, Welz (who was interned after the war for two years by the United States Forces on suspicion of war crimes) came to their apartment and, upon spotting *Wally,* insisted that she give it to him. This is what transpired, as set forth in the Complaint, based on Lea Bondi's letters:

> Welz . . . observed *Wally* hanging on the wall and insisted that he have it under the Gallery's "aryanization." Bondi responded that it was part of her private collection and had nothing to do with the Gallery. Welz continued to pressure Bondi for the painting. Bondi's husband finally told her that, as they wanted to leave Austria, perhaps as soon as the next day, she should not resist Welz because "you know what he can do." Bondi surrendered *Wally* to Welz.

Meanwhile, around that time, another Viennese art collector, Dr. Heinrich Rieger, was forced to sell his art collection to Welz; it included a number of Schiele's works. Rieger was subsequently deported to the Theresienstadt concentration camp, where he died shortly thereafter.

After the war, U.S. military forces in Austria arrested Welz and seized his artworks, including *Wally,* as well as the artworks that he had taken from Rieger. These were all transferred to the Austrian Government, as it was the policy and practice of the Allied forces to return artworks looted by the Nazis outside of Germany to the governments of the countries of origin. But in this case, there was a mix-up. According to the records of the U.S. Forces, *Portrait of Wally* was mistakenly mixed in with the seized Rieger works. The Americans were aware of the apparent error, however, and notified the Austrian Government.

Nevertheless, when the Rieger heirs later agreed to sell their collection to the government-owned Austrian National Gallery in the Belvedere, the *Wally* was still mixed in with the Rieger works shipped to the Belvedere, and the Belvedere took *Portrait of Wally* for itself. It thus became part of *its* collection, despite the fact that, as its own internal records show, it was well aware of the mistake.

It was not until years later, well after the war, however, that Lea Bondi, who then lived in London, learned that her painting was hanging in the Belvedere. In 1953, Dr. Rudolph Leopold, an Austrian Schiele collector, paid Bondi a visit and confirmed that he had seen *Portrait of Wally* at the Belvedere. Bondi asked Leopold to help her recover her painting, since her prior entreaties to the Belvedere had been ignored.

But instead of helping Bondi retrieve her painting, Leopold entered into an agreement with the Belvedere whereby he exchanged a Schiele painting from his own collection for *Portrait of Wally*, and kept *Wally* for himself. When Bondi discovered Leopold's deceit years later, she retained lawyers to attempt to convince Leopold to return her painting to her, but to no avail. She never brought a lawsuit, however, believing that it was futile to try to defeat Leopold in an Austrian legal proceeding. As she said in one of her letters, she felt that "everyone," including her lawyers, "was siding with Dr. Leopold." Lea Bondi died in 1969 without having recovered her painting.

In 1994, Leopold's art collection, including *Portrait of Wally*, became part of the newly formed Leopold Museum where Leopold himself is "Director for Life." In late 1997, *Wally* was included in an exhibit of Schiele paintings loaned by the Leopold Museum to MoMA. In the catalogue prepared by Leopold that was used for this exhibition, he changed the provenance of *Wally* that he had published in an earlier catalogue raisonné, and listed Rieger as having acquired the painting from Lea Bondi.

When Bondi's heirs learned that the painting was being exhibited at MoMA, they demanded that MoMA hold the work pending the resolution of their claim. MoMA refused, citing its contractual obligation to return the painting to the Leopold Museum at the end of the exhibition.

Robert M. Morgenthau, the District Attorney of New York County, then issued a subpoena for the painting in connection with a criminal investigation he had commenced into the matter, but the subpoena was quashed by the New York Court of Appeals a year later. Within hours of that decision, the U.S. Customs Service obtained a warrant of seizure of the painting, and Mary Jo White, the U.S. attorney for the Southern District of New York, commenced an action alleging that stolen property (the

Wally) had been knowingly imported into the United States in violation of the National Stolen Property Act and was therefore subject to forfeiture to the Government.

One important question that has repeatedly been raised about the Schiele case by certain museum representatives and others is simply this: Why is the U.S. Government involved in this case at all? Why are the Government's resources being committed to what these same critics have characterized as nothing more than a title dispute between the Leopold Museum and the Bondi family, one that should be resolved in a civil lawsuit between them?

This question is important because it really raises the issue of whether the United States and, indeed, other governments should play a significant role in trying to resolve Nazi-looted art claims. Although I cannot speak for the Government, I think that this civil forfeiture action is both consistent with and fully promotes the United States' express public policy interests regarding Holocaust-looted art.

Let us begin with the allegations in the Government's Complaint: that the *Wally* was stolen by a Nazi agent from Lea Bondi in 1939, wrongfully acquired by Leopold, and then knowingly imported into the United States in violation of the National Stolen Property Act. In other words, what is alleged against the Leopold Museum is that it knowingly trafficked in stolen property in the United States. After an exhibition at one of this country's foremost museums, the Leopold Museum was going to take this stolen property out of the country, while the heirs of the true owner, among them several U.S. citizens, stood helplessly by. The heirs could not ask a court to seize the property pending a resolution of the matter because New York State law immunizes art loaned from abroad from judicial seizure. So the U.S. Government acted, and acted quickly, to assure that the stolen property did not leave the country.

As Chief Judge Michael B. Mukasey determined, "On its face, [the National Stolen Property Act] proscribes the transportation in foreign commerce of all property over $5,000 known to be stolen or converted. Although the museum parties and *amici* would have it otherwise, art on loan to a museum—even a 'world-renowned museum'—is not exempt." Explaining further, the court added that "if *Wally* is stolen or converted, application of [the National Stolen Property Act] will 'discourage both the receiving of stolen goods and the initial taking,' which was Congress's apparent purpose." The court concluded that "there is a strong federal interest in enforcing these laws."

Indeed, when Nazi-looted art is involved, the U.S. Government's interest is even more sharply brought into focus. In 1998, the United States led the way in urging governments around the world to seek to effectuate the policy of identifying art looted from the Nazis and returning it to its rightful owners. The U.S. Government convened a conference of government officials, art experts, museum officials, and many other interested parties from around the world in Washington at that time to consider and debate the many issues raised by the continuing discovery of Nazi-looted assets, including artworks.[2] The conference promulgated eleven principles concerning Nazi-confiscated art, which were adopted by forty-four nations. One principle states that pre-war owners and their heirs should be encouraged to come forward to make known their claims to art that was confiscated by the Nazis and not subsequently restituted, and another states that, once they do so, steps should be taken expeditiously to achieve a just and fair solution, which may vary according to the facts and circumstances surrounding a specific case.

Another principle adopted in Washington encouraged the resolution of these disputes by "alternative dispute resolution," where possible, to avoid long, drawn-out litigation. There has been much hand wringing and complaining by those who say simply that the Schiele case should have been settled and that this long litigation in state and federal courts is exactly the wrong way to go about resolving Nazi-looted art claims. But let us not put the cart before the horse here. The U.S. Government brought this action and seized *Wally* before it was about to be sent to Austria and thus placed beyond the reach of any plausible attempt at resolution. The Austrian Government, while adopting a law in 1998 that purportedly was designed to ensure the careful review of claims for Nazi-looted artworks in the Austrian Government's possession, has determined that, as a "private foundation" under Austrian law, the Leopold Museum is not covered by this statute, despite the fact that the Austrian Government provides a substantial amount of its funding and appoints half of its board of directors. Moreover, in a recent decision involving a Holocaust art claim in federal court in California, the court held that the Austrian courts are an inadequate forum for determining art claims because, among other things, of their exorbitant court filing fees, which the court described as "oppressively burdensome": they would have totaled over one hundred thousand dollars, just for asserting a claim in an Austrian court.[3]

Although cases can and should be settled, it takes two to tango and the dance has obviously not ended yet—perhaps because the Leopold Museum assumed that it would succeed in having the case dismissed at the outset. But whether or not this case is ever resolved short of trial, commencing this forfeiture action without delay and securing the artwork in the United States certainly promoted the U.S. Government's interest in fairly resolving these cases and preventing the trafficking in stolen Holocaust property.

Another question that has been raised about the Schiele case has been voiced by some museums. They worry about the "chilling effect" that a case like Schiele will have on the willingness of foreign museums and others to loan art to American museums for exhibition. These museums claim that, even though potential lenders may not say why they are not loaning art, the real hidden reason for their occasional refusal is that they fear that their artwork will be unfairly seized.[4] Put that way, of course, it is virtually impossible to measure whether the Schiele case has had any such chilling effect on the frequency of art loans from abroad. But more importantly, there is something seriously illogical about this contention.

Besides the automatic immunity afforded by the law of New York and a few other states, which prevents almost all seizures of loaned artwork— but cannot interfere with the federal government's ability to seize and commence forfeiture proceedings against stolen artwork—there is much more sweeping protection available to potential lenders. Pursuant to a federal statute, any not-for-profit museum or other exhibitor may apply to the U.S. State Department for a determination that the art to be loaned from abroad for exhibition is culturally significant and that its exhibition is in the national interest. If the application is granted, the art is automatically immunized from judicial seizure at the state or federal level, including by the federal government. For some reason, however, no such application was made to the State Department with respect to the Leopold Museum loan exhibition.

The procedure that the State Department follows to determine whether the exhibition of the loaned art is in the national interest is apparently designed to ensure that Nazi-looted art and other items of questionable provenance are not granted immunity from seizure; it thus effectively balances the Government's interest in encouraging other countries to participate in the exchange of cultural property with its equally compelling interest in ensuring that Nazi-looted property is identified and returned to its rightful owners.[5] In order to obtain a determination that the loan of the artworks is in the national interest, the applicant must certify that it has undertaken professional inquiry, including independent, multi-source research into the provenance of the objects being loaned. The applicant also must certify that it does not know, or have reason to know, of any circumstances with respect to any of the objects that would indicate the potential for competing claims of ownership, or, for objects for which such circumstances do exist, the applicant must describe those circumstances as well as the likelihood that any such claim would succeed.

One assumes that if the State Department received information that demonstrates that the artwork to be loaned was looted by the Nazis and never restored to the true owner's family, the application would be denied and judicial immunity from seizure could not be obtained. Thus, any failure by a museum to apply for immunity should result either from ignorance of the procedure or from the fact that a serious question about the artwork's provenance and ownership has arisen, which causes the lender and/or the borrower to fear submitting it to government scrutiny.

From my firm's own experience advising museums both in the United States and abroad about immunity, we have found that foreign art lenders have started to *require* that borrowing museums obtain immunity determinations before loans are made, but neither the application process nor the provenance certification is difficult to accomplish in the usual case. Moreover, the large number of wonderful exhibitions of art that continue to be loaned from abroad to museums throughout the United States, as well as the numerous notices of immunized loans regularly published by the Federal Register, should be a comfort to all those who fear being chilled out of the market.

As shown by its prosecution of the case of *U.S. v. Portrait of Wally*, the U.S. Government has played an important role in trying to correct some of the terrible wrongs wrought by the Holocaust, while ensuring that the free flow of loans of cultural property to museums in this country continues at a healthy pace. Despite cries of alarm from those who fear that their interests are threatened by the efforts of the families of Holocaust victims to reclaim their property, as demonstrated above, there are ways to accommodate the varying interests involved in a fair and reasonable manner.

NOTES

1. The legal proceedings and facts alleged by the Government are recited in Chief Judge Michael B. Mukasey's opinion in the case denying the Leopold Museum's and MoMA's omnibus dismissal motions. *See* U.S. v. Portrait of Wally,

2002 U.S. Dist. LEXIS 6445 (S.D.N.Y. 2002). Several of these allegations are disputed by the other parties, and they will ultimately be determined at the trial.

2. See Proceedings of the Washington Conference on Holocaust-Era Assets, *available at* http://www.state.gov/www/regions/eur/holocaust/heac.html.

3. Altmann v. Austria, 142 F. Supp. 2d 1187, 1210 (C.D. Cal. 2001). On appeal, the Ninth Circuit disagreed with the district court's analysis and determined that the filing fees for cases in Austrian courts did not render them an inadequate forum. Altmann v. Austria, 317 F.3d 954, 972 (9th Cir. 2002), aff'd on other grounds, 124 S. Ct. 2240 (2004). A detailed discussion of this case is found in another essay in this volume. *See* E. Randol Schoenberg, "Whose Art Is It Anyway?"

4. Celestine Bohlen, "Judge Revives Case of Nazi-Looted Art," *New York Times,* April 27, 2002, at B9 (quoting Stephen W. Clark, MoMA's Associate General Counsel).

5. The State Department's website sets forth the text of the Immunity from Seizure Act as well as detailed information about applying for immunity. *See* http://www.state.gov/s/l/c3432.htm.

Chapter 26

Whose Art Is It Anyway?

E. Randol Schoenberg

My grandparents were all Austrian refugees from Hitler. My father's parents, the composer Arnold Schoenberg and his wife Gertrud, famously fled in the middle of the night from Berlin in May 1933 several weeks after Nazi culture minister Josef Goebbels announced that Jewish artists and intellectuals had to be expelled from all German universities and cultural institutions.[1] My maternal grandparents, Eric and Trude Zeisl, fled Vienna on November 10, 1938, the day after Kristallnacht.[2] My grandparents left behind not only their careers and the cultural institutions that had supported them but also large numbers of their extended families, among them my great-grandfather Siegmund Zeisl, who was later deported from Vienna to Theresienstadt and murdered at Treblinka.

I had been an avid genealogist and family historian since I was in grade school. This hobby naturally led to an interest in the Holocaust and its effect on my family. Not surprisingly, it was through genealogy that I first came into contact with the Holocaust restitution movement. An early article by Gregg Rickman,[3] an aide to Senator Alphonse d'Amato, in a genealogy magazine alerted me to the catalogue of 1938 asset declarations submitted by Austrian Jews that had been compiled by Dr. Hubert Steiner at the Austrian State Archives.[4] I immediately ordered files for twenty of my relatives, not knowing then that documents such as these would become the cornerstone for Austrian restitution efforts in the coming years.

In September 1998, an old family friend, Maria Altmann, called me and asked if I could help her with regard to her uncle's property that had been taken by the Nazis. She had just received a call from Peter Moser, the former Austrian consul general in Los Angeles (and future Austrian ambassador in Washington), who told her that there was talk in Vienna of returning the famous Klimt paintings that had belonged to her uncle and aunt Ferdinand and Adele Bloch-Bauer. In December 1997 an article by Judith Dobrzynski in the *New York Times* led to the seizure of two paintings by Egon Schiele that had been loaned to an exhibit at the Museum of Modern Art by an Austrian museum. In response, the Austrian cultural minister, Elisabeth Gehrer, decried the seizures and declared that there were no looted paintings in Austria. An Austrian journalist, Hubertus Czernin, set out to prove her wrong. In a series of stories published in *Der Standard* in the spring of 1998, Czernin described the manner in which the postwar Austrian authorities had managed to extort "donations" of looted artworks from Jewish families like the Rothschilds, Bloch-Bauers, and Lederers. Czernin quoted directly from the files of the Austrian government, which told the story in black and white. In March 1948, for example, the director of the Austrian Gallery had written to the Austrian Federal Monument Agency asking for a "delayed handling" of the Bloch-Bauer family's request for export permits "for tactical reasons." This delaying strategy effectively forced the Bloch-Bauers' attorney to give up the family's claims to five Klimt paintings in order to obtain export permits for other, ultimately less valuable works.

Minister Gehrer responded by sealing the archives and ordering an internal investigation, which resulted in September 1998 in the promulgation of a new law designed to return Nazi-looted artworks that had been obtained by Austrian federal museums under duress in the postwar period. The announcement of the new law immediately led to speculation concerning the Bloch-Bauer collection of Klimt paintings hanging in the Austrian Gallery. The portrait of Maria Altmann's aunt, Adele Bloch-Bauer, was the most famous painting in the museum, adorning the cover of the museum's official guidebook. I had known the painting and seen it several times since my first visit to Austria in 1978.

The first thing that Mrs. Altmann and I did when the new Austrian law was passed was to write to Minister Gehrer to notify her that the Bloch-Bauer Klimt paintings might fall under the new law. At the time, we did not have the documents that Czernin had discovered, but we had located internal family documents that shed some light on the situation and could not have been known to the Austrians. Minister Gehrer had responded initially to press inquiries by stating that she did not think that the Bloch-Bauer Klimt paintings would have to be returned, but the documents we had uncovered made that premature conclusion seem doubtful. We offered these documents to her, expecting that we would engage in a mutual process of determining what exactly happened to the paintings and whether they should be returned under the new law.

The Austrians had other ideas. Although the new law was touted as a model for restitution at the Washington conference, in practice the law left much to be desired. A commission was established to research the provenance of paintings that it identified as potentially subject to restitution. The law permitted no claims to be made for the return of artworks. Indeed, the victims (or their heirs) were entirely excluded from the process. Moreover, the commission rarely, if ever, sought information from victims or their families; rather, it relied only on often one-sided and misleading documents in government depositories. The provenance report was submitted to an advisory board made up of government bureaucrats. That advisory board met in secret, sought no input from the families who might be claiming the artworks, and made recommendations to Minister Gehrer as to which artworks should be returned.

In the Bloch-Bauer case, I was permitted to see the provenance report before the advisory board discussed the matter. I sent lengthy letters and requested that additional facts and documents be included, but to no avail. The advisory board was not shown my letters or many relevant documents that had been uncovered. I recognized that much of the case rested on the legal issue of whether Adele Bloch-Bauer's will, written in 1923, established a gift of the paintings to the Austrian Gallery when she died in 1925.

In her will, Adele had asked her husband to give the paintings to the museum upon his death. Ferdinand viewed this request as nonbinding, as set forth in the probate documents, because the paintings belonged to him and not her. Yet he apparently stated in 1926 that he intended to abide by her request. Under U.S. law, Adele's request would have been considered precatory and nonbinding. Ferdinand would have been free to change his mind, as he undoubtedly did when the Nazis came in 1938 and confiscated all of his property. Ferdinand fled Austria ahead of the Nazi annexation in March 1938.

In 1943, the Nazis liquidated Ferdinand's entire estate, and the Klimt paintings moved to local museums. In 1945, just after the war ended, Ferdinand died in Zurich and his heirs were unable to recover the paintings. Ferdinand had left his entire estate (consisting solely of restitution claims) to Maria Altmann and her older sister and brother. Not surprisingly, he made no bequest to the Austrian Gallery.

I asked an Austrian attorney specializing in inheritance law, Dr. Andreas Lintl, to draft an opinion letter on the issue of the will. I sent this to Minister Gehrer's section chief for culture, the chairman of the advisory board, Dr. Rudolf Wran, but (as he later admitted to me) it was not distributed to the full board. Instead, Dr. Manfred Kremser, the Austrian state attorney who was a member of the advisory board, wrote his own opinion on the matter, misstating or ignoring much of the evidence and the law.

After press reports signaled that the board might be preparing to reject restitution of the paintings, I telephoned Dr. Wran and Dr. Kremser. I was told that the advisory board had decided that it would not entertain any discussions with claimants, that claimants and their attorneys could not attend the meetings, and that I could not see or respond to any reports that had been written by Dr. Kremser. Indeed, when I offered to come to Vienna to meet with him, Dr. Kremser told me, "You can come to meet with me at any time, but I am not permitted to speak to you about the case." My entreaties for fairness and due process fell on deaf ears. Several weeks later, the advisory board recommended against restitution of the Klimt paintings, and Minister Gehrer immediately accepted and publicly announced that decision. In her defense, Gehrer stated that the paintings could not be returned because they had not been stolen during the Nazi era. She responded to my letters attempting to correct her mistake by suggesting that if we disagreed with her decision we should go to court.

So that is what we prepared to do. We first tried to file suit in Austria. There were two principal impediments to a suit in that country. First, Austria requires the payment of court filing fees in proportion to the amount in dispute. In this case, those fees would have reached almost $2 million, far in excess of Maria Altmann's assets. We therefore made an application to the court to reduce the required fees. The application was granted, in part, with the court finding that Mrs. Altmann would have to pay all, but no more than all, of her available assets. Not content with this result, Austria filed an appeal seeking to raise the fees up to the maximum level. Austria refused to respond to our requests for many months. At that point, we decided to look at our only other alternative—a suit in the United States.

The history of that suit, and the legal issues it has raised, can be seen in district court, appellate court, and Supreme Court decisions.[5] Suffice it to say that Austria has raised every procedural argument possible. By the time the case was heard before the Supreme Court on February 25, 2004, the Austrians were down to their last one—that the Foreign Sovereign Immunities Act of 1976 (FSIA)[6] cannot be applied in cases concerning acts that took place during World War II. Incredibly, the U.S. government weighed in on Austria's side.

On June 7, 2004, the Supreme Court ruled 6 to 3 that Mrs. Altmann's claims could proceed.[7] According to the decision, the FSIA could be applied to all actions, regardless of when the acts underlying the claim took place, even before the enactment of the FSIA in 1976. The Ninth Circuit had already ruled that Mrs. Altmann's claims fell under the so-called expropriation clause of the FSIA because the case concerned rights in property taken in violation of international law, where that property was owned and operated by an agency of a foreign state that conducted business in the United States.[8] Because the Austrian Gallery advertised its exhibits and sold books in the United States, it could be sued under this exception even for property not located in the United States. The Supreme Court let this decision stand and did not review it. So, after almost four years of litigation, Mrs. Altmann's case will soon proceed to trial in federal district court in Los Angeles.

Mrs. Altmann's case is now one of the most prominent cases making its way through the U.S. courts. Holocaust-related litigation is incredibly difficult and time consuming, and the prospects of success, even in exceptional cases such as Mrs. Altmann's, are very low. Nevertheless, in cases concerning Nazi-looted artworks, there is a glimmer of hope.

Editors' Postscript

In May 2005, as this volume was going to press, the Republic of Austria and Mrs. Maria Altmann agreed to settle the case out of court. Under the agreement, the dispute will be resolved by binding arbitration rather than trial. The agreement calls for each party to choose an arbitrator, with the two arbitrators then selecting a third arbitrator, and this panel of arbitrators will render a decision binding upon the parties. All three arbitrators will be Austrian nationals, and the panel will decide the case under Austrian law. Arbitration is set to be completed by November 1, 2005.

Further details can be found at the website accompanying this volume: www.holocaustlitigation.com.

NOTES

1. My grandfather had taught since 1926 the master class for composition at the Preussische Akademie der Künste, the most important music teaching position in central Europe. H. H. Stuckenschmidt, *Arnold Schoenberg: His Life, World, and Work* (Shirmer 1977), 308. He came to Los Angeles in 1934 and taught at both USC and UCLA. From there he worked tirelessly to extricate family and friends from the clutches of the Nazis, and in October 1938 penned his prescient essay, "A Four-Point Program for Jewry," in which he asked, "Is there room in the world for almost 7,000,000 people? Are they condemned to doom? Will they become extinct? Famished? Butchered?" Alexander Ringer, *Arnold Schoenberg: The Composer as Jew* (Clarendon 1990), 230. For a more detailed account see my article, "Arnold Schoenberg and Albert Einstein: Their Relationship and Views on Zionism," *Journal of the Arnold Schoenberg Institute* 10, no. 2 (November 1987), reviewed by Robert Craft, *New York Review of Books* (February 16, 1989).

2. Eric Zeisl was also a composer of classical music. Malcolm S. Cole, *Armseelchen: The Life and Music of Eric Zeisl* (Greenwood 1984).

3. *See also* Gregg J. Rickman, *Swiss Banks and Jewish Souls* (Transaction 1999).

4. Dr. Steiner is an unsung hero of the Holocaust restitution movement who tirelessly assisted Austrian Jewish families in retrieving documents from the Austrian State Archives.

5. Republic of Austria v. Altmann, 124 S. Ct. 2240 (2004).

6. 28 U.S.C §§ 1330, 1602 et. seq.

7. Republic of Austria v. Altmann, 124 S. Ct. 2240 (2004).

8. Altmann v. Republic of Austria, 317 F.3d 954, 967 (9th Cir. 2002).

Part VI

The Litigation's Legacy

Chapter 27

The Unfinished Business of the Unfinished Business of World War II

Stuart E. Eizenstat

I. Introduction

In my book *Imperfect Justice: Looted Assets, Slave Labor, and the Unfinished Business of World War II*,[1] I describe the struggle for belated justice for the victims of World War II through restitution of Holocaust-era assets and my role in that struggle as the presidential and State Department envoy on Holocaust issues during the Clinton administration. In this essay, I focus on those portions of the struggle that still remain unfinished, and offer my prescriptions for their resolution.

Most of the historic Holocaust restitution agreements we reached in the Clinton administration with the Swiss, Germans, Austrians, French, and the former communist nations in Eastern Europe are being faithfully implemented. Billions of dollars of benefits have reached over 1.5 million victims of Nazi aggression, helping them lead a more dignified life in their declining years. But major gaps continue to exist more than four years after we reached the last of the accords.

Bereft of a senior-level special envoy on Holocaust-era issues, and without the engagement of the Bush White House, much of the political and diplomatic pressure that led to landmark Holocaust restitution agreements on slave and forced labor, Swiss and French bank accounts, payment of insurance policies, and the return of confiscated property and Nazi-looted art to their owners has dissipated. Together with an American legal system that moves at a snail's pace, these factors have caused momentum to be lost in several areas, at a time when Holocaust survivors are passing away at a rate of 10 percent per year.

II. The Good News

The Office of Holocaust Assets, created during the Clinton administration, continues to function efficiently with a small staff, under the devoted leadership of Ambassador Ed O'Donnell, my former chief of staff when I was under secretary of state. Ambassador O'Donnell, supported by former secretary of state Colin Powell and Deputy Secretary Richard Armitage, has taken important steps to deal with European anti-Semitism, which, ironically, has increased since the time of our Holocaust restitution agreements, although its cause is related to the importation of the Palestinian intifada into Europe's swelling Muslim population. The Bush administration has effectively put the issue of anti-Semitism on the agenda of the Organization for Security and Cooperation in Europe. The Office of Holocaust Assets has also continued to work on a variety of issues, like the return of communally owned Jewish property and private property restitution in countries like Poland.

Much progress has been made under many of our existing agreements. For example, hundreds of pieces of Jewish communal property—synagogues, schools, community centers, even cemeteries—have been returned to the newly emerged post–Cold War Jewish communities in Central and Eastern Europe, as have thousands of pieces of Christian religious property. In several countries, such as the Czech Republic, Slovakia, and Hungary, private-property restitution funds have been established to pay modest compensation to Holocaust survivors whose private property was confiscated but cannot be returned to them because it either has been destroyed or is being used by other private interests. Moreover, dozens of Nazi-looted works of art have been returned to families from public museums and even from some private collections around the world.

In the Swiss bank case, under the direction of federal judge Edward Korman and the dedicated efforts of his Special Master, Judah Gribetz, it is likely that some $235 million in awards will be made by the end of December 2004 from the $800 million set aside for bank account claims. This represents payments to fifteen hundred people from twenty-six hundred accounts, with an average payment of around $120,000 per account. In addition, by the end of 2004, well over 250,000 people will have been touched by our Swiss agreement, receiving over $700 million, far more than we could have ever imagined when we stumbled into the Swiss affair in 1995 due to a *Wall Street Journal Europe* article that first disclosed the existence of dormant Holocaust-era Swiss bank accounts.

Thus far, under the Swiss accord, 169,739 former slave laborers have collected a total of $246 million, or $1,450 per person, supplementing the payments the laborers have received from the German settlement. In addition, 3,661 refugees have been reached, for a total of $10 million, $3,250 for those who were denied entry into Switzerland when they were fleeing from Nazi persecution and $750 if they were mistreated while in Switzerland. Moreover, some one hundred thousand people who fit within the "looted assets" class in the Swiss agreement, all economically needy people, have already received a total of $205 million. For the first time since the end of World War II in 1945, this looted asset group includes sixty thousand Romanis (gypsies) and Jehovah's Witnesses who were so grievously abused by the Nazi regime and who have never received compensation, along with forty thousand impoverished Jewish survivors, most in the former Soviet Union. In the court's allocation of looted assets money, 75 percent has gone to victims living in the former Soviet Union (FSU), 12.5 percent to those in Israel, and 4 percent to those in the United States, with around 10 percent to the rest of the world.

Following our German settlement in 2000, by far the largest at DM 10 billion (around $5 billion), 80 percent of the money has now been allocated to 1.6 million people—far more than we estimated—for slave and forced laborers, most of whom have now received the maximum payments of $7,500 and $2,500 respectively; for payment of confiscated property and unpaid insurance policies; and for the German Future Fund, which will fund projects to promote tolerance.

In our Austrian case, the government of Chancellor Schuessel has done a commendable job of expediting payments to victims. Over one hundred thousand slave and forced laborers (over 95 percent of whom were non-Jewish forced laborers) have been paid their full per capita amount, and there is $100 million left over that will be allocated. Likewise, $150 million has been already allocated to Austrian Holocaust victims whose apartments, jewelry, and home furnishings were confiscated during the war.

The last of our agreements, the January 2001 accord with the French government and French banks, has also produced some gratifying results. Under the direction of Lucien Kalfon, the prefect of the Commission for the Compensation of Victims of Spoliation Resulting from the Anti-Semitic Legislation in Force during the Occupation (CIVS), over 80 percent of the $22.5 million "Fund B" (19 million euros) we created in our negotiations has been paid to French Holocaust survivors or their families with imperfect proof of their bank accounts, involving over six thousand recommendations by the CIVS. They receive $3,000 per person. Another $2.5 million has been paid under "Fund A" for those required to provide hard evidence.

Even the much maligned (significantly unfairly) International Commission of Holocaust-Era Insurance Claims (ICHEIC), chaired by former secretary of state Lawrence Eagleburger, has made real progress. ICHEIC had a slow and costly start, in which, by July 2002, more than five years after its establishment, only around $7 million in insurance policies had been paid, and ICHEIC's chief of staff resigned. It took over two years after our German agreement (which had a substantial insurance component that was passed on to ICHEIC to administer) to get the German insurance companies, particularly Allianz, to reach an agreement on publishing policyholder lists that were essential to the claims process. But in the past two years, new management from the Cohen Group in Washington, named for former secretary of defense William Cohen and led here by Mara Rudman, and the claims procedures office in London, led by my former aide, Jody Manning, has begun to turn things around. Now, at last, over five hundred thousand policyholders' names have been published by the five ICHEIC insurers (Generali, Allianz, Zurich, AXA, and Winterthur), Dutch and Belgian companies, and seventy German insurers that belong to the German insurance association and that alone are responsible for 350,000 of the five hundred thousand names.

ICHEIC has had $500 million in its hands, $275 million of which was transferred to ICHEIC from our $5 billion German settlement. This has been split between a hard claims category, where claimants can name their deceased relatives' insurers (DM 350 million, around $175 million), and a humanitarian claims process for those who do not know the names of their families' insurance companies (DM 200 million, around $100 million). Having extended the claims filing period on several occasions, ICHEIC is on schedule to handle all claims by the end of 2005. By that time it will probably have paid $200 million in claims, on an average of some $9,000 per policy, but with several six-figure payments.

ICHEIC administrative costs have been high, about $90 million. Yet the bulk of the costs arose from verification and auditing requirements requested by the victims' representatives. In any event, this will probably amount to under 20 percent of the $500 million available to ICHEIC. Beyond the $200 million that will be paid out to claimants, the balance will go for humanitarian projects, such as the $132 million that will be provided over a ten-year period to the Conference for Jewish Material Claims against Germany (the "Claims Conference") for social welfare benefits.

Yet there are still difficult days ahead for ICHEIC. Recently, the insurance commissioners for the states of California and Washington have separately pressed ICHEIC for a performance audit. The National Association of Insurance Commissioners, a party to the original ICHEIC agreement, is considering whether to formally join in this request. This presents a difficult decision for ICHEIC, since such an audit would be expensive and time consuming, although it could help clear the air of allegations.

For all of the delays in the ICHEIC process, I continue to believe we were correct in asserting that ICHEIC should be the sole remedy for insurance claims, given the uncertainties and costs of litigation in U.S. courts.

III. The Still Unfinished Business

With all this progress, what is the problem? In fact, even more should have been done by now for a Holocaust survivor population that is aging and dying before belated justice is completed. Here are several examples of unfinished business of the unfinished business of World War II.

A. The Swiss Bank Affair

In the Swiss bank case, over $500 million of the $1.25 billion settlement is still unpaid more than six years after the Swiss settlement. The reasons speak volumes about the limits of our court system to handle settlements involving large numbers of people and the difficulty of getting the Swiss banks to cooperate once the harsh spotlight of public pressure was removed. It took many months to put the settlement into appropriate legal form and to receive the court's blessing. Appeals by dissident lawyers, representing claimants who refused to agree to the terms of the settlement with the Swiss banks, took years to resolve. Payments could not be made until they were disposed of. Establishing the claims process took a great deal of time.

But not only the American legal system, with its elaborate protections of dissenters, was responsible for the delay. The Swiss banks also bear a share of responsibility, as they exhibited some of the same behavior that had gotten them so much adverse publicity for their actions after the war.

The banks originally agreed with Paul Volcker, who served as chairman of the Independent Committee of Eminent Persons that oversaw the $200 million audit of the Swiss banks, to publish thirty-six thousand names. In the end only twenty-one thousand were published. Volcker had asked them to assemble their entire list of four million bank accounts opened between 1933 and 1945 so that claims could be matched against the widest possible database. This has never been done. The banks have finally agreed to publish an additional four thousand names, and the claims period will be reopened for another six months to permit possible matches against these newly published names.

Of the total Swiss settlement, $800 million was set aside for the payment of owners of actual Swiss bank accounts, established by those trying to shield their assets from Hitler's on-rushing army by placing them in the safest banking system in war-torn Europe. With around $235 million having been distributed in awards by the end of 2004, it is likely that hundreds of millions of dollars of unclaimed funds from the settlement will be left unspent.

Determining how to allocate this large pool of unclaimed Swiss bank funds will be one of the principal pieces of "unfinished business" from our work. This issue has created an unseemly battle over who should get the balance: the State of Israel, lawyers representing American survivors, or Eastern European survivors—those I have called the double victims of the twentieth century, having suffered through both Nazism and communism. Israel, which took little interest in helping our U.S. government–led initiative to help Holocaust survivors, despite having the largest survivor population in the world, has created a special task force, led by Cabinet Minister Natan Scharansky, seeking a larger allocation for Israelis. Scharansky has met with Judge Edward Korman to plead Israel's case. At the same time, attorneys such as Sam Dubbin in Florida have appealed Korman's initial allocations, which go largely to survivors from the former Soviet Union (FSU) and the former East bloc nations, seeking more for destitute American survivors. Their cause is supported by much of the leadership of the American Jewish Federation movement. On the other hand, the American Jewish Joint Distribution Committee has argued for continued disproportionately large payments to survivors from the FSU and former East bloc nations, given the absence of a Western-style social safety net in those nations after the collapse of communism.

There is no question that the deprivation of the Eastern European survivors, the surviving remnants of the prewar Jewish communities, remains generally worse than that of survivors in other parts of the world, including Israel, the United States, and Western Europe, all of which have stronger social safety nets. In the former communist countries, there is nothing comparable to Medicare, Medicaid, food stamps, and Supplemental Security Income. At the same time, I have become more acutely aware of the needs of many thousands of elderly Holocaust victims in the United States. I have been shocked and saddened to learn of the extensive poverty among many survivors in the United States and Israel. My concerns have been substantiated by several recent studies, including those incorporated in the National Jewish Population Survey, and in reports commissioned for ICHEIC. It appears from these studies that many of the impoverished survivors in the United States and Israel are in fact these "double victims" —but ones who emigrated from the FSU and Eastern Europe to the United States and Israel following the collapse of communism. The surveys show that some one-third of elderly Holocaust survivors in the United States and perhaps one half in New York live below the poverty line. There should be sufficient additional funds to allow a slightly larger allocation to U.S. and Israeli survivors, without harming the Eastern European survivors.

The large sum of unclaimed Swiss bank funds is not the only pot of additional money. When Judge Korman makes his Solomonic judgment about how to allocate the unclaimed Swiss funds, I hope he will take into account other large sums of unallocated money from our negotiations. These will include humanitarian funds in ICHEIC, with $132 million allocated to the Claims Conference for home care for needy American Jewish victims, and/or Holocaust education and remembrance projects.

Moreover, the Claims Conference has substantial funds from the sale of unclaimed properties in former East Germany, to which they took title after the fall of communism and the reunification of Germany. The Claims Conference has set aside 20 percent of these funds for Holocaust education and remembrance projects. I believe such projects are critically important to ensure a long-lasting remembrance of the dimensions of the Holocaust and its lessons for future generations. But with the great needs of elderly Holocaust survivors, I have urged that this figure be reduced to 10 percent, so that the vast bulk of money will be focused on elderly, impoverished survivors. They have suffered enough in their lives not to have to live their remaining days in deprivation. But the Claims Conference has reaffirmed its 80/20 split.

There is also $100 million in "excess" funds in the Austrian slave and forced labor settlement, after all claimants have received their negotiated maximum payments. The Austrian foundation board will decide shortly on how to allocate these funds. The Austrians are considering allocating 30 million euros to the six Central European partner organizations for slave and forced laborers and their heirs; 25 million euros to a scholarship foundation for descendants of forced laborers and others who suffered at the hands of the Nazis; 20 million euros to increase the size of the General Settlement Fund for lost property; and 20 million for a new Future Fund for projects of reconciliation. I would hope that less would be put in the Future Fund and more put toward meeting pressing needs of survivors. There is also as much as $540 million in accrued interest in the German fund, which has not yet been allocated.

Unfortunately, all of this is occurring without any coordination of effort. The U.S. government should convene the various groups overseeing each of the settlements in a Holocaust restitution summit, not to change existing arrangements but to try to assure that the parties to the various agreements are aware of how others are considering their allocations. Hopefully, in this way, funds can be allocated to areas of greatest need. Likewise, before Swiss bank Special Master Judah Gribetz and Judge Korman make their final allocations from the large pool of unclaimed Swiss funds, they should ask the Claims Conference, ICHEIC, the Austrians, and the Germans how their extra funds are being allocated.

B. Property Restitution in Central and Eastern Europe

Completion of the property restitution process remains an imperative. There are the synagogues, schools, and community centers that are essential to providing the decimated but determined Jewish communities the physical infrastructure and, where properties can be sold, the funds to sustain their future. This can be done all across Central and Eastern Europe, including the Czech Republic, the Ukraine, Croatia, Hungary, Belarus, Slovakia, Poland, Lithuania, Romania, and Bulgaria. Nowhere is the need for urgent, high-level U.S. government intervention more necessary. Indeed, this is where the European Union, which has been almost completely disengaged from the Holocaust justice effort, could be most effective. Their new member states, who joined the EU in May 2004, are part of the problem.

There was no one overarching agreement covering property restitution. I negotiated, with the help of my fellow U.S. ambassadors, on a country-by-country basis to obtain the recovery of communal property. There were many models of success. The Czech Republic returned most of the properties in the control of the national government, although held by municipalities. Hungary reached an agreement with the Hungarian Jewish community to create a fund in lieu of pursuing communal property. Similar funds were created in Slovakia. Hundreds of pieces of property have been restored across the European continent. The World Jewish Restitution Organization (WJRO) (with several major Jewish organizations like the World Jewish Congress and the American Jewish Joint Distribution Committee) has formed partnerships, in the form of joint foundations, with local Jewish communities in Hungary, Poland, Romania, and Lithuania, providing expertise to help the local Jewish communities research the titles to their properties and perfect their claims within the laws of each country. Files have been opened on sixty-nine hundred individual pieces of property in those countries, which could be worth anywhere from $17 million to $125 million. But converting these files into restored properties is a painful and expensive proposition. Many of the properties are destroyed or are in disrepair and expensive to bring up to standards of either use or sale.

Today, the process is mired in bureaucracy, slow and tortuous. Countries like Bulgaria ignore their own court decisions and refuse to return property or provide reasonable compensation, as in the case of the Rila Hotel in Sofia, in which the Bulgarian Jewish community has a significant ownership share. Only sustained diplomatic pressure by the U.S. government, with a hand from the EU (Bulgaria strongly desires eventual membership in the EU), can make a difference.

If returning communal property is difficult, getting back confiscated private property taken by the Nazis during World War II and/or nationalized by the Eastern European communist countries after the war is often even more difficult. Nowhere is this more evident than in Poland, now a member of both NATO and the European Union. More than a decade and a half after the fall of the Berlin Wall, Poland, traumatized by the potential cost of returning properties or compensating their owners, particularly Polish Jews, has no private property law. Its government has tried time and again but has difficulty coming up with a formula. Poland is now considering a compensation fund of around 15 percent of the value of the property but would exclude any properties in Warsaw from the legislation. Here again, diplomatic intervention by the United States and by the EU is essential to achieve some justice.

C. Austria's General Settlement Fund

Under our January 2001 Austrian agreement, $210 million was to be set aside in a General Settlement Fund (GSF) to compensate claimants, up to $2 million per person, for looted property that cannot be returned to its proper owners. This money has never been paid. This is because two cases remain pending in federal court in the United States brought by dissident lawyers who opposed our settlement. Thus, Austria does not have "legal peace"—the sine qua non for funding the GSF. The most prominent of the two cases, and the linchpin for allowing the GSF to be funded, is *White-man v. Republic of Austria*,[2] pending before federal judge Shirley Wohl Kram in New York. Angered by what the judge considers an inadequate settlement in an unrelated case against Austrian banks and egged on by lawyers with their own private agendas and by the head of the Austrian Jewish community, the case languishes year after year while the long-suffering families of Austrian Holocaust victims wait for payments in the GSF.

Here again senior political attention by the U.S. government might bring the parties to some agreement. If this cannot be achieved, I hope the Austrian government as a moral matter will begin to fund at least part of the GSF, until the cases can be finally resolved.

D. German Settlement

As efficient as the payments have been in our German settlement, many people failed to file their slave- and forced-labor claims in time to meet the German deadline. Others were unaware that they could file on behalf of their parents if they died after February 1999, when our negotiations began. Thousands of others have been turned down because they had insufficient evidence that they were slave laborers during the war, much of the proof having been destroyed over the years, some willfully in the years immediately after the war. Still others have been deemed ineligible because they were hidden during the war or did not live in a ghetto or concentration camp on the Red Cross list used for our negotiations.

It is now painfully clear that we set aside too little of our DM 10 billion settlement for victims of medical experiments—only DM 50 million (about $25 million). This has led people like Simon Rozenkier, a slave laborer and survivor of Dr. Mengele's diabolical medical experiments, to bring suit against the pharmaceutical companies that supplied the drugs used for the experiments.

Because of the tremendous number of slave- and forced-labor survivors, well over one million, we had to choose a form of "rough justice," compensating everyone the same, regardless of the duration or the severity of their labor. But for the victims of medical experiments and similar damages we decided on a different system. Because of the ghastly nature of these cases, on July 12, 2000, I obtained a "side letter" to our German agreement from my trusted German counterpart, Count Otto Lambsdorff. He reassured me that these special injury claims, unlike the more numerous slave- and forced-labor claims, would be treated on a more personalized basis, pro rata rather than per capita, although still within the DM 50 million cap.

But despite the best efforts of Lambsdorff and the Clinton administration, the German parliament—which generally but not completely incorporated our negotiated agreement into German law—did not reflect our agreement. They provided only for per capita payments for medical payments, so everyone, including Mr. Rozenkier, got the same amount. The German Foundation charged with administering the $5 billion fund has received many thousands more claims for medical experiments and personal injuries than any of us forecasted. The small amount of money set aside for this category assures disappointment.

Yet still the "rough justice" concept was far better than the alternative that Mr. Rozenkier's lawyers seek, that of prosecuting individual lawsuits in U.S courts. Individualizing justice in this type of case is virtually impossible. And we would never have gotten the massive settlement we achieved without assuring German companies that they would receive "legal peace" from all such litigation. We have to live with the unhappy realization that we cannot possibly fully compensate everyone for the massive injustices perpetrated against them during the war.

E. Nazi-Looted Art

At the Washington Conference on Art in December 1998, we negotiated eleven principles of art restitution for Nazi-looted art with over forty countries. The Germans had stolen a staggering six hundred thousand paintings, of which as many as one hundred thousand remain missing. The best of the stolen art was presented to Hitler by the SS for his future Fuhrer museum to be built after the war in Linz, Austria, where he was educated. For fifty years the issue of the return of the looted art was off the table. At the Washington conference, following similar guidelines adopted by American museums, the participating nations agreed that their public museums would research the provenance of their art for any suspicious transfer of ownership during the war years, publish their research, and develop fair and just claims processes, with liberal rules of evidence, to return the art to its rightful owners.

France has established a website with over one thousand paintings stolen from French Jews, many of which hung for decades in France's most famous museums, and many of which are being restored to their original prewar owners. Austria has incorporated the essence of the Washington Principles in its own legal structure. Hundreds of pieces of Nazi-looted art have been returned from American museums and from museums throughout Europe. The American Association of Art Museum Directors has created a website tracing the provenance of sixty-six American museums, which will facilitate the recovery of art by obviating the necessity for potential claimants to search through each of the museum inventories individually. Major art dealers and auction houses report a complete overhaul of acquisition standards for European art during the wartime period, and no respectable American museum will even look at an art object for sale from Europe unless its ownership between 1933 and 1945 is documented beyond doubt.

But on balance, outside the United States, the Washington Principles have been largely ignored. One example illustrates the problem. In Germany, a beautiful Pissarro painting was stolen by the Nazis from the grandmother of Claude Cassirer, who now lives in San Diego. In defiance of the Washington Principles endorsed by the Spanish government, the painting now hangs in the Thyssen-Bornemisza Museum, one of Madrid's great new tourist attractions. The Spanish government simply refuses to return the Pissarro, arguing that the museum is a private museum not covered by the Washington Principles, despite its receiving hundreds of millions of dollars in public funding and having government officials on its board. In any event, the Spanish argue, the Washington Principles do not override Spanish law.

As Anne Webber of the London-based European Commission on Looted Art has noted, outside of the admirable research conducted in federal museums in Austria, many museums in the Czech Republic, some in Germany, Canada, and the United Kingdom, and many in the United States, most countries have undertaken either only superficial or no research at all. In fact, only five or six countries out of the some forty nations that ascribed to the Washington Principles have done any serious work. It is important that all countries be urged to undertake provenance research from 1933 to today, using the widest definition of cultural property, to include libraries, archives, and books as well as art.

Research has little practical value unless its results are published and widely available. Here again there has been only a limited response. Some countries have published their results on the Internet, but with no common standards. Websites are in different languages with different designs, making it virtually impossible for families to search all the different websites. Some countries do not publish photographs of the paintings, making it complicated to identify a family's looted art.

One of the Washington Principles was the creation of a single database, a central registry, so a family could go to one place rather than multiple sites. This has now been done in the United States for the major museums. In December 2002 a private group, the Central Registry of Information on Looted Cultural Property, based in Oxford, England, developed a state-of-the-art single searchable database, but it is woefully underfunded. This should become the internationally recognized central registry, backed and funded by governments, NGOs, and international organizations.

Russia may have the largest collection of looted Holocaust-era art. Some they consider "trophy art," taken by the Red Army from German museums immediately after World War II as compensation for their war losses. But the rest was art stolen by the Germans from the Jews and then carted off to the Soviet Union after the war. Commendably, the Duma passed and President Putin signed a law that, while reaffirming their determination to keep the trophy art, permitted the recovery of looted art taken from Jews and Jewish institutions. A claims period was established following publication of a database of the looted art. But despite the law and a Memorandum of Understanding signed in 2001 by the Russian minister of culture and Ronald Lauder, on behalf of the United States–based Commission on Art Recovery, which he heads, the law has not been implemented. While a website has been created, materials have not been published in the official Russian registry to trigger the claims period. Rather, the materials have been published only in Russian, do not represent a complete survey of all museums, and have no common index to connect the various collections listed.

The art and cultural property area cries out for U.S. government leadership. Only if the Bush administration elevates the importance of full and faithful implementation of the Washington Principles will this happen. The administration should call for a new international conference for a "stock taking" on progress in the four years since the Vilnius Forum. The issue will fade away and art and cultural property restitution will again be put on the back burner without the spotlight such a conference would provide.

F. Israeli Responsibility

Few matters are more bizarre in the Holocaust restitution field than the issue of Israeli government responsibility. The State of Israel was founded out of ashes of the Holocaust and took in hundreds of thousands of Holocaust survivors. Yet Israel itself has unfinished business.

It appears that many European Jews put their assets in banks in prestate Palestine to protect them from the Nazi hordes. The Anglo-Palestine Bank, now Bank Leumi, was one prime location. Moreover, many European Jews who did not survive the war owned real property in Palestine. But in the decades after the war and after creation of the State of Israel, little or no effort was made to identify and locate the owners, let alone to return the property. Even after all the sensational revelations of how Swiss and French banks, the Austrians, and the Germans had failed to fully divest themselves of Jewish property in their possession, the Israeli banks and the land authorities that control the assets and property refused to return them. For two years there has been a Knesset Committee (chaired by M. K. Collette Avital) working in this area. It has produced an impressive report but with little impact on the Israeli government.

It is time for the Israeli government to insist that Israeli banks publish the names of bank account owners who established accounts before or during the war, just as the Volcker Commission, with our support, insisted of the Swiss banks. Likewise, the Israeli government should do everything possible to identify the owners and heirs of the real property of Holocaust victims that they possess.

G. America's Own Responsibility: The Hungarian
Gold Train and Bank Accounts

The U.S. government took the lead in providing justice to Holocaust victims and in insisting that, notwithstanding traditional laws limiting claims or other barriers to restitution, European countries had a moral responsibility to victims. Having held other countries up to the harsh light of history, we have a special responsibility to hold ourselves to the highest standards.

There are two areas where we have not succeeded.

First, although this occurred on nowhere near the scale of Swiss bank accounts, there were some Holocaust victims who placed their assets in American banks, particularly in New York, and never had them returned to surviving heirs. Under the laws of most states, dormant accounts revert to the state of incorporation of the bank. It is important that a thorough accounting be done of the funds that reverted to states like New York. New York governor George Pataki has been a champion for Holocaust victims and has established the nation's premier Holocaust claims office. He should initiate a study of New York State records and have New York's major banks do the same. President Clinton's Presidential Advisory Commission on Holocaust Assets, chaired by Edgar Bronfman, on which I sat, did not thoroughly examine the dormant bank account issue. It is time that we do this, if necessary at the federal level.

Second, the United States must face up to its responsibility in the Hungarian Gold Train incident.[3] During my negotiations in the Clinton administration, we insisted that European governments and corporations face up to their moral and historical responsibility to those they wronged, even if their legal responsibility was doubtful. We must do likewise when the shoe is on the other foot, as it is in the Hungarian Gold Train case, brought by Hungarian Jewish survivors against the U.S. government for alleged improper handling of assets stolen from them by the pro-Nazi regime in Hungary. Legal liability is doubtful; not so our moral responsibility. Faced with righting what may be America's mistake, the Justice Department has forgotten our own message to the world and is relying on strict legal arguments to escape responsibility.

The U.S. Army was not only heroic in helping to win World War II but also had an enviable postwar record in recovering Nazi-looted property. The "Monuments Men," cultural experts working directly for the army, helped collect, protect, and catalogue valuable paintings and cultural property, in contrast to the Soviet Red Army, which enriched itself as the victorious power. In accordance with international legal principles and American policy, art and cultural property was returned to the countries from which it had been taken. Those countries, in turn, were expected to return the property to the citizens from whom it had been confiscated.

It appears that in the Hungarian Gold Train matter, the American government followed a starkly different policy. We first surfaced this in the interim report of the presidential commission in 1999. The train, totaling twenty-four rail cars and holding the valuables of countless Hungarian Jews that had been confiscated by the pro-Nazi Hungarian regime, was seized by the U.S. Army in Austria in mid-May, just after the war ended. For decades, the postwar Hungarian government and the Hungarian Jewish organizations appealed to the American government to simply be permitted to examine the valuables. The American government refused, declaring that the Gold Train assets were "enemy property" unidentifiable as to individual ownership and national origin, making restitution infeasible. Instead, some senior American military officers requisitioned the property to furnish their apartments in Austria. Other items, such as watches, alarm clocks, and cameras, were sold through army exchange stores in Austria. More than eleven hundred paintings were transferred by the U.S. Army to the Austrian government. A substantial amount of the property was sold for auction in New York, with the proceeds transferred to the International Refugee Organization for the benefit of Holocaust survivors.

The disclosures by our presidential commission led to a class action lawsuit, *Irvin Rosner v. United States,*[4] brought by more than three thousand Hungarian Holocaust survivors against the U.S. government, seeking an accounting of the contents of the Gold Train still in government hands, as well as damages for each member of the class of Hungarian survivors.

Instead of acting as we had urged other governments and their companies to act, instead of seeking a neutral examination of the facts found by our presidential commission, the Justice Department moved to dismiss the case on the basis of the statute of limitations, the sovereign immunity of the United States, and the inappropriateness of the federal court system as a proper forum. These were the kinds of defenses made by the foreign governments with whom I dealt. The U.S. government has subjected elderly survivors to rigorous depositions and has employed the chair of Tel Aviv University's Jewish history department to contest some of our presidential commission's findings.

At the end of December 2004, a positive development occurred when at a hearing before Judge Seitz to assess progress in the mediation, she indicated that a "Christmas miracle" was in store for the parties. While this might be an unusual term to describe a settlement for Jewish Holocaust survivors, the judge was correct that a breakthrough had occurred. With her own prodding, the able mediation of Fred Fielding, a former White House counsel who was acting as mediator on the case, the assistance of Israel Singer and Edgar Bronfman of the World Jewish Congress, and adverse publicity in the press about the U.S. government's obdurate position, the Justice Department did a turnabout. They agreed to a $25 million settlement, which will be used for social services, like home health care, for some thirty thousand Hungarian Jewish survivors worldwide, who are largely in the United States, Israel, and Hungary itself. The Claims Conference, ably headed by Gideon Taylor, a key figure in my earlier negotiations, will have a major role in administering the new funds.

What was first disclosed by our presidential commission four years ago, and brought into the courts by lawyers such as Sam Dubbin and the indefatigable Mark Talisman, represents something more important than the small sum involved: accountability. With this step, the U.S. government is recognizing its own mistakes. By moving from total denial of responsibility for so many decades after the war to its settlement in late 2004, it will also enhance America's moral standing in relation to its insistence that other countries continue to fulfill their responsibilities.

IV. Conclusion

Much has been accomplished, but much remains undone. As the Bush administration begins its second term, I hope that the new secretary of state, Condoleezza Rice, and the president himself will appoint a high-level presidential envoy, indeed, perhaps dedicated Ambassador O'Donnell himself, who is invested with the authority of both officials—as I was—to finish the remaining unfinished business of World War II, and thereby is able to bring more complete justice to Holocaust survivors and their families before it is too late. We have come too far not to complete the task as best we can. And yet, it is painfully clear that as much as we try to do, there can be no final accounting for the grave wrongs that were done to so many millions. That is what "imperfect justice" is all about. But it is no excuse for failing to do everything we can while there is still some opportunity to focus the world's attention on justice for survivors of both the worst genocide and the worst theft in the history of the world.

NOTES

1. Stuart E. Eizenstat, *Imperfect Justice: Looted Assets, Slave Labor, and the Unfinished Business of World War II* (2003).

2. Whiteman v. Federal Republic of Austria, 2002 WL 31368236 (S.D.N.Y. Oct. 21, 2002), *mandamus denied sub nom.* Garb v. Republic of Poland, 2003 WL 21890843 (2d Cir. Aug. 6, 2003), *vacated sub nom.* Republic of Austria v. Whiteman, 124 S. Ct. 2835 (2004).

3. Stuart Eizenstat, "Integrity of the Restitution Process Rests on Single Standard of Justice," *Forward,* June 18, 2004, *available at* http://www.forward.com/main/article.php?ref=eizenstat200406161137.

4. See Rosner v. United States, 231 F. Supp. 2d 1202, 1204 (S.D. Fla. 2002).

Chapter 28

Poor Justice

Holocaust Restitution and Forgotten, Indigent Survivors

David A. Lash and Mitchell A. Kamin

The history of the United States has often included an unfortunate ignorance of the needs and concerns of poor Americans. Indeed, the poor often have been an invisible population, ignored by many, and this has been particularly true for indigent Holocaust survivors. The tragedy and suffering of poor survivors has been compounded by their indigency, their minority, and the desire of the world to pretend they simply do not exist. Even today, as high-profile, well-publicized Swiss bank settlements, unpaid insurance claims, and stolen property make headlines around the world, the lives of the poorest, most invisible survivors recede further and further into oblivion.

Take for example the case of Felicia Grunfeder. As a young child, Ms. Grunfeder suffered horribly at the hands of the Nazis. Trapped in the Warsaw ghetto, she watched wheelbarrows of dead bodies leave the walls every day, until her parents devised a harrowing plan for escape. She would be hidden under the bodies of her dead compatriots, wheeled to an appointed spot along the wall, and placed in a casket that was then to be thrown over the wall. She would be met on the other side by a Polish Catholic family who had agreed to assist her escape from the ghetto.

Miraculously, the plan was successful and Ms. Grunfeder eventually found her way to the United States after the end of World War II. Never able to shake the memories of her horrific childhood experiences, however, she endured tormenting nightmares that wreaked havoc on her adulthood. Eventually, she scraped together a meager living through the receipt of Social Security Disability Insurance (SSI) benefits and $228 a month in German reparations. But when her Social Security caseworker learned of the reparations payments, Ms. Grunfeder was instantly struck from the disability rolls. Ms. Grunfeder's receipt of nominal monthly payments, for having survived an experience that no human being should ever have had to endure, effectively gave her too much "income" to receive SSI disability payments. In desperate need of the subsistence income and medical care the SSI program provided, Ms. Grunfeder came to Bet Tzedek ("House of Justice" in Hebrew) for legal help.

Bet Tzedek Legal Services, established in 1974, was the dream of a group of young Jewish activists, attorneys, and rabbis. Their goal was to create a legal services office for elderly and indigent Jews and, under the distinctive banner of Jewish law and commandment, for all other needy residents in the Los Angeles community. A Bet Tzedek attorney immediately filed an administrative appeal from the decision rescinding Ms. Grunfeder's disability benefits. The appeal was lost. Bet Tzedek persevered, and after a four-year struggle the Ninth Circuit Court of Appeals issued a landmark decision declaring that reparations payments cannot be considered income for the purposes of establishing the indigency required for public benefits eligibility.[1] Reasoning that these payments were compensation for horrors suffered, opportunities lost, and nightmares survived, the Ninth Circuit concluded that these meager amounts could not be considered "income." After this lengthy struggle for justice, Ms. Grunfeder's benefits were restored.

Eventually, the U.S. Congress would codify the Ninth Circuit decision, making it applicable for the entire United States and thereby ensuring that the poorest survivors around the country would not lose the income they needed for shelter, food, and medical care. President Clinton signed the bill into law in 1994.[2] Thousands of indigent Holocaust survivors across the country benefited from this law, which helped them stave off homelessness and hunger. But to lift their cloak of invisibility and overcome the simple fact that they were easy to ignore, these survivors used the American system of justice to find salvation that decades before had been taken from them.

Recognizing that American courts could provide a forum for airing the claims of survivors, lawyers across the country eventually began other legal efforts on their behalf. As a result, a Holocaust restitution movement arose in the 1990s as various classes of survivors filed high-profile suits against Swiss banks, multinational insurance companies, and international corporations that enslaved Jews and others during World War II. But as the spotlight shone on issues such as the recovery of Nazi-confiscated real estate and artwork, dormant Swiss bank accounts shrouded in secrecy and cloaked in untold wealth, and prewar insurance policies worth billions of dollars, the poorest survivors resumed their forgotten place and still desperately needed assistance to secure the basic necessities of life. In fact, even as the world was awakening to the need for justice for Holocaust survivors, the plight of the neediest survivors continued to worsen.

One major problem was that programs that distributed reparations funds like those Ms. Grunfeder had been receiving were facing enormous practical and economic problems that few took the time to try to resolve. When the Iron Curtain collapsed in the early 1990s, the German reunification treaty specifically provided for the first time that survivors who had been living in Eastern bloc countries could, upon their arrival in the West, assert claims to German-based reparations payments. The treaty allotted monies to those survivors who were indigent and who could demonstrate that their current suffering flowed directly from their experiences during the Nazi era. The modest sums available through this program could often mean the difference between homelessness and survival for eligible survivors. Yet despite the human importance of the program, the problems faced by the poorest survivors in the former Eastern bloc in accessing these supposedly available reparations were largely, again, ignored.

The New York–based Conference on Material Claims Against Germany, an organization commonly known as the "Claims Conference" that had been administering German reparations programs since the end of World War II, was charged with managing this new program. Almost immediately, the Claims Conference seemed overwhelmed by applications from newly eligible, low-income Holocaust survivors. Throughout the 1980s and much of the 1990s, in fact, the Claims Conference took between three and six years to process the reparations claims of the poor. The cruel reality of these interminable delays was that many aged and suffering applicants simply did not survive.

While many of these elderly applicants died, the Claims Conference seemingly did not have the ability to focus on the tens of thousands of indigent survivors who so desperately needed those few hundred dollars a month. Rather, the Claims Conference immersed its resources in more high-profile matters. Drawn to the spotlight of claims over valuable real estate confiscated in prewar Berlin, large Swiss bank claims, and disputed slave labor compensation, internationally heralded leaders of the worldwide Jewish community moved the Claims Conference to focus its attention on these high-dollar, highly publicized matters. Left with no one to champion their cause, indigent reparations claimants were left to suffer quietly and alone.

While the world watched the international stage on which these more publicized issues were being played, the application process that the poorest survivors had to endure in order to get a few hundred dollars a month was fraught with silent frustration. In addition to interminable delays, application forms were difficult to secure. Those at the Claims Conference who were supposed to rule on the sufficiency of the applications had no legal training, yet were charged with interpreting foreign statutory and case authority. Consequently, the standards by which applications were judged were not well articulated, well explained, or well reasoned. The Claims Conference seemed to operate on its own unwritten guidelines, often resulting in ill-founded decisions, with no meaningful appeals process. At times, as many as sixty-five thousand elderly, indigent applicants waited for word on their long-pending applications.

Survivors, and a handful of the organizations working on their behalf, including Bet Tzedek,[3] began a campaign to exert pressure on the Claims Conference. Improvements, however, did not come until internal changes occurred at the Claims Conference itself. A passing of the torch to new leadership in 1998 awakened a new and just attention to poor survivors.

In 1999, a summit was held in the New York offices of the Claims Conference. Those in attendance had detailed exchanges and developed new priorities. As a result of these meetings—and after years of persistence—the Claims Conference finally hired trained attorneys to review the claims as well as additional staff to administer the backlog of applications and deal directly with low-income survivors whose claims were pending. The system was computerized and a directive was issued to eliminate the backlog of claims within twelve months. Due to these changes, applicants awaiting receipt of funds from the Claims Conference now need not endure any excruciating delays. Most claims are processed within six months and payments begin immediately thereafter. Consequently, fewer survivors are homeless, and more live with hope and help than ever before.

But for the indigent, even this significant victory fell short of justice. It was standard for survivors to receive their reparations payments by international wire transfer into local bank accounts. Wire transfer fees, however, devour as much as 10 percent of the value of the transaction. For the poor, the loss of this thirty-five dollars can mean lost meals, lost medication, and increased peril. Responding to this issue, Bet Tzedek began a campaign to ask banks across the country to waive these fees as a humanitarian gesture for the benefit of indigent survivors. Not surprisingly, little was accomplished at first. Few wanted to take the time to deal with an issue involving so little money. Few could relate to the human impact of so seemingly small a matter. But the effort gradually picked up steam as elected officials became involved and joined in the cry for justice. Today, most major banks in California, as well as those in Illinois and Great Britain, have agreed to waive wire transfer fees on the receipt by survivors of any reparations payments.

The California legislature recently took further steps to help resident survivors. Mirroring federal legislation, California passed laws providing that reparations not be considered income both for the purpose of calculating state income tax and for the purpose of calculating an aged or disabled survivor's eligibility for public assistance.[4]

The flurry of reparations-related activities over the past decade reflects the simple reality that the survivor population is rapidly aging and that the window is quickly closing on any remaining opportunities to bring salvation, peace, and justice to those who have experienced such suffering. A final debate is now raging around the world concerning the distribution of funds from the various settlement funds of the 1990s. Residue amounts from vast Swiss-bank, unclaimed-property, and insurance-policy settlements are the subject of a philosophical tug of war that can have no winners. There are potentially many millions of dollars available for some sort of distribution after all individual claims are paid to those who can demonstrate rightful, specific economic losses suffered by them and their families. Some make powerful arguments to disburse the funds only to those with verifiable claims, regardless of their need. Others argue that all recovered monies should be distributed on the basis of need so as to offer aid and assistance to those whose lives continue to be the most disrupted. Still others argue that after all individual claims are paid, the residue should be divided between programs for the needy and efforts designed to rebuild Jewish communities or fund Holocaust education programs.

The battle against poverty has been pitted against the battle over education. The Claims Conference has offered a compromise that seems to please no one. It has decided to divide its residue funds on an 80/20 model; 80 percent to aid the needy and 20 percent for rebuilding and educational purposes. However, as Bet Tzedek and Jewish agencies around the world continue to assist tens of thousands of survivors struggling to fight the poverty wrought by the Nazi death machine, there seems little justification in using the funds for anything other than healing the lives of those in need. While directing 80 percent of the funds to this purpose may be expedient, using anything less than 100 percent—while elderly survivors continue to live without homes or medical care—demeans the honor of their lives and the long history and tradition of Jews helping all other Jews who are in need.

Admittedly, the division and distribution of these remaining funds does not devolve into a question of right and wrong but instead sets up an unfortunate confrontation between right and right. On the one hand, there can be no doubt that education and remembrance is a critical component of the Jewish community's commitment to "Never Again!" Nonetheless, the claims of aging, dying survivors must take precedence. These living monuments to the soul of the Jewish people, who were stripped of their dignity then, must be guaranteed their dignity now; they must be enabled to leave this earth in the fullness of their natural years without being a burden to their families and with the self-respect they obviously deserve. Those who have suffered the most brutal blows of history and society— first the Holocaust and then poverty—have the greatest claim to whatever funds justice has acquired in their names.

Michael Berenbaum, the Holocaust historian, has proposed a simple and just solution. All survivors who need it or request it should have the best possible health care. They should have access to assisted living or home health care insurance to permit them to live with dignity as the ravages of age require. And, finally, they should be given funeral insurance so that as they go the way of all flesh in the fullness of time, they can be brought to Eretz Yisrael, from wherever they lived and died, with a memorial stone to mark their burial place, a right that was denied those murdered in the Holocaust.

It is true that other legitimate claims to the funds are likely to arise. Communities in the former Soviet Union and Eastern bloc countries need to be revitalized and the lives of many families living there would be immeasurably improved by funds that in the United States might seem nominal. And there are many worthy humanitarian and educational goals deserving of support as well.

In the end, however, this proposal trumps all others. It outdistances the compromise enacted by the Claims Conference and represents the greatest rights for those who have been left behind.

Those among us who have suffered the most, whose lives can still be substantially improved, deserve our immediate collective help and attention. They deserve to be forgotten no more. And, in the end, we will have overcome generations of indifference to the plight of the poor, finally setting priorities that exalt the ideals of Jewish culture and values.

NOTES

1. Grunfeder v. Heckler, 748 F.2d 503 (9th Cir. 1984).

2. *See* 42 U.S.C.A. § 1382a n.9 (1994).

3. During the 1990s, Bet Tzedek had as many as eight hundred survivor clients at any one time awaiting determination of their reparations applications.

4. *See* Cal. Rev. & Tax Code § 17155.5 (West 2000); Cal. Welf. & Inst. Code § 11008.17 (West 1999).

Chapter 29

The Holocaust Restitution Enterprise
An Israeli Perspective

Arie Zuckerman

An analysis of Israel's attitude to the Holocaust restitution and compensation enterprise must begin with an examination of the manner in which Israeli society copes with the Holocaust itself. Israel's attitude is inherently different from the attitude of Diaspora Jewry, insofar as generalizations may be drawn.

The Jewish nation endured a trauma that is unprecedented in the annals of humankind. An attempt was made to wipe a nation off the face of the earth, and it partially succeeded, as a third of world Jewry was exterminated. Consequently, the Jewish people will never be the same. The Holocaust will always accompany Jewish life in the Diaspora as a threatening shadow of insecurity and uncertainty. The specter of recurrence lingers in the air whenever the terrible events of the Holocaust are recalled. Considering the fact that the genocide originated in the most cultured of nations and in the middle of the twentieth century, we are hard pressed to classify the Holocaust as an isolated incident, or to dismiss the possibility of its recurrence in countries with Jewish populations.[1] Broaching the topic of the Holocaust brings to mind images of Jews as fragile and vulnerable individuals.

The *sabra* (native-born Israeli) views the Holocaust as a part of the Zionist story. The Holocaust and the resurrection of the Jewish state are mentioned in the same breath, as two contiguous events within a single narrative. Accordingly, the Holocaust served as a powerful catalyst for the founding of the state. Israelis look back at the Holocaust and see themselves as proud Jews who are erasing the humiliation and restoring the pride of the Jewish people.

This Israeli perspective, as Tom Segev elucidates in his book *The Seventh Million,*[2] occasionally led to a disparaging attitude and lack of understanding towards the thousands of survivors who immigrated to Israel immediately following the Holocaust. This same attitude is also evident in Israel's motivation to send army officers and pilots to visit the former concentration camps and fly jets over these sites in a show of strength and self-affirmation.

The Holocaust is not a favored topic among Israelis, as it detracts from Israel's image of power and strength. Dealing with the Holocaust transforms the Israeli into a champion of justice, not pity—into an individual who demands historic justice in the name of those who lacked the aegis of an independent Jewish state. Moreover, the Holocaust affirms the distinctiveness of the Jews vis-à-vis other nations. It proves the necessity for an independent Jewish state.

This conviction is what induced the emotional outburst over the indemnity agreement (the Luxemburg Agreement) that David Ben-Gurion spearheaded in the early 1950s. Against the desperate national need for foreign currency and the survivors' need for compensation and assistance to rehabilitate themselves in the young State of Israel stood the pride of the *sabra,* who saw the agreement itself as a humiliation. The desire to look ahead and "vanquish" the past, which symbolized destruction and weakness, led many Israelis to wage a vigorous struggle against the acceptance of German reparations. They demanded that Israel be forged on the cornerstone of the rejuvenated Hebrew might, not on the basis of the torturous Jewish past.

This perspective was advocated not only by the agreement's opponents (such as Herut, the forebear of the present-day Likud party) but also by its adherents, with Ben-Gurion, the architect of the German reparations, at the forefront. For the vast majority of Israelis, regardless of political differences, the nullification of the shameful Holocaust past of helplessness was unequivocally a central Israeli-*sabra* axiom. However, as far as Ben-Gurion was concerned, the needs of the hour overrode the intense feelings and the wounded pride that the agreement caused. Nevertheless, during the negotiations with Germany Ben-Gurion felt that it was necessary to distinguish between the acceptance of indemnities for the building of the State of Israel, a country that was absorbing Holocaust survivors, and private property restitution and compensation. It is fair to say that if not for the German condition that obligated the Israeli government to issue monthly indemnities to the injured Holocaust survivors, all the money would have been directed towards building Israel's economy and none of the survivors would have been personally compensated by the government. The need to bolster the young and fragile State of Israel was the main concern, not the individual victim. Consequently, Ben-Gurion submitted the administration of individuals' claims to an agency of Diaspora Jewry. The Conference on Material Claims against Germany (also known as the "Claims Conference") was established for this purpose and was comprised exclusively of different Jewish organizations from the Diaspora without any Israeli representation. In fact, the State of Israel did not even take part in the personal claims for property. The national interest did not encompass private property interests; therefore, Israel's participation in the process was not deemed appropriate.

The behavior of the very symbol of the new *sabra* spirit, the kibbutz movement, was emblematic of this approach. Individual survivors who were members of a kibbutz were forced to relinquish their personal indemnity payment to the good of the collective. The indemnity was considered tantamount to any other income that a member earned, all of which was turned over to the collective coffers of the kibbutz. The past, as horrendous as it may have been, was forced to surrender its place for the building of a better future.

In contrast, the revival of Diaspora Jewry among the various nations was predicated on the experiences of the Holocaust. These communities emphasized the all too immediate past in order to foster a sense of responsibility among the nations towards their Jewish communities. Similarly, the indemnity and restitution enterprise was part of the efforts to secure an admission of guilt, which obviously began with Germany itself. Not only was this process *not* frowned upon; it was deemed desirable and necessary. Accordingly, the restitution of property was an integral part of the recognition that Jews had economic rights like every other citizen and were entitled to demand what was legitimately theirs.

The reparations issue also provided an agenda and justification for the Jewish organizations and its attendant politics. Dr. Nahum Goldmann, the president of both the World Jewish Congress and the then recently established Claims Conference, ran the entire negotiations. Although there was Israeli representation on the negotiating staff, Ben-Gurion and Goldmann agreed that the latter would conduct the negotiations with Chancellor Konrad Adenauer, while coordinating all his activities with the Israeli prime minister. This arrangement was perfect for both sides. The fact that it was the Jewish organizations that negotiated with the Germans allowed the Israelis both to "save face" by avoiding direct contact with the Germans and to benefit from the agreement as well.

Goldmann navigated the negotiations and its crises utilizing all the tools at his disposal: his close ties with the American administration, his ability to work the media, and his expertise in internal German politics. The final result was that the State of Israel was compensated for general damage and for absorbing survivors, and the Jewish organizations were assigned the responsibility for dealing with matters of private property.

With the renewed activity on Holocaust restitution and compensation issues in the early 1990s, the same fundamental elements rose to the surface once again, despite the political changes that had transpired over the course of the last fifty years. The activity commenced at the initiative of the Jewish organizations under the leadership of the World Jewish Congress (WJC). Dr. Israel Singer, the secretary-general of the WJC, clearly was and remains the leading force. He employs many of the same skills and resources that Nahum Goldmann had used: his ties with the American administration, his expertise in international politics as well as the internal politics in many foreign countries (especially Germany), his ability to work the media, and his well-honed improvisational skills.

A prevalent claim that is voiced against the Jewish organizations in general, and against the WJC in particular, is that the issues that they advocate are more a justification for their existence than a raison d'être in themselves. Although the subject of Holocaust restitution may have started out as yet another one of these organizational power grabs, it quickly developed into a pertinent and justified issue in its own right. The Jewish claim was essentially one of justice and morality. The focus of the organizations was on reaching an agreement that obliged the various countries, companies, and banks to admit to the debt that they owe to the Jews and compensate them accordingly. Given the realities involved, the very act of reaching an agreement and securing an indemnity is the essence of these proceedings. While the manner in which the individual claims are considered and settled is of great significance, it was not the focal point of these negotiations. In sum, the global agreements that have been hammered out under the considerable glare of the media have indeed produced the effect of historical justice. On the other hand, the payments to individual claimants have been cast aside, postponed, and drawn out for years.

As in the early 1950s, the State of Israel again was not among the leaders of the property restitution process that began in the early 1990s. Once again, a declared and coherent Israeli position was not articulated, and not one government meeting was held on the matter. Apparently the traditional position, prescribed by the Foreign Ministry, determined the Israeli government's policy. This approach favored the continued leadership of the Jewish organizations, while the state's participation would again be limited to observing the proceedings from the sidelines.

In 1992, with the fall of the Iron Curtain and the improving ties with the former Soviet satellites, the government, together with the World Jewish Congress, decided to establish an umbrella organization that would be charged with the restitution of communal Jewish property from the nations of Eastern Europe. Accordingly, the agreement that was signed between Avraham Shochat, then the Minister of Finance, and Edgar Bronfman, the president of the World Jewish Congress, established the World Jewish Restitution Organization (WJRO). The latter was comprised of various Jewish organizations from throughout the world, and the Israeli position was again underscored by its modest role. The government decided to limit its representation in the organization to the mere status of an observer, despite the fact that it was the organization's primary sponsor. Notably, the organization is mandated to handle the restitution of communal property, not private property.

The main reason was that the Israeli government was concerned that these activities could threaten its bilateral relations with different European states. These included arms exports to Poland, the purchase of submarines from Germany, and the return of Israelis arrested for spying in Switzerland. Preserving proper bilateral relations with various European nations is a national interest that takes precedence over settling old scores with Europe. Therefore, the Israeli government refrained from situating itself at the forefront of the struggle.

However, in my opinion, this issue goes beyond these diplomatic considerations. In the early 1990s, Israel still considered these activities to be of secondary importance. Moreover, it felt that the negotiations reverted the Jew back to the status of a victim—a role that Israel has no interest in whatsoever—and it preferred to leave the negotiating to the leaders of the Jewish Diaspora.

Nevertheless, if there were economic fruits to be reaped from this effort, national interests obligated Israel to take advantage of this opportunity. Consequently, it took a greater interest in the mandate of the WJRO, especially in all matters that concerned communal property, whose proceeds are not designated for individual use but for the Jewish collective—

namely, as understood by the Israelis, the State of Israel. The issue of collective compensation, with its potential to fill the state's coffers, was thus perceived as falling under the purview of the Ministry of Finance. It is therefore no coincidence that the finance minister was the official representative on this matter. The agreement also saw to it that the proceeds of the Jewish organizations' struggle would be channeled to the benefit of the State of Israel.

Given the developments in the restitution indemnity negotiations and the fact that the negotiations were now nearing their fruition, the government decided to ratchet up the extent and adjust the nature of its involvement. Rabbi Michael Melchior, the first minister for Diaspora affairs, was assigned responsibility for this issue.[3] Consequently, restitution is no longer considered a financial or economic matter but a "Jewish" one. Israel's involvement in "Jewish" affairs in general—all the more so on the ministerial level—constituted an essential change in the government's attitude towards this issue. The implications of this change were felt on various levels, evident in an increased involvement in the various negotiations (especially those being conducted with European insurance companies and Eastern European governments). The topic of cultural and religious property has been placed on the agenda, and keeping the survivors informed of their rights as they pertain to the proceedings has become a priority. For the first time, the Israeli government entered fields that were previously the exclusive domain of the Jewish organizations, such as conducting negotiations and caring for the survivors' rights.

Israel's approach to the restitution process has indeed undergone some major revisions. While the old Israeli approach chose to eschew the issue of personal property and individual rights, the new approach, adopted by different Israeli negotiators, has in fact concentrated on the individual, addressing such issues as filing and realizing claims against the companies, trusts, and governments; determining the amount of evidence required to substantiate a claim; transferring the burden of proof onto the defendant; fully and fairly estimating the claimed funds and properties; and publishing the names of the property owners on the Internet. These issues became a central component of the Israeli agenda. The Israeli team has thus moved from a policy that was concerned exclusively with communal or unclaimed property to a policy in which the individual's private interests are now the primary consideration of the Israeli representatives. In effect, the Israeli negotiators have essentially switched hats with their colleagues from the Diaspora, whose main objective was to attain a global agreement covering the amount of the settlement, humanitarian sums, and the unclaimed properties.

On several occasions, these differences led to arguments between the two parties. Such disagreements were evident during the negotiations with Generali Assicurazioni SpA (Generali), the Italian insurance company with a long history of selling insurance to European Jews in the prewar era. The argument primarily revolved around details that concerned the welfare of the claimants. These issues were not appropriately resolved within the framework of the agreement that was signed by the Jewish organizations in May 2000. Consequently, the Israeli representatives demanded that the agreement be revoked and entered new negotiations with Generali, which ultimately led to the signing of a new and markedly different agreement in November 2000. The new agreement, in contrast to the original one, required full publication by Generali of policyholder names, lowered the standards of proof necessary to prove a claim, assured that the settlement funds would not be used to pay administrative expenses of the settlement, and assured that payouts earlier made by Generali to settle previous litigation against it were not deducted from the settlement. The new settlement also secured funds for humanitarian purposes.

As a rule, the Israeli approach to the negotiations over all Holocaust restitution claims was firmer than that of the Jewish organizations. The Israeli position was characterized by a demand for absolute justice and morality, less willingness to compromise, and greater suspicion towards the parties seated across the negotiating table. In contrast, the organizations were more pragmatic. Their objective was to reach the best possible agreement under the circumstances. The organizations claimed that, for the most part, the Israeli approach was unrealistic and that their high-minded pursuit of justice and morality would ultimately prevent them from reaching any agreement at all. Moreover, they claimed, the fact that time is running out for the survivors further underscores the importance of compromise and the need to expedite the negotiations. In contrast, the Israelis contended that the willingness to give in on "minor" points produced agreements that lack a framework with which the survivors or their heirs can process a claim and realize their rights. In fact, most of the agreements did not even stipulate the class of claimants that would benefit from the settlements and perhaps—as insinuated more than once—this was the intention of the Jewish organizations.

Notwithstanding the conflicts that have exacerbated the general effort, the two approaches ultimately assisted one another, although this was not the result of any preconceived plan. The Jewish front consisted of both a "good cop" and a "bad cop": the former, the organizations, have concentrated on the broader picture—the amount of the agreement and the external circumstances—while the Israelis have concentrated more on the details and the functionality of the accords insofar as the individual claimants are concerned. In fact, the most effective agreements (in terms of the practical aspects of reaching an agreement, the global amount, the form of the agreement, and the details on processing individual claims) were hammered out when both parties managed to cooperate. Where agreements were made without the participation of Israeli representatives, the rights of individuals became secondary. In those settlements, the funds were not allocated to the compensation of individual claimants but went to the local Jewish communities to use as they saw fit. Moreover, the amounts were small, and so the overall benefit to the local community was negligible. Potent examples of these include the settlements with Belgium, the Czech Republic, Hungary, and Slovakia. These agreements have failed to provide historical justice and a fitting indemnity to either the claimants or the entire Jewish nation.

The responsibility for the affairs of the entire Jewish people cuts to the very heart of the relationships between Diaspora Jewry and Israel, between the Jewish communities throughout the world and the manifold Jewish organizations. Who is the representative of the Jewish people? Who has the Jewish people chosen as its representative? These questions have precipitated many arguments among the different Jewish organizations and between the organizations and the Israeli government. At times, it appeared as if the European insurance companies, governments, and banks lacked a bona fide negotiating partner. They were forced to shuttle back and forth between the representatives of several Jewish organizations, and then on to the Israeli representatives. Unlike in the 1950s, now there is no consensus regarding Israel's centrality and its interests in the negotiations. While the representatives of the Jewish organizations also ran the negotiations during the 1950s, they were primarily representing Israel's interests, as Goldmann was constantly in touch and coordinated his activities with Ben-Gurion and the Israeli Foreign Ministry. Today, however, the situation has dramatically changed. Not all the organizations have accepted Israel's centrality in Jewish affairs. The historic alliance between the Israeli government and the World Jewish Congress has indeed been preserved, and the organization has worked hand in hand with the Israeli government and its representatives, but other organizations have hardly welcomed the Israeli government's encroachment onto their "territory." Different organizations have preferred to see themselves as the legitimate representatives of the entire Jewish people. Local communities similarly perceive themselves, at the very least, as the representatives of the community for which the property is being claimed. The Israeli government thus finds itself in a rather uncomfortable situation—a situation, as we have seen, that the government has effectively created with its own hands over the past fifty years.

In recent years, Israel has clearly moved towards a policy of increased involvement. This change promises to play a more substantial role during the second phase of the restitution enterprise—the distribution of the unclaimed funds that remain from the various agreements—which is now at its peak. In essence, the main objective of this effort is to remedy Israel's entire approach to the restitution issue.

It can only be hoped that this chapter in the Holocaust restitution enterprise will conclude in an honorable and propitious manner, one that unites Jews in the Diaspora with those residing in Israel. May these efforts benefit both the needs of the Holocaust survivors and the Jewish people throughout the world.

NOTES

1. Note, for example, the title of Abraham Foxman's book on antisemitism and its dangers: *Never Again? The Threat of the New Antisemitism* (Harper San Francisco, 2003).

2. Tom Segev, *The Seventh Million: Israelis and the Holocaust* (New York: Holt, 2000).

3. Prior to Melchior's appointment and creation of this ministry, the involvement of the Israeli government in Holocaust restitution was done directly by the Prime Minister's Office through his Diaspora Affairs advisor, Bobby Brown.

Chapter 30

Historical Reparation Claims
The Defense Perspective

Owen C. Pell

The use of the class action to address vast historical wrongs has come into its own over the last decade. Rather than individual plaintiffs seeking damages against the specific state officials who may have harmed them, reparation litigation has now become akin to mass tort litigation, with broadly defined classes seeking billions of dollars in damages against defendant classes sometimes comprising entire industries and generally including the largest multinational corporations in the world.

As these claims have moved from discrete to sweeping, so has the temporal reach of these suits. U.S. courts have been presented with claims relating to historical events that hearken back decades, if not centuries, including African slavery in the United States,[1] the Armenian genocide,[2] the events of World War II in Europe and the Pacific,[3] events that occurred in postwar Europe under communist rule,[4] and the former apartheid regime in South Africa.[5] While these cases are susceptible to significant defenses and almost always fail, the multi-billion-dollar settlements achieved in the Holocaust asset cases[6] created significant momentum in the plaintiffs' bar for pursuing reparation claims in the hope that some other grave historical wrong will open the way to other large settlements.

From a defense perspective the Holocaust asset cases, and historical reparation cases generally, present three distinct areas to be addressed: (1) historical issues; (2) legal issues; and (3) public relations issues. These issues are interrelated and will govern the way reparation cases are resolved and determine whether they have significant settlement value.

A crucial lesson of the Holocaust asset cases is that companies must invest heavily in historical research so that they will have control and an intimate understanding of the facts. A complete understanding of the history surrounding a claim can add to the available legal defenses and can dictate how and whether a company engages with the media regarding a reparations claim. With respect to the law, companies must understand that the legal defenses are strong, but that judges and governments may nonetheless be sympathetic to reparation claims because of the gravity of the harms alleged. The public relations lesson of the Holocaust asset cases is that, unfortunately, companies gain very little from publicly addressing the historical record. If companies do engage publicly, they must recognize the harms suffered by plaintiffs while highlighting the legal and historical perspective that supports dismissal of these types of claims.

The Nature of the Claims

Historical reparation claims brought in U.S. courts are usually premised on the Alien Tort Statute (ATS).[7] Plaintiffs in an ATS case generally must allege that they have been the victim of a tort that is either (1) a crime of individual responsibility under customary international law or (2) a crime under international law in which a defendant was a state actor or was acting under color of law (i.e., acting with the real or apparent authority of the state). Commonly recognized crimes of individual responsibility include state-sponsored murder and torture, genocide, and war crimes. Early ATS cases focused on government officials being pursued by those they had actually harmed.[8] Pursuing historical reparations in this way, however, poses a huge problem for plaintiffs.

Governments generally will have sovereign immunity with respect to grave historical wrongs committed wholly outside the United States. Either these claims will be subject to absolute immunity (if committed before 1977),[9] or they will be immune from U.S. jurisdiction under the Foreign Sovereign Immunities Act (FSIA)[10] because the tort exception to immunity requires that the relevant conduct occurred in the United States.[11] Thus, plaintiffs have increasingly turned their attention to companies that may have done business in or with nations that engage in human rights violations.

This was the paradigm for the Holocaust asset cases. Plaintiffs sued banks, insurers, manufacturers, and other businesses that had various levels of contact with Germany or its allies (including Japan) before and during World War II. The level of contact varied greatly. Some companies handled assets of Jews and others who were persecuted by the Nazis. Other companies were accused of actively participating in slave or forced labor programs instituted by the German or Japanese governments. Still other companies were accused of doing business with the Nazi regime. In all cases, plaintiffs alleged broad conspiracies among the corporate defendants so as to support claims of joint and several liability for all the wrongs committed by Germany or Japan. Plaintiffs defined broad classes of individuals who were affected by the Holocaust or other German or Japanese government actions.

Once filed, the lawsuits were used as a public relations platform to mobilize political and public opinion against the defendant companies. Congressional, state, and local political representatives used the lawsuits as a basis for subpoenas and hearings. In some cases states or cities threatened to bar defendant companies from doing further business with a state or city. This political pressure was a catalyst for the multi-billion-dollar settlements that were then brokered by the Clinton administration.

The Problem of Historical Distortion

The style of pleading used in historical reparation cases is not unique to U.S. litigation. Rather, it is premised on U.S. rules of procedure that only require the plaintiff to provide the defendant with simple notice of the nature of the claims asserted.[12] Generally, on a motion to dismiss, well-pled allegations of fact are then accepted as true. This is a pleading style designed to best allow cases to survive a motion to dismiss so that plaintiffs may pursue discovery (and keep cases alive so as to exert maximum settlement pressure). Thus, plaintiffs make allegations of fact that they assert a court must accept as true for purposes of a motion to dismiss.

The problem with this approach, however, is that often plaintiffs in reparation cases must ignore or distort history to plead a strong complaint. Reparation cases generally are premised on massive violations of human rights carried out by *governments*—not companies—that ended because of actions by other *governments*—not companies. Thus, World War II and the Holocaust implemented by the German government ended when the Allies defeated Germany. The Allies then determined that there would be the Nuremberg trials for the major German war criminals, that other war criminals would be tried in the Allied occupation zones, and that reparations of one kind or another for victims of German aggression and persecution would, through a series of treaties, be paid by Germany. In addition, it was West Germany that decided to make reparations on behalf of *all Germans* through the payment of billions of dollars to the State of Israel and to Holocaust survivors around the world. It is acknowledged that these payments have already totaled over $60 billion.

In pleading their complaints, however, plaintiffs often reduce the societal and governmental to the transactional or corporate. These complaints ascribe actions of governments to companies and assume that all defendant companies willingly conspired and uniformly participated in the crimes committed by governments. The complaints also ignore actions taken by governments *after* the alleged human rights violations have ended, including prosecuting such crimes or making reparation to victims, because it is central to plaintiffs' claims that companies that were not specifically called to account were "unjustly enriched" even where a state or group of states decided who would be prosecuted and/or what the societal reparation scheme would be. Reparation cases also generally ignore acts of resistance by corporate officers or employees because such facts undercut the mass claims asserted.

Confronting Historical Issues

To properly address reparation claims, companies must invest early in serious and exhaustive historical research. Companies must seek as much information as possible on (1) their corporate existence and activities during the period in question; (2) the role of other companies and the government in the wrongs allegedly committed; and (3) the facts surrounding the actual claims made by the named plaintiffs. A thorough understanding of the facts is crucial in showing a court, a regulator, or the media that plaintiffs' counsel is distorting historical facts and can be extremely important in getting a court to focus on the legal issues presented or in convincing a regulator not to become involved in a case. Placing facts in historical context also may convince the media that a story is not as compelling as it may have seemed.

For example, with respect to the reparation claims made against banks doing business in France during World War II, historical research developed by the French government and the defendants played an important role in the negotiation of a settlement that was much lower than that reached in other Holocaust asset cases. This data was collected and published by the French government in the so-called Mattéoli Report and included a special two-volume report on "Financial Spoliation" to which all banks operating in France contributed.[13]

In particular, documents available in French, German, U.S., and British archives established that (1) the Germans moved immediately after conquering France to inspect and inventory all safe deposit boxes in occupied France—as opposed to the banks helping to target only those held by Jews; (2) it was almost two years into the Occupation before the Germans moved to block Jewish bank accounts, during which time many banks in France allowed Jewish customers to draw down their accounts; (3) banks in France did not uniformly move to block Jewish assets before being formally ordered to do so by the German authorities; and (4) to the extent that the Germans provided advance notice of their intent to block Jewish accounts, that notice was provided only five days before the formal blocking order, and there was no evidence that all banks in France froze Jewish accounts prematurely. The Mattéoli Report also showed that the number of accounts and the account balances ultimately affected by the German blocking rules were much lower than plaintiffs had alleged. Significantly, the research also showed that after the liberation of France, a significant number of account holders (for many French banks, over 90–95 percent) sought and received restitution for amounts seized during the war.

The Legal Issues

The fundamental premise of historical reparation cases against companies has been that the ATS allows broad claims based on evolving concepts of international law that have developed since World War II.[14] The case law, however, shows that, to date, most reparation cases are dismissed at the motion-to-dismiss phase.[15] If anything, it now will be even harder for plaintiffs to advance reparation cases based on the recent ruling by the U.S. Supreme Court in *Sosa v. Alvarez-Machain*.[16]

In *Sosa*, a Mexican doctor, Alvarez-Machain, was accused of assisting a drug cartel in the torture and murder of a U.S. DEA agent in Mexico. After failing to secure his extradition, the DEA plotted with people in Mexico (including Sosa) to abduct Alvarez-Machain and bring him to the United States for trial. Alvarez-Machain was acquitted, and then sued the U.S. government under the Federal Tort Claims Act (FTCA)[17] and Sosa, now living in the United States, under the ATS.

Passed by the first Congress in the Judiciary Act of 1789, the ATS provides that "[t]he district courts shall have original jurisdiction of any civil action by an alien for a tort only, committed in violation of the law of nations or a treaty of the United States."[18] As noted above, since *Filartiga v. Pena-Irala* held that ATS claims could be based on evolving standards of international law,[19] U.S. courts have been deluged with numerous lawsuits alleging that U.S. and foreign corporations have committed or aided and abetted violations of international law.[20]

The Supreme Court took a narrower view of the ATS than the lower federal courts. The Court began its analysis by reviewing the history of the ATS. The Court found that "[d]espite considerable scholarly attention, it is fair to say that a consensus understanding of what Congress intended has proven elusive."[21] The Court found that a "narrow set of violations of the law of nations"—in particular the three specific offenses of violation of a government grant of safe conduct, infringement of the rights of ambassadors, and piracy—were "probably on the minds of the men who drafted the ATS with its reference to tort."[22]

Ultimately, a unanimous Court concluded that the ATS is "a jurisdictional statute creating no new causes of action."[23] Although the ATS did not *create* new causes of action, the Court also concluded that "the reasonable inference from the historical materials is that the statute was intended to have practical effect the moment it became law" without the need for further enabling legislation. Thus, "[t]he jurisdictional grant is best read as having been enacted on the understanding that the common law would provide a cause of action for the modest number of international law violations with a potential for personal liability at the time" (i.e., the three violations noted above).[24]

If the Court had stopped with that ruling, every ATS action brought since *Filartiga* would have been foreclosed. A six-justice majority, however, went further, holding that the federal courts were *not* limited to the three causes of action recognized in 1789, but *could recognize* other violations of international law as actionable under the ATS.[25] This holding, in turn, came with a stern warning that "there are good reasons for a restrained conception of the discretion a federal court should exercise in considering a new cause of action" and that "courts should require any claim based on the present-day law of nations to rest on a norm of international character accepted by the civilized world and defined with a specificity comparable to the features of the 18th-century paradigms we have recognized."[26]

The Court then discussed a number of reasons why "judicial caution" must be exercised in recognizing claims under the ATS. For example, the Court recognized that "[w]e have no congressional mandate to seek out and define new and debatable violations of the law of nations, and modern indications of congressional understanding of the judicial role in the field have not affirmatively encouraged greater judicial creativity."[27] The Court also found that "the potential implications for the foreign relations of the United States of recognizing such causes should make courts particularly wary of impinging on the discretion of the Legislative and Executive Branches in managing foreign affairs."[28]

To illustrate the specificity with which a crime under international law must be defined to be recognized as a tort in violation of the law of nations and thereby actionable under the ATS, the Court cited *United States v. Smith*, an 1820 piracy case.[29] In *Smith*, the Court found that the crime of piracy was "a crime of a settled and determinate nature; and whatever may be the diversity of definitions, in other respects, all writers concur, in holding, that robbery, or forcible depredations upon the sea, *animo furandi*, is piracy."[30]

The Supreme Court's reasoning in *Smith* is consistent with that applied in the recent Second Circuit decision in *Flores v. Southern Peru Copper Corp.*[31] In *Flores*, the court concluded that "customary international law is composed only of those rules that States universally abide by, or accede to, out of a sense of legal obligation and mutual [as opposed to merely several] concern."[32] In ascertaining whether a particular rule is part of customary international law, the court held that "we look primarily to the formal lawmaking and official actions of States and only secondarily to the works of scholars as evidence of the established practice of States."[33] In *Flores*, the Second Circuit expressly rejected a plaintiff's reliance on, among other things, various non-self-executing treaties (such as broadly worded international human rights conventions), nonbinding UN resolutions, and other multinational declarations of principle as sources of international law.[34]

Although *Flores* was not cited in *Sosa*, the Supreme Court endorsed similar reasoning. Thus, the Court rejected the claim that a prohibition on arbitrary arrest had attained the status of customary international law, holding that Alvarez-Machain could *not* rely on the Universal Declaration of Human Rights or the International Covenant on Civil and Political Rights as establishing a cause of action under international law. The Declaration was only a statement of principles, while the Covenant was ratified by the United States only "on the express understanding that it was not self-executing and so did not itself create obligations enforceable in the federal courts."[35]

The Supreme Court's reasoning is particularly significant to the reparation actions that have been advanced against companies under the ATS. Most of these actions have been heavily reliant on post–World War II UN conventions, but these conventions are, like the Declaration, limited to general statements of principle, and virtually every human rights treaty ratified by the United States has been expressly conditioned on a reservation that the treaty is not self-executing (i.e., does not of its own force create rights that can be enforced in U.S. courts).

Applying this reasoning, the Supreme Court included two footnotes in *Sosa* that are of particular significance to companies. In footnote 20, the Court recognized that under international law there is a question as to whether companies may be sued at all.[36] Thus, federal courts now will have to examine whether particular ATS claims apply to nongovernmental actors (as some claims under international law apply only to nations) and, if so, to corporations, as opposed to individuals. In footnote 21, the Court focused on a well-publicized pending case involving claims against companies that did business in or with South Africa during the apartheid era.[37] Both the U.S. and South African governments asked the federal district court considering the case to dismiss it, and warned that failure to do so could harm U.S. foreign affairs.[38] The Supreme Court in *Sosa* highlighted this, noting,

> Another possible limitation that we need not apply here is a policy of case-specific deference to the political branches. . . . The Government of South Africa has said that these cases interfere with the policy embodied by its Truth and Reconciliation Commission, which "deliberately avoided a 'victors' justice' approach to the crimes of apartheid and chose instead one based on confession and absolution, informed by the principles of reconciliation, reconstruction, reparation and goodwill." The United States has agreed. In such cases, there is a strong argument that federal courts should give serious weight to the Executive Branch's view of the case's impact on foreign policy.[39]

Having twice highlighted a need for the courts to avoid interfering with U.S. foreign relations, the *Sosa* decision will increase the weight of any U.S. government statement in ATS litigation.

After *Sosa* it will be harder for plaintiffs to plead (or recover on) ATS claims generally. Specifically, the Supreme Court's holding on why the Universal Declaration of Human Rights and International Covenant on Civil and Political Rights *do not* create actionable claims under international law will undercut any attempt to frame claims based on the broad array of UN-sponsored human rights treaties enacted over the last forty years. In addition, the Supreme Court has strongly admonished the lower courts to act with great restraint in recognizing causes of action under the ATS.

On the other hand, the lower federal courts have not generally exercised great restraint in ATS cases, and *Sosa* leaves the door open for judges who are so minded to attempt to interpret international law broadly. At a minimum, claims based on state-sponsored activities like genocide, war crimes, crimes against humanity, or state-sponsored murder, rape, and torture, *likely will continue* to be recognized as well established under international law. As to these crimes, *there is* also precedent from international tribunals for aiding and abetting liability (although whether these rulings constitute international law will continue to be debated). Therefore, these claims will continue to be brought. Significantly, however, no international tribunal anywhere has ever held that doing business with or lending money to a government constitutes aiding and abetting a crime under international law. Thus, after *Sosa,* claims against banks and other companies for simply doing business with repressive or violent regimes should fail.

Finally, for companies, *Sosa* also signals the beginning of an important new debate based on the Court's question of whether companies are proper party-defendants in claims arising under international law. To the extent that plaintiffs fear that it may not be possible to recover against companies, it is *highly likely* that plaintiffs now will name corporate directors and officers *in addition to* companies in ATS actions.

In addition to the issues raised by *Sosa,* reparation cases also face additional defenses that companies should raise at the outset in motions to dismiss, including standing (plaintiff's ability to link his/her alleged injury to some act by defendant that can be remedied by plaintiff's claim), statutes of limitation, whether the case poses nonjusticiable political questions, and whether the case presents issues that are inherently unmanageable by the courts.[40] Moreover, it also is highly doubtful that any reparation case could ever be certified as a class action given the individual issues relating to the harms suffered by each plaintiff, the relationship of each defendant to the plaintiffs and a given government, and/or the causal connections among any defendant, the plaintiffs, and the government in question.[41]

Given these significant defenses, companies should move to dismiss reparation cases as soon as possible. A well-presented motion makes clear to the court that the case can be addressed quickly and straightforwardly. In addition, highlighting the myriad problems faced by the plaintiffs can go a long way to reducing the public interest in a reparation case and/or plaintiffs' ability to create political or public support.

Public Relations Issues

A huge challenge posed by historical reparation cases is the threat of adverse publicity. The cases can be particularly frustrating because although the risk of loss is very low, the risk of unfavorable media attention is high. In addition, as noted above, unfavorable press also can attract unfavorable attention from regulators and consumers.

The Holocaust asset cases showed that managing public relations in reparation cases can be difficult for defendant companies. As an initial matter, it is critical that a company not speak in detail until it has done its research and understands the historical facts. It also is critical for a company to make clear that it takes these cases and the wrongs alleged very seriously. Even if, as a legal matter, the claims are untrue or readily dismissible, companies take, and must be seen as taking, the underlying harms alleged very seriously—something that must be clear in statements to employees and the public.

To the extent that a company does speak to the facts alleged in any reparation case, it must speak with precision and must be careful not to exaggerate or distort the historical record. This will help keep the media honest and prevent exaggerated or inaccurate claims about a company from gaining credence. As the Holocaust asset cases showed, once certain claims are in the public domain it is difficult, if not impossible, to counteract them. It is when such claims take on a life of their own that pressure to settle can build. To the extent, however, that plaintiffs or their counsel make false statements about historical matters, companies should consider making strong and precise responses that may reduce the credibility of plaintiffs or their counsel as press sources.

Experience seems to show that companies gain by maintaining a low profile in reparation cases. History is often very complicated and does not lend itself to sound bites. That U.S. companies, for example, kept doing business with Germany even as World War II approached is not a simple story. It requires consideration of U.S. and European politics and foreign policy, and the interplay of events involving many nations, companies, and individuals. As historians will admit, even decades later, after weighing detailed historical records, it may not be clear why certain things happened or why people acted as they did. There also are serious ongoing debates among legal and academic scholars about the efficacy of visiting on any company or nation, decades after the fact, reparations for harms committed by individuals long dead in wars long over.[42]

In short, companies may find it much easier to address these issues in court through written pleadings than in short media releases. This tactic dictates a cautious media strategy and mandates that any dealings with the media be carefully managed, with ample time given to background preparation of reporters and those speaking for the company. It also may support a media strategy in which companies encourage serious academic pieces addressing the historical perspective presented by a reparation case and thereby placing the issues in a more informed perspective.

In addition, it must be remembered that the news cycle is short and relentless. If companies refuse to conduct a public debate with plaintiffs it is quite likely that media attention will fade, as producers and editors are reluctant to continually broadcast only one side of a story. It also should be noted that litigation generates a special news cycle tied to "milestones" in a given case. The filing of a complaint can generate news and background stories, as can the filing of a brief or a court decision. The months that may pass between filing and argument, or argument and decision, however, are dead space that companies may avoid filling by simply noting that the matter is pending before the court.

In sum, "positive press" in the area of historical reparation claims is difficult to come by. What happened to the plaintiffs usually is quite real and quite horrible, and must be acknowledged as such. To the extent that companies did business with oppressive regimes, even when encouraged by their governments and in furtherance of a nation's foreign policy, these activities may not be something that any company wants to publicize today. Companies rarely gain much by engaging plaintiffs in a debate on reparations.

Conclusion

The challenge posed by historical reparation claims is that plaintiffs who have suffered real and serious harms are seeking remedies that many (including judges, regulators, and consumers) may find sympathetic. There is a great appeal to seeking some form of ultimate justice or closure, especially when history itself is nowhere near as satisfying.

Historical reparation claims do not easily fit the mold of typical tort or contract claims, and do not usually survive the motion-to-dismiss phase. As the Holocaust asset cases proved, however, these claims can take on a life of their own and can generate huge settlements on claims that probably would have failed if litigated to final judgment. The lesson of these cases is that, more than other types of litigation, they must be addressed on multiple fronts and with a keen eye to the historical record.

The ultimate challenge for companies confronted with reparation claims is to understand the detailed historical record and the law, and then work to convince the courts, press, and public to maintain perspective— both historical and legal. This perspective is critical to making it more likely that these cases will be resolved in the courts, where companies should and often do prevail.

NOTES

The author thanks Jena A. Tarleton, an associate at White & Case LLP, for her help in drafting this chapter.

1. *See In re African-American Slave Labor Descendants Litig.*, 304 F. Supp. 2d 1027, 1038–39 (N.D. Ill. 2004) (dismissing consolidated actions).

2. *Marootian v. New York Life Ins. Co.*, No. 99-12073 (C.D. Cal. filed Nov. 22, 1999).

3. *See, e.g., Burger-Fischer v. Degussa AG*, 65 F. Supp. 2d 248 (D.N.J. 1999); *Joo v. Japan*, 172 F. Supp. 2d 52 (D.D.C. 2001), *aff'd*, 332 F.3d 679 (D.C. Cir. 2003), *petition for cert. filed*, 72 USLW 3373 (U.S. Nov. 20, 2003) (No. 03-741); *In re World War II Era Japanese Forced Labor Litig.*, 114 F. Supp. 2d 939 (N.D. Cal. 2000); *Deutsch v. Turner*, 324 F.3d 692 (9th Cir. 2003).

4. *Haven v. Rzeczpospolita Polska*, 68 F. Supp. 2d 947 (N.D. Ill. 1999), *aff'd*, 215 F.3d 727 (7th Cir. 2000), *cert. denied*, 531 U.S. 1014 (2000); *Garb v. Republic of Poland*, 207 F. Supp. 2d 16 (E.D.N.Y. 2002), *vacated*, No. 02-7844, 2003 WL 21890843 (2d Cir. Aug. 6, 2003), *cert. granted and judgment vacated*, 124 S. Ct. 2835 (2004).

5. *See In re S. African Apartheid Litig.*, 346 F. Supp. 2d 538, 542–43 (S.D.N.Y. 2004) (dismissing consolidated actions).

6. *See Bodner v. Banque Paribas*, 114 F. Supp. 2d 117 (E.D.N.Y. 2000); *In re Austrian and German Holocaust Litig.*, 250 F.3d 156 (2d Cir. 2001) (per curiam); *In re Austria, German Bank Holocaust Litig.*, 80 F. Supp. 2d 164 (S.D.N.Y. 2000), *aff'd*, *D'Amato v. Deutsche Bank*, 236 F.3d 78 (2d Cir. 2001); *In re Nazi Era Cases against German Defs. Litig.*, 198 F.R.D. 429 (D.N.J. 2000); *In re Assicurazioni Generali SpA Holocaust Ins. Litig.*, 228 F. Supp. 2d 348 (S.D.N.Y. 2002). The Swiss banks litigation was settled between the parties, without involvement of the Swiss government. See *In re Holocaust Victims Assets Litig.*, 105 F. Supp. 2d 139 (E.D.N.Y.), *aff'd*, 225 F.3d 191 (2d Cir. 2000).

7. 28 U.S.C. § 1350 ("The district courts shall have original jurisdiction of any civil action by an alien for a tort only, committed in violation of the law of nations or a treaty of the United States.").

8. *See Filartiga v. Peña-Irala*, 630 F.2d 876 (2d Cir. 1980); *Kadic v. Karadzic*, 70 F.3d 232 (2d Cir. 1995), *reh'g denied*, 74 F.3d 377 (1996).

9. *See, e.g., Carl Marks and Co. v. U.S.S.R.*, 841 F.2d 26 (2d Cir.), *cert denied*, 487 U.S. 1219 (1988); *Joo*, 332 F.3d 679.

10. 28 U.S.C. §§ 1602–11.

11. *See* 28 U.S.C. § 1605(a)(5). *See also Doe v. Unocal*, 933 F. Supp. 880, 887 (C.D. Cal. 1997) (dismissing claims against Burmese military government and its state-owned company under FSIA where all torts occurred in Myanmar), *rev'd on other grounds*, No. 00-56603, 00-57195, 00-57197, 00-56628, 2002 WL 31063976 (9th Cir. Sep. 18, 2002), *reh'g en banc granted, opinion vacated*, No. 00-56603, 00-56628, 2003 WL 359787 (Feb. 14, 2003).

12. *See* Fed. R. Civ. Pro. 8(a) ("A pleading which sets forth a claim for relief . . . shall contain . . . a short and plain statement of the claim showing that the pleader is entitled to relief. . . .").

13. *See generally* Claire Andrieu and Cecile Omnes, *La spoliation financière: Mission d'étude sur la spoliation des Juifs de France, présidée par Jean Mattéoli.* Paris: La Documentation française (2000), *available at* http://www.ladocfrancaise.gouv.fr/.

14. *See, e.g., Filartiga v. Peña-Irala*, 630 F.2d 876 (2d Cir. 1980); *Kadic v. Karadzic*, 70 F.3d 232 (2d Cir. 1995), *reh'g denied*, 74 F.3d 377 (1996).

15. *See, e.g., Joo*, 172 F. Supp. 2d 52; *Burger-Fischer*, 65 F. Supp. 2d 248; *Iwanowa v. Ford Motor Co.*, 67 F. Supp. 2d 424 (D.N.J. 1999).

16. 124 S. Ct. 2739 (2004).

17. 28 U.S.C. §§ 1346, 2671, et seq.

18. *See* 124 S. Ct. at 2755.

19. *See* 630 F.2d 876 (2d Cir. 1980).

20. *See supra* notes 2–6.

21. *See* 124 S. Ct. at 2758.

22. *See* 124 S. Ct. at 2756.

23. *See* 124 S. Ct. at 2761.

24. *See* 124 S. Ct. at 2761. The Court also rejected the FTCA claim. *Id.* at 2748–54.

25. *See* 124 S. Ct. at 2761–62.

26. *Id.*

27. 124 S. Ct. at 2763.

28. *Id.*

29. *See* 124 S. Ct. at 2765 (citing *United States v. Smith,* 18 U.S. (5 Wheat.) 153 (1820)).

30. *See* 18 U.S. (5 Wheat.) at 163–80 and n.a.

31. 343 F.3d 140 (2d Cir. 2003).

32. *Id.* at 154.

33. *Id.* at 155.

34. *See* 343 F.3d at 155–56.

35. *See Sosa,* 124 S. Ct. at 2767.

36. 124 S. Ct. at 2766 n.20.

37. *See supra* note 5.

38. *See In re S. Afr. Apartheid Litig.,* 346 F. Supp. 2d at 553–54.

39. 124 S. Ct. at 2766 n.21.

40. *See, e.g., Dellums v. U.S. Nuclear Regulatory Comm'n,* 863 F.2d 968 (D.C. Cir. 1988); *Kelberine v. Société Internationale,* 363 F.2d 989 (D.C. Cir.), *cert. denied,* 385 U.S. 989 (1966).

41. *See generally* Detlev Vagts and Peter Murray, *Litigating the Nazi Labor Claims: The Path Not Taken,* 43 Harv. Int'l L.J. 503 (Summer 2002).

42. *See generally,* Elazar Barkan, *The Guilt of Nations* (Norton, 2000).

Chapter 31

The Legacy of Holocaust Class Action Suits
Have They Broken Ground for Other Cases of Historical Wrongs?

Morris Ratner and Caryn Becker

In the mid-1990s a small group of American class action counsel, including the authors of this essay, changed the history of the postwar reparations movement by commencing scores of private civil law suits in U.S. courts on behalf of victims of Nazi persecution, against Swiss, German, Austrian, French, and other European entities. To settle these suits, European governments and companies have, to date, paid more than $8 billion to these victims and their heirs.

The results in these cases have inspired victims of other historical atrocities to place hope in the U.S. judicial system—hope that they too might receive some measure of compensation for their suffering. Other victims coming forward have included braceros, Mexican temporary workers who worked in the U.S. during the war and did not receive their full pay; Japanese "comfort women" during World War II; slave laborers used by Japanese companies throughout Asia; South African victims of apartheid; and descendants of American slaves.

Unfortunately, American courts have not proved to be the path to justice for victims of non-Holocaust-era historical wrongs. Why did the Nazi-era cases not produce a wave of additional success stories for other victims of historical wrongs? The authors examine this question, first, by reviewing the Holocaust-related court decisions to see what the judges said about the prospects for these and other similar cases; second, by identifying the nonjudicial pressure points that helped produce the Holocaust-related settlements; and, third, by examining the litigation of other historical wrongs in light of these factors to see if the differences can explain their relative lack of success in achieving justice in U.S. courts.

U.S. courts have always been available for victims of human rights abuses to seek justice.[1] For example, the Alien Tort Claims Act, 28 U.S.C. § 1350 (ATCA), although rarely used until recently, was originally adopted in 1789 as part of the original Judiciary Act, and gives federal courts "original jurisdiction [over] any civil action by an alien for a tort only, committed in violation of the law of nations or a treaty of the United States." The Nazi-era cases were different from the other human rights claims, however, in part because they involved *historical* wrongs that were already fifty years old when the major wave of litigation commenced in the mid-1990s. These cases were also different from typical human rights cases in that the victims' advocates sought redress for entire populations of victims by utilizing the human rights law that had developed over the prior decades and combining it with the class action device that allows U.S. courts to aggregate the claims of large groups of persons and resolve their common disputes in a single proceeding. The Nazi-era class cases also differed from prior Nazi-era litigation in that they did not seek return of specific items of property, but instead, in most instances, involved efforts to recover nonspecific damages, typically characterized as illicit profits (such as from slave labor or the laundering of stolen gold).

What Did the Holocaust Litigation Judges Say?

Many point to the results of the Nazi-era cases—public apologies and the payment of billions of dollars by European governments and corporations —as proof of the success of that litigation. The judicial record created as a result of the Nazi-era litigation wave, however, is surprisingly limited. Of the more than one hundred Nazi-era cases prosecuted, there are only approximately twelve published decisions from the class cases.[2] Perhaps the most profound decisions that can provide hope and long-lasting support for victims of other historical abuses were issued by the courts that approved the substance and process of the Swiss banks settlement.[3]

The Swiss banks case is the only major Holocaust case that was fully resolved through a private class action and not through an international agreement. Chief Judge Edward R. Korman of the Eastern District of New York, the presiding federal judge, extended the American court's jurisdiction over a worldwide class of victims and targets of Nazi persecution for the purpose of resolving all claims against Swiss banks and other Swiss entities in one proceeding. Judge Korman oversaw an incredibly detailed and extensive worldwide notice plan (including a multi-million-dollar publication program, direct mail to survivor lists and support groups, and grass-roots community outreach) and appointed a Special Master to develop a plan for allocating the settlement funds among the many different types of class members. After holding hearings in both New York and Israel, he issued an order approving, first, the settlement and then, later, the Plan of Allocation. The Second Circuit upheld both orders.[4] The lesson from these cases is that U.S. courts *can* effectively provide a forum for resolving these kinds of extraordinary historical wrongs.

Other federal trial judges presiding over Nazi-era cases also indicated that U.S. courts would not necessarily preclude victims of historical wrongs from litigating their claims in the United States simply because the claims might involve political questions, touch upon foreign relations, or involve abuses that took place in the distant past. For example, Judge Sterling Johnson Jr. in the Eastern District of New York declined to dismiss the cases alleging Nazi-era confiscation and retention of assets by French banks.[5] Rejecting the French banks' arguments, Judge Johnson found that the issues were appropriate for U.S. courts to decide and that the claims were not time barred because plaintiffs had alleged continuing wrongs.

But not every court has been as willing to open its doors to the claims of victims of Nazi persecution. Two federal trial court judges in New Jersey who presided over the leading German slave and forced labor cases dismissed those cases largely on political question grounds, finding that plaintiffs could not have their claims heard in a U.S. court, as their claims were best left to the executive branch.[6] Similarly, the U.S. Supreme Court held that California's Holocaust Victim Insurance Relief Act of 1999 — which required insurers doing business in California to disclose the details of any Holocaust-era insurance policies—had been preempted by the executive branch's conduct of and supremacy over foreign policy, as expressed principally in the postwar executive agreements with Germany, Austria, and France.[7]

In 2004, Chief Judge Michael Mukasey in the Southern District of New York dismissed plaintiffs' claims against the Italian insurance company Generali, the only remaining defendant in the Holocaust-era insurance litigation.[8] Although he earlier rejected Generali's argument that the U.S. courts were not the proper place for plaintiffs to pursue their claims, Judge Mukasey was forced to conclude that, under the Supreme Court authority discussed above, "it appears that plaintiffs cannot use the courts to obtain recovery of benefits due under Holocaust-era policies, regardless of the theory of recovery."[9]

Although these decisions were fact specific—based upon the executive branch's involvement in the Holocaust compensation efforts—the results are unfortunate, both for the Holocaust victims who have been deprived of their day in court and also for other victims of historical abuses, as they illustrate the ability of the executive branch to hold the key to the courthouse and to justice.[10] With the reelection of President George W. Bush, who has actively sought to quash human rights cases, the future for victim groups becomes murkier.

The Supreme Court recently rekindled hope for abuse victims generally, however, by confirming that the ATCA provides jurisdiction for foreigners to seek redress in U.S. courts for the most egregious violations of the "law of nations," such as torture, genocide, crimes against humanity, and war crimes,[11] despite the serious opposition of the Bush administration and numerous business groups who all filed "friend of the court" briefs.[12]

The judicial record created by the Nazi-era litigation is therefore mixed. It provides some hope for advocates of victims of historical wrongs that U.S. courts may provide a means for obtaining justice even many years after the fact. However, it also shows that even under optimal circumstances, litigation is at best a difficult and uncertain tool for victims' advocates.

Other Factors That Contributed to the Nazi-Era Settlements

The Nazi-era litigation was simply one component of an organized political and social movement on behalf of the victims. The movement involved the use of pressure points both within the countries accused of wrongdoing and within the United States, including use of the media, the executive/regulatory branch, the legislative branch, and good old-fashioned grassroots organizing. Together, these efforts provided the pressure necessary to force perpetrators of historical wrongs to compensate their victims.

European Guilt at the Turn of the Century

Morris Ratner, one of the authors of this essay, participated directly in the negotiations that resulted in the class action settlement with the Swiss banks, and that also resulted in the executive agreements between the United States and Germany, Austria, and France, respectively. In the course of these negotiations, which took place between approximately 1997 and 2000, it became clear that as the close of the twentieth century approached, these countries sought to find a symbolic way to obtain closure for the bad acts committed by their former government's nationals during and after World War II. Indeed, the countries were psychologically ready and eager to apologize for their participation in Nazi-era atrocities and profiteering.

While this desire for atonement and closure was apparent, it was tempered by an attitude that the current generation should not have to pay today for the sins of their fathers. In some instances, especially with respect to the Austrians and the French, there was an underlying impression conveyed by the negotiators that they did not fully appreciate the victims' experiences or sense of aggrievement; at times, we had to remind them of what they did. Nonetheless, the desire for atonement and closure was clearly stronger than any countervailing reluctance to acknowledge or to take responsibility for past conduct. In the end, it was the desire to "do the right thing" that helped propel and produce these settlements. As discussed further below, it is the absence of a similar desire by governments and private institutions in the context of other historical human rights abuses that ultimately will make it much more difficult to settle those claims.

Support of the U.S. Government

The Clinton administration made resolution of Nazi-era litigation a high priority. Secretary of State Madeleine Albright—who around the time that this litigation was pending discovered that her grandparents were Czech Jews who had perished in the Holocaust—was personally involved at the highest level in supporting our efforts to obtain compensation for the victims. The U.S. State and Justice Departments had teams of persons devoted to facilitating settlement discussions between the plaintiffs in the U.S. litigation and the European governments and corporations we were suing. Until settlements intended to resolve all of the litigation claims were reached, the Clinton administration refrained from interfering with the pending litigation by declining to file papers adverse to the claims in the courts handling them.

In stark contrast, the Bush administration's approach to human rights cases has been to undermine such efforts by attacking the ATCA, the statute that formed the basis for much of the Holocaust litigation.

Media Attention

At the time of the groundswell of Nazi-era class action litigation, and during negotiations with Nazi-era defendants, media coverage of Holocaust issues was extensive. Human interest stories chronicling survivors' efforts to recover lost property or the plight of victims of slave labor or other atrocities regularly appeared.

Media attention was not limited to the written press. Dozens of pieces aired on both network and cable television. For example, in July 1998, *60 Minutes* ran a piece about a family's search for a painting stolen by the Nazis. In November 1998, *60 Minutes* and *Dateline NBC* both ran stories about the use of slave labor by German industry and the surrounding litigation. Such coverage had an impact on the governments and private institutions that ultimately paid to settle the victims' claims. Throughout the Swiss and German negotiations, the issue of the press and the negative attention generated by the litigation clearly weighed upon the negotiators.

Regulatory Pressure and Threatened Legislation

While the litigation was pending, industry regulators, such as banking and insurance regulators in the United States, applied the kinds of pressure they could uniquely bring to bear. For example, the Executive Monitoring Committee, representing hundreds of state and local financial officials and founded by New York City Comptroller Alan Hevesi, put significant pressure on European banks and insurance companies to settle Holocaust-era property claims through the use of such tactics as threatening economic sanctions against the Swiss banks and delaying regulatory approval of the acquisition by Germany's Deutsche Bank of the New York–based Bankers Trust. Such efforts served to prompt the European defendant companies doing business in the United States to compensate the persons they had injured during and after the Nazi era.

State legislatures in California, New York, and elsewhere were also active in passing legislation intended to assist victims of Nazi persecution in the prosecution of claims in their local state courts. These state statutes aimed to provide Holocaust survivors with access to local courts by giving the courts specific jurisdiction to handle Nazi-era claims and extending the time period during which the lawsuits had to be filed.[13]

In the aftermath of the dismissal of the German slave labor cases by the New Jersey federal udges, Congress began formulating statutes to strengthen the hands of victims' advocates in the U.S. courts in subsequent cases. In 1999, for instance, Senator Charles Schumer of New York introduced a bill that would have authorized federal courts to hear cases arising out of Nazi-era conduct, and would have made it more likely that other cases would survive similar dismissal motions.

Why Have Litigation Efforts by Subsequent Victim Groups Failed to Replicate the Success of Victims of Nazi Persecution?

Generally, for victims of other historical wrongs, one or more of the critical factors that led to the outcome in the Nazi-era cases has either been entirely absent, or not present with sufficient intensity to propel the perpetrators to make restitution payments like those made in the Nazi-era cases. As a result, there has not been a repetition to date of the success of the Nazi-era cases in the context of litigation efforts intended to address other historical wrongs. For example:

- In 2001, representative plaintiffs filed class actions on behalf of the Mexican braceros who worked in the United States in the 1940s, and who were supposed to have funds deposited for them in protected U.S. trust accounts as part of their compensation.[14] Those accounts disappeared, and the funds were never returned to the migrant workers or their heirs. These litigation efforts have thus far not resulted in a settlement or judgment for the braceros. However, on June 15, 2005, the Court reversed course and denied the Mexican defendant's motion to dismiss on all grounds (including foreign immunity), raising hope for a positive result and adding to the body of favorable law.
- Efforts on behalf of persons who were forced to perform slave labor for Japanese industry, or to act as "comfort women" by the Japanese government, during World War II likewise have not been successful on a class basis.[15] There is renewed hope for the comfort women claims, however, as the Supreme Court reversed and remanded the case in light of its ruling in a separate Nazi-era case on the issue of foreign sovereign immunity.[16] New motions to dismiss are pending.
- Cases filed in the United States on behalf of African-American slave

descendants seeking compensation from private entities such as insurance companies that insured slave boats, and others who allegedly profited from slavery, have not been successful either. In January 2004, Judge Charles Norgle Sr. of the Northern District of Illinois dismissed all of plaintiffs' claims on a number of grounds, including that the plaintiffs lacked standing (i.e., a direct stake with a traceable injury), that the legislative branch was the more appropriate branch to decide the issue, and that the claims were time barred.[17] Plaintiffs thereafter filed an amended complaint. It appears unlikely that these cases will pave the way to a compensation program in the foreseeable future given the uniquely difficult hurdles faced by plaintiffs (including standing, post–Civil War legislation addressing slavery, and passage of time).

- Claims on behalf of South African victims of apartheid against companies doing business in apartheid South Africa have not seen success. In November 2004, Judge John E. Sprizzo of the Southern District of New York dismissed the lawsuits on the ground that they did not state a cause of action under the ATCA.[18] The case is presently on appeal.

Of all the ingredients discussed above that produced the successful outcomes in the Holocaust litigation, the most clearly and detrimentally absent has been the desire by the defendants in the non-Holocaust cases to admit guilt and provide restitution. Instead, the defendants in the post-Holocaust cases have chosen to fight their victims to the bitter end; and, because litigation is time intensive and at best uncertain, a defendant in a complex case involving historical wrongs can use time to its advantage. For example, plaintiffs in the Japanese slave labor cases are quite elderly, and their mortality rate is high, such that few will be alive if Japan and its industry ever decide to pay compensation.

Additionally, media attention, which played a key role in the Holocaust cases and was intimately linked to the willingness of politicians and regulators to expend political capital on behalf of Holocaust victims, has been far less intensive in the post-Holocaust-litigation context. While thousands of articles appeared in mainstream papers during the apex of the Holocaust litigation, fewer than 150 stories were published about the plight of the braceros, and only hundreds appeared about the "comfort women" and Japanese slave labor cases, with many of these stories appearing in local rather than national papers. The only post-Holocaust litigation that has generated anything close to the level of media attention that occurred for the Holocaust cases is the African-American slavery reparations litigation. Much of that press had nothing to do with the litigation, however, and instead focused on the theoretical issue of whether such compensation makes sense at all, given that there are virtually no survivors, and also the difficulty of identifying heirs with precision after the passage of so much time.

The unfortunate response to the African-American slavery litigation (to date) suggests that when victims' advocates try to address wrongs that are too generalized (e.g., effects of slavery on the current African-American population), too old (e.g., more than a century), too broad (in terms of the years involved, i.e., centuries of slavery versus a few years during the Nazi era), and too closely connected to prior political activity at an official level (e.g., congressional role in abolishing slavery and aftermath), courts will be more likely to dismiss such lawsuits.

The Holocaust litigation, however, demonstrates that certain historical wrongs can and should be addressed in U.S. courts. Courageous judges will always be available to provide a forum for victims of human rights abuses to obtain justice. Nonetheless, such difficult cases face many hurdles, including courts with overburdened dockets that may find an easy out in various discretionary doctrines that permit courts to decline jurisdiction. The Holocaust litigation has not produced a flood of decisions favoring victims of historical wrongs, and the litigation effort is best made a part of a larger social movement for justice, to enhance the prospects of a favorable outcome.

Advocates on behalf of victims of historical human rights abuses need to coordinate with victim communities, interested politicians and regulators, sympathetic journalists, and other community groups to build an awareness of the need for compensation for victims, and to increase the prospects that the perpetrators of historical wrongs will feel compelled to acknowledge their misconduct and provide some measure of justice to the victims.

Moreover, given the resurgence of ATCA and the Supreme Court's recent decision affirming the use of U.S. courts to combat human rights abuses, opportunities for victims of more recent or future human rights abuses should continue to be explored, so that the U.S. courts remain a pathway for justice.

NOTES

1. For example, abuses related to torture and murder in Paraguay, abuses committed by the Marcos administration in the Philippines, and atrocities committed in the course of the Bosnian civil war have been litigated in U.S. courts. *See Filartiga v. Pena-Irala,* 630 F.2d 876 (2d Cir. 1980) (Paraguay); *In re Marcos Human Rights Litig.,* 910 F. Supp. 1460 (D. Haw. 1995) (Philippines); *Kadic v. Karadzic,* 70 F.3d 232 (2d Cir. 1995) (Bosnia).

2. This reflects the following search in Lexis for all federal and state cases: "Holocaust and overview (Holocaust or Nazi or "World War II" or wartime) and ("class action" or "Rule 23!")," then reviewed to remove any unpublished cases or cases not relating to the litigation at issue. The search captured the following opinions: *Am. Ins. Ass'n v. Garamendi,* 123 S. Ct. 2374 (2003); *Deutsch v. Turner Corp.,* 324 F.3d 692 (9th Cir. 2003); *D'Amato v. Deutsche Bank,* 236 F.3d 78 (2d Cir. 2001); *In re Assicurazioni Generali S.p.A. Holocaust Ins. Litig.,* 228 F. Supp. 2d 348 (S.D.N.Y. 2002); *Ukrainian Nat'l Ass'n of Jewish Former Prisoners of Concentration Camps and Ghettos v. United States,* 205 F.R.D. 102 (E.D.N.Y. Jan. 5, 2002); *Frumkin v. JA Jones, Inc. (In re Nazi-Era Cases against German Defs. Litig.),* 129 F. Supp. 2d 370 (D.N.J. 2001); *In re Nazi-Era Cases against German Defs. Litig.,* 198 F.R.D. 429 (D.N.J. Dec. 5, 2000); *Bodner v. Banque Paribas,* 114 F. Supp. 2d 117 (E.D.N.Y. Aug. 31, 2000); *In re Holocaust Victim Assets Litig.,* 105 F. Supp. 2d 139 (E.D.N.Y. Aug. 9, 2000); *In re Austrian and German Bank Holocaust Litig.,* 80 F. Supp. 2d 164 (S.D.N.Y. 2000); *Iwanowa v. Ford Motor Co.,* 67 F. Supp. 2d 424 (D.N.J. 1999); *Burger-Fischer v. Degussa,* 65 F. Supp. 2d 248 (D.N.J. 1999).

3. The status of the administration of the Swiss banks settlement can be ascertained by reference to its official website www.swissbankclaims.com.

4. *See Weisshaus v. Swiss Bankers Ass'n,* 225 F.3d 191 (2d Cir. 2000)(affirming the Swiss Banks settlement) and *Friedman v. Union Bank of Switzerland,* Nos. 00-9595 (CON), 00-9597 (CON), 2001 U.S. App. LEXIS 17343 (2d Cir. 2001) (upholding the Plan of Allocation).

5. *See Bodner v. Banque Paribas,* 114 F. Supp. 2d 117 (E.D.N.Y. 2000).

6. *See Iwanowa v. Ford Motor Co.,* 67 F. Supp. 2d 424 (D.N.J. 1999) and *Burger-Fischer v. Degussa,* 65 F. Supp. 2d 248 (D.N.J. 1999).

7. *See Am. Ins. Ass'n v. Garamendi,* 123 S. Ct. 2374 (2003).

8. *See In re Assicurazioni Generali S.p.A. Holocaust Ins. Litig.,* MDL Nos. 1374, M21-89, 2004 U.S. Dist. LEXIS 20569, at *20–21 (S.D.N.Y. Oct. 14, 2004).

9. *Id.*

10. *See also* David G. Savage, *White House Turns Tables on Former American POWs,* L.A. Times, Feb. 15, 2005 (describing Bush administration efforts to prevent Gulf War POWs from receiving compensation from Iraq for abuses under Saddam Hussein's regime).

11. *Sosa v. Alvarez-Machain,* 124 S. Ct. 2739 (2004).

12. The Bush administration has also filed similar papers in other human rights cases. *See, e.g.,* Human Rights Watch, "U.S.: Ashcroft Attacks Human Rights Law; Justice Dept. Undermining Key Precedent" (May 15, 2003), available at http://www.hrw.org/press/2003/05/us051503.htm. *See also* Human Rights Watch, "U.S. Attorney General Nominee Undermined Rights: Former White House Counsel Helped U.S. Circumvent International Legal Obligations" (Nov. 10, 2004), available at http://www.hrw.org/english/docs/2004/11/10/usdom9659.htm.

13. *See, e.g.,* Cal. Civ. Proc. Code §§ 354.3 (Holocaust-era artwork); 354.6 (slave and forced labor claims); 354.5 (insurance); N.Y. CLS § 2704 (extending statute of limitations and providing right of action for insurance claims); Fla. Stat. § 626.9543 (extending statute of limitations for insurance claims); *see also* N.Y. Consol. Law Tax § 13 (providing tax exemption for Holocaust compensation).

14. *Cruz v. United States,* No. C 01-00892 CRB (N.D. Cal., Breyer, J.).

15. *Deutsch v. Turner Corp.,* 324 F.3d 692 (9th Cir. 2003) (affirming dismissal of slave labor litigation against Japanese industry); Joo v. Japan, 332 F. 3d 679 (D.C. Cir. 2003) (affirming dismissal of "comfort women" claims against Japan under the Foreign Sovereign Immunities Act).

16. *Joo v. Japan,* 124 S. Ct. 2835 (2004).

17. *In re African-Am. Slave Descendants Litig.,* 304 F. Supp. 2d 1027 (N.D. Ill. 2004). At least two portions of the order are worth noting. First, the Court relied quite heavily on Holocaust-era decisions that had ruled against plaintiffs. Second, the Court focused heavily on the prior efforts by the legislature, including the Civil War amendments, civil rights acts, and its previous consideration of reparations. According to the Court, the "historical record" revealed that ". . . the issue of reparations to former slaves was one committed to the Representative Branches of the federal government." *Id.* at 1060–61.

18. In re South African Apartheid Litig., 346 F. Supp. 2d 538 (S.D.N.Y. 2004).

About the Contributors

Roland Bank was the principal legal adviser of the German Foundation "Remembrance, Responsibility, and the Future." He has been published widely in the area of international law and human rights issues, in such journals as the *European Journal of International Law,* the *Heidelberg Journal of International Law,* and the *German Yearbook of International Law.*

Michael Berenbaum is the Director of the Sigi Ziering Institute: Exploring the Ethical and Religious Implications of the Holocaust and a Professor of Theology at the University of Judaism in Los Angeles. He is the author and editor of sixteen books, including *The World Must Know* and *Anatomy of the Auschwitz Death Camp.*

Lee Boyd is a Professor of Law at Pepperdine Law School. She publishes in the area of international human rights litigation and represents plaintiffs in international human rights cases in U.S. federal courts.

The Honorable Judge *Thomas Buergenthal* serves as a judge on the International Court of Justice in the Hague. Formerly a law professor at George Washington University School of Law in Washington, D.C., and Dean of American University Washington College of Law, he has also served as Vice Chairman of the Claims Resolution Tribunal for Dormant Accounts in Switzerland. One of the youngest survivors of Auschwitz and Sachsenhausen, the Czech-born Buergenthal immigrated to the United States in 1951.

Monica S. Dugot is Director of Restitution and Senior Vice President at Christie's, where she coordinates Christie's restitution issues globally. Prior to joining Christie's, Ms. Dugot served as Deputy Director of the New York State Banking Department's Holocaust Claims Processing Office and represented New York State on art restitution matters at various international venues.

Stuart E. Eizenstat was President Carter's chief domestic adviser and served in several high-level positions in the State, Treasury, and Commerce Departments in the Clinton administration from 1993 to 2001, including being the Special Representative of the President and Secretary of State on Holocaust-Era Issues.

Eric Freedman teaches international negotiations at the University of Orléans, France, and serves as the Research Consultant for the Simon Wiesenthal Centre Europe, attached to the Drai Commission in Paris. He was a member of the legal team in the U.S. class action suits against French banks, and since 2001 has been a member of the French-American Washington Accords Oversight Committee.

Si Frumkin, liberated from Dachau at the age of fourteen, went on to become the CEO of a successful textile business in California while at the same time dedicating himself to the causes of Soviet Jewry, Holocaust education, and political activism. He is a cofounder of the Union of Councils for Soviet Jews.

Peter Hayes is Professor of History and German and Theodore Z. Weiss Professor of Holocaust Studies at Northwestern University. He is the author of numerous essays on German business and the Nazi regime, and the recently published treatise *From Cooperation to Complicity: Degussa in the Third Reich.*

Kai Hennig is the spokesperson of the German Foundation "Remembrance, Responsibility, and the Future" and is also in charge of the implementation of the compensation of life insurance policies from the Nazi era. Prior to his work with the Foundation, he worked in the German Foreign Ministry, including serving with the German Permanent Mission to the United Nations.

Roman Kent is the Chairman of the American Gathering of Jewish Holocaust Survivors, Treasurer of the Conference on Material Claims against Germany, and Vice President of the Jewish Foundation for the Righteous. He was also appointed by President Clinton to serve on the U.S. Presidential Advisory Commission on Holocaust Assets in the United States and was a key member of various negotiating committees for recovery of Holocaust-era assets.

Lawrence Kill and *Linda Gerstel* are members of Anderson, Kill & Olick, P.C. They represented plaintiff Holocaust survivors and their heirs in numerous class action lawsuits concerning Holocaust-era claims, including the first Holocaust-era insurance class action. Both are signatories to the U.S.-German agreement establishing the German Foundation "Remembrance, Responsibility, and the Future."

The Honorable Judge *Edward R. Korman* is the Chief Judge of the United States District Court, Eastern District of New York. He is presiding over the settlement of the Swiss bank Holocaust litigation, *In re Holocaust Victim Assets Litigation.*

Otto Graf Lambsdorff was the Representative of the Federal Chancellor for the "Foundation Initiative of the German Industry: Remembrance, Responsibility, and the Future." He is a former member of the German Bundestag and was Minister of the Economy of the Federal Republic of Germany from 1977 to 1984.

David A. Lash served from 1994 to 2003 as the Executive Director of Bet Tzedek, "The House of Justice," in Los Angeles, and *Mitchell A. Kamin* is the current Executive Director. Since 1974, Bet Tzedek has been providing free legal representation to thousands of elderly, indigent, and disabled residents of Los Angeles, and assists Holocaust survivors through its Holocaust Reparations Project.

Hannah Lessing is the Secretary General of both the National Fund and the General Settlement Fund of the Republic of Austria for Victims of National Socialism. She was a member of the Austrian negotiating team leading to the Washington Agreement of January 2001 and is a permanent member of the Task Force for International Cooperation on Holocaust Education, Remembrance, and Research. *Fiorentina Azizi* is the Deputy Head of the Legal Section of the General Settlement Fund. She has worked at the European Commission for Human Rights and the Lauterpacht Research Centre for International Law, and is currently on a one-year sabbatical at the Secretaría de Derechos Humanos of the Argentine Ministry of Justice.

Burt Neuborne is the John Norton Pomeroy Professor of Law and Legal Director of the Brennan Center for Justice at New York University School of Law. He currently serves as Lead Settlement Counsel in the Swiss Banks Holocaust Litigation. and is one of two U.S. appointees to the Board of Trustees of the German Foundation "Remembrance, Responsibility, and the Future."

C. *Pell* is a senior litigation partner at White & Case LLP. He has
ended clients from claims relating to the Holocaust, post–World
ar II property seizures, the former apartheid regime in South Africa,
and African slavery in the United States. He has also participated in the
successful negotiations between the United States and France to resolve
Holocaust-related claims.

Morris Ratner and *Caryn Becker* are partners at Lieff, Cabraser, Heimann
& Bernstein LLP. They represented Holocaust survivors and heirs in
many Holocaust-era class action lawsuits. Ratner and his firm served as
Settlement Class Counsel in the Swiss bank settlement. Ratner represented victims in the international negotiations and is a signatory to
the German, Austrian, and French Holocaust-era settlements.

Shimon Samuels is Director for International Liaison of the Simon Wiesenthal Centre in Paris. His work focuses on the containment of resur-
gent antisemitism, restitution claims for Holocaust victims, and international diplomacy at UNESCO, the Council of Europe, and the OSCE.
He is the author of numerous articles on combating racism, antisemitism, and prejudice.

E. Randol Schoenberg is a partner at Burris & Schoenberg, LLP. He has
been active in Nazi-looted art restitution and successfully argued the
case of *Republic of Austria v. Altmann* before the U.S. Supreme Court.

William Z. Slany was the Historian of the State Department from 1984
until his retirement in 2000. He directed the interagency group that
prepared U.S. government reports on Holocaust assets in 1997 and 1998.
He is currently researching and writing a history of the State Department from 1933.

Howard N. Spiegler is a partner at Herrick, Feinstein LLP and is cochair of
its international art law practice. He has been involved in several well-
known lawsuits brought on behalf of the heirs of Holocaust victims
and others to recover stolen artworks, including the currently pending
Portrait of Wally litigation and the action on behalf of the heirs of Kaz-
imir Malevich to recover fourteen Malevich artworks from the City of
Amsterdam.

Deborah Sturman, of counsel to Milberg, Weiss, Bershad & Schulman LLP,
conceived of the first suits in U.S. courts on behalf of Holocaust-era
slave labor victims, which led to the establishment of the German

Foundation. She has been profiled in *The Wall Street Journal* and *Financial Times,* is a columnist for *Manager Magazin,* and regularly appears as a legal commentator in various European media regarding international litigation.

Robert A. Swift is a senior member of Kohn, Swift & Graf, P.C. He served as lead counsel in the first class action human-rights litigation in history, *In re Ferdinand E. Marcos Human Rights Litigation,* and was a principal litigator and settlement negotiator in the Holocaust cases against Swiss, German, and Austrian entities.

Gideon Taylor is the Executive Vice President of the Conference on Jewish Material Claims against Germany ("Claims Conference"). The Claims Conference currently administers allocations from the German Foundation "Remembrance, Responsibility, and the Future" and the Swiss bank settlement.

Lothar Ulsamer, MA, PhD, studied sociology, economic and social history, political science, and empirical social science. He headed a project group at the Baden-Württemberg State Ministry of Labor, Health and Social Affairs; he was head of the Department of Publications, Press and Culture at Richard Hirschmann, Esslingen; he was in charge of External Relations and Speeches of the Finance/Controlling Department at DaimlerChrysler; he has been Director State and Communal Relations, Foundations/Department for External Affairs and Public Policy at DaimlerChrysler. Since 1999 he has also been head of the office of the German Economy Foundation Initiative "Remembrance, Responsibility, and the Future." He has written numerous articles as well as a number of nonfiction books and novels.

Richard Weisberg is the Walter Floersheimer Professor of Constitutional Law and Director of the Center for Holocaust and Human Rights Studies at Cardozo Law School, Yeshiva University. He was a member of the legal team in the U.S. class action suits against French banks, and since 2001 he has been a member of the French-American Washington Accords Oversight Committee.

Melvyn I. Weiss, Senior and Founding Partner of Milberg, Weiss, Bershad & Schulman LLP, was a pro bono lead counsel in the Swiss bank litigation and a lead counsel in litigation brought on behalf of Holocaust victims against German companies.

Witten is a partner at Wilmer, Cutler & Pickering and led the ιepresentation of the UBS AG and Credit Suisse Group in con-ι with litigation against Swiss banks relating to World War II and the ιιᴜlocaust; and the firm's representation of several German companies in litigation against them relating to World War II and the Holocaust, which led to the creation of the German Economy Foundation Initiative.

Sidney Zabludoff is an economist who worked for the White House, CIA, and Treasury Department for more than thirty years. Upon retirement in 1995, he has focused on issues related to restitution of Jewish assets stolen during the Holocaust era. He has published numerous studies on the issue and was the principal analyst for Jewish participants involved in Holocaust-era insurance claims.

Arie Zuckerman served between 2001 and 2003 as the head of Israel's negotiation team on Holocaust restitution. An attorney, he also lectures in the area of human rights from the perspective of the Holocaust and international law at Sha'arei Mishpat Law College in Hezlyia, Israel.

Index

About the Editors

Michael J. Bazyler is Professor of Law and The "1939" Club Law Scholar in Holocaust and Human Rights Studies at Whittier Law School, Costa Mesa, California. Author of numerous articles in international law and the book *Holocaust Justice: The Battle for Restitution in America's Courts,* he is also a former Visiting Scholar at the U.S. Holocaust Memorial Museum.

Roger P. Alford is Associate Professor of Law at Pepperdine University School of Law, Malibu, California. A former Senior Legal Advisor for the Swiss Claims Resolution Tribunal in Zurich, he is the author of dozens of articles on international law.